Rural Credit
in the Era of Globalisation

Rural Credit in the Era of Globalisation

Edited by

K. A. Rasure

MADHAV BOOKS
GURGAON (HARYANA)

First Published - 2010

ISBN: 978-81-907891-4-1

Published by

MADHAV BOOKS
F-2562, Palam Vihar
Gurgaon-122 017 (Haryana)
Phone : 0124-2365193, 9810373248

CONTENTS

FOREWORD

CREDIT is not only one of the critical inputs in agriculture but also an effective means of overall development of rural economy. A large number of agencies, such as Co-operatives, Regional Rural banks (RRBs), Commercial Banks, Self-Help Groups (SHG) and a well-spread informal credit outlets together constitute the Indian rural credit delivery system. One of the objectives of the credit policy is to minimize the role of non-institutional sources, mainly the moneylenders in the flow of agricultural credit. Several initiatives have been taken in this regard. In recent years, initiatives like Kisan Credit Card Scheme (KCCs), Special Agricultural credit plans, and RIDF schemes have been introduced to enhance the flow of credit to the rural sector. However, in spite of these efforts and initiatives, the flow of credit to the agricultural sector remains of matter of concern, and the money-lenders continue to play a dominating role in the delivery of credit to rural households, as the reach of institutional agencies has remained poor, particularly to the small and marginal farmers. The recommendations of Vaidyanathan Committee (2005) on rural credit are pathways to be followed and can be viewed holistically.

For a scientific and empirical analysis of rural credit delivery, one needs to examine at a micro level the latest development of credit delivery system. Such an analysis would be useful in understanding the reasons for approaching one type of credit institution than others by groups of borrowers. This will also help in reorienting the credit policies and programmes for a better impact. At this juncture the book entitled, *"Rural Credit in the Era of Globalisation"* is welcome and very pertinent. The volume is completely updated and comprehensive. Each chapter of this book is well written by the leading experts having long standing research experience in this field .The book occupies special advantage of excellence because it is an edited version and injects the best refined ideas of eminent social scientists and scholars from different parts of the country. I appreciate the efforts made by Dr. K. A. Rasure for meticulous compiling and editing the chapters of this book.

I congratulate authors, editors, and the publisher for bringing out this book. Hope this publication will prove useful to students, teachers, planners, researchers, and policy makers. This book will also provide guidelines to formulate strategies for better credit delivery system and development of the rural credit system.

Prof. R. G. Desai
K. K. Birla Fellow & Former Chairman,
Department of Economics
Bangalore University, Bangalore.

PREFACE

In the era of Globalisation, a great deal of attention has been devoted towards rural credit, particularly in backward agrarian economies. This is understandable in so far as the prevailing credit systems have their definite implications for the development of agriculture as also the well-being of various sections of rural population. The previous researches examining the agrarian credit markets highlighted a number of features, inadequate availability and unequal distribution of formal credit, gradual strengthening of the base of informal credit, exploitative nature of informal credit, interlinked nature of informal credit, exploitative nature of informal credit contracts, high variability of rate of interest on informal loans and so on. Each of these aspect has drawn considerable research attention over past couple of decades or so. Nevertheless, no generalized opinion could be formed regarding the actual nature and functioning of agrarian credit markets that typically display wide variation across different agrarian regimes.

In the existing multi-agency approach to rural credit despite high density of the retail outlets of formal credit institutions, some recent innovations in delivery system, and some renewed thrust on rural credit the problem of outreach, availability of adequate credit, at the right time, at reasonable cost and almost at doorstep continue to be elusive for a vast majority of the farmers. Despite progressive institutionalization of rural credit, non-institutional credit, even though exploitative in nature, continues to have a significant presence because of convenience features of its loan delivery system.

Therefore, the prime concern remains how to achieve absolute convergence on a range of issues relating to credit availability, credit delivery system and adequate credit absorptive capacity of the rural populace.

Realising the imperative need to bring out a suitable book on "Rural Credit in the era of Globalisation", tailored to meet the specific requirements of research scholars, teachers, students, planners and policy makers, who can utilize it profitably. This book contain 30 papers prepared by eminent personalities coming fairly from seats of higher learning situated in different parts of India. Therefore, I am proud and privileged to say that this volumes is of representational value on the national level. The issue covered in this book have a practical and policy significance in India. The themes have been deeply and intensively discussed by the paper writers. I have made an earnest attempt to present this book in the hands of the academic community.

I acknowledge my sincere indebtedness to Dr. R. G. Desai, Professor of Economics and K K Birla Fellow, and Former Chairman , Department of Economics, Bangalore University, Bangalore, for writing a Foreword to this book and also his able advice, and encouragement constantly in my life.

I wish to record my heartfelt gratitude to all the esteemed and learned contributors for having made their articles, completely error free, reader friendly and research related in the choice of the topics and the substance put inside them for worth reading.

Thanks are due to Sri. Baswaraj Patil Sedam, President Dr. Nagareddy Patil, Secretary, Sri. Govindlal Malpani, Joint Secretary, Sri. Ramanujdas Tapadiya, Treasurer and the members of Sri. Kottal Basaveshwar Bharatiya Shikshan Samiti, Sri. Manne Hasreddy Principal, my colleagues and non-teaching staff of Seth Sri. Tulsi Ram Gilada. Nrupatunga Arts, Commerce, Management and Science Degree College, Sedam, for the constant encouragement, advice and help extended to me.

Further, I am thankful to my wife Smt. Sujata daughter Swati for their co-operation patience and pleasing behaviour.

In the last but not in the least, thanks are due to Sh. S. K. Jha, Serials Publications, New Delhi for taking active interest in the publication of this book.

K. A. Rasure

CONTRIBUTORS LIST

Kanak Kanti Bagchi, Professor & Head, Department of Economics, North Bengal University, Raja Rammohunpur, Darjeeling, W.B. *E-mail: kkbagchi@hotmail.com*

Goutam Ghosh, Lecturer (Selection Grade), Department of Commerce, Malda College, Malda, W.B.

Dr. Birendra Kumar Jha, Reader & Head, Deptt. of Economics, D. B. K. N. College, Narhan (Samastipur, Bihar).

Dr. Jagannath Lenka, Professor of Economics, North Orissa University, Baripada, Orissa, India.

Prof. D. Pulla Rao, authors belongs to the Department of Economics, Andhra University, Visakhapatnam, (AP).

Prof. M. Sundara Rao, authors belongs to the Department of Economics, Andhra University, Visakhapatnam, (AP).

Vipla Chopra, Professor of Economics, Punjabi University Patiala.

Dr. A. Gunasekaran, Reader and Head, Post-Graduate and Research Department of Economics, Sir Theagaraya College, Chennai.

Dr. Praveen Sharma, Ass. Professor, Department of Economic Administration and Financial Management (EAFM) University of Rajasthan, Jaipur.

S. N. Yogish, Reader, Department of Economics, Jnana Sahyadri, Shankaghatta.

Dr. R. R. Biradar, Sr. Lecturer, Department of Economics, Karnataka University Dharwad, Karnataka State (India).

Mr. Venkatappa Naik and Mr. P.M. Pargonda, M. Phil Students Department of Economics, Karnataka University Dharwad, Karnataka State (India).

Girija Yabannavar, Lecturer in Economics, Smt.KSJ Arts & SMS Commerce College for Women, Dharwad.

Hosamani S.B., Head, Agri Business & Export Knowledge Centre & Professor of Agril. Economics, UAS, Dharwad

Kulkarni B.S., Research Associate, Agri Business & Export Knowledge Centre, UAS, Dharwad.

Dr. P. Loganathan, Reader in Economics, Kandasami Kandar's College, Velur, Namakkal.

K. Saravanan, Lecturer in Economics, (SS), Kandasami Kandar's College, Velur, Namakkal.

S. K. Dhage, Reader and H.O.D. of Economics, Baburaoji Gholap College, Sangvi, Pune.

B. G. Lobo, Lecturer of Economics, Sinhgad Institute, N.B. Navale College of Commerce, Lonavala, Pune.

V. Muniraju, District Statistical Officer, GoK, Siddagangamut Building, Rajajinagar, Bangalore.

V. Ramakrishnappa, Research Associate, Centre for Public Policy (CPP), Indian Institute of Management, Bangalore.

Dr. K. A. Rasure, Reader in Economics, Nrupatunga Arts, Commerce, Management and Science College, SEDAM, Dist. Gulbarga (Karnataka).

Dr. (Mrs.) Pushpa Sinha, (Lecturer), Dept. of Economics, Patna Women's College, Patna.

Mrs. Ratna Mitra, (Lecturer), Dept. of Economics, Patna Women's College, Patna.

Smt. Pushpa S. Abbigeri, Senior Scale Lecturer, Department of Commerce, S.K.S. Jigalur Arts and Dr. (Smt) S. M. Sheshgiri Commerce College for Women, Dharwad. Karnatak State Women University, Bijapur.

Dr. S. Mahendra Kumar, Reader, Department of Studies in Economics and Cooperation, Manasagangotri, University of Mysore, Mysore.

R. Ramakrishna, Professor and Former Head, School of Economics, Andhra University, Visakhapatnam.

Dr. N. Subba Rao, Asst. Professor, Dept. of Rual Development, A.U. Campus, Srikakulam.

D. Tata Rao, Doctoral Fellow, School of Economics, Andhra University, Visakhapatnam.

Dr. N. Subba Rao, Faculty Member, Department of Rural Development, AU Campus, Etcherla, Srikakulam District.

Dr. B. Vijaya, Reader, Department of Commerce, Gulbarga University, Gulbarga.

Veerendrakumar, Research Scholar, Department of Commerce, Gulbarga University, Gulbarga.

Dr. S. V. Padmini, Guest Lecturer Department of PG Studies Economics & Research School of Business in Economics, Kuvempu University, Shankaraghatta, Shivamogga (D).

V. Basil Hans, Selection Grade Lecturer and Head, Department of Economics, St Aloysius Evening College, Mangalore, Karnataka, India. *E-mail: vbasilhans@yahoo.com*

N. S. Mugadur, Research Scholar, Department of Economics, Karnatak University, Dharwad.

H. H. Uliveppa, Professor and Chairman, Department of Economics, Karnatak University, Dharwad.

A. Marimuthu, Lecturer in Economics, R.D. Govt. Arts College, Sivagangai.

A. Bose, Lecturer in Commerce, Govt. Arts College, Melur, Madurai.

D. Bose, Reader & Head, Department of Economics, A.N.J.A. College, (Autonomous), Sivakasi, Virudhunagar, District.

Channabasavanagouda P., Research Scholar, Department of Economics, Gulbarga University, Gulbarga, Karnataka, India.

Dr. Sherly Kurien, Reader, Department of Economics, Avinashilingam University for Women, Coimbatore.

Dr. Anjali Jain, Assistant Professor, Department of Economics Sarojini Naidu Govt. Girls' Post Graduate Autonomous College Bhopal, (M.P.).

Dr. Mona Khare, Professor (Economics), Department of Regional Planning & Economic Growth, Barkatullah University, Bhopal, (M.P.).

Dr. C. S. Singhal, Professor, CHRD, National Institute of Rural Development, Rajendranager, Hyderabad, *E-mail:singhalcs@yahoo.co.in*

Dr. Jayasheela, Reader, Department of Economics, Mangalore University, Mangalagangothri.

Dr. Shoukat Ali M, Principal, Besant Evening College, Managlore.

Dr. K. P. Kumaran, Associate Professor, NIRD, Hyderabad.

1

RURAL CREDIT AND REGIONAL RURAL BANKS

K. A. Rasure

Introduction

Rural India virtually includes the cultivaters, the village craftsmen and agricultural labourers. One of the serious and unrelenting problems faced by the Indian farmers, households has been indebtedness. Despite substantial improvement in agricultural output and distribution of credit, Still majority of the farmers are suffering from this major economic malaise called indebtedness along with lack of timely and adequate farm credit. Agricultural distress witnessed in the country occasionally takes the form of suicides by farmers.

Rural finance is a matter of great concern in an agrarian economy like India where 70% of the population depends upon agriculture for their livelihood. Moreover 40% of our GDP is contributed by the rural sector. Economic development of our country can be achieved only with the upliftment of the village folk consisting of artisans, agriculture labourers, farmers, rural industry workers etc. Finance being the lifeline of every commercial venture, availability of adequate funds at reasonable terms is a must to ensure speedy economic development in the village. Among the various institutional agencies engaged in rural finance, Regional Rural Banks play a significant role in financing the target group in the rural sector. They are specially designed financial institutions working under the guidance of NABARD and the parent commercial banks, spread in rural areas with a close network of branches serving a particular district or region.

Organisation and Management

The Regional Rural Banks came into existence by the Regional Rural banks Act, 1976 as a part of the efforts of the Govt. to devise alternative agencies to provide institutional credit to rural people. As per the recommendations of the working group on Rural Banks, the first five RRBs were established on 2 Oct 1975 under a presidential ordiance, which followed the promulgation of the Act in April 1976.

As per the Act, each RRB is to be sponsored by a public sector banks. The RRBs were established at the initiative of the Central and State Govt. The initial issued capital was Rs. 25 lakh with Rs. 1 Crore as authorized capital shared between the Central Govt, the State Govt and the sponsor bank in the ratio of 50%, 35% and 15% respectively. The Regional Rural Banks Act, 1987 has enhanced the authorized capital of RRB to Rs. 5 crore with up capital of Rs. 1 crore.

The management of the RRB is vested in the Board of Directors consisting of nine members including the Chairman who is appointed by the Central Govt. of the rest three, are appointed by the Central Govt, two by the State Govt, and three by the sponsor bank. In addition, the RBI and NABARD also nominate one director each to the Board. With the formation of NABARD in July 1982 the affairs of the RRBs are being looked after by this Central agency.

At present there are 196 RRBs spread over the 22 states in India with the maximum member (40) in Uttar Pradesh followed by Madhya Pradesh (24) (before bifurcation), Bihar (22) etc. These Regional Banks are sponsored by 28 scheduled banks. There are 14,400 branches of these RRBs, spread across 511 districts. The deposits were Rs. 45,000 crores and advances Rs. 19,000 crores. Their combined profits were Rs. 608 crores but the total accumulated losses amount to Rs. 2,700 crore by 2005.

The RRBs were set up with a view to develop rural economy by providing credit facilities for the development of agriculture, trade, commerce, industry and other productive activities in rural areas. Such facility was intended mainly for small and marginal farmers, agricultural labourers, artisans and small entrepreneurs. These banks are expected to provide cheap and liberal credit facilities to the poor and the marginalized, to inculcate banking habit, credit employment opportunities among these people and save them from the clutches of moneylenders.

The data given above indicates the scale of operation and the performance outcome of the RRBs. The accumulated losses amount to Rs. 2800 crore which is being wiped off with the recapitalisation help by the Govt. Out of the 196 banks, 43 banks had made losses during the year. The causes for loss have been reported as poor quality of advances, poor recovery and mounting overdues. Consequently the menace of non performing assets is really grave, affecting the solvency position of these banks.

Growth and Development

The performance of RRBs right from its inception indicating the key elements of growth such as number of banks and branches, districts covered, deposits and advances over a period ranging from 1975 to 2003 are given in Table 1. The number of RRBs grew into 196 in the year 1991 itself and remains the same there after. A steady growth is seen in the number of branches from 4795 to 14527 during the 10 year period between 1981 and 1991. There is a downward trend in the number of branches after 1991. More and more district are brought under the purview of RRBs resulting in tremendous growth in the deposits and advances. The deposits mix of RRBs during the year 2002-2005 shows that, of the total deposit 56.5% belongs to the term deposit category, 39.7% savings bank account and only 3.8% falls under current deposit. Cost of funds in these banks is bound to be high due to very low level of current deposit.

Table 1
Peformance Indicators of RRBs

Year	Number of RRBs	Districts covered	Number of Branches	Deposits Rs. Cr.	Outstanding Advances (Rs. Cr.)
1975	6	12	17	0.20	0.10
1981	107	182	4795	336.00	406.59
1991	196	381	14527	4989.24	3535.35
2001	196	451	14475	22189.00	9861.00
2005	196	511	14400	45000.00	19000.00

RRBs versus Commercial Banks

The comparative position of RRBs in our banking sector is made clear by means Table 2. Compared to all other Banks, the deposit and credits of RRBs appear to be quite meager. The CD ratio is found much below the satisfactory level. As the lending level is poor these banks resort to investments on a large scale. And this situation is not going to help the rural sector.

Table 2
Share of Deposit, Credit and CD Ratio of banks

Banks	Deposits %	Credit %	CD Ratio %
Public Sector Banks	50.6	46.8	54.8
SBI & Associated Banks	24.0	24.0	59.7
Other Scheduled Banks	17.0	19.2	66.9
Foreign Banks	4.5	7.0	94.1
Regional Rural Banks	3.9	3.0	46.4
Total	100	100	-

Rural Finance

Rural India has a vast potential for increased banking activity. Only 30% of the rural household have so far availed of banking facilities. Remaining 70% of the families do not know what is banking. Atleast 50% of them can be given finances for self employment schemes, housing and other non farm activities. The lack of proportion between lending in rural and other sector is very clear out of the total borrowers of 5.42 crores, 45% are in rural India but they account for only 13.4% of outstanding loans. As against this, 15% of the loans from metros got 54% of overall lending. 98.5% of the rural borrowers operates small borrowal accounts with credit limit below Rs. 1 lakh. Total agricultural advances as on March 2005 by PSBs was only 15.34% and private sector banks 10.78% against the target of 18%. Credit/Deposit ratio in rural areas by all banks was very low–PSBs. 42.70% and private banks 33.32%. Bank branches in rural centers have been reduced from 35,329, to 32,481 in 8 years since 1994 where as urban and metro branches have gone up from 14,584–19,004.

Table 3
RRBs: A Profile

Total No. of RRBs	196
Deposits	Rs. 50,100 crores
Borrowings	Rs. 4,800 crores
Investments	Rs. 33,000 crores
Outstanding Advances	Rs. 22,200 crores
Loans Issued	Rs. 12,600 crores
Accumulated losses	Rs. 2,800 crores
Net Profit	Rs. 520 crores
No. of Banks that made profits	156
NPA	14.50%
Recapitalisation help given by Government	Rs. 2200 crores

Problems Faced

RRBs face multifarious problems due to their peculiar nature and tasks involved. The main issues are as follows:

(1) Poor recovery rate and the resultant, mounting losses.
(2) Delay in decision making on account of different agencies being involved in the management process.
(3) Capital inadequacy.
(4) Staff incompatibility as they find it difficult to cope with rural surrounding and business opportunities.
(5) Restrictions in respect of deposit mobilization and scope for investment.

Suggestions

In the light of the foregoing analysis and the report of the study group on RRBs, the following suggestions are made, considering the need for strengthening intermittent supply of rural finance and effective operation of the RRBs in the days to come.

Ownership and Control

Instead of these banks working as extensions of sponser banks, they must be made to work independently as a separate entity. The capital investment must be restructed to deal with the existing contribution of 50:35:15. These banks should be given specific designation, entity and role to play as different from, that of the parent institution. The number of hierarchy level must be reduced to state level co-ordination and RBI–Central Govt. level regulation and control.

Formal regulatory measure can be chalked out at the apex body where as the functional policies may be framed at the state level, in conjunction with state policies, priorities, needs and peculiar conditions. These banks should have absolute operational freedom to decide their course of action and execute general management without any kind of persistent interference from the other agencies except through policy guidelines and other banking regulations.

Management of Funds

Strict guidelines are to be issued as regards the deployment of funds, the wide areas of operation and the kind of debts to be serviced. It is rural sector reforms that should be born in mind. A flexible approach on the part of these banks will achieve sumptuous dividends. Policies must be adequate to effects deposit mobilization, finance poverty alievation, programmes, support self help groups to organize self employment projects, promote prominent rural industries suitable to the specific area and wage in viable socio-economic activities to lift up the block/village from the shackles of unemployment, poverty, illiteracy and other socio-economic evils.

Target and Motive

Advances target should be fulfilled at any cost. Almost all the advances must go to the rural sector. No question of the rural funds being siphoned off to other sectors. There must be flexibility in the interest rates between different kinds of loans such as crop loans, villages housing loans, cottage industries, SSIs service industries and others depending upon loan duration, rist factor, priority, government schemes etc. Profit should not be the only motive of these banks functioning for the welfare of the poor and the marginalized. They must function on service motto. After the financial reforms the commercial banks have visibly shifted from social banking to profit banking and in the transition, the priority sector is left in the lurch. Now the question arises on the part of the public sector banks as to whose child the priority sector is. It does not mean that the lending principles can be thrown to the winds. The proper cost-volume profit analysis is necessary. Economy and efficiency of operation should not be sacrificed. It is in the interest of survival of the bank that it should work profitably and diligently.

Coverage Area and Branch Expansion

India has about 5 lakh villages. As the Scheduled Banks have already diverted their attention to urban and metro cities resulting in closure of many rural branches, the only alternatives is RRBs, barring the co-operatives. It is essential that all these villages, panchayats, blocks, taluks must come under these banks. A close network of the branches situated on a regional basis would plug under competition, complacency and duplication of efforts and promote competence. Hence it is essential to multiply the number of branches to cover the entire rural area of our country.

Staffing and Training

The appointment and training of the staff working in these rural oriented institution should be given much attention. Every branch should have on it staff, at least one person from the same locality so that it will be easy for the bank manager to learn about the local conditions and people. Generally, numbers from rural communities only should be appointed in these banks so that the employees do not appear to be out of place in the rural setting. Also they can serve better in the familiar surroundings. It is hoped that at least 5 lakh jobs can be created for the rural educated youth on account of these banks. Effective training is to be imparted to the employees on a regular basis to orient their activities in the proper mode. Monetary and non-monetary incentive can be tried to bring about added enthusiasm and target attainment.

Development of Agro-based Industries

Unemployment and underemployment persist especially in rural areas due to crop failure on account of drought situations, sickness engulfing the tiny, cottage and SSI sectors with the advent of globalization, lack of infrastructure facilities etc. Banks would find it very difficult to function under such a setting unless agro-based industries and fostered. Setting up of such units will be beneficial to the banks as well as for the economic well being of the locality. The banks can expand their avenues of operation with the industrialization of the rural sector. Thus, development of suitable industrial units in particular localities would help in efficient functioning of RRBs.

As Market Leader

The RRBs should have the status of the market leader of rural finance. The number of other players must be restricted. Almost all the requirements of the rural population must be met through the RRBs themselves, except preferably, long-term needs, capital investment, housing etc. Other agencies such as SIDBI, SFC, NABARD etc can contribute in specific areas or in arranging refinance facility. The RBI could help by arranging additional flow of funds.

Higher Capital

The existing 196 RRBs must raise their capital to cope with the additional volume of business to deal with at least 50% of the population. Around 1,00,000 branches will have to be opened, though on a smaller scale, in order to cover the vast rural population. Accordingly, the capital base is to be enhanced either with the Govt. contribution and/or public issue

Refinance facility by various agencies will come handy in their respect.

Conclusion

As institutional finance is inadequate in rural areas, moneylenders rule the roost and the rural population ever in the shackles of debt and bondage. The commercial banks are closing down rural branches and concentrating or profitability rather than service to the rural poor. Organizing lending through Govt. institutions is to be reinforced to help the villages recover from debt and poverty and improve employment and productivity. In this context, the RRBs, are specially suited to work solely in the rural areas to channelise funds and monitor regional development. At present, there are multifarious kinds of schemes and organizations to serve the rural sector. What is needed is synergy of these institutions policies and projects to achieve the overall growth of the region. A target oriented timebound, realistic and regional approach is needed for optimum results.

References

Parameswaran, R. & Natarajan, S. (2002), Indian Banking, S. Chand & Company Limited, New Delhi.

Report of the Working Group to Suggest Amendments in The Regional Rural Banks Act, 1976.

TNBEF HERALD, Tamil Nadu Bank, Employees Federation, Chennai, Vol. III, Issue 8, Aug. 2003, Vol. IV, Issue 3, March, 2004.

2

ROLE OF INFORMAL SECTOR LENDERS IN AGRICULTURAL AND RURAL DEVELOPMENT—AN EMPIRICAL STUDY

KANAK KANTI BAGCHI & GOUTAM GHOSH

Introduction

THE business of money lending to the farmers by individuals has sometimes been accused of charging usurious rate of interest on the credit given to the farmers. Again, money lenders' activities have been regarded as activities conducive to the development process of rural areas. Whatever be the actual role of the money lenders in the sphere of socio-economic advancement of rural India, it cannot simply be inferred that money lenders have always played a negative role in the development process.

The negative image of money lenders has developed over the ages in different cultural contexts under the influence of social, economic and political factors. Money lenders in India have both negative and positive image, which has been simply accepted, in the development field. Now we make an attempt only to take a quick look at the socio-economic construction of the money lenders in India from a historical perspective in order to trace out the positive image and its survival upto the present rural credit market with due importance.

In Europe and West Asia. the money lender was regarded as abominable by Christian and Muslim societies, which had support of religious sanction on usury. Mughal ruler Akbar did not have an unfavourable disposition towards moneylending. Religion was, thus, the underlying factor generating the negative image of money lenders. Bouman (1990) entwined Hinduism with other major religions, i.e. Christianity, Muslim and Buddhism in the religiously 'stigmatizing of money lenders' in the case of India during the Hindu rule (Pre-Islam period i.e. pre-12th century, AD), money lenders were accorded due respect as a part of the Hindu caste of traders/businessmen, and as a class carrying out its assigned social role.

Traditionally the money lenders had an important position in the village economic and social structure. Seth points out that: "The money lenders occupied an important 'niche' in the structure of ancient Indian society. He was rather an indispensable constituent in the social set-up, in as much as it had been laid down in Niti ('Laws') that a person, ought not to take his residence at a place where the 'five essentials' i.e. raja, ('king'), dhanika, ('money lenders'), shrotiya, ('scholar of Vedas'), vaidya, ('physicians') and nadi ('river') did not exist. The place of money lenders was thus next only to that of the king by no means an unenviable position".

Gandhi's assessment of the money lenders was also positive. As Catanach notes, by 1917 Gandhi had gained practical experience of conditions in rural areas and his experience in Champaran had made him question the 'accepted opinion' of the money lenders.

'I have found him to be not always relentless not exacting of the last pie. He sometimes serves his client in many ways or even comes to the rescue in the hour of their distress. My observation is so limited that I dare not draw any conclusions from it, but I respectfully enquire whether it is not possible to make a serious effort to draw out the good in the *mahajan* (money lenders) and help him or induce him to throw out the evil in him. May not he be induced to join the army of co-operation or has experience proved that he is past praying for? (Catanach, 1970). This questioning of the 'accepted opinion' by Gandhi subsequently became a part of Gandhian thought wherein this culturally bound traditional institution was regarded as a necessity for the rural economy.

The money lender was not universally perceived to have a negative image and the positive image that existed under the surface, was never reflected in policy while most administrators and economists in British India held negative attitudes towards money lenders. There is also some record of dissenting attitudes.One observer precedes the current thought of the Ohio school in his assessment that the money lender carries out an important economic function and moreover, can not be considered usurious - the high rate of interest understandable because of his high risks.

The simple village economy is entirely based upon the dealings of the village *mahajan* (money lenders), whom it is sometimes the fashion to decry as a usurer but also who is often the only thrifty person among an improvident population. If his rate of interest is high, it is only proportionate to the risks of his business (Hunter 1871 Quoted in Krishetha, 174-75).

Even Sir Darling admits that: financing the village marketing, its produce and supplying its necessities, the money lender in India frequently stood between the cultivator and death; and, as Sir William Hunter remarks, he represents the one thrifty person among an improvident population", without whose help the cultivator would have had nothing to depend upon but the harvest of a simple year'. Whenever, therefore, we are tempted to revile him, we should remember that by his assistance to agriculture for 2500 years he has made life possible for millions who must otherwise have perished or never been born (Darling 1938; 200).

Thus, for centuries there is a great controversy over the image of money lender in the socio-economic development process. But there is no consensus that money lender is completely a parasite in the rural economy. It is true that, during the post-Independence period, the Government has adopted so many policies to institutionalize the rural credit market to liberate the rural poor, particularly, the poor farming population from the exploitative clutches of money lender. The money lenders' share of contribution to the total rural credit market is still remarkable.

The establishment of various institutional credit agencies has, to some extent, curbed the dominance of money lender in rural credit market. Though the influence of money lender is declining, yet they are still dominant and important in the development process of rural India and their role in rural economy, particularly, agriculture economy cannot be negated.

The paper is organized as follows. Section I traces out the evolution of money lending business in brief. Section II deals with the nature and characteristics of informal sector loan providers for agricultural and non-agricultural purposes in certain selected villages of Uttat Dinajpur district of West Bengal. Section III portrays the exploitative nature of business of informal sector lenders in our study villages. Section IV explores the causes of the existence of informal sector lenders in our study area in spite of the presence of formal sector lending institutions. Finally in section V we have suggested certain measures to curtail the role of informal sector lender in order to free the borrower farmers from the clutches of informal sector money lenders.

Nature of Informal Finance

In the context of our of our discussion about the nature of informal credit in rural areas under the present study we should specifically find out who the informal lenders are and who borrow from what type of informal lenders. In course of our field study we have seen that informal sector lenders in rural credit market have a strong base till today. In our study we have found that till now 31 per cent of the total loan cases come from informal sources of credit.

There are many players in the informal credit market in the rural area of our study. They are the village money lenders, traders, input-sellers, friends and relatives and big cultivators.[1] In fact all of these players taken together can be called money lenders.

Now let us see how the players in the informal rural credit market are playing their role in the village of our survey.

It is evident from Table 1 that input-sellers as informal lenders rank first position in terms of lending in the villages of our survey. Out of 112 borrower-farmers 43 take loan from input-sellers. So, they provide loan to 33.39 per cent farmers in the villages of our study. Next in importance come the big cultivators who supply credit to 42 farmers, which is 37.5 per cent of the total borrower-farmers of the surveyed villages. Village money lenders served 12 out of 112 loanees. They provided credit to 10.71 per cent of the total loanee-farmers of the surveyed villages. Traders also meet the credit need of the farmers. They serve 10 borrower-farmers out of 112. It is 8.93 per cent of the total loanee-farmers. Friends, relatives and neighbours also meet credit need of the farmers. They meet credit need of only 4.46 per cent of the total loanee-farmers. So far we have analysed the Table 1 according to the role of different players in the informal rural credit market of the surveyed villages. A pie chart is drawn to show the share of different informal lenders in the informal rural credit market in the surveyed villages.

Table 1
Distribution of Informal Credit Cases by Borrower-Lender Types (per centage)

	Type of Lenders					
Type of Borrowers	*Village money lenders*	*Traders*	*Input sellers*	*Friends & relatives*	*Big cultivators*	*Total*
Marginal farmers	12.50	3.57	12.50	3.57	67.86	100 (56)
Small farmers	7.31	12.19	15.85	65.85	4.88	1900 (41)
Large farmers	13.39	20.00	60.00	6.67	0.00	100 (15)
All	10.72	8.93	38.39	4.46	37.50	100 (12)

Source: Field Survey
Note: Figures in the parentheses indicate total informal loan cases.

It can be generalized from the above discussion that big cultivators and input sellers are the most dominant factors as informal lenders in the surveyed villages and the dominance of the village money lenders as informal lenders in the surveyed villages of this district is not as significant as big cultivators and input sellers were. It may be due to the fact that people engaged in money lending, as village money lenders are not feeling good in this profession. Besides, new avenues for income are coming up day by day and the people engaged in this profession are feeling better to invest their money therein.

Now, let us proceed to show the lender-borrower relationship through the data as gathered in our survey.

As per the land holding pattern in the district of Uttar Dinajpur the farmers are classified into five categorizes as follows:

(i) Marginal farmers: Farmers having an amount of land below 1.0 acre (most of the marginal farmers work as agricultural labour).

(ii) Small farmers: Farmers having an amount of land from 1.0 acre and above, but less than 2.0 acres.

(iii) Semi-medium farmers: Farmers having an amount of land of 2.0 acres and above but less than 4.0 acres.

(iv) Medium farmers: Farmers having an amount of land of 4.0 acre but less than 10.0 acres.

(v) Large farmers: Farmers having an amount of land of 10.0 acres and above.

But for convenience we have placed them in three categorizes:

(i) Marginal farmers: Farmers having an amount of land upto 2.0 acres;

(ii) Small farmers: Farmers having an amount of land upto 5.0 acres;

(iii) Large farmers: Farmers having an amount of land above 5.0 acres.

It is can be seen from Table 1 that big cultivators provide 37.5 per cent of the total informal loan. This Table also shows that big cultivators supply 67.86 per cent of their credit to the marginal farmers. The marginal farmers are generally supposed to have large number of family members, who also work as agricultural labours. The big cultivators give credit to the marginal farmers to ensure the supply of agricultural labour in their agricultural field during peak agricultural seasons. In most cases, big cultivators interlock their credit with labour service of the marginal borrower-farmers. These borrower-households generally repay their loan by giving labour services to the cultivator-lenders.

The input-sellers have also much dominance in the informal agricultural credit market. They are seen to be the most important source of informal farm lending. They provide 38.39 per cent of the total informal farm credit and it is the highest among the informal lenders. It is evident from Table 1 that the small farmers take 65.85 per cent of their informal farm credit from input-sellers and the large farmers also obtain 60 per cent of their informal farm credit from the same source. The main advantages of credit from input-sellers are that such credit may be repaid either in cash or kind.

Figures presented in Table 1, indicate that the position of the money lenders are now far behind the big cultivators and input-sellers as far as the provision of loan is concerned. The money lenders charge exorbitant rate of interest and their credit is to be repaid in cash only. Generally, they do not want to have their credit repaid in kind. The money lenders are found to have advanced only 10.78 per cent of the total informal credit while the traders have a share of 8.93 per cent of the total informal credit. The friends and relatives are not much important in the informal credit market as their share is only 4.46 per cent. It appears from Table 1 that the big cultivators have a preference to supply fund to the marginal farmers while the input-sellers have a tendency to serve all categories of farmers.

For the purpose of our discussion on informal lending tried to find out the answer to the question whether there is any relationship between the type of informal lenders and the purposes for which loan is taken.

Table 2
Lender Types and Purposes for Informal Loans
(Percentage of Loan Cases)

		Type of Lenders					
Category of Households	*Purpose of Loan*	*Village Money lenders*	*Traders*	*Input-sellers*	*Friends & Neighbours*	*Big cultivators*	*Total*
Marginal	Production	20.52	7.69	38.46	7.69	25.64	100 (39)
Farmers	Generalised Consumption	29.41	5.88	-	17.65	47.06	100 (17)
Small	Production	12.50	9.38	59.38	15.63	3.13	100 (32)
Farmers	Generalised Consumption	55.55	11.11	-	22.23	11.11	100 (9)
Large	Production	9.09	18.18	63.64	9.09	-	100 (11)
Farmers	Generalised Consumption	25.00	25.00	-	50.00	-	100 (4)

Note: (i) Figures in the parentheses indicate total amount of loan cases.
(ii) Generalised consumption includes expenditure for consumption, health, social & religious ceremonies and, construction & repairs of houses.

Source: Field Survey.

It is evident from Table 2 that the village money lenders provide credit to the farmers both for production and consumption purposes, but they have a tendency of providing more loan for consumption purpose. This Table reveals that all categories of farmers are attended by input-sellers but they provide fund only for production purpose while the big cultivators prefer marginal farmers to provide them consumption loan. They do so for the purpose of getting labour services from the family members of the marginal farmers to their own agricultural field during busy agricultural seasons. It could be seen from Table 2 that friends and relatives also provide informal credit to all categories of farmers, but in large number of cases, they supply credit for consumption purpose.

In respect of collateral on informal lending we should see what type of informal lenders prefers what type of collateral.

It is notable that informal lenders take both marketable and non-marketable collateral from the borrower-farmers.

Table 3 below shows the performance of types of colleteral by different types of informal lenders.

Table 3

Type of Lenders and Collateral Preference Irrespective of the Category of Households (Farmers)

Type of Lenders	*Total no. of loan cases*	*Per cent of Distribution of collateral based loans according Collateral*				
		Land	*Silver & Gold*	*Product*	*Labour*	*Total*
Village Money lenders	12	-	81.82	18.18	-	100
Traders	10	-	33.33	66.67	-	100
Input-sellers	43	12.82	-	87.18	-	100
Friends, Relatives and Neighbours	5	75.00	25.00	-	-	100
Big cultivators	42	13.51	-	5.41	81.08	100

Source: Field Survey.

According to the nature of collateral Table 3 reveals that the traders and big cultivators are more interested to accept non-marketable collateral like product and labour while advancing loans to the farmers. It also emerges from Table 6.3 that village money lenders and friends & relatives have a tendency to advance loan to the farmers against deposit of marketable collateral like land and gold. It is experienced while conducting field survey that in most cases friends, relatives and neighbours do not seek any collateral from the borrower, but if they seek any collateral, land is most preferred by them. In these cases it is observed that the lender retains the portion of land, which is mortgaged as collateral by borrower-farmers, until the repayment of loans is completely made. Under such cases crops of the mortgaged land are taken away by the lenders.

Exploitative Nature of Informal Sector Lenders

The well-known saying in the country: "The Indian farmer is born in debt, lives in debt and dies in debt", indirectly depicts the exploitative picture of money lenders. In 1951-52 nearly 93 per cent of the total rural credit requirements were from the source of money lenders, according to the All India Rural Credit Survey.

It is believed in Marxian economics that money lenders enter into lending transactions linked with other factor markets. These interlinked transactions are devices of the dominant party to subjugate the poor and to increase their political and economic power in the village economy. So, they lend money to consolidate their class position in the rural credit market.

Money lenders are associated with so many malpractices which exploit the borrower farmers to a great extent. Some of the malpractices as transpired to us in course of our interview with the borrowers are noted below:

(i) Money lenders deliver credit to the needy farmers and obtain bonds or promissory notes or sometimes they get a blank paper signed by the loanee-farmers and enter in the blank paper an amount of loan larger than actually delivered. Moreover, they charge a rate of interest much higher than the rate settled verbally at the time of delivering credit. If the cultivation goes well the loan is repaid though with tremendous miseries, and if cultivation is betrayed or the loanee-farmers face in any financial trouble, the loan is not repaid in time. By this time the amount of loan along with interest becomes so huge that the loanee-farmer cannot afford to repay. As a result, the farmers have to sale their land to the landlord. Thus, the money lenders grab the land of the loanee-farmers by ill tricks.

(ii) The money lenders give no money receipts to the loanee-farmers on the repayment of loan and often the money lenders deny the receipt of repayment of loan by the loanee-farmers. Such malpractice keeps the loan amount intact in spite of repayment. Thus, in practice, the loanee-farmer can rarely pay-off his dues. Even after his death the loan-amount is carried forward to his next generation who does not know anything about the burden of loan he has to shoulder. Thus, the popular saying: "The Indian farmer is born in debt lives in debt and dies in debt", has emerged.

(iii) Money lenders give loan against standing crops. They interlink credit with output. In this way, they exploit the loanee-farmers by two ways:

 (a) Charging exorbitant rate of interest on the amount of loan given to the farmers.

 (b) Making profit from the crops of the farmers as the money lenders, before delivering credit, give condition to the farmers to sell their crop to them (money lenders) at the price lesser than the prevailing market price.

(iv) Sometimes, money lenders exploit the loanee-farmers by advancing loan in lieu of mortgaging of land of the loanee. Here the money lenders take possession of the land of the loanee for cultivation, and until the entire amount of loan is repaid by the farmer, the money lender will continue to cultivate the land of the loanee. So the loanee-farmers' land remains mortgaged to the money lender, and as a result, the farmer finds no way but to work as agricultural worker or otherwise. In many cases the loanee-farmers do not get back their land by paying-off their dues, and the money lender cultivates his land year after year. He falls in deep poverty, which leaves him with little surplus to pay-off his old debts. Ultimately he has to sell the land to the money lender. In this way, he becomes a landless labourer.

(v) Money lender's credit is available for both productive and unproductive purposes. In many cases it could be found that money lenders exploit loanee-farmers by delivering them credit on the condtion that they have to supply labour in time of peak agricultural operation at a lower rate than what prevails in the labour market. If any able member of the loanee-farmer's family is found to hesitate to work as labour in the money lender's land or work elsewhere in spite of the demand by the money lender; the latter tortures the former both mentally and physically to force him to pay-off his dues even before the stipulated time.

(vi) Sometimes, while delivering credit to the farmers, the money lenders compel the borrower-farmers to buy agricultural inputs from them at a price higher than the market price and give them (borrowers) condition that they will have to sell their output at a lower price. Thus, the money lenders exploit the borrower-farmers both through selling of input and buying of output.

Causes of Existence of Informal Sector Lenders

Since pre-nationalization period government has made efforts to drive out the informal money lenders from rural credit market, but still today the presence of informal money lenders in our rural credit market is very much felt and their role appears to be very important from the point of view of supply of rural credit. The conventional notion about rural credit market has drastically been changed, now it is widely accepted that "credit transacted outside the banking circuit is quantitatively huge and qualitatively critical, especially in developing countries" (Floro and Yotopoulos, 1991).

A lot of reasons may be attributed to the existence of informal lending in our agricultural credit market. Some major ones are noted below:

(1) The systems and procedures of institutional credit are very rigid and complicated. Since large portions of our farmers are still poor and illiterate,.they dare not approach the institutional lenders.

(2) The lending formalities of institutional credit are time consuming. As a result, it increases the transaction cost of the rural borrowers, viz., cost of repeated visits to the branch of bank, cost of obtaining quotation for loan, cost of getting land ownership certificates from the competent authority and so on.

(3) It is a fact that at present 70.82 per cent of the farming population of the district of Uttar Dinajpur belongs to marginal and small category of farmers. They do not have sufficient marketable collateral for obtaining formal loan as additional security. In such cases the bankers have negative attitude towards lending to the poor farmers. They think that lending to agriculture is not profitable; rather it is a very risky venture. It is noteworthy that though the provision of collateral for of amount upto Rs. 50,000 is not needed as per rule, the bankers do not want to deliver credit without collateral.

(4) Since most of the staff of institutional credit houses do not reside in the place of branch, no personalized relations between the borrower-farmers and the formal lenders is built up. But money lenders live in the village of borrower-farmers and have a personalized relation with borrower-farmers and in some cases it is seen that the informal money lenders have been in close touch with the farmers over generations. On account of the personalized relation over generations, the borrower-farmers cannot think but to approach for credit to the informal lenders.

(5) As approaching for loan to the money lenders requires no formal procedures, the borrower-farmers have easy accessibility to money lenders.

(6) Informal lending is still influential in rural credit market as it delivers credit for both productive and non-productive purposes. No loan for non-productive purpose is delivered by the formal sector.

(7) A farmer, whose agricultural expenses are not covered by the formal sources due to the rationing of credit and strict requirements of collateral against credit, can easily borrow from informal sources. For getting loan from informal sources, he is not asked any question regarding the purpose of loan. Besides, he is not required to pledge any marketable collateral like land.

The only thing he has to do in this regard is to pledge his crop. Such type of informal sources interlinks credit with output, and the borrower is benefited in two ways: He gets ready market for his crop and he requires no place for storage or buyer to find out.

(8) Timely delivery of credit is not always done by the formal sector. Sometimes it is so delayed that the purpose for which loan is sought becomes fruitless when the loan is due to be disbursed.

(9) Every branch of commercial banks in the district of Uttar Dinajpur has to work with a geographical area of 3140 sq. km. and a population of 49832 people as per the census of 2001. Under such circumstances, it becomes quite impossible to a branch to search the persons who are in search of credit. Most of the branches of commercial banks in rural areas are two-staff branch. But as the money lenders confine their lending activities to a limited number of people, they can get the information that are in need of credit. Whenever they get the information, they rush to the door of the needy farmers and give credit instantly. Such type of work banks cannot do. Banks have to maintain heaps of papers before issuing any loan. Naturally banks trail behind the money lenders.

(10) The rigidity of the repayment schedule of loan provided by the formal sector institutions sometimes discourages the farming people to obtain loan from the formal sector.

(11) In many cases the so-called prominent persons of the locality discourages or insist on the borrower-farmers not to obtain loan from institutional sources. Such types of persons are the agents of the money lenders. So, according to Lipton (1976), "urban interests conspire against the rural poor and deny them access to significant amounts of formal credit."

(12) The price of land is not valued as per present market price by the formal sector lending institutions. So, it is

undervalued. Only Rs. 10,000 is given as loan for crop per acre of land. It is too meager for the farmers to carry out their activities. But informal sector lenders a larger amount of loan per acre of land. This is why; informal sector lenders are preferred by the borrower-farmers.

Suggested Measures to Reduce the Role of Informal Sector Lenders

On the basis of our field investigation we would like to suggest the following remedial measures to minimize the role of the informal sector lenders in order to lessen the degree of exploitation of the borrower farmers:

(i) The number of institutional credit agencies should be increased to such a level that the institutional credit houses reach to the doorstep of every farming households to meet their credit need.

(ii) The nature of collateral should be diversified. The institutional credit agencies grant loan to the borrower-farmers only on the basis of marketable securities, i.e. land, gold, silver etc. But the money lenders deliver credit on the basis of both marketable and non-marketable collateral like crop, labour, utensil, cattle etc. It is a fact that still a large number of farmers in our study area do not have any legal title deed of their own land. In our study area in some cases land is bought and sold on the basis of verbal agreement. They do not care to get their land registered by the competent authority. The farmers possess land orally in terms of actual possession but they do not legally possess it. So, they are deprived of getting loan from any institutional credit houses on the basis of the legal possession of land. This is why the institutional credit houses should deliver credit on the basis of both marketable and non-marketable collaterals against loan like the money lenders.

(iii) The amount of loan per acre of land should be increased. As mentioned earlier, at present only Rs. 10000 is granted to the borrower-farmers as loan per acre of land. It is too meager an amount.

(iv) Institutional credit agencies deliver loan only for productive purposes. But the borrower-farmers need loan not only for production of crops, but also for consumption and other non-productive purposes. The non-institutional credit agencies offer loan to the borrower-farmers for any purpose. To make control over diversion of loan amount, the institutional credit agencies should specify the category of credit for both production and non-production purpose with some specific rules regarding the rate of interest, mode of payment etc. In some cases we found that the farmers take loan from money lenders for an emergent need at a high rate of interest and at last fails to repay the loan along with huge amount of interest and until and unless the whole amount of loan is repaid, the borrower-farmer is debarred from loan from other sources. Thus, the money lenders bind him in a chain of debt for a long time or till his death.

(v) The area of operation of the branch of a bank should be limited. As per the figure in 2002 every branch of a bank, on an average, has to operate with 49,332 people in the district of Uttar Dinajpur, as compared to 15,000 people at the national level. Practically it is very difficult for the rural branch of a bank to look after the credit need of this huge number of people in a situation when the number of staff per branch in our rural area does not exceed four.

(vi) The money lender gives credit to them who are in the close contact with the him and whom he meets almost daily being resident of the same village or of an adjacent village. Generally, the staff of the rural branch of a bank does not reside in rural areas; they come from urban area and do not have any privilege to meet the villagers beyond their office hours. So, no social relation is built-up between the bankers and the borrower-farmers. Under such circumstances the farmers hesitate to approach for loan to the bank staff. Therefore, we suggest that the staff of a bank should reside near the branch in the same village so that a scope of building up social contact with the farmers is possible. If it is successfully done, the farmers will not hesitate to approach for loan to bank in time of need.

(vii) There should be strict follow-up of the existing rules regarding the unauthorized or unlicensed money lenders operating in the rural credit circuit to curb their dominance in the rural credit market.

(viii) Frequent holding of farmers' 'Awareness Camp' should be organized to make the farmers aware of different economic facilitates easily available from institutional credit systems and also about the exploitative attitude of the money lenders.

(ix) The loaning procedures of institutional credit agencies should be easy, prompt, flexible and less paper-based. As still most of our farming population is illiterate, they dare not approach for loan to the bank for the fear of complicated paper work.

Note

1. *Village Money lenders:* Village money lenders lend money to the farmers at high rate of interest and their primary source of income is lending. Generally money lenders' loan is repaid in cash. As per our survey (Table 1) 10.71 per cent of players in the informal credit market belong to the cases of village money lenders. *Traders:* They meet the financial requirements of the farmers for productive purposes much before the crops mature. They generally force the farmers to sell their product to them and they also charge high rate of interest. *Input-sellers:* 8.93 per cent Input-sellers supply credit to the farmers in kind, particularly in the form of seeds, fertilizers, pesticides etc. The borrower-farmers

repay their credit either in cash or in kind. *Big cultivators:* They give loan to the marginal and small farmers mainly. Generally they interlink their credit with labour services. The big cultivators give credit to the marginal and small farmers who have greater number of family members. They advance credit to such group of farmers from whom they are assured of the supply of labour during the busy agricultural seasons. They also charge interest on credit. Primarily they are interested in farming but they carry on moneylending as a side business. *Friends, Relatives and Neighbours:* Farmers generally borrow from their friends, relatives and neighbours in cash or kind in order to tide over temporary difficulties. Generally they charge low interest or no interest, but such loan is repaid just after the harvest.

References

Agarwal, G. D. (1955), "Role of Moneylenders in Agricultural Finance, *Indian Journal of Agricultural Economics,* Vol. 32, No. 2, p. 41.

Bandyopadhyay, A. Kumar (1984), "Economics of Agricultural Credit with Special Reference to Small Farmers in West Bengal", *Agricole Publishing Academy.*

Barman, K. K. (1994), "Financial Sector Reforms: Some Implications for Rural Credit", *Indian Journal of Agricultural Economics,* Vol. 49, No. 3, Conference No. July-Sept.

Bouman F. J. A. (1990), Informal Rural Finance: An Alladin's Lamp of Information, *Sociologica Ruralis,* Vol. xxx 2.

Catanach, I. J. (1970), Rural *Credit in Western India 1875*-1930, University of California Press, Berkeley.

Degaonkar, Chaya K. (1994), "Agricultural Finance in a Backward Region," *Asian Economic Review,* Vol. 36, No. 1, p. 35.

Floro, S. L. and Yotopoulos, P. A. (1991), *Informal Credit Markets and the New Institutional Economics, 'The Case of Phillipine Agriculture,* Westwind Press, Inc. Boulder.

Ghate, P. *et al* (1992), Informal Finance, Oxford University Press, Delhi.

Jodhka, Surinder S. (1995), "Who Borrows? Who Lends? Changing Structure of Informal Credit in Rural Haryana, *Economic and Political Weekly,* Vol. xxx, No. 39, Sept. 30, pp. A-123 to A-132.

Lipton (1987), "Variable Access to Food", in J. Price Gittinger, Joanne Leslie and Caroline Hoisington (eds.), *Food Policy: Interacting*

Supply, Distribution and Consumption, John Hopkins University Press, Baltimore.

Ray Debraj, *et.al.* (1989), "Interlinkages and the Pattern of Competition," in Bardhan, P.K. (ed.), *The Economic Theory of Agrarian Institutions,* Oxford University Press, New York.

Sarap, Kailas (1991), *Interlinked Agrariar, Markets in Rural India,* Sage Publications India Pvt. Ltd., New Delhi-48.

Yunus, Muhammad (1987), *Credit for Self-Employment: A Fundamental Human Right,* Gramin Bank, Dhaka, Bangladesh.

3

RURAL CREDIT FOR RURAL DEVELOPMENT IN THE GLOBAL ERA

BIRENDRA KUMAR JHA

"THE main challenge before a developing nation was to foster sustainable growth. For growth or its recovery the nation's productivity has to be strengthened and expanded. In the development agenda, an important issue relates to the problem of the provision and delivery of financial services and credit to the poor so that the poor emerge out of their poverty through meaningful productive activities (Rangarajan, 1999) India is the second fastest growing economy of the World after China. The Central Statistical Organization (CSO) estimated the country's gross domestic product (GDP) growth rate at 8.7% in the current financial year 2007-08 whereas China has witnessed 10.7% growth rate in the same year. This is, undoubtedly, much better performance than expected on the back of high domestic savings and increased spending on capacity expansion. Although the growth of 8.7% is lower than 9.4% GDP growth recorded in the financial year 2006-07 which was the best performance in 18 years of global era but reaching double digit growth is not possible without rural development to a desirable extent.

The 'big push' and 'trickle-down' approaches adopted as development strategy during the planning period have generated inequalities across regions, sectors and rural-urban locations. The policy makers have believed in trickle-down economics. But it is not true that a rising tide lifts all boats'. Sometimes, a quickly rising tide, especially when accompanied by a storm, dashes weaker boats against the shore, smashing them to Smithereens. Pauperism seemed to grow in the 19th century England even though the country as a whole prospered. Growth in America in the 1980s, provided the most recent dramatic example. While the economy grew, those at the bottom saw their real income decline (Joseph E. Stiglitz, 2002). R. B. Singh (2005) has rightly observed that if tricke-down economy didn't work in England or recently in America, why would it work in developing countries and while it is true that sustain reduction in poverty cannot be attained without robust economic growth, the converse is not true, growth need not benefit all.

Socio-economic Reality in Rural India

The much talked about 'feel-good factor' among the economically privileged sections of urban population should not blind us to the fact that we have the largest number of poor living in rural areas where job famine is now becoming the most serious socio-economic, socio-political challenge. The robust demonstration of its strength by the Indian economy during the last four years has brought a cheer to the planners and finance minister. A plethora of central and state schemes and programmes are under implementation for the benefit of the common man, but the growth of urban conglomerates and the exodus from villages to cities indicate that the intended benefits of development have not reached the needy. The magnitude of the problem of rural poverty faced by the country is immense. According to UN studies, the largest number of World's poor are living in India (HDR, 2003) and, that amounts to one-fourth of the world poor. Rural people living BPL in the mid-fifties, was 54% or 184 million persons. At the dawn of 21st century the people living BPL were brought down to

27% rural and 24% urban. But the number of persons living BPL did dramatically increase to 193 million rural and 67 million urban and 260 million total (India SDR, 2006). Liberalization, Privatization and Globalization (LPG) syndrome did promote international economic growth, especially that of developed countries. However, it is noted that LPG is increasingly failing to generate new and better jobs could lead to people's empowerment and poverty reduction in developing countries. According to ILO Key Indicators of Labour Market (KILM) Report, 2005, half of the world's workforce i.e. 1.38 billion are not able to earn enough to lift themselves and their families above poverty line at $2 or more a person a day. Obviously, the constituents of the Indian labour force are the worst affected one.s That is why, the post liberalization growth of India is aptly termed as jobless growth (V. Govinderajulu 2008). The new economic policy initiated by Indian government in 1991 has also affected the government capacity to mobilize resource to finance the rural development activities.

Needless to say that India's rural scenario is dismal as it is characterized by falling contribution to GDP, migration of labour to urban areas in search of job-opportunities, sucking of villages by cities, diversification of crop patterns and so on. The fact is 70% of the country's population is now contributing to less than 20% of GDP reflecting lesser income for the masses and greater concentration of wealth in fewer hands in the cities. No doubt, the recent prime challenges for the policy makers have been to sustain the growth momentum but one of the most disturbing features of the growth process is that despite high growth of overall GDP and per capita income after launching of economic reforms in 1991 the growth rate of Indian agriculture has decelerated significantly. The Economic Survey 2007-08 pronounces a performance of Indian agriculture at only 2.6% in 2007-08. It is needless to say that acceleration of growth of agriculture sector which is the mainstay of rural India, where 70% of the country's population resides, will not only push the overall GDP growth upwards, it would also make the growth rate inclusive. Raising productivity of all the pursuits in which rural people are engaged is highly desirable for rural development. At the start of the 1970s, 62% of India's national income was generated in rural areas and only 38% of it arose in urban locations. Today, the urban population earns a little more than half of national income, accordingly the rural population now earns a little less than half. Thus, in income generation terms, the centre of gravity in Indian economy has shifted fairly recently from rural to urban areas. The vast majority of income earners, however, continues to live and work in rural places. One result is that urban per capita income in 1999-2000 had risen to almost two and a half times rural per capita income a figure some what higher than the corresponding figure for 1970-71, and substantially higher than figures for the intervening period. During the 1970s and 1980s, the rural-urban per capita income gap had narrowed considerably, only to widen again, rather suddenly, during the second half of the 1990s. A change in the income growth trajectories of rural and urban areas led to this deepening of the rural-urban divide. This does not augur well for the future economic welfare of rural India's population. Most rural income is still generated in agriculture, although the share has gone down by more than 20 percentage points since 1970-71. Agriculture now accounts for only half of all rural incomes (Sheila Bhalla, 2005).

Rural Development

Economic development of a country entails development of all segments of its population, whether living in metropolitan and urban areas or in semi-urban and rural locations but we all know that most of India lives in the rural areas. And so overall economic development of the country, therefore, depends upon the development that takes place the rural areas which are characterized by abject and widespread poverty which is reflected in low per capita income, less access to education, health, housing, water supply and other essential services. It is needless to say that rural development is essentially dependent on agricultural development. Once income from agricultural pursuits increase, rural people's standard of living will increase, poverty will banish, unemployment and under-employment will diminish, agricultural labourers will get more income and employment. In fact, rural development in all aspects will get momentum to the extant of agricultural development and consequential income generation. This is reason behind confusion. Rural development is often confused with agricultural development. Agricultural development, no doubt, constitutes the heart but not the whole of rural development. Rural development of the rural life changes in a desired direction and in sympathy with the other components. It means structural changes in the socio-economic set-up of the rural areas within the framework of the national goals and objectives and without prejudice to the development of urban areas of the country, provided that urban development is not prejudicial to rural development. According to Bowles Chester, "Rural area means not only the villages and their surrounding farm areas, but also the rural towns, ranging from two or three thousand population to many thousands, which serve as marketing centres for the peasants and landless labour of the countryside". He defined rural development in these words", "Rural development means only agricultural expansion but the growth of small industry, schools, training centres, improved communications, rural electrification, public health, population control centres and even the stimulation of rural cultural awakening" (Bowles Chester, 1963).

Phases of Rural Development

The first moorings of rural development were founded during British time when Lord Curzon encouraged Justice Ranade and Sir William Wedderburn who prepared the first scheme for cooperative credit banks to provide loans to farmers. In 1892 late Sir Frederick Nicholson assigned by the then government of Madras, prepared a report on starting system of land banks and recommended cooperative societies on Reiffeisen Model, German concept of Agricultural co-operative Movement and thus, rural development started in India at once as an agricultural movement and co-operative movement. Statutorily the cooperative movement which was visualized as a social force and a powerful instrument of economic transformation and a sort of organizational training ground in increasing the strength of working class, was firmed up through the Cooperative Societies Act of 1904 but it gave no legislative protection to societies other than credit, to the central agencies, banks, unions which were gradually coming into existence to finance and supervise the primary credit societies. Thus, the seeds were sown and in a predominantly rural economy with 5.78 lakh villages and 70% of populace living on agriculture, the stress was on development of Agricultural cooperatives and agricultural sector has been key to rural development (P. Krishanaji, 1986).

In the post independence period rural development programme has passed through several phases. The first one began with the inception of the community development programme. Launched on October 2, 1952 in the First Five year Plan period and starting with 55 pilot projects, the programme covered within 13 years by the Third Plan period, the length and breadth of the country. The seed of the present day IRDP lay in the then CDP as CDP concept aimed at many sided development or balanced regional development of the present day Area Approach as distinct from intensive development of particular aspects. Initially, a community development block covered an area of about 1300 sq. km. with about 300 villages and a population of 0.2 million. The pattern was revised in 1958 when a block was made to cover 620 sq.km. only with 110 villages and a population of about 92,000 persons. Supply of fund for the blocks remained primarily the responsibility of the central government till the end of 1966 after which the programme was transferred to the state sector of the plan. This considered slowed down the progress of CDP and relegated it to low priority projects.

Another notable development of the planned economy has been local self government (LSG) or the panchayat raj so to speak which was the administrative machinery to implement the national programme viz CDP and other programmes that were to follow. The panchayats and cooperatives were to plan and implement the CDP with the aid of the government agencies at village level. But this experiment in democratic decentralization was however not taken in right spirit as the Asoka Mehta committee reviewing the performance found that the working of panchayat raj administration was vitiated by political factionalism, corruption and inefficiency. Soon the project had to be side tracked due to unanticipated fall in food production during the sixties and India which was to have launched on, to the proverbial Rostowian 'Takeoff' into self sustained growth stage' ran a ground. Emphasis on 'Grow More Food' (GMF) campaign and HYVs to raise food output attracted and in this process the concept of area development approach of community development got diluted and it became synonymous with agricultural development which constituted the third phase of rural development.

In the fourth phase of rural development planning, the large scale awareness of expanding food grain production to cut down the large scale imports of food grains from abroad especially wheat from U.S.A. and rice from Burma and Thailand, through what is now legendary 'Green Revolution' and HYVs and IAD programmes was found but its fall-out on rural development was not very heartening. The capital intensive method of agricultural operation led to built up deformities in the socio-economic structure of rural communities which, in the long run resulted in widening the disparity between the rich and the poor and even regional disparity widened because the new agricultural strategy could be directed only to the favourable pockets. To counteract these problems the fourth plan aimed at diffusing the benefits of modern technology in agriculture to the weaker sections of community and the underdeveloped regions of the country through programmes intended to tackle special regional or individual problems and for which government of India launched a number of rural development schemes like crash scheme for Rural Employment, Minimum Needs Programme, Antodaya, Small Farmers Development Agency, Drought prone Area Programme, Farmers' Training programme, Rural Industries projects, and so on. These programmes helped to accelerate the overall development of the country but with every increase in farm as well as factory production, the disparity between those who owned the productive assets and those who did not have grew wider.

The fifth phase of rural development began in 1978-79. Prior to the fifth phase we find that the main weakness of the programme arose mainly due to their being primary concerned with the development of primary sector and so only those who owned land could be benefited from programmes. The various target group oriented or area oriented programmes were not comprehensive whilst the expectations of the people were rising. A large number of rural households below the poverty line belonged to agricultural labour, rural artisans, non-agricultural wage earners and other self-employed persons were left outside the scope of these programmes and so this realization necessitated the adoption of the new strategy of rural development known as Integrated Rural Development programme (IRDP). But the result of IRDP have not shown as much promise as expected.

The next phase of rural development aimed at revitalizing district administration as a spring board for local planning. Panchayat Raj is expected to be revamped and people's participation encouraged and motivated. The Eight plan adopted the grass root planning as an important component of the national plan. What is highly desirable for rural development is the development of local resource based economy which will provide additional employment and employment to people living in rural areas. Muhammed Yunus (2004) stated that less from the experiences of other developing countries like Bangladesh, Indonesia, Bolivia and Philippines motivated India, too to start experiencing innovative scheme of SHGs which are also called as thrift and credit groups'. Of course, the SHGs is a brainchild of Grameen Bank of Bangladesh which was founded by Prof. Muhammed yunus of Chittageng University in the year 1975 but the real effort was made after 1991-92 from linkage of SHGs with the banks. The IRDP that was planned with good thinking had inherent weakness in terms of monitoring and evaluation. Nonetheless, it was the first major initiative in the right direction. The recent programmes like the SSA, SGRY, NFFWP, NREGP, PMGSY, SJGSY and NRHM have been launched with substantial funding. The effectiveness of these programmes will depend on the implementation by convergence and synergy.

The planning commission has set ambitious targets of generating seven crore new job opportunities during the 11th plan period and to double the per capita income during the next ten years to remove poverty and improve living conditions of the people. This could be achieved only if the growth rate crosses 10%. The rural economy has to grow at double the present pace of growth of less than 3%. Alongwith several other such steps a second 'Green Revolution is the urgent need to improve rural economy for rural development. The Economic Survey 2007-08 reveals the fact that," Maintaining growth rate at nine per cent will be a challenge and raising it to two digits will be an even greater one". Mr. Chidambram, the Finance Minister admits himself there are several challenges to inclusive growth namely agriculture, infrastructure, education and skill development. He says" we have to ensure that the benefits of the growth percolate to the most marginal and vulnerable segments of the society. Hereby it is worth noting that Bharat Nirman Programme envisaged bringing an additional one crore hectares of un irrigated agricultural land. under assured irrigation; all weather road connectivity for all habitations having a population of one thousand (500 in hilly and tribal areas), provision of safe drinking water to all villages and habitations in the country, electrification of all the remaining villages and hamlets, construction of sixty lakh houses for the rural poor and telephone connectivity to all the remaining villages in the country. For these a number of programmes have been designed specifically to enlarge the flow of credit to the poor particularly living in rural India.

Role of Credit for Rural Development

"In any design of rural development, an efficient credit delivery system has to be integral part....... The role of credit and credit institutions in augmenting production and productivity is well recognized. The main thrust of Indian public policy towards rural credit has, therefore, been to ensure that sufficient and timely credit, at reasonable rates of interest, is made available to as large a segment of the rural population as possible". (Rangarajan, 1999).

For rural development we have been planning since 1950s and merely chugging along with limited success. Bunker Roy in his article 'Freedom from Poverty mentions Einstein's interesting definition of insanity. "Endlessly repeating the same process hoping for different results,' A powerful formula for bringing prosperity to rural India is Providing Urban Amenities to Rural Areas (PURA). Our mission to uplift a large number of rural people living below poverty level and provide them with improved quality of life necessitates the spread of the development process to the rural sector. That is what PURA programme involving four connectivities namely physical, electronic and knowledge leading to economic connectivity envisages physical connectivity through quality roads and transport, electronic connectivity through telecom and high bandwidth fibre optic cables; knowledge connectivity through education, skill training for farmers, artisans and craftsmen and entrepreneurship programmes and these three will lead economic connectivity through starting of enterprises with the help of banks, micro credit and marketing of products. Undoubtedly PURA proves instrumental in the process of rural development but it cannot forgotten that lack of access to financial services for the vast majority of India population is the biggest hurdle in realizing the full growth potential of economy in rural India. As Prof. Muhammad Yunus said, "credit is a kind of key, a passport to explore the potential of a person. Credit was the real missing link between people and their creative potential. I want to make credit available to more and more poor people to give them the chance of better future" (Quoted by S. Kumar & S. Anand in Kurukshetra, 2007). Indeed, the role of credit for rural development is crucial, and financial institutions are one of the important catalytic agents in the process of development but they may play an increasingly critical role in triggering off development, particularly in rural areas only when, as Mrs. Indira Gandhi said, "an institution, such as the banking system, which touches and should touch the lives of the millions has necessarily to be inspired by a larger social purpose and has to sub serve national priorities and objectives". (quoted by Pranab Mukherjee, 1985). Despite high density of the retail outlets of formal credit institution, the presence of informal agencies for credit continue to exist although their share has been declining over the years. Informal agencies largely extend credit for consumption and social ceremonies and their interest and other terms of conditions are onerous, yet they coexists with the formal financial institutions mainly due to their proximity, feel-at-ease, timely and quick services, all time access, purpose free credit, flexibility in loan repayments and low transaction costs. According to All India Rural Credit Survey, non-institutional sources supplied 91.27% of the total rural credit in 1951-52. This share has declined to 71% in 1971-72 and further to around 36% in 1990-91. Despite a perceptible increase in the flow of rural credit from institutional sources, financial needs, primary credit, are still primarily met by informal sources on exploitative terms. In 2002 the share of non-institutional credit was around 43% of the total rural credit.

Institutional sources include set of multi agency institutions namely cooperative Banks, commercial Banks, Regional Rural Banks and Micro-Finance Institutions. India having a large number of people below poverty line is place in a unique situation which necessitates a number of credit-based poverty alleviation programmes. Cooperative banks as well as commercial banks are already involved in these programmes; the RBI and the NABARD, besides providing policy guidelines, have been playing an important role in enlarging the flow of credit to these programmes by providing refinance assistance to participating banks. The strategy of developing rural financial services is a three pronged one consisting of (i) expansion of the institutional structure (ii) directed lending; and (iii) concessional or subsidized credit. (Rangarajan, 1999). This approach has resulted in an impressive growth of rural banking of India in terms of its outreach, credit disbursement and support to the poverty alleviation programmes.

The credit goes to the report of the All India Rural Credit Survey of 1954 for laying down the foundations for the building of a broad credit infrastructure for rural credit. Ensuring the provision of timely and sufficient credit to as large a segment of rural population as possible has been one of the major policy initiatives which has guided the formulation of public policy in the country. The rural credit system in India has evolved through different phases as a result of these initiatives and there has been a substantial broadening of the infrastructure for credit delivery resulting in increased outreach and reduction in the influence of informal agencies. The major policy in the sphere of rural credit has been its progressive institutionalization so as to ensure timely and increased flow of credit to the farm sector, reduce regional imbalances and to provide increased credit support to the special programmes.

The practice of extending institutional credit to agriculture can be traced back to that period when farmers were provided with such credit by the government during drought years. Of course, co-operatives could be seen as the premier institutions for disbursing rural credit "For some decades, that is since long before the organization of the Reserve Bank, great faith has been placed in India in the potentialities of the co-operative organization to serve the credit needs of the country, especially of the rural sector". (RBI 1970: 68) It was in 1935 that the Reserve Bank was founded and during the period between 1935 and 150 the Reserve Bank was very active in continuing the attempt to re-invigorate the co-operative credit movement through a variety of initiatives. Besides providing financial accommodation to the co-operative movement, the RBI played a central role in the task of building the co-operative credit structure, which gradually evolved into two separate arms, one for short term credit and another for long term credit - a structure that still exists today. Co-operative credit structure in India consists of a 3-tier structure. At the apex are the state Co-operative Banks followed by District Co-operative Banks at the district level and Primary Agricultural Credit Society at the grass root level. The committee of Direction that conducted the All India Rural credit survey (1954) observed that agricultural credit fell short of the right quantity, was not of the right type, did not serve the right purpose and often failed to go to the right people. The committee, therefore, recommended an integrated scheme of rural credit based on the co-operative credit system as an exclusive agency for providing agricultural credit supplanting the moneylender. Despite the implementation of the recommendations of All India Rural Credit Survey (1954), the co-operative credit system was found to be wanting and inadequate to meet the new and growing needs. In 1950-51 co-operatives provided only 3.1% of total rural credit, which has increased to 22.7% in 1970-71. The amount of aggregate credit, both short and long term, was 28,94,7 crore in 2005-06 as against Rs. 24 crore in 1950-51. The number of Primary Agricultural Credit Societies, supplying short term credit is around one lakh and the number of co-operative land development bank is around 750. The credit co-operatives have played a vital role in channeling credit to the farmers and therefore summed up that "co-operation has failed, but co-operation must succeed". But at the same time the co-operative system was beset with some serious problem like dominance of large farmers, weak financial position due to large overdue and low recovery rate, poor management and efficiency in working methods, inadequate and unsatisfactory agencies for dispensing production-oriented credit etc.

The All India Rural Credit Review Committee (1966) undertook a comprehensive review of the supply of rural credit in the context of the Fourth Plan in general, and the requirements of the intensive programmes of agricultural production in different parts of the country, in particular, and to make recommendations for improving the flow of agricultural credit. After a comprehensive review, the specific recommendation of the committee was: "The requirement of the agricultural sector was so large and diverse that commercial and co-operative banks can both play a mutually complementary role without getting into conflict with each other." Thus, the merit of the co-operative banking system was found in fulfilling the twin objectives of (i) providing a credit delivery system operating at the doorsteps of the farmer and (ii) making such credit available at relatively cheaper rates in view of the economy in the operating costs but credit cooperative did not function too well in meeting the need for credit and so it needed the support of commercial bank.

Our commercial banking system had only a limited responsibility of providing working finance to trade and industry and the share of commercial banks in rural credit was very low. According to All India Rural Credit Survey, share of banks in rural credit was only 0.9% in 1951-52 which was further reduced to 0.7% in 1961-62. Since the nationalization of the 14 major commercial banks in 1969, the banking industry has traveled a long way to emerge as one of the accredited agencies of rural development. Efforts are also being made to being about an orientation in the lending policies, procedures and practices of the banks so as to enlarge the flow of credit to the smaller borrowers, particularly to the rural poorer sections of the society. Towards this end six more banks were nations allied in 1980 (Pranab Mukherjee, 1985). Banking in India has now moved from class banking to mass banking. The number of branches in rural areas has increased from 1833 in 1969 to 33004 in 1995 recording almost 18 times increase during this period. The share of rural branches has increased from 22% to 53% during the same period. Credit deposit ratio for rural areas has increased from 37.5% in 1969 to 48.50% in 1995. However, the expansion and promotion of banking in rural India has taken a backseat after reforms taken place in 1991. The trend of bank expansion has got reversed after 1991. Though the number of total bank offices has increased during this period, the number of branches in rural India has decreased from 35,329 in 1994 to 32,481 in 2002. Credit-deposit ratio has also declined from around 50% in 1994 to 41.8% in 2002. The number of rural credit accounts has also declined from 3.22 crore in 1991 to 185.73 lakhs in 2004. However, rural deposit has increased during this period. The proportion non-institutional debt in rural areas has also gone up from 9.8% in 1991 to 15.5% in 2001. This reversal in trends might be possible because of the new polices adopted by commercial banks. In order to become more competitive and financially viable, these banks start reducing their non-performing assets most of these banks adopted the policy of mergers and acquisitions which in turn reduced the number of branches and other banking operations like advancement of loan etc. in rural areas. The decline in CD ratio between 1991 and 2001 shows that deposits mobilized from rural India are being utilized elsewhere. Also, the commercial banks have failed to fill the gap generated by cooperatives in availability of credit for rural people (S. Kumar & S. Aanad, 2007).

Regional Rural Banks are specialized rural financial institutions for catering to the credit needs of the rural sector. The working group with Sri M. Narsimham as the chairperson recommended establishing state sponsored, regionally based and rural-oriented banks. In the light of the recommendation of the working group, the government passed the Regional Rural Bank Ordinance in 1975 which was later replaced by the Regional Rural Bank Act, 1976. The observation of the Narasimham Working Group reveals the main motivation behind setting up the RRBs:

The main disabilities in the co-operatives in purveying the needed quantum of credit arise from their inability to mobilize adequate deposit resources, their managerial weaknesses and the character of their functioning marked by dominance of the vested interests which have come in the way of their efficient functioning, especially effective supervision of credit and the inadequate coverage of the small and marginal farmer. Yet another weakness has been of the limited absorptive capacity from the higher tiers of the co-operative credit structure urged repeatedly and attempted over the last two decades don't appear to have yielded because of inadequate non-overdue cover efforts at rehabilitation of the co-operative credit structure any appreciable results and there was probably an urgent need to try out new experiments, specially in credit-starved areas of the country........ the commercial banks suffered from two basic weakness in dispensation of rural credit i.e. (i) their high cost structure and (ii) their attitudinal character basically urban oriented.... in a country of the size and regional diversity as India, no single pattern, be it commercial banking or co-operative credit, can be expected to meet all the emerging requirements in all areas. A degree of adaptation and improvisation is called for and the range of institutional alternatives widened.

RRBs were expected to combine local feel and familiarly with the rural problems which the co-operatives possessed on the one hand, and the degree of business organization and modernized outlook of commercial banks, on the other. (Rangarajan, 1999). RRBs are empowered to extend all banking activities under clause (b) of section 5 of the Banking Regulation Act, 1949 and can also undertake one or more types of business described in sub-section (i) of section 6 of the same Act.

There are 196 RRBs operating in 26 states across 518 districts with a network of 14446 branches as on March 31,2004, majority of the branches of RRBs are located at rural areas.

Even though the RRBs are providing better services to the rural poor, they have only limited resources and concentration on a small geographical area. This is the time of globalization. In the global world the Indian banks face competition from the foreign banks. The RRBs face competition from other PSCBs and also from private sector banks. It creates under competition among banks under the same ownership (A Subbiah & M. Salvakumar, 2006). The most worrisome is the decline in the number of RRB from 196 in 1990 to 104 by 2006.

Another major landmark in the history of development of rural credit in India was the establishment of the National Bank for Agriculture and Rural Development (NABARD). Following the recommendations of the committee to review arrangements for institutional credit for agriculture and rural development, NABARD was set up in 1982, which took over the entire undertaking of the ARDC and the refinancing functions of the RBI in relation to state co-operatives and RRBs until the establishment of the NABARD, the refinance facility was made available directly by the RBI. Since its inception, the NABARD has played a central role in providing financial assistance, facilitating institutional development and encouraging promotional efforts in the area of rural credit Pranab Mukherjee (1985) has pointed out that "It is expected that NABARD will develop as a fully autonomous statutory organization providing the necessary leadership to banks to play their proper role in integrated rural development". Realizing the potential of village industries the NABARD constituted a Task force to look into the various aspects of this sector's development which made several important suggestions relating to credit and promotional support for village industries. Based on the tenor of these suggestions, the NABARD has opened several new lines of credit for investment in production as well as for infrastructure support. In keeping with the well-established principle of multi-agency lending, refinance facilities have been made available through all banking channels, etc. co-operative banks, scheduled commercial banks, regional rural banks and state land development banks. Of course, the NABARD is an apex institution in the field of rural credit by merging the Agricultural Refinance and Development corporation, the Agricultural credit department and Rural credit and planning cell of the RBI During 2004-05 the total disbursement of credit by NABARD was Rs. 1,25,309 crore. In 2005-06 ground level credit flow to agriculture and allied activities was Rs. 1,57,480 crore. The NABARD has also initiated several innovative projects like Rural Infrastructure Development Fund (RIDF), Kisan Credit Scheme and Watershed Development Fund etc. The government of India in the Union Budget of 1995-96 had taken a unique step in according priority for creation of rural infrastructure through the Rural Infrastructure Development Fund (RIDF) administered by NABARD. Among the major steps that are taken by the NABARD in the extension of refinance facilities to scheduled commercial banks and to state-central co-operative banks, mention should be made of "financing tiny industries in rural areas under the Automatics Refinance Facility". This scheme has been devised to assist the tiny industries set up by individuals, proprietory /partnership concerned or groups of individuals' including companies and corporate bodies, for them loan/composite up to a maximum of Rs. 5 lakhs (S. N. Pradhan, 1986). Besides, the NABARD has extended its refinance facilities to RRBs in addition to those already enjoyed by SCBs and CBs for financing the setting up of biogas plants under the National Project for Biogas Development. The NABARD has set up a soft loan Assistance Fund for Margin Money for providing assistance to those entrepreneurs who are unable to bring in the required down payment wherever stipulated. The NABARD has also devised schemes for assisting the voluntary organisations in conducting Entrepreneurial Development Programme (EDPs,) based on non-farm sector activities. As part of its promotional effort, the NABARD is also organizing workshops/training programmes for the functional managers of DICs/DRDAs and officers of commercial banks to impress upon them the need for developing non-farm activities and making them aware of the various facilities available to beneficiaries. Thus, the NABARD as an apex development bank has been charged with the responsibility to promote integrating rural development in the rural areas. Towards facilitating this, the NABARD has been providing refinance support to commercial and co-operative banks for increasing the production, productivity and employment generation in the rural areas through both on-farm and off-farm activities.

Now-a-days micro credit is a world-wide scheme and it is broadly established to uplift the rural poor for rural development. Muhammed Yunus (2004) stated that lessons from the experiences of other developing countries like Bangladesh, Indonesia, Bolivia and Philippines motivated India too to start experiencing innovative scheme of SHGs which are also called as' thrift and credit groups'. The SHG is a brainchild of Grameen Bank of Bangladesh which was founded by Prof. Muhammed Yunus of Chittageng University in the year 1975. According to Muhammed Yunus, "If we are looking for one single action which will enable the poor to overcome their poverty, I will focus on credit," Micro-credit programmes extend small loans to very poor people for self employment projects that generate income allowing them to care for themselves and their families. The micro-credit programme which made a modest beginning in the year 1992-93 is now implemented in 31st states and Union territories covering 572 districts of the country. As on 31st March, 05, as many as 1,618, 456 SGHs were linked with 41,082 branches of 573 banks (27 public sector, and 20 private sector commercial Banks, 196 RRBs and 330 cooperatives) and provided credit amounting to Rs. 68984.60 million. The World Bank estimates that more than 87% of India's poor cannot access credit from a formal sources and therefore they are not borrowing at all or have to depend on money lenders who charge them interest rates ranging from 48% to 20% per annum or sometimes much higher. In recent years micro-credit has become a buzzword among the development practitioners. The rationale of its emergence has its roots in the failure of the formal credit institutions in effectively meeting the credit needs of the rural poor. Micro-credit holds a big promise to generate income and employment, to empower the poor particularly women and alleviate poverty, to improve the living standard of the rural people and eliminate exploitation done by money lenders. to make optimum cum utilization of rural resources and mobilize rural savings, to engage inactive human resources and make easy access to institutional credit facilities. Thus, micro credit engages rural people in development process of the country.

In promoting micro credit non-government organizations play an important role in India both as promoters and financial intermediaries in bringing the gap between the un-reached micro-enterprises and the formal banking system. At the formal level NABARD and Small Industries Development Bank of India (SIDBI), the apex level financial institutions are promoting, supporting and financing micro credit programmes in India. Involvement of NABARD in promoting finance through the concept of Self Help group (SHGs) started in 1987 with a sanction of Rs. 10 lakh as grant assistance from the R & D fund to Mysore Resettlement and Development Agency (MYRADA) for providing seed money to the credit management group promoted by it whereas the other apex level institution in micro-credit, SIDBI launched its micro-credit scheme in 1994 for extending financial assistance to the rural poor, particularly women, through NGOs. Undoubtedly, micro-credit proves instrumental for rural development but according to the World Bank, the major challenges for micro-credit in India can be summarised as improving governance, professional management, improving internal transparency lowering costs, better targeting of the poor, expanding beyond credit to meet the diverse needs of borrowers, and a better financial infrastructure in order to scale up.

Global Era Analysis

Globalization has become a household name in all corners of the World. To some, it is an inescapable and primarily benign process of global economic integration, in which countries increasingly drop border restrictions on the flow of capital goods and services. Globalization, connoting pervasiveness, inclusiveness and sweepingness with epidemic and pandemic, implications in international trade and financial relations, is a new avatar of the 18th century imperialist, colonization and exploitation and the 20th century new-liberal economic fundamentalism. Distinguishing this current wave of globalization from earlier ones, author Thomas Friedman has said that today globalization is "farther, faster, cheaper and deeper". Globalization has become the most fastionable world today. Meenu Agrwal (2008) has quoted Kofin Annam's observation in this concern "It has been said that arguing against globalization is like arguing against the laws of gravity."

The World Commission on Social Dimension of Globalization (2004) reveals the fact that "Our primary concerns are that globalization should benefit all countries and should raise the welfare of all people throughout the world. This implies that it should raise the rate of economic growth in poor countries and reduces world poverty and that it should not increase inequalities or undermines socio-economic security within countries." In India globalization has commenced ever since the commencement of the economic reforms in 1991 which were crisis driven. It is widely believed that globalization which simply means the integration of the

Indian economy with the world economy, has been deemed as the panacea for solving all problems (B. K. Jha, 2005). They overlook fact that it is widely seen as unbalanced and unequal, a process that benefits only a minority of people and of countries, leaves many excluded and brings real disadvantage to some particularly developing countries like India (B. K. Jha, 2008). A Buddhist proverb is appropriately applicable to Indian case. The key to the gate of heaven, goes the proverb, is also the key which could open the gate of hell. Indeed, danger and opportunities are so intricately intermingled in the liberalization of Indian economy that the journey to the promised land of well functioning market economy could easily turn into a hellish nightmare of poverty and widening inequality for the majority and creating a gap between the urban and rural regions.

Since July 1991, the Indian economy has been witnessing wide range of reforms in all sectors of the economy viz. financial, industrial, fiscal, trade, agriculture etc. The Indian banking system has come from a long way from being a sleepy business institution to a highly proactive and dynamic entity and credit for this transformation goes to the large dose of liberalization and economic reforms that allowed banks to explore new business opportunities rather than generating revenues from conventional streams. The major challenge of the reform has been to introduce elements of market incentive as a dominant factor gradually replacing the administratively coordinated planned a actions for development. Greater competition has been infused in the banking system by permitting entry of private sector banks and liberal licensing of more branches by foreign banks and the entry of new foreign banks. With the development of a multi-institutional structure in the financial sector, emphasis is on efficiency through competition irrespective of ownership. Since non-back intermediation has increased, banks have had to improve efficiency to ensure survival (Y. V. Reddy, 2003). In the post global era the financial sector displayed rapid changes. With passing decades, the Indian banking sector is considerably fully mature, in terms of supply of credit, product range and reach and thus it is reaping lucrative incomes for itself but rural India still has to be covered. No doubt, globalization has brought with it major technological advances which have benefited the global system greatly. Aggressive use of ATMs, telebanking, net banking and mobile banking has reduced cost to fraction of conventional amounts. Industry estimates assume teller costs at Rs. 1 per transaction, ATM cost at Re 0.45 phone banking at 0.35 and debit cards for 0.10 per transaction. Such has been the impact of ATMs that ICICI customer base has grown from 2 million to 5 million from 2002 (T. Banerje & S. Sharma, 2008). Undoubtedly, growth in bank credit accelerated from 22.8% during 2004-05 to 27% during 2005-06. The credit to GDP ratio grew rapidly from about 10% at December 1969 to about 40% by end March 2005. The impact of globalization is visible when we come to know the fact that almost 36 foreign banks have entered into the Indian market and they have almost 206 branches, though mainly concentrated in Mumbai. These banks are earning higher profit per unit of business handled in comparison to Indian banks. Thus, foreign banks are posing a treat to indigenous banks. Indian banks having operations abroad has remained at 9, the total branches being 93, representative offices to have risen to 17, due to opening of more branches of ICICI and HDFC banks. SBI has nearly 52 offices spread over all times zones in 31 countries. The process of globalization and economic liberalization has brought the issue of customers to the forefront and a successful banker will be judged by his ability to manage the expectations of his customers as well as exceed them. A revolutionary innovation in technological advancement is the use of simputer which can be used for a variety of applications in rural areas but what devices like simputer can do when basic infrastructure and utilities don't exist in rural India.

What May be

Now the question is what may be, when low income groups of rural India generally don't have the necessary capabilities to deal with organized credit institutions? No doubt, one aspect of rural credit is credit to the poor but the factors which constrain the capacity of the poor to borrow from organized credit institutions are : lack of skills, unawareness of economic opportunities and of markets, what they are capable of producing and their inability to overcome bureaucratic requirements.

Gunnar Myrdal has termed credit as an accelerator of development and so ensuring the provision of timely and sufficient credit to as large a segment of rural population as possible has been one of the major policy initiatives which has guided the formation of public policy in the country but what may be when every rupee spent on rural development reaches the intended beneficiaries is doubtful? What may be when only 15% of the real value of the schemes reached the genuine beneficiaries and the rest was lost due to redtapism?

What may be when "The combination of the rural rich and the bureaucracy is formidable and fed as it is on the mounting corruption, claiming 50 per cent to 80 per cent of the huge, programmes funds (nearly Rs. 1500 crores per annum, earmarked for the poor)" (L.C. Jain, B. V. Krishnamurthy P. M. Tripathi, 1985).

Is it not true that those who are entrusted with the functions of implementation of policies are urban-oriented ? And there is a visible distance between them and the people for whom the programme and being implemented. No doubt, realising this gulf, initiatives have been taken to bridge this gap by introducing the Panchayati Raj institutions; but it made only a halting progress.

Besides the above, globalization which was set into motion in India in the early 90s brought into its wake both opportunities for growth and challenges for overcoming the weakness on all fronts of the national economy. The overall objective of the various steps that have since been initiated has been to add to the competitive strength of our economy so that we are not driven away from the markets, domestic and overseas. Those who are in favour of globalization have ultimate faith in market, believe that market is solution for all problems. For them market is God and God is market. But this

God, like other Gods, has also failed It has failed to deliver equality and justice between the rich and the poor, the urband and the rural. There is no denying the fact that this God shows his own favouritism, justifying it in the name of the survival of the fittest, when the God fails, who pays for this failures ? Undoubtedly, the market failure cost is paid mainly by rural India. What can rural credit do for rural development when China-made items have flooded the Indian market and many village small-scale as well as cottage industries have been forced to shut doors, more are in line? Is it not true that lord Ganesha, also made in China, worshipped all over the country during Ganapati festival, comes in different shapes and sizes, for more attractive than the traditional ones. It is but true that over Rs. 1 million worth of China-made consumer durables are sold in India everyday. Thus, how can rural development possible when rural people are loosing their livelihood in this way and how far rural credit proves instrumental in achieving its target of upgrading the standard of livings of rural people in this scenario created by globalization? Undoubtedly, the issue of linking formal credit institutions with the rural poor through intermediaries such as self-help groups and voluntary organizations has raised some hopes in this concern but the provision of rural credit and the way in which rural credit is tailored to suit the requirement of the rural people are equally important.

References

Rangaranjan C. (1999), Indian Economy: Essay on Money and Finance, UBSPDD, New Delhi.

Mishra Jagannath (1997), My Vision for India's Rural Development Vikas Publishing House, New Delhi.

Mukherjee Pranab (1985), Beyond Survival: Emerging Dimension of Indian Economy, Vikas Publ. House, New Delhi.

Joseph E. Stliglitz (2002), Globalization and its Discontents, Penguin Books.

Singh R. B. (2005), Globalization and Indian Economy in Globalization and Contemporary Economic Scenario ed by R. K. Singh Abhijeet Pub., New Delhi.

Bhalla Sheila (2005), India's Rural Economy: Issues and Evidence, Institute for Human Development New Delhi.

Jha B. K. (2005), Gandhian Economic versus Globalization in Globalization and Contemporary Economic Scenario (ed by R. K. Singh) Abhijeet Publ. New Delhi.

Jha B. K. (2008), Impact of Globalization on Poverty and Unemployment, Evidence from Uttar Pradesh Impact of Globalization on Development ed by Meenu Agrawal Deep & Deep Pub., New Delhi.

Govindarajuhi (2008), *Bharatiya Samajik Chintan*, Vol. VI, No. 4, Jan-March.

Jain L. C., Krishnamurthy B. V., Tripathi P. M. (1985), Grass without Roots-Rural Development under Government Auspices Sept.

S. Kumar Sandeep & Anand Smita (2007), *Kurukshetra*, Vol. 55, No. 12 Oct.

Benerji. T. & Sharma S. (2008), Globalization and its Impact on Banking Sector in Impact of Globalization on Banking Sector in Impact of Globalization on Development (ed by) Meenu Agrawal Deep & Deep Publ. New Delhi.

Reddy Y. V. (2003), *Southern Economist*, Vol. 41, No. 17, Jan. p. 23.

Pradhan S. N. (1986), *Khadi Gramodyog*, Vol. XXXIII, No. 2, Nov. p. 104-107

Subbiah A. & Selva Kumr M. (2006), *Kurukshetra*, Vol. 54, No. 8, p. 19-21.

90th IEA Annual Conf.

Different *Yojanas*.

Bowles Chester (1963), Lecture at Delhi School of Economics.

Krishnaji P. (1986), Challenges and Responsibilities of Banks in Rural Development Khadi Gramodyog, Vol XXXII, No. 12, Sept.

4

INDEBTEDNESS OF RURAL FARMER HOUSEHOLDS: AN ANALYSIS OF THE MAJOR STATES IN INDIA

JAGANNATH LENKA

Introduction

THE principal objective of this paper is to highlight the incidence of debt of the rural farmer households and relative role of the institutional and non-institutional agencies in financing the rural indebtedness across the major states in India as revealed by the results of the 59th round survey conducted by the National Sample Survey Organisation, Government of India. An overview of the surveys on debt and investment of rural households is given in section-II. Materiais and methods are presented in section-III. The salient feature on the indebtedness of rural farmer households is discussed in section-IV. The concluding section presents a summery of the findings and suggests policy implications.

Surveys on Debt and Investment of Rural Households: An Overview

The benchmark event in the history of rural credit was the launching of the All India Rural Credit Survey (AIRCS) by the Reserve Bank of India in the year1951-52.In fact, the main purpose of the survey was not to compile the national estimates of indebtedness or credit requirements, but to collect data for suitable policy formulation. The survey was conducted in 75 selected districts and covered about 1, 25,000 families from 600 villages. According to the findings of AIRCS, the money lenders played a dominant role in financing the rural households at high rates of interest. Furthermore, the supply of agricultural credit was far behind the demand requirements was not of the right type, did not serve the right purpose and failed to reach the right people.

The committee suggested the need for a constant review of all the main features of the credit situation in the rural sector through annual investigation in the nature of sample enquiries of moderate scope and more elaborate large scale surveys at longer intervals of time. As per recommendation of the AIRCS, the second decennial All India Rural Debt and Investment Survey (AIRDIS) was conducted in the year 1961-62 with the objectives of arriving at statistically valid estimates of various economic characteristics of rural households such as pattern of borrowing and payment, composition and value of outstanding debt, asset holdings etc.

However, due to administrative and other inconveniences, it was decided that field work of the All India Debt and Investment Survey (AIDIS), 1971-72 be entrusted to an outside but expert agency. NSSO was requested to take up this task. Since then NSSO has been conducting the field survey while the responsibility of processing and publication of the results is rested with the RBI.

Materials and Methods

The present analysis makes use of the secondary data, which was first collected by the NSSO. Particularly the data pertains to the 59th round of the survey conducted by the NSSO in the year 2003 and published in the month of May 2005.The approach is empirico-analytical in nature with an objective to bring out the salient features of the indebted rural farmer households across the major states of India. Simple statistical tools like percentages and proportions are used for comparative analysis.

Salient Features of the Indebted Rural Farmer Households

The results of the 59th round survey conducted by the NSSO throw up a number of interesting points that are discussed below.

Magnitude of Rural and Indebted Rural Farmer Household

Estimated number of rural households, rural farmer households and indebted rural farmer households are presented in Table 1. It may be observed from the table that farmer household constitute 60 per cent of the rural households in India .This speaks about the importance of agriculture in spite of the fact that the contribution of this sector to GDP is gradually declining.

Table 1

State-wise Distribution of Indebted Rural Farmer Households

States	*No. of Rural House-holds*	*No. of Farmer House-holds*	*No. of Indebted Farmer House-holds*	*Farmer House-holds as % of Rural House-holds*	*Indebted Farmer Households Farmer as % of Households*
	(00)	*(00)*	*(00)*		
Andhra Pradesh	1,42,512	60,339	49,493	42.34	82.02
Bihar	1,16,853	70,840	23,338	60.62	33.00
Gujarat	63,015	37,845	19,644	60.05	51.91
Haryana	31,474	19,445	10,330	61.78	53.12
Karnataka	69,908	40,413	24,897	57.80	61.61
Kerala	49,942	21,946	14,126	43.94	64.36
Madhya Pradesh	93,898	63,206	32,110	67.31	50.80
Maharastra	1,18,177	65,817	36,098	55.69	54.85
Orissa	66,199	42,341	20,250	63.96	47.83
Punjab	29,847	18,442	12,069	61.79	65.44
Rajasthan	70,172	53,080	27,828	75.64	52.43
Tamil Nadu	1,10,182	38,880	28,954	35.29	74.47
Uttar Pradesh	2,21,499	1,71,575	69,199	77.46	40.33
West Bengal	1,21,667	69,226	34,696	56.90	50.20
All India	14,78,988	8,93,504	4,34,242	60.41	48.60

As expected, the maximum number of households is found in less developed states. Utter Pradesh leads the list of percentage (77.46%) of rural farmer households followed by Rajasthan (75.64%), Madhya Pradesh (67.31%). Orissa(63.96%) and Bihar(67.31%) . Developed states like Punjab and Haryana are also found to have this percentage above that of the country as a whole. It may be pointed out here that the developments of these two states are mainly due to their agricultural development.

In contrast with this, Kerala is found to have the lowest percentage (43.94%) of farmer households in the country. States having rural farmer households less than the national percentage are Andhra Pradesh, Gujarat, Karnataka, Maharastra Tamil Nadu and West Bengal.

Looking to the indebted farmer households as proportion of rural farmer households, it is seen that overall situation in the country is disheartening. Despite the fact that there is comfortable GDP growth and agricultural prosperity, nearly half (48.60%) of the farmer households in the country are indebted though in varying degrees.

What is startling and disturbing is the fact that the rate of indebtedness of farmers is seen to be unrelated with economic growth or agricultural prosperity. Andhra Pradesh, one of the biggest producer of food grains in the country is found to have sheltered the largest number (82.02%) of indebted farmers. Similarly,agriculturally the most prosperous state Punjab is seen to harbour 65.40 per cent of the indebted farmer households .Tamil Nadu which has become the darling of industrial investment in recent times, has the second largest prevalence rate of indebtedness among the farm households at 74.50 per cent.

On the other hand the low income states are observed to have less percentage of indebted former households with Bihar having 33.00 per cent, U.P, 40.33 per cent and Orissa 47.83 per cent.The rest of the states under study have this figure above the national percentage.

Thus a contrasting feature is noticed that the poor states have less percentage of indebted rural farmer households while the rich states have more. It may be due to the fact that the former category states have not diversified and commercialised their agriculture and accordingly the credit requirement is less or lending institutions shy away of the farmers in these states where agricultural yield is less compared to developed states. On the other hand the farmers of the latter category states have aggressively diversified their agriculture in favour of the commercial crops with the support of large scale credit and in the case of crop failure or distress sale, they are trapped into indebtedness.

Socio-Economic Status of the Indebted Rural Farmer Households

The social group and land holding size of the indebted farmer households are shown in Table 2 and Table 3 respectively. It is seen from Table 2 that at the national level the indebted farmer households stand in the order of 10 per cent ST, 18 per cent SC, 43.9 per cent OBC and 28.1 per cent others .The overwhelming presence of the socially disadvantaged people in the indebted list is in itself the indication of the reason for such massive indebtedness of the Indian farmers .Almost in all states it is observed that the socially less progressive farmers are trapped in indebtedness.

Table 2
State-wise Distribution of Indebted Rural Farmer Households According to Social Groups (in %)

States	*ST*	*SC*	*OBC*	*OTHERS*
Andhra Pradesh	10.8	16.8	47.7	24.7
Bihar	2.9	17.0	59.8	20.4
Gujarat	22 .8	6.6	36.2	34.4
Haryana	0.5	21.8	32.6	45.1
Karnataka	9.8	10.8	43.0	36.4
Kerala	1.6	4.5	49.6	44.3
Madhya Pradesh	15.9	18.6	47.8	17.6
Maharastra	9.3	8.6	34.5	47.7
Orissa	23.3	14.2	44.1	18.5
Punjab	0.2	26.1	15.8	57.9
Rajasthan	20.8	16.5	47.0	15.7
Tamil Nadu	4.2	21.9	72.9	1.0
Uttar Pradesh	1.8	25.7	55.7	16.8
West Bengal	5.7	29.6	7.4	57.3
All India	10.0	18.0	43.9	28.1

It may be observed from the Table 3 that in every 100 indebted farmer households, 61.1 belong to marginal farmers, 19.8 belong to small farmers, 6.4 belong to medium farmers and the rest 1.2 belong to large farmers. Looking to prevalence rate of indebtedness it is also found that 45.1 per cent marginal farmers, 51.0 per cent small farmers, 52.8 per cent of semi-medium farmers, 65.1 per cent of medium farmers and 66.4 per cent of large farmers are indebted in various degrees. Thus there is a direct relationship between holding size and the prevalence rate of indebtedness while an inverse relationship exits between the percentage of indebted farmer households and the size of land holding. Thus the marginal and small farmers in the lower strata of the society are the real victims of indebtedness.

Table 3
Distribution of Indebted Farmer Households According to Size of Land Holding

Land Holding Size (in hectare)	*No of Farmer Households*	*Indebted Farmer Households*	*% of Indebted Farmer Households*	*% of Prevalence Indebted Rate*
	(00)	*(00)*		
0.01-1.00	5,89,071	2,65,031	61.1	45.1
1.01-2.00	1,60,602	81,920	18.8	51.0
2.01-4.00	93,504	54,409	12.5	58.2
4.01-10.00	42,581	27,734	6.4	65.1
> 10.00	7,748	5,148	1.2	66.4
All sizes	8,93,504	4,34,242	100	48.5

Purpose of Borrowing

A cursory glance at Table 4 reveals that much of the borrowing is made to meet the agricultural requirements. At the national level 37 per cent of the indebted farmer households borrowed to meet their expenditure in farm business. Loans taken for this purpose is most common in Gujarat where 56 per cent of the indebted farmer households borrowed to meet their current

Table 4
State wise Distribution of Indebted Farmer Households According to Purpose of Borrowing (in %)

States	*Capital Expenditure in Farm*	*Current Expenditure in Farm*	*Consumption*	*Nonfarm Business*	*Marriage Ceremony*	*Edn.*	*Med.*	*Others*
Andhra Pradesh	26	51	26	3	9	1	4	9
Bihar	21	12	30	7	10	1	6	25
Gujarat	13	56	13	2	13	0	5	8
Haryana	32	35	19	4	14	0	4	14
Karnataka	21	52	19	3	7	1	1	7
Kerala	16	17	27	12	12	4	8	34
Madhya Pradesh	30	41	25	4	17	0	5	4
Maharastra	30	53	13	5	6	0	4	6
Orissa	26	36	21	8	8	0	4	8
Punjab	17	37	27	5	14	1	4	12
Rajasthan	28	29	32	3	16	1	5	8
Tamil Nadu	20	38	34	4	9	3	7	12
Uttar Pradesh	28	27	19	5	15	1	11	10
West Bengal	22	34	25	9	7	1	8	15
All India	24	37	23	5	11	1	7	11

farm expenses. In Maharastra it is 53 per cent and in Andhra Pradesh, 51 per cent.

The next important purpose of borrowing was capital expenditure in farm business. At the national level 24 per cent of the indebted farmer households are found to have borrowed for this purpose. The states also show more or less the same picture.

Though borrowing to meet consumption expenses stand at 23 per cent for the country as a whole, the variation ranges from 13 per cent in Maharastra to 34 per cent in Tamil Nadu. It may be pointed out here that since the purposes of loan are not mutually exclusive, the households might have borrowed for more than one purposes and exact magnitude of borrowing for different purposes is not a part of the present study.

Sources of Borrowing

The sources of borrowing are presented in Table 5 .It is a matter of concern that the dominant source of fund is the professional money lenders. At the national level, 29 out of every 100 indebted farmer households borrowed from this source. Among the states the incidence of borrowing from this source is highest in Andhra Pradesh followed by Tamil Nadu. As many as 57 per cent farmer households in the former and 52 per cent in the latter borrow from professional money lenders. Banks and cooperative societies are next to important sources of funds for the farmers.Kerala is observed to have the highest incidence of bank credit while co-operative societies are the main source of funds for the farmers of Maharastra. 61 out of every 100 Maharastraian farmers have borrowed from this source. What is most disturbing is the fact that even after a decade of economic reforms, the financial institutional have not been able to meet the demand of the farmers and the professional money lenders have been successful as they find less competition from institutional sources. Except Maharastra and Gujarat, the professional money lenders have tightened their grips over the small and marginal farmers across the country.

Table 5

Statewise Distribution of Indebted Farmer Households According to Sources of Borrowing (in %)

States	*Govt.*	*Co. Op. Society*	*Banks*	*Ag Prof. Money Lenders*	*Traders*	*Relative Friends*	*Other Prof.*	*Others*
Andhra Pradesh	3	20	31	57	9	6	1	4
Bihar	2	4	17	44	5	26	2	7
Gujarat	0	40	23	8	10	29	1	1
Haryana	2	44	30	29	9	9	2	1
Karnataka	2	23	32	34	5	12	1	3
Kerala	8	46	42	16	6	12	1	5
Madhya Pradesh	4	37	23	22	23	17	2	2
Maharastra	2	61	29	7	6	11	2	4
Orissa	2	30	36	23	4	16	0	3
Punjab	1	38	19	28	18	21	1	2
Rajasthan	2	15	21	40	23	14	2	2
Tamil Nadu	3	33	23	52	2	11	0	2
Uttar Pradesh	4	13	30	26	9	28	3	4
West Bengal	10	19	22	15	29	23	2	4
All India	3	26	27	29	12	18	2	3

Summary and Suggestion

The main findings that emerged from the aforesaid analysis are enumerated below:

- Nearly half of the rural farmer households in the country are indebted in various degrees and agriculturally prosperous states have become home to a large number of indebted farmer households.
- Most of the indebted farmer households belong to the category of marginal and small farmers and are concentrated in the disadvantaged social groups such as SC, ST and OBC.
- Rate of indebted rural farmer households appears to have no relation with overall economic prosperity. Developed states are found to have harbored more indebted farmers compared to less developed ones.
- More than 60 per cent of the rural farmer households are found to have utilised their borrowings for agricultural pursuits. However, loans to meet consumption expenditure are as high as 23 per cent which is a matter of concern.
- The most important feature of the survey is that even after a decade of economic reforms, professional money lenders dominate the source of funds for the poor rural farmers across the country.

Since large scale indebtedness has constrained some rural farmers to commit suicide in recent years, the government must gear up the machineries to protect the rural farmers from the clutches of the professional money lenders. The Rs. 60, 000-crore farm loan waiver can at best provide short-term relief to farmers who are covered by the institutional credit mechanism. However, about 30 per cent of the borrowing of rural households is sourced from money lenders (NSS 59th Round), even though moneylenders are notorious for the high interest rates they charge and coercive methods they use to recover outstanding. It may be noted here that moneylenders provide access to credit in areas where institutional credit mechanism has not made inroads. Even where banks and co-operatives have a presence, people prefer to go to moneylenders as they have almost no paper work and disburse funds quickly. Moreover weak enforcement of money lending legislation by states is partly responsible for the exploitative practices of a large section of these informal credit providers.

Clearly, curbing money lending is not the solution to the problem that would hurt the poor who have no other access to credit. One part of the solution involves expanding the reach of the formal credit mechanism so that monopolistic practices of the moneylenders can be curbed. But it must be recognised that borrowing in rural areas is not just for agricultural needs but also for consumption including expenses on education, healthcare and weddings. Borrowings for consumption will come down only when farmers get more remunerative prices for their produce and are thus able to save for at least minor emergencies. That apart, the risks arising from crop failures must be covered adequately.

Realising the need to enhance credit flow to agriculture, the government in consultation with the RBI, NABARD and commercial banks announced a credit package for agricultural sector in June 2004.The RBI also set up an Advisory Committee on the flow of credit to agriculture under the chairmanship of Prof. N.S. Vyas which submitted its report on June 30, 2004. Several recommendations of the committee have been accepted. But what is most important is not the policy but their implementation within a given time frame which has never happened in our country. Policy backed by strong political will may help to overcome the tragedy and bring smile to a large number of rural poor farmers across the states. More importantly, strategies are required to be implemented that would accelerate the shift of people in rural areas to non-agricultural activities.

References

Agricultural Credit Review Committee, RBI (1984), A Review of the Agricultural Credit System in India, RBI, Bombay.

Bardhan, P.K and Ashok Rudra (1978), "Interlinkage of Land, Labour and Credit Relations–An Analysis of Village Survey Data in East India". *EPW*, Feb. Annual Number.

Clive, Bell (1990), Interaction between International and Informal Credit Agencies in Rural India, *World Bank Economic Review*, Vol. 4, No. 3 Sept.

Dandekar, M.N. (1989), Farm Credit in India, in Sunita, R.K (ed), *Economic Development Planning and Policy in India,* Vol. VII, Deep & Deep Publications, New Delhi.

Dantwala, M. L. (1989), Agricultural Policy in India since Independence, Sunita, R.K. (ed) *Economic Development Planning and Policy in India,* Vol. VII, Deep & Deep Publications, New Delhi.

Govt. of India (2005), Economic Survey, Ministry of Finance, New Delhi.

Mahanti, T. K. (2005), Rural India in Debt-trap, *The Economic Times,* June 6.

National Sample Survey Organization (2005), 59th Round, Report No.498, Govt. of India.

Rangarajan, C. (1996), Rural India, The Role of Credit, RBI Bulletin May, Mumbai.

RBI (1956), All India Rural Credit Survey, 1951-52, Vol. I, II & III, RBI, Bombay.

RBI (1956). All India Rural Debt and Investment Survey, 1961-62. RBI, Bombay.

Subba Rao, K. G. K. Ramachandra Rao and A. K. Tripathi (1997), Indebtedness of Rural Households–A Profile, RBI Occasional Paper Vol. 18, No.-2&3, RBI, Bombay, pp. 525-551.

Tandon, P. K. (1988), A Profile of Rural Indebtedness, Social Scientist, April.

5

MICRO FINANCE TOWARDS EMPOWERMENT OF RURAL WOMEN: A STUDY OF TEKKALI MANDAL IN SRIKAKULAM DISTRICT OF ANDHRA PRADESH

D. Pulla Rao & M. Sundara Rao

Introduction

In India over the centuries, a very large number of women in the rural regions, have been carrying in the burden of poverty ignorance, outmoded customs and traditional women have been laying down and surrendering all their comforts for the welfare of the children. Rather than rural men, the rural women performs a hope of activities and these activities range from child rearing to house hold affairs and farm operations. In terms of economics benefits many of theses activities are not visible and flexible even then rural women pay a crucial role in the rural economy. To leave about the extent of knowledge, the women participation can be solicited in the Indian economy. Such activities are so needed to the rural life and the women. Collecting fuel and fodder gathering seed from forests, fetching drinking water, cooking for the house hold, child rearing, a host of household and form operation have been performed by women because of the traditions customs and usage which have insisted the women to assume responsibility and compared men, these are all markedly different.

Against this background the India Governments have been vigorously working for the empowerment of women in general, rural women in particular by launching various developmental programmes of which Development of Women and Children in Rural Area (DWCRA) is prominent one. Therefore an attempt has been made to look through the impact of the above said scheme on alleviation of poverty of rural women. One such effort is the DWCRA scheme which was introduced in 1982 as a subcomponent of IRDP to accelerate the integration of women with the rural development programmes. The primary objectives of the DWACRA scheme is to focus attention on the women members of rural families below the poverty line with a view to providing them with opportunities of self employment as sustained balls. The SHG programme in India is initially introduced in 50 selected districts. Later, it was extended to more districts in a phased manner.

In this regard the study of Venkata Ramana, M. (1995) comparatively studied the functioning and performance of DWCRA groups, by way of observing two successful groups and failed groups. Hemalatha Prasad, C. (1995) has carefully examined the socio economic factors that make a DWCRA group successful in a case study undertaken in Gurgoan Dist. of Haryana. Manimekala and Rajeswari (2000) examined the empowerment of women through SHGs in rural micro enterprises in Tiruchinapalli district of TamilNadu. Based on both primary and secondary data, Datta and Raman (2001) studies SHGs under Rastriya Seva samithi (RASS) at Tirupati. From these studies it is revealed that the Self Help Groups (SHGs) are viable alternatives is to achieve the objectives of rural development and to get community participation in all the rural development programmes SHG is a viable organisation set up to disburse micro credit to the rural women for the purpose of making them enterprising women and encouraging them to enter into entrepreneurial activities. The women led SHG and DWCRA have successfully demonstrated how to mobilise and mange thrift, appraise credit needs, maintain linkages with the bank and enforce financial self-discipline.

These studies also reveal that an in depth analysis of DWCRA scheme is very essential to find out whether such a programme is contributing for women enlistment economically and socially. There is also a need to identify the loopholes in the scheme for making them operationally successful. The above analysis shows that SHG is on of the important programme to rural women and it is a boon to the rural women-folk. The studies in the context of working patterns of SHGs in Srikakulam district are very few. On the other side the earlier studies have more gaps and not covered the determinants of productive activities various independents and appropriate statistical tools to analyze the study. The need for rural development programmes specifically for the development of rural women is much imperative in a backward region like Srikakulam District. Hence an attempt is made in this study to evaluate the SHG programme in Tekkali Mandal of Srikakulam District.

Methodology

This study is based on both primary as well as secondary date sources. The Tekkali mandal of Srikakulam district is selected for the study because it is one of the most backward areas in the state. The selected mandal has high poverty, lowest female literacy rate, high birth and infant mortality rates, poor health status and large socially disadvantaged sections of population (SC, ST& BC). Thus the Tekkali mandal is a typical case for analyzing the social dynamic operating against the emancipation of women through social mobilization and economic support and self-employment programmes. Secondary data on status of SHG programme in the Tekkali mandal have been collected from annual reports of IRDP, district year books published by Chief Planning Officer and women and child development offices, Srikakulam. The study is limited to Tekkali mandal of Srikakulam district of Andhra Pradesh.

To select the sample Multi Stage Random Sampling technique is applied in sample selection. The process of selection involves stage-I selection of village, stage-II selection of Self Help Groups and stage-III selection house hold. In stage-I from Tekkali mandal three villages Ravi Valasa, Lingala Valasa and Seetha Puram selected. At stage–II from each village 6 SHGs are selected. At stage-III from each selected SHG ten member house holds are selected. Totally 18 SHGs from Tekkali mandal are selected for evaluating the functioning of SHGs at group levels. For purpose of studying the impact of SHG on socio economic conditions of the SHG members 10 members from each SHG, a total of 180 households are selected by following the Multi stage, Probability Proportionate Sampling (PPS). Data was ascertained from each selected SHG member with the help of a structured questionnaire by Personal Interview method.

Functioning of Selected SHGs

The center and state Governments have been implementing the DWCRA scheme with a sacred objective of alleviating the poverty among downtrodden sections and women section of the society. In this study an attempt has been made to evaluate the performance of DWCRA scheme. More specifically an attempt has been made to study to what extent the scheme is helpful to increase the awareness of the rural women in the Tekkali mandal of Srikakulam district.

SHGs Participation in Developmental Activities

At the outset to assess the functioning of selected SHGs important aspects like participation of SHG members in various developmental activities, the level of, matching/grant/ revolving fund drawn and amount fertilization particulars, amount repaid by the SHG members in the study area have been discussed. Along with thrift, the SHG/DWCRA has been giving priority to health, family welfare, literacy, and social awareness activities like convergence activities as a basic determinant of the families' economic development and welfare. These activities also recognized by SHGs of Tekkali mandal in Srikakulam District. Table 1 shows the active role played by SHG members in various developmental activities like participation in Mahila Mandal meetings, craft centers, thrift movement, health & family camp, prohibition literacy complain, and Pallebata etc. in the study area.

Table 1
SHG Members' Participation in Developmental Activities

Topic	*R. Valasa*	*L. Valasa*	*S. Puram*	*Total*
Mahila mandal activities	51	43	30	124
	(65.00)	(71.67)	(50.0)	(68.89)
Craft centre	30	14	8	52
	(50.0)	(23.33)	(13.33)	(28.89)
Health and family welfare	55	26	14	85
campaign camp	(91.67)	(43.33)	(23.33)	(47.22)
Literacy campaign	50	30	24	104
	(83.33)	(50.0)	(40.0)	(57.78)
Thrift	60	44	32	132
	(100.0)	(73.33)	(55.67)	(73.33)
Praja padam/Pallebata	40	30	21	81
	(66.67)	(50.0)	(35.0)	(45.00)
Total	60	60	60	180

Note: Figures in the parenthesis are percentage to column total.

It is found from the Table 1 that, a majority of respondents participated in thrift (73.33 per cent), family welfare and health campaign and Mahila mandal activities (68.69%), Prajapadam, pallebata (45%) and literacy aspects (57.78%) respectively. Among the three villages SHGs the proportion is relatively higher in Ravi Valasa groups ranging from 65 per cent in Mahila Mandal and in thrift (100 %). In the case of Lingala Valasa groups the selected SHG members ranging from 23.33 per cent in literacy aspects and 73.33 per cent in thrift Across the Seetha Puram groups they are ranging from craft centers (13.33 %) and in thrift (53.32 %). It is observed from the table that, the thrift activities have occupied a good position in all aspects of SHGs. Thrift concepts linked with bank linkage and bank loans. So it may be a reason behind well performance of the SHG members in thrift activities rather than in other activities. As a whole it is observed that, a major number of the respondents have participated in village development activities for the free of cost and they consist of 61.17 per cent of the total respondent. It is so because everybody wants to keep his/her village in a good position. It may not be continues process. In the leisure time every one ready to participate in the village development programme

SHGs Participation in Different Activities

The selected SHG members of all the selected three villages participating in different programmes. The information relating to their participation in different activities and programmes are presented in Table 2.

Table 2
SHG members Participation in Different Programmes

Topic	*R. Valasa*	*L. Valasa*	*S. Puram*	*Total*
Mahila mandal activities	50	20	8	78
	(83.33)	(33.33)	(8.87)	(43.33)
Thrift	60	45	28	133
	(100.0)	(75.0)	(46.67)	(73.89)
Family planning	52	38	18	108
	(86.87)	(63.33)	(30.0)	(60.00)
Health aspects	58	30	14	102
	(96.97)	(50.0)	(23.33)	(56.67)
Literacy aspects	42	23	13	78
	(70.0)	(38.33)	(21.67)	(43.33)
Praja padam/Pallebata	40	29	19	88
	(66.67)	(48.33)	(31.67)	(48.89)
Total	60	60	60	180

Note: Figures in the parenthesis are percentage to column total.

From the Table 2 it can be noticed that, the selected SHG members are participating in the discussion on various developmental aspects to be organized by them. Among the SHG members, majority of respondents discussed about thrift (73.89 per cent), followed by family planning and health (60 per cent), participating in the programmes like pallebata to place their problems before the administration (48.89 per cent) ,literacy aspects (43.33 per cent) and Mahila Mandal activities (43.33 per cent). From the above table it is revealed that the

Self Help Groups (SHGs) are viable alternatives to achieve the objectives of rural development and to get community participation in all the rural development programmes.

Financial Assistance Received by Selected SHGs from Different Sources

SHG is a viable organisation set up to disburse micro credit to the rural women for the purpose of making them enterprising women and encouraging them to enter into entrepreneurial activities. The women led SHG and DWCRA have successfully demonstrated how to mobilize and mange thrift, appraise credit needs, maintain linkages with the bank and enforce financial self - discipline. The theoretical aspects of protection are necessary to built the sector or at gross root level. In this regard an attempt is made to analyze the revolving fund utilization sanctioned by Government .through DRDA. Matching/revolving fund is the amount provided by Government as the simple payment worth of Rs. 10,000 to 15,000 per group. The amount to be drawn for two purposes viz. economic or productive purpose and unproductive purpose or daily transaction. The SHGs are also attempt to the demand for money for the above purposes. But they are living in poor economic conditions. Hence they may depends on financial support which they were created them selves called Self-Help Groups fund (SGHGR) these fund may includes, matching grant, SHG Fund, financial recovery of debts, interest on borrowing saving, Government special grants, special grant from NGOs, profits from SHG activities, in some cases donations to the groups, in centres etc. SHG is a right organization to provide money when they need for money.

The drawn money by the SHGs may be used for productive and non-productive purposes. In rural areas the families are very poor and they are unable to reach their daily transactions they needed money for, health, marriages, functions, cloth, education, house repairs, unforeseen distress, deliveries and maintenance of old age people child care etc. These people are depending more on moneylenders. SHGs attacking the situation and releasing money to their own needs taking into consideration the needs of respondents pushed them to draw funds from the financial institutions. In this context the details pertaining to the amount drawn by the selected SHG members has presented in Table 3.

Table 3

Amount drawn from Matching Grant fund by the selected SHGs.

No. of times drawn	*R. Valasa*	*L. Valasa*	*S. Puram*	*Total*
1st time	30,000	24000	20000	53000
	(75.0)	(60.0)	(50.0)	(44.17)
2nd time	33000	21000	15000	69000
	(82)	(52.50)	(37.50)	(57.50)
3rd time	39000	26000	14000	84000
	(97.50)	(65.0)	(35.0)	(70.0)
4th time	40000	15000	-	55000
	(100.0)	(37.50)		(45.83)
Total	40000	40000	40000	120000

Note: Figures in parenthesis are percentage to column totals.

From the Table 3 it can be observed that the selected SHGs are able to tap Government support. The selected SHGs raised their resources to the tune of Rs. 88.235 as matching grant from DRDA, Srikakulam. But the above grant was kept with the concerned banks in the form of fixed deposits according to the Government rules. In recent months, by the pressure of SHGs releasing the money basing on the rate of saving and matching grant to income generating activities to eradicate middle men and bogus group formation in field, the DRDA made a policy they released matching grant in the name of groups and kept with Banking institutions as the group avail credit linkage with the bank. Total amount of matching grant of SHGs is Rs. 1, 20,000 and drawn in 4 times. The drawn amount utilized for productive purposes and little portion of amount is also used to un-productive activities like family maintenance expenditure. The pattern of matching grant drawn during 1st to 4th times is registered as 44.71 per cent, 57.50% 70% and 45.83 per cent respectively by unanimous decision of all SHG members. In the case of three villages, the proportion of the amount drawn during the said period, Ravi Valasa groups drawn higher compared to the two categories. It is ranging from 75 to 100 per cent.

Regarding Lingala Valasa groups the percentages indicating a fluctuating trend in the drawn position. The highest amount is drawn in the third time and later it is recorded to 35.50 per cent. On the other hand the amount drawn by Seetha Puram groups in each time has shown a declining trend from 50 to 35 per cent.

Utilisation Patterns

The concerned Banks have not able to release or accept to draw amount if the saving position of SHGs are not in good position and if they are not able to fulfill the required ratio with matching grant. It is found that Ravi Valasa groups are better in saving position in the study area. In addition to the matching grant, SHGs have bank linkage facilities. The concerned branches extended their support to SHGs in the form of credit advance. The three selected villages SHGs have receive the bank facilities but Ravi Valasa village stood in first place in utilizing the amount to income generating productive activities. The utilization patterns of bank finance towards productive and other purposes are presented in Table 4.

Table 4
Amount Utilization on Productive & Consumption Purposes by SHGs

Productive and Consumption	*R. Valasa*	*L. Valasa*	*S. Puram*	*Total*
Sheep rearing	75000 (18.34)	80000 (26.14)	-	155000 (16.65)
Vegetable Cultivation and vending	60000 (14.67)	45000 (14.71)	65000 (30.01)	170000 (18.26)
Jute based products	86000 (21.03)	65000 (21.24)	-	151000 (16.22)
Dairy	45000 (11.0)	-	-	45000 (4.83)
Petty trade	28000 (6.85)	-	61000 (28.24)	89000 (9.56)
Agar batti production	55000 (13.0)	50000 (16.34)	-	105000 (11.28)
Consumption purpose	60000 (15.0)	66000 (21.57)	90000 (41.67)	216000 (23.20)
Total amount utilization	409000 (80.0)	306000 (65.81)	216000 (54.68)	931000 (67.91)
Total amount sanctioned	511000	465000	395000	1371000

Note: Figures in parenthesis are percentage to column totals.

From the Table 4 it can be noticed that the total amount sanctioned to SHGs is recorded ate Rs. 1371000, but only 67.91 per cent of amount is utilized in various income generating productive activities viz; sheep rearing, vegetable cultivation and vegetable vending, jute based products, dairy, petty trade and agarbathi production. The proportion of amount utilized on the above-mentioned productive economic activities is 67.91 per cent. Out of which 16.65 percentage of amount utilized on sheep raring, petty trade has occupied 9.56 per cent of amount. The remaining amount is utilized for vegetable cultivation and vegetable vending (18.26), Jute based products (16.22%), Agarbathi Production (11.28%) and Dairy (4.83%). Among the three village SHG members, large proportion of amount is utilized in Ravi Valasa (80.0%) and second place got by Lingala Valasa followed by Seetha Puram (54.68). Except Seetha Puram groups remaining groups have taken 4th time bank linkage. From the Table 4 it can be noticed that the total

Repayment Position

The repayment patterns of selected SHGs are presented in the following Table 5.

Table 5
Amount Repaid by Selected SHG Members

Particulars	*R. Valasa (N=60)*	*L. Valasa (N=60)*	*S. Purim (N=60)*	*Total*
Amount taken	409000	261000	216,000	931,000
Amount repaid	409000	269.00	149,000	8,27,000
	(100.00)	(87.91)	(68.98)	(88.83)
Out standing	-	37,000	67,000	1,04,000
		(12.09)	(31.02)	(11.17)

Note: Figures in parenthesis are percentage to column totals.

Amount repaid by SHG members of bank loans including, Bank linkages, bank micro enterprises credit loan. presented in the above Table 5 shows that the loan repayment performance of the SHG members out of the total amount taken by the groups is quite satisfactory, as a whole the proportion of amount repaid is 88.83 per cent and the remaining 11.17 per cent is recorded as out standing registered with the institutions. Among the selected villages SHG members, the proportion of amount repaid is cent per cent in case of Ravi Valasa village groups, the repayment of Lingala Valasa groups is recorded as 87.91 per cent and 68.98 per cent is recorded in case of Seetha Puram groups. Similarly the amount out standing is recorded as zero in case of Ravi Valasa groups, 12.09 per cent in case of Lingala Valasa groups and 31.02 per cent in case of Seetha Puram Groups. This situation explains that the proportion of amount out standing is different from one village to village. Low level of incomes, returns, high consumption may be attributed as the reasons behind the poor recoveries of loans in the Seetha Puram and Lingala Valasa villages.

It is observed from this study that the amount drawn by different SHGs in different villages shows that, the SHGs in Seetha Puram village drawn finance from the banks on the name of productive activities and the amount are utilized for consumption purposes. The SHGs in Seetha Puram are spending the loan amounts received by them for consumption purposes. Hence this study suggests the need for providing proper guidance and supervision to all the SHGs in the adoption of productive and income generating activities.

Conclusion

There are several benefits being bestowed by the different activities under the DWCRA scheme. According to the study, the women respondents are receiving both the employment opportunities and the income under the scheme in the study villages. Among the villages, the respondents of Ravi Valasa are able to get more employment opportunities and incomes as the resources are available at cheaper rate for their activities when compared to other villages. Regarding activities, the vegetable marketing activity, kirana business activity and dairy activity under this scheme are providing more employment opportunities and incomes to the rural women in the study area. The findings of this study ultimately indicate that micro finance is playing very vital role in the upbringing of the living conditions of rural women. The findings of this study ultimately suggests that, In view of fast changing scenario in rural areas, a vision for self reliance and urge for development has to be inculcated in rural societies especially in the women folk. These vital changes can be accomplished by establishing thrift and credit societies. Adult literacy centers, DWACRA groups have to be established in al the interior rural villages. The local organisations have to be empowered and guided properly in functioning and maintenance by women liaison workers and community coordinators.

References

Agarwal, B. (1998), Patriarchy and the Modernizing State: An Introduction; in Bina Agarwal (ed.) Structures of Patriarchy: State Community and Household in Modernizing Asia, New Delhi, Kalifor Women, pp. 1-28.

Batliwala Srilatha (1997), "Empowerment Women", Seminor No: 449, New Delhi, p. 89.

GOI (1974), Towards Equality, New Delhi.

GOI (1989), National Perspective Plan for Women, New Delhi.

GOI (1999), 9Th Five Year Plan Document, New Delhi.

Government of Andhra Pradesh (2001), 'Strategy Paper on Women's Empowerment', Department of Women Development and Child Welfare, Hyderabad.

Hall C. M. (1992), Women and Empowerment: Strategies for Increasing Autonomy, Hemisphere Publishing Corporation, Washington.

Hasan Zoya (ed.) (1994), Forging Identities: Gender Communities and the State, New Delhi, Kalifor Women.

Jet Buss maker and keep van Kersbergan (1994), "Gender and Welfare States: Some Theoretical Reflection" in Gendering Welfare States, ed by Diane Sainsbury, London, Says Publication.

Kate Young (1993), Planning Development with Women: Making a World of Difference, Mac Millian, p. 157.

Kosambi Meera (1997), "Gender Reform and Competing State Controls Over Women: The Rakhmabai lax (1884-1988) in Social Reform, Sexuality and the State (ed. by) Patricia Uberoi, New Delhi, Sage Publications.

Marilee Karl (1995), Women and Empowerment: Participation and Decision Making, London, Zed Books Ltd.

Maithreyi Krishna Raj (2000), Public Policy: An Agenda, IAWS, Hyderabad.

Patricia Uberoi (ed.) (1996), Social Reform, Sexuality and the State, New Delhi, Safe Publication, pp. 6.

Sangari, K. and Vaid, S. (Eds.) (1999), Recasting Women: An Introduction is Recasting Women: Essays in Colonial hystony New Delhii, Kalifor, Women, pp. 1-26.

Stephen, F. (1997), "Women's Empowerment: A Process of Restricting Power Relations", *Search Bulletin,* XII, PP. 4-13., Quoted by B.V. Jaya Lakshmi (2001), Women's Empowerment Published by IDPS, Visakhapatnam.

6

RURAL CREDIT IN INDIA: RECENT DEVELOPMENTS

VIPLA CHOPRA

IN India nearly 72 per cent (census 2001) of population lives in villages and is mostly dependent for their livelihood on rural areas Despite such a high predominance, the share of agriculture and allied activities in India's GDP is only about 25 per cent. Although there has been decline in poverty ratio in rural areas from 56.4 per cent in 1973-74 to 27.1 per cent in 1999-2000, the absolute number of poor still remains quite large. Lack of adequate and cheap source of finance to the weaker sections in rural areas has been one of the major factor responsible for poverty. Provision of sufficient and timely credit at fair rates of interest has therefore, to be considered as an integral part of agricultural development.

Till independence, money lenders and the landlords were the principal source of rural credit in India. But over the years, their share in rural credit declined and the share of institutional credit rose sharply. The credit delivery system in rural areas remained mostly confined through cooperatives during 50s and 60s. Then came the phase of Multi-Agency Approach with the participation of commercial banks and Regional Rural Banks (RRBs). During the phase of reforms (90s), the Government of India introduced some new schemes related to the supply of rural credit so as to benefit the rural economy of the country. NABARD, which is an apex organisation in the field of rural credit, has taken several initiatives in this regard. Introduction of kisan credit card (KCC) scheme and the linkage of the self help groups (SHGS) with banks are the two notable developments that have taken place in recent years. With this background, an attempt has been made in the present paper to examine

1. the growth of institutional and non-institutional sources of credit in rural India,
2. main features and scope of Kisan Credit Card (KCC) scheme and
3. growth of Micro credit in India.

Section–I

Credit is one of the crucial inputs for realizing the full potential of agriculture. Credit requirements of the farmers have increased over time. Flow of institutional credit and non-institutional credit to agricultural sector can be seen from Table 1.

Table 1
Borrowing of Cultivators from Different Sources (Percentages)

Sources	*1951-52*	*1961-62*	*1971*	*1981*	*1995-96*
Non institutional					
Money Lenders	69.7	49.2	36.1	16.1	7
Traders	5.5	8.8	8.4	3.2	5
Relatives and friends	14.2	8.8	13.1	8.7	3
Land lords and others	3.3	14.5	10.7	8.8	10
Sub-total	92.7	81.3	68.3	36.8	25
Institutional					
Government	3.1	15.5	7.1	3.9	5
Co-operatives	3.3	2.6	22	29.9	40
Commercial and rural banks	0.9	0.6	2.6	29.4	30
Sub-total	7.3	18.7	31.7	63.2	75
Total	100	100	100	100	100

Sources: 1. All India debt and Investment Survey, 1961-62.
2. All India Debt and Investment Survey, 1981, Sarvekshana July, 1986.
3. Economic Survey, 1998-99

Among all the different non-institutional sources the contribution of moneylenders was highest and that was to the extent of 69.7 per cent in 1951-52. They charged exorbitant rates of interest. The government enacted various legislations to regulate their activities. The most important move to free the farmers from the clutches of the moneylenders was the expansion of institutional credit to agriculture. The contribution of moneylenders slowly declined to 49.2 per cent in 1961-62 to 36.1 per cent in 1971 and further to 7 per cent in 1995-96.

Total contribution of non-institutional source towards agricultural credit has slowly dwindled from 92.7 per cent in 1951-52 to 81.3 per cent in 1961-62 and further to 25.0 per cent in 1995-96. On the other hand the share of institutional sources to the agricultural credit has risen from 7.3 per cent in 1951-52 to 18.7 per cent in 1961-62 and further to 75 per cent in 1995-96. Co-operatives provided only 3.1 per cent of total rural credit in 1951-52. However, its progress afterwards has been quite impressive. The co-operatives provided 40 per cent of total rural credit in 1995-96. The share of commercial banks and regional rural banks in rural credit was merely 0.9 per cent in 1951-52 and 0.6 per cent in 1961-62 which further increased to 30 per cent in 1995-96. After nationalization, the commercial banks have played an important role in providing rural credit. To supplement the efforts of the commercial banks and co-operatives in extending credit to weaker sections in rural areas, regional Rural Banks (RRBs) were established.

Table 2 depicts the agency-wise flow of institutional credit to agriculture in recent years. The total institutional credit (comprising cooperative banks, Commercial banks and Regional rural banks) flow for agriculture and allied activities rose from Rs. 52, 827 crore in 2000-01 to Rs. 69,560 crore in 2002-03 and further to Rs. 2,03,297 crore in 2006-07. Among the various agencies disbursing agricultural credit, the amount of loan advanced by cooperatives has risen from Rs. 20,800 crore in 2000-01 to Rs. 23,716 crore in 2002-03 and further to Rs. 42480 crore in 2006-07. Since 1975 Regional Rural Banks were advancing direct loans to small and marginal farmers, agricultural labourers and rural artisans for productive purposes. The share of Regional Rural banks to the total agricultural credit has grown from Rs. 4,220 crore in 2000-01 to Rs. 20435 crore in 2006-07. Again the share of commercial banks to the total agricultural credit rose sharply from Rs. 27,807 crore in 2000-01 to Rs. 1, 40,382 crore in 2006-07.

The share of co-operatives in total credit to agriculture has declined from 39.37 per cent in 2000-01 to 20.89 per cent in 2006-07. On the other hand share of RRBs rose from 7.99 per cent to 10.05 per cent during the same period. Similarly proportionate share of commercial banks in total credit grew sharply from 52.64 to 69.06 during the corresponding period. Thus the main story in the extension of rural credit has been the ascending of commercial banks along with RRBs with a corresponding fall in the share of cooperatives.

Table 2

Flow of Institutional Credit to Agriculture in Recent Years

(In Rs. Crore)

Agency	*2000-2001*	*2001-2002*	*2002-2003*	*2003-2004*	*2004-2005*	*2005-2006*	*2006-2007*
Cooperative	20800	23604	23716	26995	31424	39404	42480
Banks	(39.37)	(38.04)	(34.09)	(30.99)	(25.07)	(21.83)	(20.89)
Regional Rural	4220	4854	6070	7581	12404	15223	20435
Banks	(7.99)	(7.82)	(8.73)	(8.71)	(9.90)	(8.43)	(10.05)
Commercial	27807	33587	39774	52441	81481	125859	140382
Banks	(52.64)	(45.86)	(57.18)	(60.30)	(66.03)	(69.74)	(69.06)
Total	52827	62045	69560	86981	125309	180486	203297

Source: NABARD
Economic Survey, 2007-08, 2006-07, 2005-06.
Figures in parenthesis are percentages.

Table 3 shows the flow of institutional credit to agriculture on the basis of time. The short term institutional credit rose from Rs. 11, 271 crore to Rs. 40, 961 crore (nearly 4 times) during 1993-94 to 2001-02 and that of long term institutional credit also increased from Rs. 5223 crore to Rs. 23039 crore (more than 4 times) during the corresponding period. In percentage terms the flow of short term institutional credit to agriculture which was 68.4 per cent in 1993-94 gradually declined to 64.0 per cent of the total credit in 2001-02 and that the share of long term credit grew from 31.6 per cent in 1993-94 to 36.0 per cent in 2001-02.

Thus rural credit has played a vital role in supporting farm production in India. Though the amount of rural credit have increased over times, several weaknesses have crept in like problems of over dues, neglect of weaker sections. Unfortunately much credit has grown to rich and influential large farmers, neglecting the bottom levels. To provide the rural poor accessibility to credit from the banking system and for alleviating poverty, GOI introduced SHG-Bank Linkage programme in 1992 and Kisan credit card scheme in 1998-99.

Table 3
Flow of Institutional Credit to Agriculture

(Rs. Crore)

	Short Term		*Medium and Long Term*	
Year	*Amount*	*Per cent*	*Amount*	*Per cent*
1993-94	11271	68.4	5223	31.6
1994-95	7938	42.3	10806	57.7
1995-96	14526	65.9	7507	34.1
1996-97	16998	64.4	9413	35.6
1997-98	20640	64.6	11316	35.4
1998-99	23903	64.8	12957	35.2
1999-2000	28862	64.6	15750	35.4
2000-01	33283	63.1	19431	36.9
2001-02*	40961	64.0	23039	36.0
2002-03 $	44929	54.7	37144	45.3

* Estimated
$ Target

Source: Economic Survey, 2002-03, P. 167.

Section–II

Kisan Credit Card Scheme (KCC)

For the development of agriculture sector various schemes have been introduced in banking scenario like Agriculture Cash Credit (ACC) for short term requirements, Agriculture Term Loan (ATL) for long term requirements Kisan Credit Card (KCC) scheme is the modified and improved version of

ACC. Before the launch of the kisan credit card, the farmers under the agriculture cash credit had to produce bills for every activity such as purchase of fertilizers, seeds, pesticides levelling of farms etc. This caused a lot of inconveniences to the farmers. It was also a costly affair for farmers. To mitigate the problems faced by the farmers, the Government of India in 1998-99 through National Bank of Agriculture and Rural Development (NABARD) and RBI directed the public sector banks, cooperative banks and Regional Rural Banks (RRBs) to launch a simplified scheme for farmers known as kisan credit card. The scheme aimed at provision of adequate and timely support from the banking system to the farmers for their cultivation needs including purchase of inputs in a flexible and cost effective manner. The scheme is being implemented in all the states and union territories by all commercial banks, RRBs, state co-operative banks, and primary agricultural co-operative societies.

Kisan Credit Card Scheme started with the following features.

- Eligible farmers to be provided with a KCC and pass book or card-cum-pass book.
- Provision of revolving cash credit facility with unlimited with drawls and repayments.
- Meet the production credit need, cultivation expenses and contingency expenses of the farmers.
- Limits based on the basis of operational holdings, cropping pattern and scale of finance.
- Fixation of sub-limits at the discretion of banks.
- Credit Card valid for three years subject to annual renewals.
- Withdrawals through Slips/Cheques accompanied by card and passbook.
- Security, margin, rate of interest, etc. as per RBI norms.
- Each with drawls to be repaid within 12 months.
- Credit Limits can be enhanced depending on performance and needs.

Thus all rural farmers having land and a good financial track record of two years are eligible for this scheme. However, new borrowers could also be included if they provide proof of operational land holding from the area patwari. The farmers will be evaluated by the bank on financial grounds by looking at his past record with the bank and on personal grounds by looking at his reputation in the village.

The Kisan credit card scheme is an innovating mechanism for facilitating the flow of timely and adequate short-term credit to the farmers. The KCC scheme is an ongoing scheme. The progress in issue of KCC by cooperative banks, regional rural banks and Commercial banks can be seen from Table 4. The total number of cards (KCCs) issued has increased from 7.84 lakh in 1998-99 to 96.8 lakh in 2004-05 (i.e about 13 times). Up to November 2007, total number of cards issued were more than 707.55 lakh. Out of which cooperatives banks contributed 341.10 lakh (48.21%) followed by commercial banks 273.32 lakh (38.63%) and rest 93.13 Lakh (13.16%) by RRBs. During 2006-07, the total number of KCCs issued were 85.11 Lakh and the amount sanctioned was Rs. 46729 crore. For 2007-08 the amount sanctioned was Rs. 25263 crore. The amount of loan sanctioned by cooperative banks, commercial banks and regional rural banks, jointly has risen from Rs. 2314 crore in 1998-99 to Rs. 21785 crore in 2003-04. At the end of September 2004, the cumulative progress in respect of amount of loan sanctioned since 1998-99 was to the extent of Rs. 111459 crore (Economic Survey, 2004-05), Kisan Credit card holders are also provided personal accident insurance cover for death and disability.

The Kisan Credit CArd scheme (KCC) has benefited both the farmers as well as banks. Some of the benefits of the KCC scheme to farmers and banks are:

- Helped in augmenting the flow of short-term crop loans for seasonal agricultural operations.
- Access to adequate and timely credit to farmers.
- Enlargement of the scheme to include term loans for agriculture and allied activities along with a component to meet the consumption needs.

- Full year's credit requirements of the farmers taken care of.
- Flexibility to draw cash and buy inputs.
- Minimum paper work.
- Sanction of the facility for three years subject to annual review.
- Assured availability of credit at anytime enabling reduced interest burden for the farmer.
- Simplification of documentation for withdrawal of funds from the bank.

Table 4
Agency-wise KCCs Issued

(lakh)

Year	*Cooperative Banks*	*RRBs*	*Commercial Banks*	*Total*
1998-99	1.56	0.06	6.22	7.84
1999-00	35.95	1.73	13.66	51.34
2000-01	56.14	6.48	23.90	86.52
2001-02	54.36	8.34	30.71	93.41
2002-03	45.79	9.64	27.00	82.43
2003-04	48.78	12.75	30.94	92.47
2004-05	35.56	17.29	43.95	96.80
2005-06	25.98	12.49	41.65	80.12
2006-07	22.97	14.06	48.08	85.11
2007-08[a]	14.01	10.29	7.21[b]	31.51
Total	341.10	93.13	273.32	707.55
% Share	48.21	13.16	38.63	100.00

Source: NABARD and RBI.
Economic Survey 2007-08.

- Reduction in work load for bank staff by avoidance of repeated appraisal and processing of loan papers.
- Improvement in recycling of funds and better recovery of loans.
- Reduction in transaction cost to the banks.
- Better banker–client relationships.

NABARD had advised banks to extend coverage through expanding their outreach by lending to more farmers including non-willful defaulters, oral lasses, tenant farmers, share croppers who may have been outside the fold of the scheme, as also new comers (Economic Survey, 2007-08). Further, from January 31, 2006, the KCC scheme has been extended to all kinds of loan requirements of borrowers of state cooperative Agriculture Rural Development Banks (SCARDBs). It covers short-term/medium term credit and long-term credit and a reasonable component of consumption credit within the overall limit sanctioned to the borrowers.

Thus the introduction of Kisan, Credit Card KCCs was a significant innovation in the rural credit delivery mechanism. However, the outreach of the KCCs to cover all eligible farmers under the scheme has been hampered by the lack of updated land records, small landholdings and illiteracy of borrowers etc.

Section–III

Although India has one of the largest networks of bank branches in the world, yet the hundreds of millions of poor are largely out of it. But those locked out of the banking world have found a way out. It is called micro credit. Micro credit as the name itself indicates, is small amount of credit to lower income groups which comprise small and marginal farmers, landless labourers, hawkers, rural artisans, petty shop owners etc. A significant instrument of promotion of micro credit in India in a sustainable manner has been the Self-Help Groups (SHGs) Programme and its linkage with banks.

National Bank for Agricultural and Rural Development (NABARD) set up in 1982 is a pioneer in conceptualizing and implementing the concept of SHG through the SHG-Bank Linkage programme since 1992. This programme has emerged as the largest micro-credit programme in the country in recent years. The objectives of this programme relate to encouraging banking thrift and credit among the poor, evolving supplementary credit strategies for meeting the credit needs of the poor, building mutual trust and confidence between the bankers and the rural poor, members of SHG save and contribute to a common fund from which small loans are made to the needy members as per decisions of the group. With modest beginning of 500 SHGs in 1992, this project steadily progressed in terms of number of SHGs financed, bank loans disbursed, number of SHGs refinanced and refinance disbursed. All the major categories of the banks, viz. commercial banks, cooperative banks and regional rural banks (RRBs) are participating in delivering of micro finance services. In all, three distinct linkage models are being followed.

(i) SHG Bank Linkage Model I (Bank as SHPIs) envisages the bank itself as self help group promoting institutions (SHPIs)

(ii) Under SHG-Bank Linkage Model II groups are formed, nurtured and trained by NGOs or by Govt. agencies. The bank provides credit directly to the SHGs after watching their operations.

(iii) Under SHG-Bank Linkage Model III, NGOs act as both facilitators and microfinance intermediaries, NGOs promote the groups, nurture and trained them and get bulk loans from banks for on lending to the SHGs.

Out of all these three models currently in vogue, Model II turns out to be most acceptable (Table 5). As on March 31, 2004 about 20 per cent of SHGs were financed by banks (model I), 72 per cent SHGS were formed by NGOs/Govt. agencies and financed by banks (Model II) and the remaining 8 per cent were financed by banks with the intervention of NGOs. More than 80 per cent of Bank loan has been given to SHGs formed

Table 5
Model-wise Linkage Position (As on March 31, 2004)

Model	*Type*	*Number of SHGs*	*Bank loan (Rs. Crore)*
1	SHGs formed and Financed by banks.	2, 17, 624 (20)	549.87 (14)
II	SHGs formed by NGOs/Govt. agencies, etc and financed by banks	7,77,326 (72)	3, 164.72 (81)
III	SHGs financed by banks using NGOs formal agencies as financial intermediaries	84, 141 (8)	189.62 (5)
	Grand Total	10,79,091	3,904.21

Figures in brackets show percentages.

by NGO/Govt. agencies. It is interesting to observe that more than four-fifths of SHGs have been linked with NGOs, in one way or the other. Thus NGOs often, play an important role in the linkage process however they usually don't play a financial role. They promote and train the groups, and assist them through the qualifying process of saving and internal lending.

Table 6 depicts the progress made by SHG-Bank linkage programme since its inception in 1992. Credit linkage between the SHGs and the banks forges an alliance between the informal SHGS and the formal banks As on December 31,2007 bank loans of Rs. 20,114 crore was availed of by 30.51 Lakh SHGs from the banking system compared to bank loans of Rs. 57 crore availed of by 32,995 SHGs in 1998-99. As on December 31, 2007 the average bank loan availed of per SHG and per family amounted to Rs. 65 924 and Rs. 4708 respectively Cumulatively, till March 2006-07, loans of Rs. 18041 crore have been disbursed by banks to 30.51 Lakh SHGs as compared to loans of Rs.480. 87 crore disbursed by banks to 2.64 lakh SHGs with refinance support Rs. 400.74 crore till March 31, 2001. In all 495 banks (50commercial banks, 96 amalgamated RRBs and 352 Cooperative banks) are actively participating in the programme (Eco. Survey 2007-08).

Table 7 depicts Agency-wise Linkage position as on March 31, 2004. Total number of SHGs financed by commercial banks, RRBs and cooperatives Banks were 50%, 38%, and 12 %respectively. Recently there has been modest involvement of commercial banks in SHG Bank linkage programme. Some of the characteristics of SHGs like strong sense of ownership, voluntary participation, and non bureaucratic and committed leadership have helped in achieving progress.

The government of India is very much optimistic about the recent development of MFIs, particularly the SHGs in providing a productive base for the rural economy. The mission of NABARD is to link one million SHGs with the overall banking system by the year 2008, facilitating access of 100 million rural poor to formal credit system.

Despite credit linkage of more than 1 million SHGs and mobilization of about Rs. 3000 crore as credit from the formal

Table 6
SHG-Bank Linkage Programme

	Total SHGs financed by Banks			Bank Loan[a]			Refinance		
	During the Year			During the year					
Year	Number %	Growth	Cumulative Number	Amount (Rs crore)	Growth %	Cumulative Amount	Amount (Rs crore)	Growth (%)	Amount (Rs. crore)
1992-93	255	-	-	0.29	-	-	0.27	-	-
1998-99	32,995	-	32,995	57	-	57	52	-	52
1999-00	81,780	148	1,14,775	136	138	193	98	88	150
2000-01	1,49,050	82	2,63,825	288	112	481	251	156	401
2001-02	1,97,653	133	4,61,478	545	89	1026	396	58	796
2002-03	255,882	29	717,360	1,022	87	2049	-	-	-
2003-04	3,61,731	41	10,79,091	1856	81	3904	705	13	2124
2004-05	539,365	49	16,18,456	2994	62	6898	-	-	-
2005-06	620,109	15	2,238,565	4499	50	11,398	-	-	-
2006-07	686408	11	2987441	6643	47	18041	-	-	-
2007-08[b]	126068	-	3051041	2073	-	20114	-	-	-

a. Includes repeat loans to existing SHGs.
b. As on December 31, 2007

Sources: 1. Economic Survey: 2005-06, 2006-07, 2007-08
2. Report on Trend Progress of Banking in India, 2003-04, RBI

Table 7
Agency-wise Linkage Position (As on March 31, 2004)

	Number of SHGs		*Bank Loan (Rs. Crore)*	
Agency Cumulative Position	*2003*	*2004*	*2003*	*2004*
Commercial Banks	3, 61, 061 (50)	5, 38,422 (50)	1150 (56)	2255 (58)
RRBS	2,77, 340 (39)	4,05,998 (38)	727 (36)	1278 (33)
Cooperatives	78,9 59 (11)	1,34, 671 (12)	172 (8)	371 (9)
Total	7, 17, 360 (100)	10,79, 091 (100)	2049 (100)	3904 (100)

Figures in brackets show percentages.

financial institutions, micro-finance still forms a small proportion of the total bank credit in India. What is particularly welcome is that SHGs have significantly empowered women as over three-fourths of the SHGs are managed by women. The main advantages of the programme are timely repayment of loans to banks, reduction in transaction costs both to the poor and the banks, doorstep "saving and credit facility for poor and exploitation of the untapped business potential of the rural areas.

Micro-finance initiatives have shown that banking with the poor is a viable proposition. Micro-credit has been hailed as the best method of creating additional employment and removing poverty NABARD has been playing a catalytic role in terms of promotional support to NGOs and also in nurturing quality SHGs.India's demand for micro credit is Rs. 500 billion, and only Rs. 18 billion of this amount has been generated so far there is still a long way to go.

Moreover micro credit movement has not spread uniformly throughout the country. Andhra Pradesh, West Bengal, Rajasthan, Tamil Naidu are some of the states which have fared better compared to other states like Punjab, Himachal Paradesh, Manipur, Goa, Haryana etc. (Table 8). Another criticism levied against this programme is that the poorest of the poor are not the beneficiaries of this programme.

Table 8
Self-Help Group and Bank Linkages

End-March 2003

	Commercial Banks		Regional Rural Banks		Co-operative Banks		Total	
Region/State	No. of SHGs	Bank Loan	No.of SHGs	Bank Loan	No. of SHGs	Bank Loan	No. of SHGs	Bank Loan
(1)	(2)	(3)	(4)	(51	(6)	(7)	(8)	(9)
Northern Region								
Haryana	359	2.6	1165	4.3	-	-	1524	6.9
Himachal Pradesh	3451	4.5	1365	2.4	4059	10.1	8875	17.1
Punjab	330	1.5	141	1.1	371	1.4	842	4.0
Jammu & Kashmir	405	0.8	315	0.5	168	1.1	888	2.4
Rajàsthan	8807	16.1	11526	24.8	2409	5.4	22742	46.3
Delhi	52	0.4	-	-	-	-	52	0.4
Sub-Total	13404	25.9	14512	33.1	7007	18.0	34923	77.1
North Eastern Region								
Assam	282	0.3	3158	4.2	37	0.1	3477	4.5
Manipur	162	0.5					162	0.5
Meghalaya	62	0.6	117	Neg.	-	-	179	0.5
Sikkim	24	0.1	-	-	-	-	24	0.1
Tripura	2	Neg.	96	0.1	6	Neg.	104	0.1
Nagaland	-	-	15	0.1	-	-	15	0.1
Arunachal Pradesh	108	0.2	-	-	-	-	108	0.2
Sub-Total	640	1.6	3386	4.4	43	0.1	4069	6.0

Contd...

	End-March 2003							
	Commercial Banks		*Regional Rural Banks*		*Co-operative Banks*		*Total*	
Region/State	*No. of SHGs*	*Bank Loan*	*No.of SHGs*	*Bank Loan*	*No. of SHGs*	*Bank Loan*	*No. of SHGs*	*Bank Loan*
(1)	(2)	(3)	(4)	(51	(6)	(7)	(8)	(9)
Eastern Region								
Bihar	2873	4.4	5197	7.3	91	0.4	8161	12.1
Jharkhand	4518	19.5	3247	7.1	-	-	7765	26.7
Orissa	12451	12.7	24621	31.8	5200	6.6	42272	51.0
West Bengal	7731	5.8	8287	10.2	16629	14.4	32647	30.5
A & N Islands (UT)	-	-	-	-	48	02	48	02
Sub-Total	27573	42.5	41352	56.4	21968	21.5	90893	120.5
Central Region								
Madhya Pradesh	5054	13.0	8326	13.6	1891	4.1	15271	30.7
Chhatisgarh	565	0.4	4286	3.7	1912	1.2	6763	5.4
Uttar Pradesh	17151	13.3	35644	73.1	901	1.0	53696	87.5
Uttaranchal	4780	17.4	811	3.2	262	0.1	5853	21.1
Sub-Total	27550	44.1	49067	93.7	4966	6.9	81583	144.7
Western Region								
Goa	194	0.8	-	-	46	0.3	240	1.1
Gujarat	8535	9.4	4120	5.3	1220	1.36	13875	16.1
Maharashtra	14989	41.3	9339	20.4	3737	8.0	28065	69.7
Sub-Total	23718	51.6	13459	25.7	5003	9.6	42180	86.9

Contd...

	End-March 2003							
	Commercial Banks		*Regional Rural Banks*		*Co-operative Banks*		*Total*	
Region/State	*No. of SHGs*	*Bank Loan*	*No.of SHGs*	*Bank Loan*	*No. of SHGs*	*Bank Loan*	*No. of SHGs*	*Bank Loan*
(1)	(2)	(3)	(4)	(51	(6)	(7)	(8)	(9)
Southern Region								
Andhra Pradesh	174992	634.1	99558	322.2	6788	19.1	281338	975.4
Karnataka	23680	43.8	21929	60.5	16569	39.7	62178	144.0
Kerala	14068	40.3	4218	9.1	2726	15.1	21012	64.5
Tamil Nadu & UTP	55436	265.6	29859	122.2	13889	41.8	99184	429.5
Sub-Total	268176	983.8	155564	513.9	39972	115.7	463712	1613.4
Total	61061	1149.5	277340	727.2	78959	172.0	717360	2048.7

Neg.: Negligible.
Note: Components may not add up to the total due to rounding off.
Source: RBI Annual Report, 2002-03

The poorest are generally let out, as they are not confident about participating in the programme. Another problem facing self-help groups is their sustainability. They cannot survive unless they are operationally and financially sustainable. Most of the self-help groups are dependent on NGOs which have sponsored them and once they withdraw from the scene, the self-help groups might not survive.

The outreach of MFIs in terms of the proportion of poor households served is also very small covering less than 5% of India's rural poor (as compared to 65% in Bangladesh). Issues relating to structure and sustainability, funding, regulations and capacity building for micro credit delivery are engaging the attention of Reserve Bank of India. NABARD also recently initiated a programme to involve private banks in micro finance.

Thus we have seen that there are significant opportunities for banks in micro-credit. Every SHG and MFI in India has been through a great learning experience in the last few years. Although micro finance in India has been growing millions of poor people are yet to be touched by its magic. The biggest challenge for India is to scale micro finance up, as it is an integral part of the strategy for poverty alleviation. For this some of the suggestions are:

(1) Design appropriate institutional mechanisms that are sensitive and responsive to the needs of the poor so that they can save and use credit in a productive manner.

(2) Social intermediation is the need of the hour for organizing the poor into SHGs. For this adult education programmes should be arranged and skills should be imparted. In view of the low literacy rate of women, social intermediation assumes special importance. This task should be assigned to NGOs.

(3) For strengthening micro credit movement, a national policy framework should be devised.

(4) Lending to the poor has to be regulated just like other lending, perhaps even more carefully considering their already weak economic standing.

(5) There is need to change the bankers' mind set so that they start extending loans to SHGs as their normal banking activity.

(6) India being a vast country. A single model may not be suitable in all the regions of the country. A model best suited to local conditions must be adopted so that rural poor can be approached expeditiously.

(7) To make available micro credit quickly and without any hassle the banks should be given complete freedom to disburse the loans on the spot and at easy terms and conditions.

Micro credit could help eradicate poverty only if it is complemented with other measures like healthcare, literacy etc. A number of measures are needed to promote sustainable growth of micro- credit. Self help groups cannot survive unless they are operationally and financially sustainable. They must be able to earn enough to cover the operational costs and also they should be able to manage without depending on subsidized input on a continuing basis.

In the end we can say that if these programmes can be implemented successfully then the prospect of rural credit structure would be quite bright in future. The government should take urgent steps to boost credit flow to the agricultural sector.

References

Banerjee, Amalesh and K. S. Shrawan ed. (2002), *Banking and Financial Sector Reforms in India,* Deep and Deep Publications, Pvt. Ltd., New Delhi.

Datt. Ruddar (2001), *Second Generation Economic Reforms in India,* Deep and Deep Publications, Pvt. Ltd., New Delhi.

Fisher, Thomas and M. S. Sriram ed. (2002), *Beyond Micro-credit: Putting Development Back into Microfinance,* New Economic Foundation, London.

Government of India, *Economic Survey,* Various Issues, New Delhi.

Hermes, Niels and Robert Lensink (2007), "Impact of Microfinance, A Critical Survey," *Times News,* Network, June 15.

Kainth, G. S. (2007), "Rural Finance in India", *Yojana,* February.

Meenakshy B. S. (2007), "Microcredit to Nobel", *Yojana,* Vol. 51, March.

Murthy, Laxmi (2005), "International Year of Micro-credit", available *at http: //in fochangeindia-org/micro*

Pandey, M. C. and Subodh Kumar ed. (2005), *Banking: Trends and Practices,* Anamika Publishers and Distributors (P) Ltd., New Delhi.

Prasad, C. S. ed. (2006), *Sixty Years of Indian Agriculture 1947 to 2007,* New Century Publication, New Delhi.

Rao, Subha, K. G. K. (2007), "Financial Inclusion: An Introspection," *Economic and Political Weekly,* Feb. 3, pp. 355-360

Ray, Debraj (2006), *Development Economics,* Oxford University, Press, New Delhi.

Reddy, A. R. (2004), *Rural Banking and Over Dues Management,* Mittal Publications, New Delhi.

Reserve Bank of India, *Report on Trend and Progress of Banking in India,* 2003-2004.

Sarkar, A. N. (2005), *Strategic Business Management and Banking,* Deep and Deep Publications, Pvt. Ltd., New Delhi.

Sreekantaradhya, B. S. (2004), *Banking and Finance: Perspectives on Reform,* Deep and Deep Publications, Pvt. Ltd., New Delhi.

7

MICRO FINANCE AND POVERTY REDUCTION: ANALYTICAL ISSUES IN TIRUCHIRAPPALLI DISTRICT, TAMIL NADU

A. Gunasekaran

The rational is that economic empowerment of the poor through strengthening the income generating capacity, equips the poor to access all the development requirements to get out of the multifaceted dimensions of poverty. Addressing poverty is the most significant challenge in this millennium, clearly reflected in the Millennium Development Goals that seeks to have global poverty by 2015. Self Help Group (SHG) methodology is the most dominant form of micro finance in India. The formation of SHGs for women around thrift and credit has emerged as one of the more effective methods for poverty reduction and women empowerment. Over the past 10 years, nearly one million SHGs have been formed in India. The SHGs have been increased with almost 80 per cent in South India especially in Tamil Nadu and Kerala. There has been an exponential growth in the number of SHGs from the year 2005.

Microfinance and Economic Development

The real idea of micro-finance is to help increase income of poor people particularly women. It is based on the notion that with small-scale loans and access to other financial and business services, the poor can help themselves to generate income by creating or expanding small businesses. It is estimated that nearly out of 400-500 million people worldwide, about 80 percent of those who are in need of financial services are yet outside the mainstream of formal financial systems. In order to reduce the poverty among the village people, Micro Financial Institutions come forward to provide financial services to the needy people. Asia is the most developed continent in the world in terms of volume of Micro Finance Institutions (MFI) activities.

Review of Literature

The district of Mahabubnagar is highly drought prone and poverty stricken; with 45 per cent of its rural households living below the poverty line it has the largest concentration of poor households in the state. Within this backdrop the state government has pro-actively pursued the SHG-bank linkage program as a significant component of its wider poverty-alleviation strategy for Mahabubnagar. The result is that with over 20,000 SHGs, Mahabubnagar has the second biggest and perhaps the fastest growing linkage program in the state *(Government of Andhra Pradesh 1996).*

The use of credit for poverty alleviation is not a new phenomenon in China. As part of the Chinese government's poverty alleviation measures in the eighties, a number of countries gave small loans to households in poor areas, based on an assessment of whether or not the household was capable of making use of the loans. The repayment rate of these loans in the later half of the eighties has been estimated as somewhere between 30-65per cent. Not an impressive figure, but an analysis by Rozelle *et al.* (1998) suggests that these loans were actually a very efficient way of combating poverty since they led to a substantial growth in agricultural productivity. Because of the low repayment rates, these loans were less popular during the early half of the nineties where the policy shifted its emphasis from household loans to other revenue-generating and growth-oriented strategies.

As most Grameen members are women, one of the results is that women have had title deeds transferred to them, often from their husbands, to obtain these loans. This has also reduced the incidence of divorce since women as; owners of their own homes cannot be easily evicted (Yunus 1998).

Need of the Study

Tamil Nadu is one of the predominate state to encourage to form SHGs next to Andhra Pradesh and Kerela. The NGOs and Banks are providing credit facilities to SHGs members. But the roles of NGOs are larger than banks to facilitating credit to poor people, because the banks are not extending to this service to the poor. Many studies estimate that the micro finance is one of instrument to remove poverty in rural areas. However, in backward states and districts organized supports from NGOs were lacking. But National Bank for Agricultural and Rural Development (NABARD) is also experimenting to include SHGs. The promotional efforts especially undertaken by NABARD in the last two years have resulted in a significant growth of programme beyond expectation. The adoption of SHGs-Micro Finance concept as primary anti poverty, self-employment generation programmes by central government and NGOs. The study is made an attempt to analyse the role of micro finance to remove the poverty in Tiruchirappalli district.

Objectives

1. To examine micro credit organized and nurtured by NGOs and NABARD in Tamil Nadu and India,
2. To study the social and economic profile of the SHG members in sampled areas district of Tiruchirappalli,
3. To estimate the income changes of SHG members through micro credit in the sampled areas.

Hypotheses

The hypotheses for the study are

1. The women's participation in SHG activities influence the decision making in the family

2. The participation in SHG members increases the participant household's income.

Methodology

Source of Data

The objectives of the study stated above have been verified with the use of both primary and secondary data.

The necessary secondary data have been obtained from various published works such as books, reports, journal articles, magazines, periodicals and electronic web materials. In addition to this the researcher has made use of the data and other information pertaining to micro finance, the growth of self-help group, and performance of SHGs-NABARD Bank Linkage and others from NABARD Annual Reports.

Methods

Multi-stage, simple random sampling method was used for selecting the SHGs and respondents. In first stage, Tiruchirappallai was selected for conducting sample survey. The total of 30 divisions, only 3 divisions were randomly selected for the research purpose. The names of the divisions are Pandamangalam, Kottapattu and Kottai Colony. At the third stage two Self Help Groups were selected from the each divisions. Thus a total of 6 SHGs and a sample of 78 members representing the sample SHGs were selected for the study.

The Evolution of SHG System in India

The Self Help Groups (SHGs) is the newly emerged concept. Due to non-availability of credit and in order to remove clutches of moneylenders, the members form a group of around twenty members. The group formation process may be facilitated by an NGO or by the MFI or bank itself, or it may evolve from a traditional rotating savings and credit group (ROSCA) or other locally initiated grouping. The SHG members decide to make regular savings contributions. The collected amounts are kept by the head of the members in cash, or in kind, or they may be banked. The details of micro credit provider in terms of borrowers in India are furnished the Table 1. The mean value of loans is provided by micro finance a provider is 112. It is interesting to note that BASIX dominates to provide credit to its members when compare to other micro credit agencies. For instance the mean value of loan amounts are provided by BASIX is 145 and the mean value of loan provided by SPANDANA is 142.

Table 1
Micro Credit Providers in Terms of Number of Borrowers in India

Micro Credit Providers	*No. of Borrowers*	*Gross Loan Portfolio (US$)*	*Average*
Spandana	385,996	54,621,671	142
SHARE	368,996	40,218,274	109
Sanghamitra	112,029	3,482,305	31
Basix	89,593	13,009,883	145
Bandha	82,260	4,629,266	56
Total	1,038,874	115,961,399	
Mean	207,775	23,192,280	112

Source: NABARD Bank, Annual Reports, 2004-05.

Outreach of SHG-NABARD Bank Linkage

While the SHG-bank linkage programme was slow to take off, in recent years it has expanded exponentially. By the end of March 2005, its coverage had more than doubled over the previous year to 24.25 million families in nearly 5,39,385 lakh SHGs, with 90 percent women members. These SHGs had availed of Rs. 6,776.10 crores in cumulative bank loans. The average loan per SHG was Rs.125, 626 and per family Rs. 2794. On-time repayment by SHGs was reported to be over 95 per cent.

Analytical Framework

The present study is concerned with the socio-economic profiles of the sample of Self Help Group Members in Tiruchirappalli. The topics covered are the demographic particulars and general characteristics of sample of Self Help Group Members and economic conditions of sample members. This chapter also attempts to provide an alternative to the sponsor-led impact assessments.

SHG-member Survey

An accompanying survey collected detailed information from 78 women belonging to the 6 SHGs in the 3 survey divisions in Tiruchirappallai. These interviews were carried out during the survey period in 2007. In order to compare the performance of the SHGs, three divisions are selected in the sample areas. They are Pandamangalam, Kottapattu and Kottai Colony. Two groups are selected from each division. The Shahidhya Magalir Self Help Group and Sri Kamalavalli Natchiyar Women's SHGs selected from Pandamangalam divisions, Roja Women's SHGs, ASA Women's SHGs from kottapattu divisions and Gangai Women's SHGs, Lilly Women's SHGs from Kottai Colony. Table 2 summaries the agencies providing loans to Self Help Groups.

Table 2
Name of the Self Help Groups and Micro Credit Agencies

	Name of the Agencies		
Name of the Self Help Groups	*NABARD*	*NGOs*	*Total*
Shahidhya	13		13
	100.0%		100.0%
Sri Kamalavalli Natchiyar		13	13
		100.0%	100.0%
Roja		13	13
		100.0%	100.0%
Asa		13	13
		100.0%	100.0%
Gangai	13		13
	100.0%		100.0%
Lilly		13	13
		100.0%	100.0%
Total	26	52	78
	33.3%	66.7%	100.0%

Source: Survey Data, 2007.

It is inferred that out of 78 sample SHG members, 66.7 per cent (52 members out of 78) of members are borrowing loans with help of Non-Governmental Organizations (NGOs). The remaining 33.3 percent (26 members out of 78) of the members are receiving credit from the National Bank for Rural

Development (NABARD). The reason is that NGOs have initiated to facilitate credit to the rural poor at the early of eighties but the NABARD-Bank Linkage Programme was started to provide loans to rural people during the nineties. However, The NGOs provides financial assistance to three SHGs namely, Sri Kamalavalli Natchiyar Womens Self Help Groups, ASA Women's Self Help Groups and Lilly Women's Self Help Groups. Thirteen members are selected from the each group in order to give equal representation of members.

Measurement of SHGs' Performance

Out of 78 SHGs respondent's 77 respondents (98.7 per cent) received loans from banks with the help of NGOs and NABARD. The survey analyse the purpose of the loan, which obtained from banks. The respondents are getting loans for the three purposes consumption purposes, income purposes and others purposes. Out of 78 respondents, 30 respondents (38 per cent) borrowed loan for the purpose of consumption. Out of this, 70 per cent (21 respondents) respondents borrowed for the purpose of education expenditures whereas only meager percent of the loan utilized for purchase of clothing and festival expenditure.

This survey also consists of the total loan amount borrowed from the banks for the purpose of consumption activities. Nearly 33.3 per cent of the respondents borrowed from banks in the total loan amount between Rs. 3000 and Rs. 5000. ASA SHGs is receiving higher amount than the other SHGs. At the same time 16.7 per cent of the respondents received loan in the range of more than Rs. 12000. Kamalavalli and Lilly SHGs is borrowing higher amount than any other groups in the loan amount Rs.12000. It accounts for only 3 groups received loan in the range of less than Rs. 3000 when compared to the loan amount range of Rs. 5000 and Rs. 7000.

In order to understand the relationship between income and loan amounts that borrowed from the banks, the study is analysed the loan amount for the purpose of the income generation activities. Out of the 46 respondents, 21 SHGs members (45.7 per cent) borrowed loan a sum of Rs.10000, the five members belongs to Lily SHGS and seven members belongs to Shahidhya SHGs members whereas 26.1 per cent (12 SHGs Members) received loan a sum of Rs.15000 those are belonging to each three members in the SHGs of Shahidhya, Kamalavalli and Lilly.

Household Income and Borrowing Loans

In this study is made an attempt to find out the changes in household income before borrowing loans and after borrowing loans from the banks. The details of Details of Household income before borrowing loans are provided in Table 3. It is interesting to note that out 78 respondents, 40 SHGs members (51.3 per cent of respondents) belonging to the income category of Rs. 3000 to 5000. Only 15.4 per cent of the respondents belong to the range of below Rs. 3000.

Table 3
Details of Household Income before Borrowing Loans

Household income	*Frequency*	*Per cent*	*Valid Per cent*	*Cumulative Per cent*
Below 3000	12	15.4	15.4	15.4
3000 -5000	40	51.3	51.3	66.7
5000-7000	9	11.5	11.5	78.2
7000-9000	6	7.7	7.7	85.9
9000-12000	2	2.6	2.6	88.5
Above 12000	9	11.5	11.5	100.0
Total	78	100.0	100.0	

Source: Survey Data, 2007.

In order to estimate the performance of the bank loans, the survey undertakes borrower opinions after receiving the loans from the banks. It is inferred that nearly 93.6 per cent of (73 out of 78 respondents) expressed response to change in their household's income after they received loans from the various banks. The remaining 6.4 per cent of the respondents have been given consent against the change in their household's income. Table 4. explains the details of household income after borrowing loans. The study finds that the respondents belong to below Rs. 3000 households were only 3 respondents at the same time it was 12 respondents before taking loans from the banks. It is understood that there is change in the income of the SHG members. Further it indicates that out of 93.6 per cent, 33.3 per cent of the respondents those who are belongs to in the income category of Rs. 5000 to 7000 whereas approximately, 29.5 per cent of the respondents income are in the range of Rs. 3000 to 5000.

Table 4
Details of Household Income after Borrowing Loans

Household income	*Frequency*	*Per cent*	*Valid Per cent*	*Cumulative Per cent*
Below 3000	3	3.8	4.1	4.1
3000 -5000	23	29.5	31.5	35.6
5000-7000	26	33.3	35.6	71.2
7000-9000	8	10.3	11.0	82.2
9000-12000	2	2.6	2.7	84.9
Above 12000	11	14.1	15.1	100.0
Total	73	93.6	100.0	

Source: Survey Data, 2007.

When the loan amount increases, the household's income also increases. It is argued that the higher amount loan gives the high amounts income to the respondents. For instance, 14.1 per cent respondents are in higher income category. It indicates that details of household's income, the respondents borrowed loans with help of NGOs and Banks. Out of the 73 respondents, nearly 49 respondents (67.1 per cent) received credit with support of NGOs whereas 24 respondents (32.9 per cent) borrowed credit with the help of banks in the sampled areas. As a result increase the credit ratio; it would be effect on the household's income. On an average 35.6 per cent of (26 out of 73) the SGHs members earn income in the range of Rs.5000 to 7000, meanwhile 69.6 per cent (16 out of 26) of respondents received credit with the support of NGOs and 38.5 per cent (10 out of 26) with help of banks. It is understood that there is positive significance between change in households income and credit facilities.

Null Hypothesis (H_o)

There is no significant difference in the change of household's income and loans borrowed from banks

Alternative Hypothesis (H_a)

There is significant difference in the change of household's income and loans borrowed from banks.

Table 5
Test Statistics

Test Statistics	*Income Changes*	*Total Loan Amount*
Chi-Square	22.479	85.289
df	33	8
Asymp. Sig.	.916	.000

a. 34 cells (100.0%) have expected frequencies less than 5. The minimum expected cell frequency is 2.1.

b. 0 cells (.0%) have expected frequencies less than 5. The minimum expected cell frequency is 8.4.

Source: Survey Data, 2006.

The calculated value is higher than the tabulated value. The value is higher than the tabulated value. The value is significant. Hence it can be concluded that there exist a significant difference between in the change of household's income and loans borrowed from banks. Therefore the null hypothesis is rejected and the alternative hypothesis is accepted.

Null Hypothesis (H_o)

Members of the SHGs are not inversely related to decision-making in their family.

Alternative Hypothesis (H_a)

Members of the SHGs are inversely related to decision-making in their family.

The data demonstrates that the decision making power of the SHG members have been increased. In order to find the relationship between the SHG members and decision-making powers, Karl Pearson's Correlation coefficient is worked out.

The value of Correlation coefficient is .921 at zero level of significance indicates that the women has more power than the men to decide in their family.

Conclusion

The SHG-Bank linkage approach is found to be an effective instrument by which very poor people can access hassle free formal credit without any collateral security and simultaneously improve their thrift habits. The approach also contributes to a social empowerment of the women However, the linkage and its impact can be made sustainable with the sincere interventions by the promotional agencies particularly the banks and Block authority in the areas of awareness building, skill development and training, and continuous.

The self-help groups in Tiruchirappalli not only provide a means of survival for poor women, but also serve as nascent institutions for the building up of women's specific social capital, which can serve a long-term sustainability function in poverty reduction. Apart from increasing women's networks and fostering trust, it enables them to acquire skills in conflict management, and organised participation in forums like the Gram Sabha, which will also have a long-term effect on enhancing women's overall ability to address poverty.

It is important to ensure that the government micro finance initiatives do not go the way of their several well-intentioned predecessors. The biggest challenge in development, however, is the simultaneous development of investment potential and improvement of skill levels of the borrowers. A glut of low skilled services is an unwelcome substitute for scarcity of credit. As micro credit alleviates the credit availability problem, the need for micro consulting, business planning and services like marketing, are being felt with greater acuteness.

Suggestions

Technical assistance has been provided through other government departments such as the Department of Industrial Promotion (for basic business skills training and trade promotion activities such as exhibitions) and the Ministry of

Health (for occupational health such as proper lighting). At the household level, family members have been mobilized to help in packaging and transport, and the younger members (including young men) help in designing goods. At the community level, some members of the women's groups are reportedly engaged in local community management structures and issues. The objective of standards has to be towards an improvement of MF programmes rather than provide cut-off values to be used as a basis for denial of funds and support. There is also a need is to develop the capacity of SHGs.

Reference

Chen and Snodgrass Chen, Martha A., and Snodgrass, Donald (2001), "*Managing Resources, Activities, and Risk in Urban India: The Impact of SEWA Bank.*" Washington, D.C.: AIMS.

Christen R. and Drake D. (2002), "Commercialization: The New Reality of Micro finance". *In:* Drake D. and Rhyne E., eds. *The Commercialization of Microfinance: Balancing Business and Development,* Connecticut, USA: Kumarian Press.

Government of Andhra Pradesh, "*Study of SHGs in AP*", Hyderabad, India, 1996.

Krishnaraj, Maithreyi and Thelma Kay (2002), "Report of Review of IFAD Gender Mainstreaming Projects in Asia", Unpublished Paper Prepared for IFAD.

Lalitha, N. and B. S. Nagarajan (2002), *Self-help Groups in Rural Development,* New Delhi, Dominant Publishers and Distributors.

NABARD (2001), *Progress of SHG-Bank Linkage in India 2000-2001.* NABARD Publications.

NABARD, Annual Reports, 2005.

Puhazhendhi, V. and Satyasai, K. J .S. (2000), Microfinance for Rural People: An Impact Evaluation. Mumbai: National Agricultural Bank for Rural Development, *Journal of Micro finance,* Volume 4 Number, 2 244.

Rozelle, Scott, Albert Park, Vincent Benziger and Ren (1998), Changing Targeted Poverty Investments and Economic Growth in China. *World Development Report,* Vol. 26, No. 12, pp. 2137-2151.

Yunus, Muhammad, with Alan Jolis (1998), *Banker to the Poor: The Autobiography of Muhammad Yunus* (London, Aurum Press).

8

MICRO CREDIT AND WOMEN EMPOWERMENT THROUGH SELF HELP GROUPS: A CASE STUDY OF CHENNAI CITY

A. Gunasekaran

In the recent years, empowerment has been recognized as the central issue in determining status of women. Since women become more potent source of development empowering them is prerequisite for over all development. By empowering women not only make them to share in the development progress but also bring out their lasting efficiency. In those days women were neglected to participate in economic activity and the perception has changed over and they are proving their efficiency by actively participating in all the sectors of the economy. Education is the key instrument to the women to make use of their power. To achieve rapid economic development women must be brought into focus and they must be empowered.

Empowerment of women is sin qua non to achieve the goals of social development. It is necessary that women must be brought in the main stream of national development programmes by empowering them to discharge all types of roles. Empowerment of women cannot be ignored while devising various policies for socio economic development. The economic status of women is now accepted as an indicator of an economy's level of development. However, this does not mean that economic development necessarily results in improving the women who constitute about 50 per cent of the population. Empowerment of women has multiple role benefits not only for the environment but for humanity as well. Ensuring sustainable development requires women empowerment and their full, equal and beneficial involvement in the decision making process related to sustainable development. Women's role in development is an indispensable factor as in the case of community development in which the participation of women and their contribution is remarkable. If women are not involved in the process of development activities, there is no advancement in their lives and there is no meaning in socio economic development of women.

Empowerment is the recent approach articulated by the third world countries women. It seeks to meet women's strategic gender needs, due to their subordinate position to men, through bottom up mobilization around practical gender need according to their accepted role in society. it aims at increasing women's power in terms of their self-reliance and internal strength to determine choices in life and to influence the direction of change.

According to human development report of 1995, empowerment is about participation in development process. It identifies empowerment with development and defines it as "development must be by people, not only for them. People must participate fully in the decision and process that shapes their lives, but as the same time promotes a rather instrumentalist view of empowerment. Investing in women's capabilities and empowering them to exercise their choices is not only valuable itself, but is also the surest way to contribute to economic growth and overall development. (UN report 1995).

Thus, empowerment is a process of awareness and capacity building, leading to greater participation in greater decision-making power and controls the transformation action. The empowerment of women covers both individual and collective transformation. It strengths their innate ability through capacity acquiring knowledge, power and experience.

The objective of national policy for women empowerment were to create an environment for women through economic and social policies, equal access in decision making and social sector needs, protection rights and legal machinery and foreign partnership within civil society. Bringing together women from poor families teaching them to cooperate with each other, helping them to understand democratic decision-making and sustaining these collectives has been a challenging task for women organizations.

Women Empowerment and Self Help Groups (SHGs)

The role of micro finance in women empowerment is a unique one, through services to poor women. Micro finance is increasingly seen as a tool for empowerment of women. Women are often most victimized from poverty, having to deal with inability to provide adequately for their children and with male suppression in society, women are left forgoing their own needs to satisfy needs of family. Though a lack of voice, they face various kinds of discrimination from household and community given the potential that more finance is believed to have in empowering women; many organizations are adopting this strategy of targeting their services to women.

The empowerment of women through SHGs would lead benefits not only to the individual women but also for the family and community as a whole through collection action for development. These SHGs have collection action. Empowering women is not just for meeting their economic needs but also more holistic social development. The SHGs empower women and train them to take active part in socio-economic progress of the nation.

Formation of SHGS with women has empowered them largely. SHGS are now gaining acceptance as an alterative system credit delivery, for meeting the credit needs especially to the people who are the poorest of poor generally comprising small/marginal farmers/and landless agricultural labors.

Greater access and sustainable flow, of credit is critical for empowerment of poor. The credit needs of the rural poor are determined by a compiled, socio-economic pillar where it is dependence of the rural poor as money lenders continue in many areas, especially for meeting the emergent needs of rural poor. Under the circumstances, it is difficult for a non-formal agency to adopt project-lending approach as usually following by banks and where the dividing the between credit for consumption and productive purposes is blurred. Despite repaid pace of expansion of financial system encompassing spheres of social and mass banking, the credit supply to the poor, in the form of SHG could emerge as promising partner to the credit system.

Origin and Concept of Self-help Group

The origin of self-help group can be traced is from Grameen bank of Bangladesh, which was founded by Mohamed Yunus. SHGS were started and formed in 1975. In India, NABARD initiated in 1986-1987. In TamilNadu, Chinnapillai an illiterate women live in parparanpatti, Madurai District, initiated the feed bank of SHGS in the stats. She was honored by the former Prime minister of India, honorable Atal Bihari Vajpayee, for forming a group and nurtured saving habits among the illiterate women in the village.

The absence of institutional credits, available in the rural area has led to the establishment to SHGS. The concept of self help groups has been evolved to organize the rural poor to meet their productive and consumption needs out of their savings.

A self help group is a small economically homogeneous affinity group of the rural poor voluntarily coming together to save small amounts regularly, which are deposited in a common fund to meet members emergency needs and to provide collateral free loans decided by the group (Abhaskumar Jha, 2000).

SHG is a medium for the development of savings habit among women (S. Rajmohan, 2003). SHGs enhance the quality of status of women as participants, decision makers and beneficiaries in the democratic, economic, social and cultural spheres of life. (Ritu Jain, 2003).

Self help is the most significant traditional activity. It is a process, group or organization comprising people coming together or sharing an experience or problem, with a view to individual or mutual benefit. A SHG is a voluntary group of poor not exceeding twenty in number formed usually by on external agency to accomplish certain common goals. Its members are expected to have similar social identity, heritage or similar occupations in order to maintain its coherence and smooth functioning without much conflict.

Aims of Self Help Groups

- To provide saving mechanism and develop cost effective credit delivery system at gross root levels to poor who have no access to the formal financial institutions.
- To equip the members with basic skills and knowledge required for understanding and operationalising transactions the groups through capacity building programmes.
- To provide forum for members for discussing their socioeconomic problems.
- To develop decision making capacity and leadership qualities among members.
- To generate awareness among the members about the ongoing development programmes into the area.
- To enable its members to become self dependent and self reliant.

Principles of SHGs

- The self help group is a network of members who fulfill location criteria. They are resident in the area and are homogenous.
- They have rules/norms regarding their functioning.
- Savings first, credit thereafter personalized services suiting the requirement of the members are ensured.
- Self Help Group hold regular meeting to ensure participation of members in the group activities.
-

- SHGs maintains accounts
- Group leaders are elected by members and rotated periodically.
- Market rates of interest on savings and credit are charged. Functions of self help groups.
- Identification of poor families and awareness building.
- Forming groups.
- Guiding groups in developing procedures and systems in savings and credit operations.
- Helping the groups in maintenance of books and account.
- Training the members in groups functioning and management.
- Addressing social and infrastructure needs of the members.

Magnitude of Self-group in the State

In Tamilnadu SHGS were started in 1992. As on august 2005, 226379 self-help groups are formed and the women enrollments are 3775541. As on Aug 2005, there are 164902 SHGS are financed by the banks of Rs.132597.39 lakhs. NABARD also planned to link one million SHGS gave been linked through various banks under aegis of NABARD and an amount of Rs.150 crores as been present aims to some objectives.

The objectives of present study are.

1. To explain the socio-economic conditions of women in SGHs.
2. To portray the occupation and employment status of the women in SHGs.
3. To describe the extent of decision making power of women after joining in SHGs.
4. To analyze the income and expenditure pattern of women in SHGs.

Methodology

The present study is both descriptive and analytical. The study has used both primary and secondary data for getting necessary information. In order to evaluate the objectives of the study the using purposive samples were drawn.

Field observation was also used to accumulate supporting information and the researcher himself personally collected the same data. During the survey, questions were translated in to the regional vernacular for the sake of respondents' convenience. Further, the participant observation technique has been used to avoid the extreme point lf view on the pat of the information by from checking.

This study was empirical in nature and was based on primary data. This study was more in the nature of case study. However, care was taken in designing the methodology of investigation and the framework for analysis.

Tools of Analysis

The collected information were systematically edited, classified and have been put into various statistical techniques. The statistical tools used include percentage analysis chi square and 't' test.

Results and Discussion

Most of the respondents i.e., 48 per cent of the respondents are come to know the SHGs through friends and relatives. Next, agencies involving to create awareness about the SHGs among the women, 33 of the respondents have known about SHG through non government agencies several anon government. 11 per cent of the respondents have taken own efforts to know about SHGs and the remaining 8 per cent of them known SHG through other sources which includes newspaper media and politician.

The enrolment rate of women in the SHGs is increasing due to so many reasons. It is observed from the study most of the respondents joined in SHGs to improve their socioeconomic conditions, whose percentage was 54, which is high. 35 per cent joined due to poverty. The remaining respondents joined in SHGs for unemployment and provide employment to others, whose percentage was seven and four respectively. The basic reason for the emergence of SHGs is to make women to be an independent.

The study shows that out of total samples 91 per cent were happy because they were not facing any problem being members in SHG while 9 per cent were facing problems being members in SHG. 85 per cent felt that they were not harassment by their husbands only 15 per cent were facing harassment by their husbands. It is observed that women in SHGs are enjoying their life comfortably.

There is strong support for women to join as a member in SHGs. The study reveals that 54 per cent respondents' family members were strongly encouraged them to join in SHGs and 25 per cent respondents family member don't mind about their membership in SHGs, 12 per cent respondents family members mildly encouraged them and the remaining 9 per cent respondents family members discouraged them. Women play an important role in family bur she is not allowed to partake with decision making process. However, after joining in SHGs their opinions are also taken for consideration in decision making process. About 52 per cent were influencing vital decisions in family and the family members neglect the remaining 48 per cent of the respondents in taking vital decisions.

Further the collected information has been tested with the statistical tool like chi-square statistic to know the dependency of the variables. The chi square value is 11.39 which is greater than the table value at five per cent level of significance for income and occupation level of the respondents.

Again the same technique has been applied to validate the hypothesis of no dependency between income and educational status of the members. The test value is 1.73 which is lower than table value at five per cent level of significance. As a result, it is accepted that there is relationship between income and education level of the respondents.

In the present study t test was used to test the employment status with respect to respondent's income. The calculated t value is 2.18 which shows significant at 5 per cent level and has been concluded that the two variables income and employment status significantly related with each other.

Conclusion

The role of self help groups is instrumental in the promotions of women empowerment. The social and economic status of women would ne still improved only if the self help groups could be enhanced to the best positive extent. There will be definite improvement in the social and economic aspects of women if such changes are brought independently or in a cooperative manner. As it has been already pointed out that through women empowerment, community development could also be achieved. Hence the SHGs scheme could be an effective instrument for the empowerment of women.

References

Sachidananda and Niraj Kumar (2004), "Empowerment of Women Through Self Help Groups in Bihar", *IASSI Quarterly*, Vol. 22, No. 4, pp. 5-14.

Abhaskumar Jha (2000), "Lending to the Poor: Design for Credit", *EPW*, Vol. XXXb, No. 8 and 9.

Rajmohan, S. (2003), "Activities of Self Help Groups in Virudhunagar: A Case Study", TNJC, pp. 25-29.

Ritu Jain, (2003), "Socio-economic Impact Through Self Help Groups", *Yojana*, Vol. 47, No. 7, pp. 11-12.

Tamil Nadu Corporation for Development of Women (TNCDW), pp. 23.

9

RURAL AGRICULTURE CREDIT IN THE POST-REFORM PERIOD SOME CONCERNS

PRAVEEN SHARMA

IN developing countries like India, the development of agriculture sector is important for variety of reasons. Agriculture is still a source of livelihood for majority of people in rural areas. It provides demand for industrial goods and in India whenever agriculture sector has grown at 3-4 per cent; industrial sector has grown at 6 plus per cent. It has been observed that the required growth of productivity in agriculture means that more capital must be invested in it. Farmers need much more capital than they can afford to save. If agriculture has to develop, its appetite for capital should be satisfied. In agriculture, *capital* represents a host of items like machinery, lives tock, irrigation systems, farm build mgs, wells, etc. In fact, the more developed the agriculture, the more capital the farmers would demand. Credit is a condition that enables a person to extend his control over his ownership of resources. It represents mobilisation of the savings by intermediaries or government from the people and through such credit operations financial savings are transformed into capital. Though credit is not capital, the money obtained through credit provides a command over enough funds to exploit opportunities.

It has been argued that credit itself would not contribute to agricultural growth unless other inputs are made available, along with credit. This is the paradigm of farm finance. The opinion has been expressed that credit plays the role of an accelerator for agricultural development provided it is adequate in quantity, cheap and development oriented It has also been observed that at a certain stage in agricultural development, agricultural credit clearly does become a strong force for further improvement. The present paper thus looks at the agriculture credit in India in the post -reform period and raises some concerns.

Indian Agriculture: A View

Indian agriculture has undergone structural changes in recent times. The nature of Indian agriculture has geared towards small farms. In 1995-96 small and marginal farmers operated 36 per cent of cultivated area, a 11 per cent increase over 1990-91 (Table 1). Given this trend, presumely has not only continued but accelerated. This meagre base of Indian agriculture is vulnerable (Vyas 2004).

Table 1
Area Operated by Operational Holdings (Million Hctares)

Type of Holdings	*1990-91*	*%*	*1995-96-*	*%*
Marginal	24.89	15.04	28.12	17.21
Small	28.82	17.42	30.72	18.81
Semi-medimn	38.37	23.19	38.95	23.84
Medium	44.75	27.04	41.39	25.34
Large	28.65	17.31	24.16	14.79
All Holdings	165.48	100	163.35	100

Source: Indian Agriculture in Brief.

Another aspect of Indian agriculture that requires mention is the significant changes in the output mix and thereby input mix (Tables 2 and 3). These changes reflected in a shift in area from food grains to non-food grains, and within food grains from coarse cereals to finer cereals. During the nineties, the area under food grains has declined by over 4 per cent. The shift towards non-food grains is observed across states with

Table 2
Area Under Food Grains Across States (000 Hectares)

States	*TE 1990*	*TE2002*	*Difference%*
Andhra Pradesh	7944.83	7289.33	8.25
Assam	3548.87	2834.60	-20.13
Bihar	2556.03	4770.03	86.62
Chhattisgarh	6626.43	4894.37	-26.14
Gujarat	4686.10	3256.77	-30.50
Haryana	4074.47	4277.27	4.98
Himachal Pradesh	869.17	831.00	- 4.39
Jammu& Kashmir	881.47	889.83	0.95
Jharkhand	1843.17	1223,97	-33.59
Karnataka	7294.33	7540.63	3.38
Kerala	605.57	365.07	-39.71
Madhya Pradesh	12216.17	11401.80 .	-67
Maharashtra	14418.93	13272.30	-7.95
Orissa	6917.37	5318.93	-23.11
Punjab	5551.77	6231.10	12.24
Rajasthan	12358.73	11674.73	-5.53
TamilNadu	3962.97	3852.67	-2.78
Uttar Pradesh	18972.20	20084.03	5.86
Uttaranchal	979.70	992.13	1.27
West Bengal	6396.87	6632.30	3.68
India	127427.30	122021.87	4.24

Source: Computed from CMIE, Agriculture February 2004.

the exception of Bihar, Haryana, J&K, Karnataka, Punjab, Uttaranchal, Uttar Pradesh and West Bengal (Table 2). The maximum shift way from food grain crops is visible in Kerala followed by Jharkhand, Gujarat, Orissa and Assam. In Bihar, 87 per cent increase in food grain crop acreage has been observed. In certain quarters, it is argued that sleeping giant has awoken. The decline in the area under coarse cereals is much sharp and is a widespread. Oilseeds, cotton, tobacco and sugarcane have gained at the expense of cereals. In terms of area (Vyas 2004). These crops have strong links with the market. The credit requirement also goes up with these changes. Changes in cropping pattern towards such crops influence change in input structure. As the modem technology spreads (GM seeds), input requirement changes. The relative prices of inputs too have changed in the nineties as a result of reduction in subsidies on power fertilisers, etc. Farmers expend sizeable part of resources on purchased inputs. Table 3 shows that value of inputs have almost doubled from Rs. 55401 crore in 1993-94 to Rs. 103555 crore in 1999-2000.

The farmers have to take recourse to credit to a much larger extent than in the past for purchase of inputs. The flow of SAO credit during the same period has improved from Rs. 9752 crore to Rs. 23694 crore, a 2.5 times increase. The crop loan from all financial institutional to agriculture covered 17.6 per cent of input cost in 1993-94 and about 23 per cent ill 1999-2000. However, it has more or less been stagnant since 1996-97. This means that even today less than quarter of input cost is covered by formal sector credit. The result is that farmers have to depend on other sources of credit including own savings to meet more than three-fourth of the cost of material inputs.

Table 3
Value of Inputs, Output and, Credit (Rs. crore at Current prices)

Year	*Value of Output*	*Value of Inputs*	*Flow of SAO Credit on*	*4as% of 3*	*4as% of 2*	*3as% of 2*
1	2	3	4	5	6	7
1993-94	204874	55401	9752	17.60	4.76	27.04
1994-95	236607	63654	11932	18.75	5.04	26.90
1995-96	256698	72026	15273	21.20	5.95	28.06
1996-97	302744	74415	16956	22.79	5.60	24.58
1997-98	319586	83125	18632	22.41	5.83	26.01
1998-99	387546	93005	20601	22.15	5.32	24.00
1999-00	405576	103555	23694	22.88	5.84	25.53

Source: Vyas. 2004.

On the other hand credit, as a percentage of gross value of output has almost been around 5 per cent when in puts, as a percentage of value of output has fluctuated between 24 and 28 per cent. This situation warrants correction if agriculture has to continue its sjgnificant contribution to the economy.

Need for Credit

The demand for agricultural credit arises due to (a) lack of simultaneity between the realisation of income and act of expenditure, (b) lumpiness investment in fixed capital formation and (c) stochastic surges in capital needs and (financial) saving that accompany technological innovations. This is the most significant factor contributing to the demand for credit. From the development perspective, both forms of agricultural credit viz., crop loans and the term loans are important in sustained absorption of technological innovations. Initial surge in technology adoption in India got a complimentary support from the institutional credit with term lending forming a major proportion of private fixed capital formation in agriculture, Because of variations in development and deployment of technology, the credit requirements across space and time keep changing. Some recent estimates (Planning Commission 1996) of demand for credit by the agriculture sector, considering the future potential and demands, for the Ninth Plan (1997-98 to 2001-02) put it at Rs. 229750 crore (both short-and long-term). This meant a 16 per cent annual growth rate of credit flow during the plan. The short-term demand was put at Rs.149400 crore while that of long-term at Rs. 80350 crore. The Working Group had further put the share of small and marginal farmers at 47.25 per cent: 55.6 per cent for short-term and 31.7 per cent for long-term. The Task Force on Agricultural Credit (GoI 2001) provided estimates on the magnitude of demand for agricultural credit for the Tenth Plan. The demand for production credit was estimated to lie between Rs.86000 crore to Rs. 122928 crore. The bulk of growth in demand is likely to come from the groups that presently receive little or no institutional finance. The diversification process shall add the spurt in demand as much as for investments in the post-harvest facilities, such as marketing yards, cold stores, warehouses and handling equipment. It is assumed that the annual growth rate of credit flow would be 24 per cent. All along it has been expected that as there is need to supply credit to small farmers to promote capital formation, due attention needs to be paid by credit institutions. With progressive change in technology in agriculture, the gradual exposure of agriculture to the international markets, promotion of agricultural exports, the role of horticulture crops, floriculture and agro-processing, storage and marketing, growing value addition in agriculture, demand for agricultural credit may increase manifold in future. The agriculture in the near future may become more capital intensive.

Recent Credit Flow to Agriculture

Since independence the Indian credit delivery system had two main players in the formal sector i.e., co-operatives and commercial banks. Co-operatives were more important but under social banking regime commercial banks began to spread. However, with the advent of financial sector reforms under liberalisation, the role of commercial banks is beginning to get redefined. Under Basel norms, banks have to adopt prudential norms and become more efficient in the process. Government of India also pumped in resources to put on rails the weak banks. However, format-sector credit flow acted as a facilitator of green revolution since the mid-sixties. Agriculture lending became priority lending. Of the net bank credit 18 per cent was earmarked for agriculture. As banking sector spread to rural areas, credit flow increased. A slow down process started with reforms in the banking sector. Table 4 shows that in 1990-91 the priority sector lending to agriculture sector was Rs. 16750 crore and it continuously increased to Rs. 90541 crore by *2003-2004,* a more than 5 times increase in credit flow to agriculture sector during the reform period. The growth in net bank credit has been almost 7 times during the same period. The priority sector lending itself has increased by more than 6 times. However, share of agriculture sector in total net bank credit that was 15.33 per cent in, 1990-91 decline & to 11.85 per cent by 2003-2004. In none of the years the target of 18 per cent has been fulfil1ed. Since 1996-97, the share did not even cross 12 per cent. This shortfa1l is a concern and many committees and groups have commented on it. There are two major reasons for this sorry affair.

One, permission to public sector banks to park unspent funds to the tune of 1.5 per cent shortfall of agriculture sector priority sector lending in RIDF on which they have been earning assured interest (Singh 200l) and second, addition of

Table 4
Priority Sector Lending to Agriculture (Rs. crore)

Year	*Priority Sector*	*Agriculture*	*3 as % on*	*Net Bank Credit*	*3 as % of 5*
1	*2*	*3*	*4*	*5*	*6*
1990-91	42915	16750	39.03	109298	15.33
1991-92	45425	18157	39.97	117443	15.46
1992-93	*49832*	19963	40.06	141800	14.08
1993-94	53880	21208	39.36	152501	13.91
1994-95	64161	23983	37.38~	192424	12.46
1995-96	73329	27044	36.88	228198	11.85
1996-97'	84880	31442	37.04	245999	12.78
1997-98	99507	34869	35.04	297265	11.73
f998-99	114611	39634	34.58	339477	11.68
1999-00	131827	44381	33.67	398205	11.15
2000-01	154414	51922	33.63	467206	11.11
2001-02	175259	60761	34.67	535063	11.36
2002-03	211609	73518	34.74	668576	11.00
2003-04	263834	90541	34.32	763855	11.85

Sourm' RBI.., 2003-2004. Handbook of Statistics on the Indian Economy.

many new activities under priority sector lending like information technology sector etc. The ill-health of co-operative sector also complicated the matter (Singh 7003a; 2003b). Bankers have also become, more cautious in lending to agriculture sector due to non-performing assets.

Delving further, Table 5 shows the flow of institutional credit to agriculture. A structural change in credit flow is observed. Of the three players in rural finance, co-operatives had a share of 38.53 per cent at the start of economic reforms that went up to 61.82 per cent when financial sector reforms were initiated. Since then with the exception of 1997-98, a continuous decline in share of co-operative movement is witnessed. By 2003-04, the share reduced to 30.99 per cent. The main reason for this decline is ill health of the co-operative sector due to variety of reasons. The share of commercial banks that include regiona1 rural banks has almost touched the 1990-91 peak of 61.47 per cent in 2003-04. Regional rural banks had a share of 8.72 per cent in 2003-04 (a continuous increase since 1996-97). In absolute terms, the credit flow to agriculture sector improved from Rs. 8846 crore in 1990-91 to Rs. 86981 crore, almost 10 times increase over the period. In case of co-operative sector, the increase is 8 times compared to 10 times jump in commercial bank credit. It is also observed that there are wide variations in annual growth of credit flow to agriculture sector. It has been as low as 4.4 per cent in 1995-96 over 1994-95 and as high as 35.4 per cent in 1992-93 over 1991-92 (beginning of the financial sector reform period). Considering, the period 1992-93 to 1999-2000, per hectare credit has improved from Rs. 818 in 1992-93 to Rs. 2494 in 1999-2000 (Table 6). This is three times increase during the period. The prime reason is the diversification agriculture and widening of priority sector lending.

Table 5
Institutional Credit to Agriculture (Rs. crore)

					Share in Total			*Total*
Years	*Coop*	*RRBs*	*CBs*	*Total*	*Coop*	*RRBs*	*CBs*	*% Increase*
1990-91	3408		5438	8846	38.53		61.47	
1991-92	5800		5402	11202	51.78		48.22	26.6
1992-93		9378	5791	15169	61.82	38.18	35.4	
1993-94	10117		6377	16494	61.34		38.66	8.7
1994-95	11915		9197	21113	56.43		43.56	28.0
1995-96	10479		11563	22032	47.56		52.48	4.4
19%97	11044	1684	12783	26411	41.82	6.38	48.40	19.9
1997-98	14085	2040	15831	31956	44.08	6.38	49.54	21.0
1998-99	15957	2460	18443	36860	43.29	6.67	50.04	15.3
1999-00	18363	3172	24733	46268	39.69	6.86	53.46	25.5
2000-01	20801	4219	27807	52827	39.38	7.99	52.64	14.2
2001-02	23604	4854	33587	62045.	38.04	7.82	54.13	17.4
2002-03	242%	5467	41047	70810	34.31	7.72	57.97	14.1
2003-04	26959	7581	52441	86981	30.99	8,72	60.29	22.8
2004-05	24471	9176	52038	85686	28.56	10.71	60.73	

Note: Figures for 2004-05 are up to only December. From 1990-91 to 1995-96 data for RRBs included in CBs.
Coop- co-operatives, RRBs- regional rural banks, CBs- commercial banks.

Source: Economic survey, various years.

Direct Credit

Agriculture sector requires credit for crop production and capital formation. The dependence for crop loan is largely on co-operative sector while commercial banks tries to satisfy demand for capital investment. Capital formation in agriculture over the years has slowed down for a variety of reasons. However, Table 7 presents the flow of credit both in the short-term and long-term by institutions. The total loans issued to agriculture sector by RfIs have multiplied by 4 times since 1990-91. In case of co-operatives, the increase in credit flow has been from Rs. 4819 crore in 1990-91 to Rs. 18202 crore in 2001-02, about 3.8 times increase. Commercial banks in all the years had a lower contribution till 1998-99, a reversal took place there after. The growth in loans issued has been slightly higher than the co-operative sector. This period saw significant jump in lending by regional rural banks.

Table 6
Per Hectare Credit Flow to Agriculture (Rs.)

Year	*1992-1933*	*1993-1994*	*1994-1995*	*1995-1996*	*1996-1997*	*1997-1998*	*1998-1999*	*1999-2000*
GCA	185487	18M20	188053	186561	189543	190570	192620	189740
Credit	15169	16494	21113	22032	26411	31956	36860	46268
Credit/ Hec.	817.79	889.23	1138.25	1187.79	1423.87	1722.82	1987.20	2494.41

Note: GCA-Gross Cropped Area in thousand hectares and credit in Rs. crore.

Source: Economic Survey, various years and CMrE.

The crop loan delivered by co-operative sector has in all the years much higher than that delivered by commercial banks, but the gap

has been narrowing over time. The short-term loans issued by co-operative sector increased by roughly 4 times when those by commercial banks by more than 6 times. This means that commercial banks have improved their performance vis-a - vis co-operative sector in case of short-term loans. In case of long-term loans issued, the opposite has happened. In the recent years co-operatives have almost equally contributed to capital formation in agriculture. Table 8 shows that funds from co-operative sector have, been mainly for short-term (more than 70 per cent in all the years with exception of two years)

Table 7
Direct Institutional Credit for Agriculture (Loan Issued) (Rs.00 crore)

	Short-term				*Long-term*				*Total*				
Year	*Coop*	*SCEs*	*RRBs*	*Total*	*Coop*	*SCEs*	*RRBs*	*Total*	*Coop*	*States*	*SCEs*	*RRBs*	*Total*
1990-91	34.48	20.48	1.25	56.21	13.72	26.28	2.10	42.10	48.19	3.59	46.76	3.34	101.88
1991-92	39.34	23.41	3.37	66.12	18.63	24.65	2.60	045.88	57.97	3.39	48.06	5.96	115.38
1992-93	43.94	24.32	4.51	}2.77	20.89	25.28	2.47	48.64	64.84	3.89	49.60	6.98	125.31
1993-94	60.39	28.60	4.76	93.75	24.45	25.40	2.76	52.61	84.84	3.77	54.00	7.52	150.13
1994-95	69.96	38.42	6.88	115.26	28.79	35.66	3.95	68.40	98.76	4.07	74.08	10.83	187.74
19'95-96	92.43	46.28	8.49	147.20	32.40	46.47	5.32	84.19	124. 83	5.54	92.74	13.81	236.92
19%-97	94.89	56.25	11.74	162.88	37:65 .	SO.SO	5.75	93.90	132.54	6.68	106.75	17.48	263.45
1997-98	100.84	62.33	14.57	177.74	40.75	53.04	6.45	100.24	141.59	8.58	115.37	'21.03	286.57
1998-99	106.89	77.42	17.50	201.81	44.01	69.21	7.65	120.87	150.90	4.20	146.63	25.15	326.88
1999-00	113.84	95.05	22.85	231.74	47.31	68.45	7.00	122.76	161.15	5.20	163.51	29.85	359.71
2000-01	121.35	107.04	30.95	259.34	51.00	57.36	8.71	117.07	172.35	4.87	164.39	39.66	381.27
2001-02	129.23	126.61	38.10	293.94	52.79	59.77	7.36	119.92	182.02	4.59	186.38	45.46	418.45

Source: RBI. 2003-2004.

Table 8
Distribution of Institutional Credit (%)

Years	Share of Short-tenn Credit in total Credit			Share in Short-term Credit			Share in Long-term Credit			Share in Total Credit			
	Coop	SCBs	RRBs	Coop	SCBs	RRI3S	Coop	S€Bs	RRJ3s	Coop	States	SCBs	RRBs
1990-91	71.55	43.80	37.43	61.34	36.43	2.22	32.59	62.42	4:99	47.30	3.52	45.90	3.28
1991-92	67.86	48.71	56.54	59.50	35.41	5.10	40.61	53.73	5.67	50.24	2.94	41.65	5.17
1992-93	67.77	49.03	64.61	60.38	33.42	6.20	42.95	51.97	5.08	51.74	3.10	39.58	5.57
1993-94	71.18	52.96	63:30	64.42	30.51	5.08	46.47	48.28	5.25	56.51	2.51	35.97	5.01
1994-95	70.84	51.86	63.53	60.70	33.33	5.97	42.09	52.13	5.77	52.60	2.17	39.46	5.77
1995-96	74.04	49.90	61.48	62.79	31.44	5.77	38.48	55.20	6.32	52.69	2.34	39.14	5.83
1996-97	71.59	52.69	67.16	58.26	34.53	7.21	40.10	53.78	6:12.	50.31	2.54	40.52	6.64
1997-98	71:22	54.03	69.28	56.73	35.07	8020	40.65	52.91	6.43	49.41	2.99	40.26	7.34
1998-99	70.83	52.80	69.58	52.97	38.36	8.67	36.41	57.26	6.33	46.16	1.28	44.86	7.69
1999-00	70.64	58.13	76.55	49.12	41.02	9.86	38.54	55.76	5.70	44.80	1.45	45.46	8.30
2000-01	70.41	65.11	78.04	46.79	41.27	11.93	43.56	49.00	7.44	45.20	1.28	43.12	10.40
2001-02	71.00	67.93	83.81	43.96	43.07	12.96	44.02	49.84	6.14	43.50	1.10	44.54	10.86

Source: Computed from Table 7.

and remained almost constant. In case of commercial banks, in 1990-91 the share of short-term loans issued was 44 per cent that improved to 68 per cent by 2001-02. Regional Rural Banks observed an increase in share of short-term loans from 37 to 84 per cent, a remarkable improvement. Table further reveals that as far as short-term loans are concerned, the contribution of co-operative sector has dwindled, a decline of 17.4 per centage points. Commercial banks and regional rural banks have compensated this decline in share. In case of long-term loans issued the share of co-operative sector has improved over the years. This means that reforms have impacted the structural change in credit flow to agriculture sector.

Credit by Farm Size

A number of scholars have attempted to assess inequity in the distribution of agricultural credit in the past. Some scholars have pointed out that institutional credit forms small part of the credit needs of the small farmers. Athers have argued that small farmers have received more than their proportionate share of total institutional credit *vis-a-vis* their share in land. Credit absorption is technology determined. What has been the situation during the reform era? Table 9 shows that share of small and marginal holdings in direct finance in 1990-91 was almost 55 per cent declined to 44 per cent in 2001-02. This is because the share of small and marginal holdings in number of accounts reduced from 78 to 56 per cent. This implies that the reforms have had adverse impact on formal sector lending on small and marginal farmers. This does not augur well for Indian agriculture. This is complicated by the fact that size of loan itself has gone up across holding sizes over the period. For instance, holdings up to 2.5 acres observed an increase in per farm finance from Rs. 6024 in 1990-91 to Rs. 16247 in 2001-02, a 170 per cent increase. In case of holdings of 2.5 to 5 acres, the average loan expended has improved from Rs. 7813 in 1990-91 to Rs. 22610 in 2001-02, a 190 per cent increase. The average loan issued in case of holdings beyond 5 acres increased from Rs. 19824 to Rs. 32130, only 62 per cent increase. This means a

Table 9
SCBs Direct Finance to Farmers According to Size of Holdings (Disbursements)

	Accounts	*Loans*	*Share in Total (%) Accounts*	*Loans*	*Accounts*	*Loans*	*Average Finance (Rs. per account) Holding Size (Acres)*			
Year	*Upto 2.5 acres*		*2.5 to 5.00 acres*		*Above 5.00 acres*		*Upto 2.5*	*2.5- 5*	*Above 5*	*Total*
1990-91	48.07	30.16	29.89	24.32	22.04	4.55	6024	7813	19824	9600
1991-92	45.42	28.79	31.43	24.87	23.15 4	.63	6295	7858	19878	9930
1992-93	44.47	27.83	31.76	24.55	23.76	4.76	6257	7729	20035	9999
1993-94	42.68	28.79	30.35	25.80	26.97	4.54	6959	8768	17367	10315
1994-95	42.24	27.57	31.54	24.02	26.22	4.84	8325	9715	23548	12754
1995-96	37.38	26.14	31.18	25.50	31.44	4.84	9885	11560	21748	14137
1996-97	37.77	24.25	30.49	25.50	31.74	5.03	10485	13656	25856	16331
1997-98	39.44	24.01	33.95	25.32	26.62	5.07	10873	13319	33991	17856
1998-99	39.48.	23.56	32.12	26.89	28.39	4.96	12075	16941	35328	20240
1999-00	40.42	23.82	32.30	24.74	27.28	5.14	14253	18528	45612	24188
2000-01	40.79	25.76	31.85	25.09	27.37	4.92	15697	19575	44632	24851
2001-02	38.43	26.70	27;73	26.81	33.84 4	.65	16247	22610	32130	23386

Source: Computed from RBI. 2003-2004.

slower growth in finance in large holdings compared to small and marginal holding. These changes are reflective of changing cropping patterns as observed in an earlier section. The demand for institutional credit is thus increasing across farm sizes during the reform period.

Scale of Credit

A related aspect to the above discussion is the scale of credit flow to agriculture sector. Scholars have been arguing that demand for institutional credit by-various categories of Indian farmers is not large. Besides, changes are occurring since the inception of reforms. Table 10 reveals that commercial banks advances to agriculture sector are observing significant structure changes. We have noticed above that the average credit demand of the Indian farmers is well below Rs. 25000. It is disturbing that since 1990-91, the share of borrowers in up to Rs. 25000 is showing a significant declining trend, and it was 55 per cent in 1990-91 and 24 per cent in 2002-03. The gainers are those borrowing Rs. 25000 to Rs. 2 lakh, the share improved from 26 to 34 per cent while in case of those borrowing Rs.10 crore or more, the increase has been from just 1.7 per cent in 1990-91 to 14.4 per cent in 2002-03. Table also shows that the share of those borrowing Rs. 2 lakh or more went up from 19.2 per cent to significant 42.1 per cent during the same period. This reinforces the above arguments that bias during the reforms of commercial banks is towards large borrower at the expense of small borrowers. This also means that there is a visible shift in lending from crop production to agro-processing. This is a result of widening of priority sector in the recent times. The policy reform has also forced the banks to take care of bad debts and so made them reluctant lenders to small borrowers. Banker has become a cautious lender at the cost of Indian agriculture, which still supports 54 crore small and marginal farmers. This lowers the transaction costs and reduces NPA of banks. In this scenario, one really wonders how doubling of credit to agriculture sector (as expounded by the Finance Minister) will take place. Even if it is made possible the small and marginal borrowers will be by passed by commercial banks. The recommendations of *yays committee* may help in augmenting credit flow to agriculture.

It has asked to waive margin/security requirements up to Rs. 50000 for crop loans and up to Rs. 5 lakh for agri-business and agri-clinics, dispense with the restrictive provisions of Service Area Approach, and aligning NPA norms for direct agricultural advances to the cropping seasons of short duration and long duration crops. What also is required is that restructuring/rescheduling of loans of farmers be allowed so that farmers become eligible for fresh loans. Need is also for rescheduling of the debts of farmers in arrears and making them eligible for fresh loans. On the pattern of industry, there should be one time settlement (OTS) for small and marginal farmers and then considering them for fresh loans. There should also be redemption of past debts from non-institutional lenders. This would help improve the present worrisome situation.

Regional Aspects of Agriculture Credit

From the onset of economic reforms, Indian agriculture had certain regions and sections that were by passed by the formal sector financial institutions. What has happened to regional dispersal of credit during the reforms? We have seen in the first section that agriculture is observing changes across states and so the credit requirement should also be expected to change. Table 11 shows that regional imbalances continued to exist since the initiation of economic reforms. Four states viz., Andhra Pradesh, Karnataka, Maharashtra and Uttar Pradesh accounted for 41 per cent of all agriculture credit flow from commercial banks in 1990-91. The share of big four stood at 44 per cent in *2002-03*, a gain of 3 percentage points. If we include Madhya Pradesh, Tamil Nadu, Punjab and Rajasthan, then these 8 states account for 71 per cent of all credit flow. The northeast region is largely bypassed region. Banks appear to be reluctant to lend there. Half the Indian States/union territories have a share of below one per cent in credit. There is uneven flow of agricultural credit across states in India and this needs rectification.

Table 10

Distribution of Outstanding Credit of SCBs in Agriculture by Size

Years	*Total*	*<25000*	*25000- 2 lakh*	*2-5 lakh*	*5-10 lakh*	*10-25. lakh*	*25-50 lakh*	*50 1akh- 1 crore*	*1-4 crore*	*4-6 crore*	*6-10 crore*	*10> crore*	*Above 2 lakh*
		Size of Credit (Rs.)											
1990-91	100	55.16	25.68	2.82	1.62	2.42	3.57	2.39	2.97	0.83	0.87	1.67	19.16
1991-92	100	'55.22	25.69	2.65	1.39	2.01	2.74	2.07	3.37	0.78	0.95	3.12	19.08
1992-93	100	52:69	25.92	2.63	1.43	2.09	2.80	2.19	4.10	0.85	1.08	4.22	21.39
1993-94	100	53.19	26.08	2.88	1.60	2.41	2.85	2.11	3.91	1.07	0.99	2.90	20.73
1994-95	100	52.04	26.04	3.30	1.85	2.67	2.80	2.15	3.68	0.84	1.09	3.54	21.92
1995-96	100	49.48	25.38	4.11	1.68	2.60	2.71	2.33	4.47	1.30	1.09	4.85	25.14
19%-97	100	47.02	25.92	5.50	2.01	2.82	2.88	2.75	4.77	1.55	0.97	3.80	27.06
1997-98	100	46.18	26.77	6.59	1.88	2.61	2.66	2.47	4.60	1.35	1.66	3.23	27.05
1998-99	100	38.26	29.74	7.90	1.77	2.22	2.44	2.41	4.10	1.13	1.44	8.58	32.00
1999-00	100	35.19	32.41	9.79	1.91	2.33	2.23	2.09	3.77	1.38	1.50	7.39	32:39
2000-01	100	32.73	33.29	10.62	1.91	2.29	1.94	1.74	3.59	1.35	1.55	8.99	33.98
2001-02	100	26.05	32.59	11.45	2.44	2.61	2.29	2.30	4.68	1.56	2.23	11.80	41.3
2002-03	100	23.59	34.36	11.71	2.30	2.35	2.00	1.95	3.85	1.45	2.09	14.36	42.06

Source: Computed from CMIE 2004, Fenruary.

Table 11
Distribution of SCBs Credit Flow to Agriculture Across States (%)

States	1990-1991	1991-1992	1992-1993	1993-1994	1994-1995	1995-1996	1996-1997	1997-1998	1998-1999	1999-2000	2000-2001	2001-2002	2002-2003
Andaman	0.01	0.01	0.01	0.01	0.01	0.01	0.01	0.01	0.01	0.01	0.01	0.05	0.04
AP	12.10	11.95	11.48	12.06	12.28	12.95	13.21	13.03	14.76	12.47	12.30	11.83	11.38
Arunachal	0.04	0.03	0.04	0.03	0.04	0.04	0.03	0.04	0.05	0.04	0.03	0.03	0.03
Assam	1.35	144	1.22	1.20	1.28	1.11	1.06	0.87	0.75	0.63	0.54	0.60	0.62
Bihar	5.11	4.87	5.17	5.38	5.54	4.95	4.72	3.95	4.20	3.12	3.35	3.32	2.69
Chandigarh	0.50	0.40	0.52	1.27	0.44	0.48	0.47	0.49	0.45	0.56	0.70	0.89	1.51
Dadra	0.01	0.01	0.01	0.01	0.01	0.01	0.01	0.01	0.01	0.01	0.01	0.01	0.00
Daman	0.01	0.04	0.41	0.42	0.01	0.01	0.01	0.01	0.01	0.00	0.01	0.00	0.00
Delhi	0.85	0.73	0.97	1.19	0.99	3.09	1.25	0.86	4.36	1.52	3.07	3.39	4.76
Goa	0.22	0.18	0.16	0.13	0.14	0.15	0.13	0.14	0.15	0.15	0.11	9:07	0.07
Gujarat	5.04	6.19	7.51	5.64	5.32	5.38	4.84	5.39	6.33	5.21	5.04	5.87	5.38
Haryana	4.48	3.99	3.91	4.02	3.77	3.46	3.62	3.43	4.16	3.79	3.67	4.28	4.11
HP	0.54	0.44	0.38	0.42	0.49	0.34	0.39	0.34	0.41	0.40	0.38	0.46	0.54
J&K	0.54	0.50	0.32	0.36	0.32	0.30	0.2S	0.36	0.40	0.32	0.33	0.35	0.33
Karnataka.	9.34	9.14	8.98	9.51	10.12	9.82	10.20	10.30	12.22	11.57	10.16	10.46	10.23
Kerala	4.31	4.20	4.11	4.25	4.58	4.46	4.43	4.84	5.24	4.66	4.80	4.20	4.03
Lakshadweep	0.00	0.00	0.00	0.00	0.00	0.00	0.00	0.00	0.00	0.00	0.00	0.00	0.00
MP	6.44	6.29	6.48	6.41	5.61	6.05	6.45	6.99	7.81	7.01	6.77	6.65	6.47
Maharashtra	8.67	8.80	8.71	7.88	8.41	9.79	10.26	9.79	11.28	10.41	9.63	10.19	9.83
Manipur	0.06	0.05	0.05	0.05	0.06	0.05	0.07	0.06	0.07	0.04	0.05	0.03	0.03

Contd...

States	*1990-1991*	*1991-1992*	*1992-1993*	*1993-1994*	*1994-1995*	*1995-1996*	*1996-1997*	*1997-1998*	*1998-1999*	*1999-2000*	*2000-2001*	*2001-2002*	*2002-2003*
Meghalaya	0.15	0.12	0.10	0.10	0.22	0.13	0.09	0.08	0.08	0.07	0.05	0.07	-0.05
Mizoram	0.05	0.03	0.04	0.04	0.06	0.03	0.03	0.02	0.02	0.02	0.02	0.03	0.01
Nagaland	0.13	0.11	0.10	0.10	0.12	0.09	0.08	0.07	0.06	0.05	0.03	0.04 .	0.03
Orissa	2.38	2.22	1.24	2.40	2.40	2.38	2.27	2.53	2.36	2.06	1.98	1.94	1.70
Pondicheny	0.16	0.14	0.13	0.14	0.14	0.16	0.31	0.33	0.14	0.11	0.10	0.11	0.09
Punjab	6.54	6.38	5.83	6.14	6.42	5.80	5.77	5.06	7.15	6.79	6.86	6.28	6.24
Rajasthan	4.67	5.00	5.17	4.82	5.07	3.98	4.80	5.03	6.08	5.93	6.14	6.39	6.39
Sikkim	0.02	0.02	0.03	0.04	0.03	0.02	0.02	0.02	0.02	0.02	0.02	0.01	0.02
TamilNadu	10.96	10.85	10.44	11.14	11.08	11.58	11:68	12.43	11.97	9.48	9.00	7.90	8.21
Tripura	0.18	0.21	0.21	0.22	0.22	0.21	0.21	0.19	0.20	0.16	0.13	0.12	0.12
UP	11.85	11.49	11.14	11.28	11.68	10.00	10.32	10.68	12.21	11.01	12.11	11.48	12.25
WE	3.29	4.12	4.12	3.32	3.14	3.15	3.01	2.64	2.96	2.40	2.61	2.93	2.87

Source: Computed from CMIE data.

At the all India level, the credit per hectare by commercial banks has more than doubled between 1992-93 and 1999-2000 and has continuously increased (Table 12), In most of the states there are yearly fluctuations. In 1992-93, 9 states (of 25) had per hectare credit of above the national level while in 1999-2000, 7 states exceeded the national average. The difference between the lowest and the highest average credit in 1992-93 was Rs. 2919 and this gap widened by 1999-2000 to Rs.6441. This means that regional inequality in credit flow has in creased during the reform period. This should be a cause of concern.

Table 12
Per Hectare SCBs Credit by States (Rs.)

States	*1992-1993*	*1993-1994*	*1994-1995*	*1995-1996*	*1996-1997*	*1997-1998*	*1998-1999*	*1999-2000*
ApdhraPradesh	1994	2591	2397	2860	3116	3785	3820	4370
ArunachaPradesh	1353	231	451	484	454	512	688	640
Assam	703	723	823	810	844	769	.675	707
Bihar	1225	1314	1400	1424	1472	1393	1474	1426
Goa	2233	1878	2177	2661	2467	2899	3170	3988
Gujarat	1511	1215	1181	1538	1392	1704	2086	2342
Haryana	1480	1589	1576	1668	1885	1970	2323	2870
Himachal Pradesh	859	992	1263	1013	1293	1209	1508	1894
Jammu & Kashmir	664	775	753	810	819	1159	1299	1337
Karnataka	1603	1756	2102	2365	2616	3107	3501	4366
Kerala	2987	3210	3750	4189	4640	5754	6329	7081
Madhya Pradesh	600	591	564	693	801	946	1059	1220
Maharashtra	918	847	982	1323	1498	1588	1795	2125
Manipur	589	603	752	868	1094	1092	1083	955
Meghalaya	963	985	2318	1538	1176	1135	1015	1162
Mizonun	774	887	1323	724	761	779	741	989
Nagaland	1008	1087	1308	1154	101	885	762	837
Orissa	528	566	615	708	875	1033	988	1100
Punjab	1710	1851	2081	2155	.2328	2278	3260.	3758
Rajasthan	568	575	621	583	734	794	1002	1403
Sikkim	479	660	468	503	528	607	622	686
TamilNadu	3272	3576	3914	322	5721.	6681	6372	6635
Tripura	1046	1085	1185	1404	1432	1386	1480	1485
Uttar Pradesh	961	1015	1132	1117	1249	1446	1685	1921
West Bengal	1069	879	899	1012	1049	1005	1124	1149
India	1194	1232	1327	1544	1669	1850	2123	2405

Source: Computed from CMIE data.

Interest Rates: The Issues

Demand is inversely related to average interest rate on crop loans. The demand for crop loans is inversely related to its price, i,e., average nominal interest rate on these loans, and so to the average farm size. It is often discussed in financial circles that agriculture is provided credit at subsidised rates. Desai and Namboodiri (2001) also point out that on interest rates for rural credit there is no subsidy (rates are positive in real terms) The reform period has observed higher rates being charged from farmers compared to the consumer goods sector customers. Table 13 shows, that the agriculture sector lending during the period 1990-91 and 2002-03 has concentrated in the interest band of 12-16 per cent. There is no doubt that till 1996-97, the interest rates have been in the band of 14-17 per cent. The downward shift is due to removal of one tier in the co-operative sector. It reinforces the argument that deregulation of interest rates had no impact. It has led to increase in their levels as well as instability in them especially for small borrower. On average an Indian farmer pays higher rate of interest compared to consumer loan customer of commercial bank.

Competing Sectors

There are many competitors for credit and when resources are mobilised at a cost then many considerations arise. In India, agriculture and industry have been the two major clients, but now other sectors like housing and trades are seeking their pound of flesh. There are not many studies that have tried to address this issue. The policy directions over the period have also favoured a few sectors like agriculture, small industries, weaker sections of the society etc. One of the principal objects of nationalisation of commercial banks was to bring about certain structural changes in the credit deployment. To begin with we look at the trends in the credit disbursement across sectors. Since the 1990-91 though the share of industry in gross bank credit has come down from 54.4 to 47.5 per cent in 2001-2002, it is still the largest user of credit, Table 14. The share of agriculture sector in gross bank credit was 14.8 per cent in 1990-91 and it declined to 11.8 per cent in 1999-2000 to recover to be

Table 13
Distribution of Outstanding Credit of SCBs in Agriculture by Interest Rates

		Interest Flates (%)									
Years	*Total*	*<6*	*6-10*	*10-12*	*12-14*	*14-15*	*15-16*	*16-17*	*17-18*	*18-20*	*20>*
1990-91	100	1.47	2.50	13.96	34.59	33.22	4.33	5.91	2.67	1.11	0.23
1991-92	100	0.88	1.72	7.98	18.11	16.98	31:43	6.87	4.60	5.39	6.04
1992-93	100	0.52	1.23	5.11	11.58	8.27	38.56	7.56	9.96	9.61	7.60
1993-94	100	0.67	1.05	3.51	9.65	11.74	41.22	10.63	11.48	5.74	4.31
1994-95	100	0.81	1.05	3.07	8.44	23.27	31.17	13:95	9.72	5.09	3.44
1995-96	100	0.00	0.41	1.90	9.31	30.95	18.45	7.88	14.44	10.73	5.94
1996-97	100	0.02	0.34	1.70	7.44	37.48	13.73	8.33	12.78	13.02	5.17
1997-98	100	0.07	0.27	2.12	22.05	26.83	12.72	12.67	10.16	10.67	2.42
1998-99	100	0.05	1.44	4.74	24.95	12.40	15.22	17.81	11.72	9.72	1.95
1999-00	100	0.04	0.71	8.58	21.36	17.61	19.98	16.50	7.76	6.01	1.45
2000-01	100	0.04	0.56	11.57	25.24	19.73	16.73	14.38	6.66	3.83	1.27
2001-02	100	0.01	2.12	16.60	26.66	19.49	17.06	11.51	3.19	2.54	
2002-03	100	0.01	5.30	18.28	32.62	18.35	11.57	9.61	1.36	2.20	0.70

Source: Computed from CMIE 2004.

12.6 per cent in 200f-2002. It is surprising that in all the years under study, the share of other sectors has been higher than agriculture sector. The other sectors that include housing activities and other consumer loan are fast emerging as a major sector. The share of this sector has almost observed a 10 percentage point jump between 1990-91 and 2001-2002. The downward trend in the interest rates for these sectors contributed significantly towards this buoyancy. Thus structural change has occurred-1n credit deployment due to policy directions. It is argued that it is essential to allow for difference between the credit requirements of agriculture and commodity industry because the latter has relatively smooth flow of purchases of inputs and sales of outputs over the year. Agriculturists, on the other hand, systematically require to buy inputs and to commit themselves to payments several months before their products are harvested. This latter feature renders it inappropriate to view the ratio of inputs to outputs in commodity industry than in agriculture as justifying a larger ratio of credit to net product. It also suggests that even the criterion of same ratio of credit to NNP in each sector is too kind to commodity industry. Commodity industry, besides this need less credit per unit of output than agriculture because both input and output flows are smoother over the year. It is also organised in larger units with more access to internal savings and to the private capital market. It is also less liable to the draining of production credit towards the funding of slack season family consumption. Unlike agriculture, it seldom turns credit-financed inputs into subsistence products which are consumed by the family that owns the firm and which thus however efficiently produced do little to help repay trade credit.

Table 14
Commercial Banks Credit Flow (%)

Year	*Agriculture*	*Industry*	*Trade*	*Others*	*Total*
1990-91	14.76	54.35	5.21	25.69	100
1995-96	12.18	56.26	5.39	26.17	100
1999-00	11.83	53.35	4.48	30.34	100
2000-01	12.10	50.99	4.16	32.75	100
2001-02	12.59	47.54	4.24	35.63	100

Source: RBFReport on Trend and Progress in Banking. various years.

Kisan Credit Cards

The scope for dispensation of institutional credit to millions of famers, for their seasonal agricultural operations, is enormous. The multi-agency approach introduced by the RBI no doubt had helped to augment the institutional credit flow for agriculture manifold, but the traditional systems and procedures, documentation, etc. adopted by the banking system have rendered availability of credit by the farmers rather cumbersome. Given the enormity of the credit requirements on the one hand and the vagaries of nature on the other, financing for agriculture has been a gigantic task for banks. The access to institutional credit for a large number of farmers, particularly small and marginal farmers continues to be a challenge to the Indian banking industry. The process of financial reforms also highlighted the need for innovative credit interventions from institutional agencies to support farmers. Any credit facility to the farmers should not only be timely, but also be available in adequate quantum besides ensuring an in-built flexibility. Against this backdrop, Kisan Credit Card (KCC) emerged as an innovative credit delivery mechanism to meet timely and hassle free production credit requirements of the farmers.

The KCC Scheme was introduced during 1998-99. It has reportedly smoothened the flow of credit to the farmers overcoming many of the problems arising out of procedural delays in sanction and release of loans. Farmers eligible for production credit of Rs. 5000 and above can apply for a Kisan Card and a passbook or a card-cum-pass book is issued. Revolving cash credit facility involving any number of withdrawals and repayments within the credit limit is allowed. Credit limit is fixed after taking into account the entire production credit needs for the full year plus ancillary activities related to crop production. Limit is fixed on the basis of operational land holding, cropping pattern and scale of finance. It is proposed that allied activities and non-farm credit needs also should be considered. Each withdrawal has a repayment period of twelve months. The card is valid for 3 years subject to annual review. As incentive for good performance, credit limits could be enhanced to take care of increase in costs, change in cropping pattern, etc. Conversion/ re-scheduling due to natural calamity is permissible wherever warranted. The RBI norms are applicable for security, margin and rate of interest. There is flexibility in the system as card can be operated at the issuing branch or, at the discretion of the bank, through other designated branches or PACs in the case of cooperatives. Cash withdrawals through slips/cheques accompanied by card and passbook are allowed. KCC are envisaged as improvement in the loan disbursement procedure making it less cumbersome. As at the end of 31 March 2004, 353 DCCBs, 192 RRBs and 27 Commercial Banks were participating in the scheme. The Kisan Credit Cards issued till September 2004 by all the banks increased to 4.356 crore from about 7.85 lakh as at the end of March 1998-99. Of the 4.356 crore KCC issued the share of commercial banks is 1.324 crore, the Cooperatives 2.586 crore and RRBs have issued 44.6 lakh cards. The total sanctioned amount is Rs.111459 crore that means on an average Rs.25587 per cardholder. The situation till September 2004 is presented in Table 15. The pace of implementation of the scheme is significant in some states like Andhra Pradesh, Bihar, Puajab, Haryana, Kamataka, Maharashtra and Uttar Pradesh.

Table 15
Number of KCC Issued and Amount Sanctioned
(Rs. crore and No. in lakh)

	1998-9		*2003-04*		*Cumulative up to*	
Agency	*Cards*	*Amount*	*Cards*	*Amount*	*Cards*	*Amount*
Coop. Banks	1.55	826	48.78	9855	258.6	5233
RRBs	0.06	11	12.74	2599	44.6	11265
Comm. Banks	6.24	1477	31.00	9331	132.4	34961
Total	7.85	2314	92.50	21785	435.6	1119

Source: GOI. (2001). Economic Survey 2000-2001 and 2004-05.

The in-house studies of NABARD reveal that KCC is meeting credit requirements of cultivation of crops for the whole year and also assuring availability of credit to the farmer whenever the credit is needed. KCC scheme has helped in making available adequate quantum of credit to the farmer, it provides flexibility to the farmer to draw cash from branch other than issuing branch and to buy inputs from any supplier of his choice. There is reduction in quantum of interest to the farmer due to frequent drawl and repayment of loans. The transaction cost of the farmer for the loan from the bank is reduced. Besides, KCC provides insurance cover at a very low premium rate. However, banks are adopting cautious approach in extending facility to only those beneficiaries with good past track record. Some banks are not issuing cards to illiterate, rain fed and tenant farmers. Mono-cropping areas are also being excluded and there is insistence of opening of saving bank accounts before KCC is issued. Disbursement of kind component also in cash under KCC is perceived by co-operatives as a possible threat to the existing co-operative marketing structure of selling agri-inputs. As cash disbursement is done only at the DCCB branch level in some states, borrowers are required to travel long distances for drawl of cash from branches of DCCBs. Some banks still have apprehension that transaction cost and workload would increase and additional staff strength would be required at DCCB level. There is lack of uniform accounting procedure both at PACS as well as DCCB level. In some states, commercial banks/RRBs are levying costly service charges for loans of KC cards to farmers (Rs. 100 to Rs. 300). RRBs are charging 2 per cent commission in case of withdrawal from designated branches other than issuing branch. Besides, some states are levying stamp duty for loans under KCC and not for normal crop loans. Few banks have fixed minimum land holding as eligibility. criteria for issue of KCC. Banks debit interest rate at half-yearly or quarterly basis amounting to compounding of interest under KCC accounts. Earlier, kharif and rabi loans were sanctioned separately and interest rates fixed on slab basis (up to Rs. 25000 and above Rs. 25000 and up to Rs. 21 lakh etc.), but after introduction of KCC, interest is charged at higher rate than earlier. Banks are still fixing the due dates for repayment of loans on the old pattern of lending. Over and above this, some banks are also insisting on land mortgage even for small loans and collateral securities in the shape of fixed deposit receipts, etc., before sanctioning the limit.

A more recent study shows that KCC has led to enhanced flow of credit to agriculture sector. It has also substantial reduced the exclusive borrowing from the informal sector for short-term needs, a significant saving in time spent on availing of short-term agricultural loans and an over all reduction in cost of credit delivery (Sharma 2005). There is, however, a need for fine tuning viz., restrictions imposed on the issuance of KCCs by security conscious banks; restrictions of the use of KCCs only at card issuing branches; non-availability of incentives/rewards to borrowers for timely repayments; low credit limits to meet the farmers' requirements and low awareness level regarding the provision of the personal accident insurance scheme.

Conclusions

The era of economic reforms has led to structural changes in credit delivery system and credit flow to agriculture sector in India. Lower end borrowers are being biased against. Farmers still pay high interest rates despite the fact that there had been a tendency of interest rates to decline till recently. There is an increased tendency on the part of the, bankers to go for large borrowers at the expense of crop producers. This would hurt the Indian agriculture in the long run. It was widely assumed that the liberalisation of financial sector would facilitate growth through a reduction in the degree of credit rationing which will follow the removal of interest rate and other restrictions. *It has been argued that* strategy which simultaneously relaxes restrictions on the credit and tenancy market, in particular those. relating to the security of land tenure, may yield greater benefits. The removal of these restrictions, which have had the effect of encouraging short-term leases in the past, would allow households to pool irrigation resources optimally through long-term tenancy contracts, and hence may significantly improve levels of rural income. Differences in behaviour among farmers facing similar technologies and risks would have to be explained by differences in their constraint sets such as access to credit, marketing, and extension etc. Since credit constraints have been widely postulated and since lack of borrowing by small holders is also frequently observed this view has to be taken seriously. Why small farmers are more severely burdened by credit constraints than larger ones?

It has been argued that if merely availability and not costs were the problem, the moneylenders would have developed the rural sector long ago. It should be remembered that the small farmer operates under a law level of equilibrium and hence there is the danger that raising the cost of credit by even 2 to 3 percentage points may convert the viable farm into the nonviable farm. Obviously, a farmer who cannot afford the cost of exploiting his land rationally, by applying fertilisers and pesticides, can not expect high returns. The Indian agricultural credit scene at this juncture reminds of what Joseph Stiglitz said that there are infinite number of charlatans out there willing to take other people's money and use it for themselves and on projects that are not good. There are four critical factors in the exercise of contexualisation of the rural credit in the future development strategy. They are food security, task of ensuring sustained agricultural growth in the coming years is far more daunting than what it was during the green revolution strategy, employment and a wide range of hi-tech segments have emerged recently in the rural sector as growth centres and these need full exploitation. It will be worth while to mention that in 2004, NPA of public sector banks due to agriculture sector was 14.44 per cent compared to 17.62 per cent due to small-scale industries (RBI 2005).

References

Desai, Bupat and N.V. Namboodiri (2001), *Organisation and Management of Rural Financial Sector: Text, Cases and Exercise,* New Delhi, Oxford and IBH.

GoI. (2001), *Report of the Task Force on Agriculture Credit for Tenth Five Year Plan, 2002-2007* (Chairman: Y.C. Nanda), New Delhi.

Gulati, Ashok and Seema Bathla (2001), "Capital Formation in Indian Agriculture: Revisiting the Debate", *Economic and Political Weekly,* 36: 1697-1708.

Gulati, Ashok and Seema Bathla (2002), Institutional Credit in Indian Agriculture: Defaults and Policy Options", Occasional Paper 23, Mumbai: NABARD.

Karmakatf, K. G. (1998), "Capital Formation in Agriculture and Role of Institutional Credit", *Journal of Rural Development,* 17:37-52.

Misra, S. N. and R. Chand (1995), "Public and Private Capital Formation in Indian Agriculture: Comments on Complementarily Hypothesis and Others", *Economic and Political Weekly,* June 24.

Planning Commission (1996), *Report of the Working Group on Agriculture Credit and Co-operation (including Crop Insurance) for Ninth Five Year Plan, 1997-98 to 2001-02* (Chairman: P. Kotaiah), New Delhi.

RBI (2000), *Report of the Task Force to Study the Co-operative Credit System and Suggest Measures for its Stengthening* (Chairman: Jagdish Capoor), Bombay.

RBI (2005), *Report on Trend and Progress in Banking in India,* Mumbai.

Sharma, Anil (2005), The Kisan Credit Card Scheme: Impact, Weaknesses and Further Reforms, New Delhi, NCAER.

10

RURAL CREDIT IN THE ERA OF GLOBALIZATION

S. N. Yogish

Introduction

The overall thrust of the current policy regime assume that credit is a critical input that affects agricultural/rural productivity with productivity and credit important enough to establish causality with productivity. A brief review of the recent policy directions from the State assume that de-dogging credit for agriculture is desirable. The thrust of doubling agricultural credit in three years through the banking channel, revival of co-operative credit structure through the package recommended by the Vaidyanathans committee and policy response to farmer suicides, including the vidarba package are excessively skewed towards intervention in the agricultural operations through intervention in credit. There have also been committee set up by state and or the Reserve Bank of India to look the aspect of financial inclusion, farmer indebtedness, integrating moneylenders with the mainstream market and on farmer distress.

The vulnerability of the Indian economy to the performance of the agricultural sector despite in strength is well known, for example, the Indian economy grew at an estimated 3.7 per cent in 2002-03 against 5.6 per cent during

2001-02. this was largely because of the negative growth of 4.4 per cent in the agriculture sector.

Just prior to the current swing into election campaigning, policy pronouncements of the Government were largely agriculture and rural center. The contribution of a farmers commission is one among them Rural credit is emerging as a focal issue and this can be gleamed from the fact that the Government earmarked Rs.15.000 crore in the Interim Budget to revitalize the co-operative structure. The Tenth plan (2002-2007) has set an ambitious average GDP growth of 8 per cent per annual.

To achieve this it is important to revitalize and revamp not only the agricultural sector but also rural financial institutions. An annual average growth of 7 per cent from this sector alone in the next five years is crucial for achieving the GDP target. The Task Force on Rural credit for the Tenth plan has projected institutional credit flow to agriculture and allied activities at Rs. 7.36.570 crore for 2002-2007, which is more than treble (32 per cent) the credit flow (Rs. 2.29.853 crore) during the Ninth plan (1997-2002).

Current Trends in Rural Banking and Credit

First let's look at some broad banking data. The 2001 census figures brought out an alarming picture about the urge of banking services among Indian house holds in Urban and rural areas despite the wide banking network in the country. The following table reinforces the conclusions about the low level of banking usage among Indian households in general 935.5%) and rural households in particular (30.1%) and also reflects the latent demand for general banking needs in rural as well urban segments.

Table 1
Usage of Banking Services by Indian house holds (HHs)

	Total No.	*5 of HHs*	*Rural*	*5 of total HHs*	*Urban*	*% HHs of total*
Total No. of HHs	19.19	100.0%	13.83	72.0%	5.36	28.0%
No. of NNs which use banking services	6.8	35.5%	4.16	30.1%	2.65	49.5%

Source: Census of India 2001.

The absolute member of bank branches has seen an increase in urban areas, which there has been decline in the areas.

Review of Literature

While we look at the rural credit. It might be pertinent to review some recent papers that touch on this theme.

An important paper that examines the possible relationship uses panel data on rural poverty and spread of bank branches argue that increase in access to credit has helped to reduce rural poverty. They conclude that the fact that banks open branches makes formal credit accessible and in the long run seems to have had a positive import on poverty (Burges and Pandey, 2003).

Capital formation in agriculture and the type of current investments being made in agriculture in the content of farmer suicides is examined in detail to see if there are any inter-linkages (Vaidyanathan 2006). This paper also does not indicate any direct relation-ship between investments and productivity. Infant the author argues that some of the recent trends in investments in agriculture could be conceived and thus could lead to a negative special.

Another paper examine the overall growth of agriculture and the role of credit (Rakesh Mohan 2006). Agreeing that the overall supply of credit to agriculture as a percentage of total disbursal of credit is going down, he argues that this should not be a cause for worry as the share of formers credit as a part of the agricultural GDP is growing.

Agricultural Credit

An equality important concern that needs attention is the flow of institutional credit to agriculture. The growth of commercial banks lending to agriculture and allied activities witnessed a substantial decline in the 1990s as compared with the 1980s. Agriculture's share in scheduled commercial banks total out standing credit as on 31-3-02 was only Rs.64,008 crores or 9.8 per cent. Even if we include loans for food manufacturing and processing (Rice, Sugar, edible oil, tea, fruits and vegetable processing), this share works out to Rs. 84.750.22 crores or 12.90

per cent, way below the stipulated largest of 18 per cent. The total agricultural lending by commercial banks (as on 31-3-2002) is now lower than even, their out standings in " Personal loans" (Rs. 82,518 crores in 17.59 millions of accounts) Portfolio comprising loans for housing , consumer durables, and so on.

Table 2
Trends in Rural Lending: Post-Reforms

Loans and Advances	*1994*	*2002*
Priority sector accounts of scheduled commercial banks (No. of accounts) % of rural advances of scheduled	34.6 million	26.16 million
commercial Banks	13.90 %	13.37 %
No. of Agricultural Accounts of scheduled commercial Banks	25 million	20.35 million
Loans Accounts < Rs. 25.000/- of scheduled commercial Banks	55.8 million	37.32 million
(No. of Accounts % of small loans (< Rs. 25.000) to total loans Accounts	18.30 %	5.9 %

Source: various RBI Publications.

Similarly, post reforms, the banking system has mobilized more deposits from farmers and extended less credit to decline number of farmers as illustrated here under:

Table 3
Farmers, Reliance on the Banking System

Year	*Farmers Deposit (Rs. Cr)*	*Farmers Borrowing's (Rs. Cr)*	*No. of farmers assisted (in lakhs)*
1992	26.211	17.835	273
1993	29.825	19.493	257
1994	36.583	19.669	251
1995	43.341	21.334	198
1996	47.433	23.813	194
1997	53.611	27.448	188
1998	57.442	29.442	173
1999	78.881	33.094	169
2000	91.009	36.466	162
2001	99.812	43.42	195
2002	1.08.233	47.43	197

Source: Statistical tables relating to Banks in India (various Issues), RBI compiled by Shri N.K. Thingalaya, former CMD Syndicate Bank.

Many scheduled commercial banks are shying away from agriculture and priority sector lending. For example, the commercial banks have an excess investments portfolio beyond the required limits of 25 per cent. He table below illustrates the decline penetration in rural banking post-reforms, compared to an excess investments of scheduled commercial banks in treasury securities (gilts).

Table 4
Scheduled Commercial Banks: Credit vs Investment in Gifts

Outstanding on	*Net demand and time liabilities (NDTL)*	*SLR investments*	*Excess investment**	*Credit*
9-10-98	7,17.783	2,48,209 (34.58%)	68.763	3,34,514
8-10-99	8,33,811	2,91,093 (34.9)	82.64	3,88,075
6-10-99	9,70,608	3,34,225 (34.4)	91.573	4,75,456
5-10-01	11,55,225	4,14,917 (35.9)	1,26,111	5,42,538
4-10-02	13,70,161	5,05,007 (56.8)	1,62,467	6,73,112
3-10-03	15,35,966	6,21,807 (40.4)	2,37,816	7,52,068

* Investment above 25 % SLR requirement.

Furthermore, schedules commercial banks are resorting to the soft window option of investing in the Rural Infrastructure Development Fund (RIDF) of NABARD. Contributions to the corpus of RIDF are received by NABARD by way of deposits from scheduled commercial Banks against their shortfall in priority sector/agricultural lending during the preceding year. The out standings at the end of March 2003 stood at Rs. 12,159,23 crores.

Table 5
Deposits *Received under RIDF As on 31 March 2003

Year	*Total (Rs. in crores)*
1995-96	350
1996-97	1,042.30
1997-98	1,007.04
1998-99	1,337.95
1999-2000	2,306.63
2000-2001	2,653.64
2001-2002	3,590.72
2002-2003	3,857.09
Total	16,145.37

Compound Growth rate 36.98%

Source: NABARDA Report 2002-2003.

Government's Response to the Rural Credit Scenario

While the current situation may not look promising for rural credit, it isn't that governments have been inactive all the way. In fact, in the early 1970s itself the central Government observed that despite a wide banking network and developmental initiatives in the first 25 years since independence, a critical gap still existed in meeting the credit needs of the rural poor. To find a solution, the Government appointed a working group on rural credit the Narashimha committee, in July 1975. The committee observed that the cost structure of commercial banks, the attitude of bank employees and the lack of a professional approach in the co-operative credit system were the main stumbling blocks to rural credit. The committee also observed that the deposits collected by banks from rural areas were not totally deployed there. The panel, therefore, recommended the creation of a new set of regionally-oriented rural which would combine a co-operative's local feel and a commercial bank's business assumes.

Challenges for Rural and Agricultural Credit in the Post Reforms Era

The agriculture sector to a large extent was excluded from general economic reforms initiated in 1991. However, the reforms introduced in industry, finance, banking and other sectors over the last decade have had considerable import on the agricultural sector. The financial sector reforms have created a level playing field between rural financial institutions (RRBs and cooperatives) and other scheduled commercial banks in treatment and in complains of regulatory norms, without any reforms in agricultural sector.

In the meantime, the agriculture sector is emerging as part of the new economic order arising out of globalization and implementation of the Agreement on Agriculture (AOA) under the World Trade Organization (WTO). If some agreement is reached at the WTO negotiations, the agriculture sector in the country would be poised for a radical transformation. To withstand the global competition enhanced productivity and sustainability of the sector has become imperative.

The agricultural credit provided by co-operative banks, commercial banks, RRBs and other agencies research Rs. 70810 crores during 2002-03,a growth over 14.3% over the previous year. Public sector investments in agriculture had increased from Rs. 3919 crore during 2000-01 to Rs.4794 crore during 2001-02, breaking the earlier declining trend. The private sector investments in agriculture and allied sectors increased from Rs. 14, 605 crores during 1995-96 to Rs. 24.257 crore during 2000-01 at current prices. The proportion of such capital formation financed by institutional credit increased from 59.6 to 71.5 per cent during the period between 1995-96 and 2000-01.

Non-Agricultural Rural Credit

In addition to the issue of agriculture, it is important to look at the other sector s. the rural economy is not homogenous to be amenable to schematic lending. Indeed our data from three states indicates that it might be appropriate to look at credit as a part of a basket of financial services. However, across regions we the following characterize rural transactions:

- The exchanges have a large non-magnetized element. While exchanges are on the basis of rupee value, transactions do not settled frequently. For instance one might agree on a daily wage rates but ultimate settlement takes place through a few cash exchanges that might be settled in kind. The cash exchanges are less. We find this practice prevalent with migrant workers and their mutaddanus.
- The income diversification of individual households is limited, with most households depending on one or two significant streams of income.

  Though, which we look at the rural markets from the demand side, it is possible for us to offer an array of need based interventions that would make an impact on the cash flows, increase magnetization and the participation of the formal sector, making exchanges discover market mechanisms.

General Issues Pertaining to Rural Credit

It is evident that the needs of rural credit are not being met by a single agency. The nature of relationships is quite diverse as described below:

- Borrowing from social networks based on reciprocity; there is no appraised. Paper work or collateral. Several times these loans are interest free. This is works on unorganized social capital.
- Forming SHGs and carrying out financial intermediation through them, disproves the notion that the poor cannot save. The paper work is minimal, collateral is absent and interest margin remain within the community. This works on the organized and formalized social capital.
- Borrowing from informal money-lenders happens when the amount is larger than what social networks can offer. This attracts a high interest, but is timely, quick and flexible, collateral is negotiated. This disproves the notion that the poor cannot service a high interest rate loan.
- Tied credit- loans tied to complementary non-financial transactions in land, labour and commodities. The lender deads with the borrow is a 'non- lending' capacity as well, the terms are opaque tend to be exploitative, even though the transactions costs of borrowing are low.
- Formal financial institution on the semi-regulated space like companies, chit funds, and micro finance institutions.
- Formal finance institutions with state support and patronage in the regulated space like co-operative and banks.

The question is whether it is desirable to have are dominated source of credit for the rural areas. While it might be desirable to move the financial transactions from the informal sources to the formal space, the agreement that it should be from a single source needs to be examined. It might not be practically possible for a single source to finance the diverse needs of the rural population. Based on our study in the three states we were able to map out the purpose of borrowing and the source from which the households, borrowed as indicated by our data. The mapping is reproduced below.

Chart 1
Pecking Order of Savings/ Loan Outlets and Purpose of Savings / Borrowings

Informal				*Formal*
Cash starved/ informal	Semi formal money lender traders	SHGs/semi formal	Neighbor hood institution co-operatives/ post offices	"Outsiders" Banks, companies, chit funds, NBFCs.
Emergency and health needs	Consumption social consumption asset purchase	Consumption social consumption asset purchase education	Withdrawal for social consumption. Borrowing for working capital assets purchase	Largely asset purchase, including assets that result in private capital formation

The chart indicates patterns on low the rural population manage their finances. There are emergency needs at one end and asset purchase at the other. The households straddle between multiple sources for different purposes. Moneylenders seem to be cutting all across the segments, because they are accessible.

Programmes of Rural Credit

The burden of indebtedness in rural India is great and falls mainly on the households of rural working people. The exploitation of this group in the credit market is one of the most pervasive and persistent features of rural life in India, and despite major structural changes in credit institutions and forms of rural credit in the post-Independence period, Darling's statement (1925), that " the Indian peasant is born in debt, lives in debt and dies in debt", still remains true for the great majority of working households in the country side.

Rural households need credit for a variety of reasons. They need it to meet short–terms for working capital and for large-term investment in agriculture and other income-bearing activities. Agricultural and non- agricultural activities in rural areas are typically seasonal, and households need credit to smooth out seasonal fluctuations in earnings and expenditure. Rural households. Particularly those vulnerable to what appear to others to be minor shocks with respect to income and expenditure, need credit as an insurance against risk. In a society that has no free, compulsory and universal education or health care and very few general social security programmes, rural households need credit for different types of consumption. These include expenditure on food, housing, health and education. In the Indian content, another important purpose of borrowing is to meet expenses for a variety of social obligations and rituals.

If these credit needs of the poor are to be met, rural households need access to credit institutions that provide them a range of financial services, provide credit at reasonable rates of interest and provide loans that are unencumbered by extra-economic provisions and obligations.

Historically, there have been four major problems with respect to providing credit to the Indian countryside. First, the supply of formal sector credit to the countryside as a whole has been inadequate. Secondly, rural credit markets in India themselves have been very imperfect and frequented. Thirdly, as the forgoing suggests, the distribution of formal sector credit has been unequal, particularly with respect to region and class, caste and gender. Fourthly, the major source of credit to rural households, particularly income-poor working households, has been informal sector loans, which are usually advanced at very high rates of interest. Further, the terms and conditions attached to these loans have given rise to an elaborate structure of coercion-economic and extra-economic-in this countryside.

That these factors constitute what may be called the "problem of rural credit" has been well recognized in official evaluation and scholarship since the end of the nineteenth country. Given the issues involved, the declared objectives of public policy with regard to rural credit in the post-Independence period were, in the words of the Governor of the Reserve Bank of India, "to ensure that sufficient and timely credit, at reasonable rates of interest, is made available to as large a segment of the rural populations possible" (Rangaarajan, 1996, p. 288).

The policy instruments to achieve these objectives were to be, first, the expansion of the institutional structure of formal-sector lending institutions; secondly, directed lending and thirdly, confessional or subsidized credit (*ibid*). Public policy was thus aimed not only at meeting rural credit needs but also at pushing out the informal borrowers (chavan, 2001, pp. 5-7 passim). Rural credit policy in India envisaged the provision of a range of credit services, including long 0-term and short-term credit and large scale and small-scale loans to rural households.

Main Problems in Rural Credit System

- There is considerable unmet demand for rural credit. Local money-lender continue to provide credit to the rural families, as the reach of institutional agencies to weaker sections has remained poor. Meeting the credit needs of 25 million non-farm informal sector enterprises continues to be a challenge to the rural financial Institutions (RFIs). Though the coverage of micro- finance scheme has expanded, still around 70% of the poor are out of this network. The micro-finance sub-sector of institutional credit has not explicitly targeted the agricultural sector. RFIs have bypassed tenants and share croppers.morethen 6% of the farm families is yet to receive the Kisan Credit Cards.
- Up to the middle of the 1980s, regional rural banks (RRBs) enjoyed a cost advantage *vis-à-vis* the commercial banks but by the late 198s they lost this advantage. Their transaction costs have also now gone up to 6% or 7% of advances. They are too strongly tied to their sponsor banks and have little freedom of operation.

- There is also a problem of inter-regional differences in research of RFIs. In the north-eastern states, the network of RFIs is relatively weak. The micro-finance program is also concerned in a few states.
- Another problem is of delays in processing loans applications. Particularly by commercial banks received 746,696 loan applications. Sanctioned only 451,458 and made actual disbursement to only 419,995 applicants. Matters were reported to be even work during 2004-05.

Priority Areas in Rural Credit

Several committees have been constituted in the recent past to suggest ways to improve the flow of institutional credit in rural areas. These include the expert committee on Rural credit (V.S. Vyas), committee on Agricultural credit though commercial Banks (R.V. Gupta), committee on co-operatives (Vikhe patil), Advisory committee on flow of credit to Agriculture (V.S. Vyas), and Task force on Revival of co-operative credit institutions (A. Vaidyanathan). The Government has implemented several of their suggestions. However, based on n analysis of current status and identification of concerns in the earlier sections of this paper, five areas of policy reforms and priority action are as follows:

Credit Policy

- There should be no attempt for a uniform RFI system throughout the country. The system should be flexible and decentralized, sited to the local socio-economic milieu.
- Policy emphasis on small borrowers showed continues, otherwise they may get systematically further discriminated against in credit allocation.

Increasing Credit Flow and Reducing Risk

- Promotion of groups of homogeneous borrowers.
- Linking production credit with credit for post-harvest operations like sorting, growing, packaging, and making in groups.

Lending by Commercial Banks

- With greater autonomy and private sector participation in public sector Banks; the institutional structure of branch network should not be diluted.
- The requirement that lending for storage unit is treated under indirect lending only it is located in rural areas should go.
- The mandatory target of 18% and 40% should be revived every five years.

Lending by RRBs

- RRBs should be given greater autonomy and flexibility in planning and lending policies, to restore their comparative advantages in rural lending.
- They should take the inciative in organizing farmers in to homogeneous groups or farmer, companies for linking credit with input supply and output marketing.

Lending by Co-operatives

- States should be allowed to borrow from RIDE for meeting their share for recapitulation of co-operative banks.
- States should be persuaded to take follow–up action on the multi- state co-operatives Act, passed in 2002.
- For imparting greater autonomy and accountability to cooperative, states should adopt the model Bill suggested by the Chuadary Brahma Prakash committee. Also, co-operative. Banks should be brought under the supervisory control of RBI/NABARD.

Conclusion

Attempts to strengthen Indian Agriculture must address farm production (farmers) but also processing, marketing, trade, and distribution. We must link farmers to markets. In this endeavor, marketing and rural credit systems are extremely important. Indian rural credit systems have undergone several changes, during the last decade.

In the field of credit delivery, the financial institutions are under stress, particularly since the financial sector reforms of 1992-93. The credit policy should continue to emphasize small borrowers. Credit policy that attempts to deal with the enormity of the problem of rural indebtedness in India must provide a range of credit services to the countryside, and on a scale that the problem demands. The objective of the rural credit policy in respect of small-scale loans to the poor in India should be to build on the strengthens of the rural banking system, not to undermine or weaken this important national asset.

References

M. S. Sriram (2007); Productivity of Rural Credit: A Review of Issues and Some Recent Literature, Indian Institutes of Management Ahamadabad-380015, Indian, pp. 3-19.

Burgees, Robin and Rohini Panday (2003), "Do Banks Matter; Evidence from Indian Social Banking Experiment", BREAD Working paper No. 37.

Mohan, Rakesh (2006), Agricultural Credit in India Status, Issues and Future Agenda. *Economic and Political Weekly,* Vol. 41, No. 12, 1013-1021.

Acharya, S. S. (2004), Agricultural Marketing in India, Volume 17. Millennium Study of Indian Farmer, Government of India, Academic Foundation, New Delhi.

Gulati, A. and S. Bathla (2002), Institutional Credit to Indian Agriculture, Defaults and Policy Options, Occasional paper 23, NABARD.

www.indiatogether. Org/2004/apr/eco-rural bank. Htm, pp. 1-11.

Bhaduri, A. (1982), The Role of Rural Credit in Agrarian Reforms with Special Reform to India in Economic Bulletin for Asia and the Pacific 3, 2, pp. 341-352.

Nair, T. (1999), Rural Financial Intermediation and Commercial Banks: A Review of Recent Trends, in Gujarat Institutes of Development Research working paper, No. 112, May (Ahumedabad).

11

POVERTY ALLEVIATION THROUGH MICRO-CREDIT PROGRAMME OF SHGs:

A CASE STUDY OF *SABALA* IN BIJAPUR DISTRICT OF KARNATAKA

R. R. Biradar, Venkatappa Naik & P. M. Pargonda

Introduction

Alleviation of poverty and unemployment has always been accorded top priority in development paradigm since the inception of planning era in India. Since the 1970s, a series of poverty alleviation programmes have been implemented. Nevertheless, the incidence of poverty continued to be persistent and widespread. Even today a substantial segment of the population at the lower rungs of income spectrum does not get sufficient food both in terms of quality and quantity. Most of the rural people do not have equal and easy accessibility to jobs, land, credit, market, natural resources and civic amenities. Unfortunately, all are not treated equally in the rural socio-economic hierarchy. Many of the poor do lack dignity, autonomy, self-respect, self-esteem, power and freedom to make decisions and choices (WB, 2000; Deepa *et al*, 2000; Nussbaum 2000; Sen, 2001).

The places of the poor, *ipso facto*, are congested, risk-ridden, covered with pollution, sewages and crime, too close to waterways, drought prone, isolated and vulnerable to the vagaries of worst weather. Many of the poor do not have physical well-being; they often speak of being hungry, weak, sick, exhausted, mentally distressed and hence they are "skeleton-like figure" in appearance (WB, 2000; Deepa *et al*, 2000). Poverty is not just low income but encompasses various disadvantages, deprivations and wants of human life. The multiple disadvantages and deprivations quite often tend to interlock to keep the poor and drive the not-so-poor into the vicious circle of poverty or lead to further impoverishment and foster deprivation trap, especially in the case of the scheduled castes (SCs) and scheduled tribes (STs), the socially marginalised and economically disadvantaged sections of the society. This can be largely attributed to lack of productive assets (land or capital) and capabilities of the poor to take active participation in mainstream development process on the one hand, and convert growth impulses into opportunities which give them sustained income and hence improvement in their socio-economic well-being.

An important question, however, is that how to break the "vicious circle of poverty" and convert into the "virtuous cycle of well-being" among the socially marginalised and economically disadvantaged sections of the society. In view of limited success of many approaches tried by the Governments to alleviate poverty and improve the socio-economic well-being, the provision of micro credit through NGOs/SHGs to the poor and not so poor has become a popular strategy of recent times in most of the poverty-stricken countries like India. Therefore, the strategic intervention for sustained reduction of poverty through NGO/SHG-provided micro credit calls for thorough understanding of, in what fallows, different aspects of poverty.

Conceptualization of Poverty

What is Poverty?

What is poverty? How is it measured? Who are the poor? Why are they poor? Some of these typical questions are too difficulty to conceptualize. There are many views and many people who talk and write about poverty around the globe, without reaching an agreement as to what they are actually saying. The concept of poverty is rather complex, dynamic and multi-dimensional phenomenon. It must be understood with reference to circumstance and level of progress of a country. It varies across the time, space and social stratification. It does not wear uniform face, shape and magnitude. In common parlance, the term poverty is defined as the inability of a certain section of the society to obtain minimum income to meet the basic necessities such as food, cloth, shelter, health care and education. In the Indian context, the poverty is officially defined as a nutritional baseline measured in calories intake. As per the Planning Commission, the poverty is defined as per capita monthly expenditure of Rs. 328 in rural and Rs. 454 in urban areas at the 1993-94 all-India prices. The aforesaid per capita expenditure is believed to be sufficient to derive a daily intake of 2400 calories by a person in rural and 2100 in urban areas. The person who does not meet these calories norms falls below the poverty line and considered to be the poor.

The concept of poverty and the discussion of its causal explanations, however, have been broadened. As the consumption/income approach in defining poverty has come under increased criticism, it has been suggested that in the analysis of poverty, common property resources and state-provision of commodities should be taken into account and the concept of poverty should be broadened to include lack of assets, dignity and autonomy. Baulch (1996) has proposed the following pyramid to schematize the range of poverty concepts, where PC is private consumption, CPR is common property resources, and SPC is state-provided commodities (Chart 1). Line 1 on top of the pyramid represents the narrowest definition of poverty while line 6, or the base of the pyramid represents the broadest.

The concept of poverty had expanded to include accessibility CPR, SPC, assets, dignity and autonomy. The first two are mainly related to survival, the second two are concerned with security and the last two are related "inclusiveness". The poor try to attain first and then the rest of the requirements.

Chart 1
Pyramid of Poverty Concepts

PC 1

PC + CPR 2

PC + CPR + SPC 3

PC + CPR + SPC + Assets 4

PC + CPR + SPC + Assets Dignity 5

PC + CPR + SPC + Assets + Dignity + Autonomy 6

Source: Baulch (1996).

Who are the Poor?

Most often it is pretty difficult to identify who are the poor for many of the poverty-alleviation programmes of the governments. It can be observed that the incidence of poverty is not uniform across different sections of the society. Going by occupational classification, a greater incidence of poverty tends to fall among those who work in casual wage employment as compared to that of self-and regular employment in government/private sector. Going by gender, it is the women who are more likely to experience higher incidence of poverty as compared to men. Across educational attainments, the illiterates and literates at lower levels are more likely to experience the incidence of poverty as compared to the literates and literates at higher levels. As regards size of landholdings, it is the small and marginal farmers and also landless agricultural labourers who experience a greater incidence of poverty. Going by social groups, the persons belonging to the STs/SCs are more likely to bear the brunt of poverty as compared to that of others.

The signs of poverty in most of the above said socio-economic groups could be observed in terms of lack of shelter, poor housing condition, poor health status, lack of clean water and sanitation, high rate of illiteracy, limited or non-accessibility to medicines, high rate of mortality, high illness prevalence rate (IPR), malnourishment/undernourishment, high incidence of unemployment, high incidence of child labour and school dropouts, etc. These sings of poverty would result due to low income and hence low monthly per capita expenditure. Most of the above said economic and non-economic dimensions of poverty indicators are interlinked and mutually reinforcing with each other to keep the poor or drive the not so poor in the vicious circle of poverty. The greatest worry of the most NGOs is not only just reduction of income dimensions of poverty but also non-income dimension by building their capabilities through micro-credit approach.

Why they are Poor?

The sustained reduction of poverty, *de facto,* requires thorough understanding of the root cause of poverty. A greater incidence of poverty, be it income or non-income, may be due to several economic and non-economic factors. It can be hypothesised that the economic factors such as lack of productive assets (land or capital), lack of human capital measured in terms of educational attainments, lack of accessibility to qualitative employment such as regular employment in government/ private sector or self-employment either in agriculture or non-agriculture, entry barrier to rural non-farm activities; wage discrimination, under utilisation of government funds allocated for poverty alleviation schemes, indebtedness and the like may be the important factors contributing to house a greater incidence of poverty, especially among the SCs/STs as compared to others (Biradar, 2005; Biradar and Jayasheela, 2006). Similarly, the non-economic factors such as alcoholism, playing cards, long-illness resulting in a loss of employment, etc are also equally important factors resulting in further impoverishment among them. More importantly, lack of accessibility to credit, market, natural resources and skill-building institutions like NGOs/SHGs are also important factors, which quite often prevent the poor from taking up income generation activities. All these factors tend to combine and reinforce to foster what can be described as "deprivation trap" (Chamber, 1983).

As higher incidence of poverty acts a major bottleneck to achieve sustainable growth with social justice and equity and also poverty anywhere is a threat to prosperity everywhere, the World Bank has also committed to reduce poverty at much faster rate than ever before, by involving the peoples' institutions such as NGOs/SHGs in the mainstream development process across the globe. The important questions, for which the entire study is designed, are that whether micro credit programme of NGOs/SHGs can break vicious circle of poverty and deprivation trap and foster spiraling virtuous cycle of well-being for the poor? And also is micro credit approach sustainable in doing so?

Brief Review of Literature

Several studies have been carried out to examine the impact of micro credit on employment, income generation and thereby poverty reduction. The results of the studies are divergent. A few studies have found that the provision of micro credit enabled the poor to take some income generation programme and contributed to decline poverty, asset improvement, improvement in their educational and health attainment (Viswanat, 1993; Narasimhan, 1999; Rao, 1999; Rajasekhar, 2000a; Rajasekhar and Biradar, 2004; Sridhar and Biradar, 2004).

The impact of micro credit on poverty reduction and women's empowerment is not always positive. A few studies have found that the tangible improvements translating into intangible improvement in women's empowerment is something, which is not apparently taking place (Rajasekhar, 2000b; Rao, 1999; Namerta, 1998). It is clear from the case studies that some SHG women are still subjected to the mercy of their husband. Their husband may dictate their involvement in SHGs, to ask for loans, terms of repayment, selling of assets given under the micro credit programme and attending meetings being conducted by SHGs. Some of them still depend on husband to make even household decisions, often relinquish control over their own earned income, face objection from their spouse in their participation in community/public activities, eventually leading to less utilisation of the credit and less impact on poverty reduction. It has been argued (Rajasekhar, 1996) that the ability of micro-credit programmes to provide credit to the poorest was limited due to structural and technical reasons. The emphasis on savings linked to credit, collateral requirements, and short-term credit, prevented the poorest from accessing credit, but it enabled the less poor with assets access to credit. A study by Namerta (1998) found that less than half of the sample women borrowers were economically empowered or benefited in terms of increased incomes due to micro-credit. But more than half of the sample lost control of the loans and incomes from the micro-enterprises as they were taken over by the male family members. It is argued (Namerta, 1998) that the NGOs did not perform better than the government in income generation programmes, as the participation of women was minimal in programme planning, implementation and monitoring. It appears that the micro-credit programme has not always benefited the poor in terms of reduction of poverty and improvement in women's economic empowerment. This can be largely ascribed to lack of job-oriented skills/training, knowledge, awareness and lack of psychological and mental assertiveness before provision of credit and unsustainability of micro-credit programme. From this indicates that there is need to discover the process that foster poverty, assetlessness, poor health and education attainment and isolation or social exclusion by taking up some case studies. There are not many studies focusing on these issues in a more detailed and root-cause-seeking manner. Against this background, the present is designed with the following objectives.

Objectives of the Study

Objectives of the study are to:

- examine the factors contributing to the incidence of poverty;
- identify the activities that are taken up by the poor to overcome poverty;
- examine the impact of micro-credit on income and poverty reduction;

- examine the changes in asset position and accessibility to education and health care facilities after provision of micro-credit; and
- offer policy prescriptions for better implementation of micro-credit programme of NGOs and bring about faster and sustained reduction of poverty.

Database and Limitations

The present is based on the case study method. The primary data were collected by conducting focus group interview held with some randomly selected members of SHGs formed by SABALA in Bijapur district of Karnataka. SABALA is a non-profit, non-government organization working for the upliftment of the weaker sections of the society specially lambanis & dalits in poverty stricken areas of Bijapur districts mainly covering Bijapur, Basavan Bagewadi and Sindagi taluks.

SABALA was chosen purposively to examine the impact of micro credit on poverty reduction and improving the socio-economic well-being of the poor. Although a large number of villages were served by SABALA, only 3 villages, namely, Aheri, Aainapur and Minchanal were randomly selected to conduct the case studies of SHG members. From each village, two sample members of SHGs were randomly selected for collection of data. The data relating to the reasons for poverty, savings, micro-credit, name of the income generating activities, its impact on the annual income of the household, impact of increased income on household asset acquisition, impact on their access to education, health and housing, etc., were collected by personal discussion with the randomly selected SHG members formed by SABALA. Due to shortage of time and resources, only six cases of SHG members were considered to examine various issues relating to the incidence of poverty.

Results and Discussion

Sabala

SABALA is a non-profit, non-government organization, working for the weaker sections of the society since 1986 in

Bijapur district. Bijapur district is drought-proven area, though it is called "Punjab" or "*punch nadigal bidu*" wherein five rivers tend to flow from the west to east in the region. During 1999-2000, the incidence of poverty was quite significant, accounting for more than 32 per cent of the people living below the poverty line as against 20 per cent of the State (GoI, 2006). Agriculture and also industries were not adequately developed in the region. Due to lack of livelihood opportunities in the region, a number of people generally migrate to nearby States such as Maharashtra or Goa in search of their livings. It is in this context that SABALA seemed to have come into the existence with a vision: Empowerment of women and other marginalised communities to have access to sustainable livelihood opportunities.

The important objectives of the organization are to educate women on social and economic issues, create awareness and provide self-employment; strengthen women's groups for undertaking development programmes; build their own societies in order to sustain over all development; create employment opportunities by developing and managing natural, physical, social, financial and human resources; and conduct programmes and provide awareness to improve health and nutritional aspects of mother and child in order to reduce child mortality, antenatal and anemia in the region.

With a view to realise its objectives, the important activities are: organization of SHGs for women's empowerment and networking; livelihood promotion; skill development and skill upgradation training; establishment of training-cum-production centre; marketing support; housing for houseless families; watershed management and sustainable agriculture; training to peoples' representatives; establishment of micro finance institutions; mother and child health care and AIDS education; and bio-intensive gardening and land appropriation. It is evident that the organization has begun to initiate a series of activities for the advancement of the poor, especially belonging to the lambanis and dalits, who are the worst victims of poverty. A brief profile of SABALA is presented in Box 1.

Box 1
Profile of Sabala in Bijapur District of Karnataka State 2006

Area of operation	*Bijapur, Basavan Bagewadi and Sindagi*
Target groups	Lambani women (tribal community of North Karnataka), dalits, shepherds and backward communities
Total No. of Villages	38
Total No of Self Help Groups	210
Total No of Members	1786
No of Active Members	1692
Total Savings (Rs.)	12,50,920
No of Loanable groups	125
Average loan disbursed to SHGs (Rs.)	70,000
Financial Assistance received	• SIDBI, Bangalore Rs. 20.00 Lakhs • RMK Delhi Rs 7.50 Lakhs
Loan Repayment Rate	98 per cent

Source: SABALA

Poverty Alleviation Through Micro Credit

Case Study 1: Sitabai

Sitabai, a resident of Aheri village in Bijapur taluk, belongs to the scheduled caste and is a marginal farmer with two acres of dryland. She lives in her own katcha house with her husband, two daughters, a son and aged father-in-law and mother-in-law. Sitabai, aged 36 years, studied only up to the second standard, while her husband is illiterate. Her first and second daughters are studying at the 9th and 4th standard, respectively; her son is studying at the 6th standard. With a view to meet their basic needs of the life, the household has diversified its activities among the limited working members. She takes care of cloth business, while her husband takes care of cultivation of two acres of land and also works as a casual labour in agriculture.

The life of Sitabai was quite piteous about 10 years ago. When she was married off to Mr. Babu Jadhav, a resident of Aheri village, the condition of the house was much worse than what it is now. Before joining the SHG, the socio-economic status of the family was marginalized and disadvantaged to access many benefits from the Government and/or communities. In the year 1997, she approached the bank to obtain a loan of Rs 15,000 to start a small cloth business in the village. But due to lack of adequate assets and influence she was denied of the loan by the bank. Under such situation, Sitabai joined "Mahalaxmi Self-Help Group" in 1998, formed by SABALA with a primary objective to gain access to micro-credit and set up a business. Accordingly, she started cloth selling business in 2005 with an initial investment of Rs. 3000 borrowed from a local money lender at 3 per cent rate of interest per month. Subsequently, she obtained a loan of Rs. 9,000 as it was admissible for her, but actually she had required a loan of Rs. 15,000. The total investment in cloth business was estimated at Rs. 12,000; of which Rs. 9,000 was fixed and Rs. 3,000 was variable or working capital. The total annual income earned from cloth business was estimated at Rs. 24,000 and Rs. 4000 from wage employment by her husband and about 4 bags of jowar were obtained from cultivation of 2 acres of land. These four bags of jowar were kept for home consumption. The total income of the household was estimated at Rs. 28,000. As she reported, before joining the SHG, the income of the household was much lower, even unable to meet their day-to-day expenditure. It has been reported that after joining the SHG, the asset possession of the household has been improved. Before joining the SHG, there were very few assets such as radio, broken tape recorder, a wall clock and bicycle. After joining the SHG, he purchased a small TV, table and chairs, fan and gas stove. This implies that the increased income has resulted in an improvement in the acquisition household assets. She felt that after joining the SHG, her income, savings capacity, access to education, health care services, banking institutions and market have improved. She reported that she has been greatly involved in major decision making activities. The life style of the household has been relatively better-off. Her socio-economic status within and outside the household is said to have improved.

Case Study 2: Lalitabai

Lalitabai, aged 30 years, is a small farmer living in Aheri village of Bijapur taluk. She lives in a Government provided house with her husband (34 years), two sons (7 and 4 years), a daughter (14 years) and father-in-law (60 years). Lalitabai and her husband are the only breadwinner of the household and rest of them are dependents. Both husband and wife seemed to have been forced to take up multiple activities such as agriculture, craft works or hotel business, and wage employment. The household had little endowments and exchange entitlements. She had about 3 acres of dryland, one buffalo and two goats. Lalitabai involved in craft works (preparation of lambanis dress, pillow covers, cushion covers, wallets, vanity bag, etc.), dairy farming and she also works as a labour in agriculture, whereas her husband takes care of cultivation of two acres of land and also hotel business set up in the village. Before joining the SHG, Lalitabai and her husband used to migrate to Pune in Maharashtra in search of employment during the slack season of agriculture and they had to struggle hard to obtain their substance. The average annual income of the household was estimated at Rs. 29,800 which is reported to be sufficient for their life to lead. In the year 1998, Lalitabai joined "Shree Laxmi Self-Help Group" formed by SABALA with the basic objectives to gain access to credit, knowledge and seek markets support to their handicraft products. In 2005, she obtained a credit of Rs. 10,000 to establish a hotel business in the village and accordingly, the hotel business was started with a financial assistance obtained from the "Shree Laxmi Self-Help Group". It was mainly managed by her husband. In the year 2006 the annual income derived from the hotel business was estimated at Rs. 18,000. The income earned from the hotel business enabled her to purchase a buffalo for the purpose of dairy farming. From the dairy farming, by way of selling milk and milk products, she earned about Rs. 2000. Agriculture wage employment and craft works are other important sources of income for the household, from which she earned an income of Rs. 2,500 and Rs. 3,000, respectively. She obtained six quintals of jowar, of which four quintals were retained for home consumption and two quintals were sold out at Rs. 800 per quintal. The annual income from agriculture was thus estimated at Rs. 4, 800 and Rs. 2,000. The average annual income of the household was estimated at Rs. 29,800 which is reported to be sufficient for their life to lead.

It has been observed that after joining, the SHG, there has been an improvement in the household assets. She purchased a radio, tape recorder, TV, fan and a couple of chairs. She also purchased a buffalo and a couple of goats. Her socio-economic status has been immensely improved as told by her. She has also been respected in the family and even outside too. Her knowledge relating to the importance of their children's education, health care and women's role in the society has been improved as weekly meeting are conducted by the SHG, in which such issues are being discussed. The household is now in a position to lead a better life and able to gain access to better education, health, market and banking institutions. The increased income has resulted in an improvement in their consumption pattern, expenditure on education of their children, heath care services.

Case Study 3: Jubalamma

Jubalamma, aged 45 years, is a resident of Minchanal village of Bijapur taluk. She lives in her own semi-pucca house with her husband (50 years), two sons (22 and 18 years) and two daughters (14 and 12 years). Both of them were not educated, but her first son studied up the to 8th standard and discontinued due to severity of poverty around 8 years back, and her second is studying at the 12th standard and two daughters are also studying at the 8th and 6th standard. On our discussion, Jubalamma says "we had not been educated by our parents due to abject poverty experienced by them, but our children should not be deprived of education......If they wish to study higher levels of education, we would certainly send them however difficulty we face........." . She had only two acres of dryland. She mainly involves in handicrafts activities initiated by SABALA and also takes care of kirani shop and occasionally works as a labour in agriculture. Her husband largely involves in management of kirani shop and her son who discontinued education against their will works as labour in agricultural as well as non-agricultural activities in the village.

Her father and mother in-laws and her husband, before marriage, used to migrate to near by states like Maharashtra or Goa. After her marriage and partition from father-in-law, she had to face lots of difficulties to lead life independently with her husband who was little bit an adamant guy. They seemed to have struggled a lot to lead married life for about more than 15-20 years. When SABALA made intervention in the village in the year 1998, she became the member of a group known as "Rukmini Self-Help Group" with an objective to gain access to micro credit and take up income generation activities. Accordingly, she obtained a loan of Rs. 8,000 for the purpose of establishing kirani shop in the village. The total investment made for kirani shop was estimated at Rs. 20,000. Out of this, Rs. 8000 was from the group and Rs. 12,000 was from their own sources. In 2006, the annual income from this business was estimated at Rs. 20,000. The income from wage employment in agriculture and non-agriculture by her son was estimated to be around Rs. 4,500 and by her it was Rs. 2,500. From the handicraft works sponsored by SABALA, the annual income was estimated at Rs. 5,000.In she obtained three bags of jowar from cultivation of two acres of land and retained them for home consumption. The average annual income of the household was estimated to be around Rs. 32, 000 in the year 2006.

The increased income has resulted in an improvement of household assets. After joining the group, she purchased tape recorder, wall clock, bicycle, fan, table and chairs and also a couple of goats. She felt happy about her association with SABALA and the group to which she belongs. She said that she has been now respected in the house and also outside and invited her to take participation in some of the community-based functions. Her knowledge about children's education, health and banks has improved. The expenditure towards education, health and better housing has increased. She has been involved in major decision making activities by her husband and other family members; though the major decisions are not taken by her. She feels that she is now confident of her life to lead and does not foresee any difficulty in near future.

Case Study 4: Gangamma

Gangamma, aged 35 years, is a small farmer, residing in Minchanail village. She lives in her own katcha house with her husband (40 years), two sons (20 and 18 years), a daughter (16 years) and father in-law (70 year). Gangamma belongs to the schedule caste (Rathod) she had 3.20 acres of dryland in the village. Gangamma and her husband were not educated, as they were borne in a poor household and also due to lack of their parents' knowledge. While her first son is illiterate due to inability to send her son to school, as they had to migrate in search of their bread and butter a few years ago. Her second son is studying at the 12th standard and daughter at the 10th standard. The main occupation of the family is hotel business established in the village, along with the cultivation of land and craft works. Her husband looks after hotel and agriculture and Gangamma mainly works for crafts.

The life of Gangamma was really miserable soon after her marriage with Sri Gopu Chavan, a resident of the same village. Until the entry of SABALA in Minchanal village, Gangamma, like many other people in the village, used to make temporary migration in search of bread and butter, especially during the slack season of agriculture. In order to set up a hotel in the village, she approached the nearby bank to get loan. But, due to lack of collateral security and influence, she was denied formal credit. This made her to join the group. In the year 1998, Gangamma joined "Laxmi Women Self-Help Group" formed by SABALA with a view to empower herself and come out of vicious circle of poverty. Since her joining, the group, several times small loans were obtained to meet their consumption needs. In the year 2005, she obtained a loan of Rs. 10,000 for the purpose of hotel business. The total investment made for hotel business was estimated at Rs. 15,000; out of which Rs. 10, 000 was from the group and Rs. 5000 from her own source.

In 2006, the average annul income from the hotel business was estimated at Rs. 25,000 after deducting all variable expenditures. She obtained six quintals of bajra and marketed at Rs. 600 per quintal and total income from agriculture was estimated at Rs. 3,600. From craft works, the total income, she earned, was estimated at Rs. 3,500. The total annual income of her household was estimated at Rs, 32,100. It has been observed that the increased income has resulted in an improvement of household assets and also in access to education, health care facilities and better housing conditions. After her joining the group, she purchased a radio, tape recorder, TV, bicycle, and a couple of table and chairs. She reported that after her joining the group, the consumption pattern has changed in favour of superior goods and services and expenditure towards education, health and housing facilities has increased. Her overall life style and status has been improved significantly. She has also reported that after her joining the group, her outside mobility tended to increase and mingling with her community people and attending certain group meetings conducted by SABALA also increased. She has been respected within and outside the house and involved in certain important decision making activities. She has gained confident of life to lead due to her association with the group.

Case Study 5: Kamalabai

Kamalabai, aged 33 years, belongs to the *lambani* community and resides in Ainapur tanda of Bijapur taluk. She lives in her own katcha house with her husband (35 years) and four sons. She was not literate, whereas her husband studied up to the 7th standard and discontinued due to poverty. Her first son is studying at the 3rd standard and second son at the 2nd standard. She had no land and no education, but knowledge of craft works. When she was married off to sri Kasu Rathod resident of Ainapur tanda, about ten years ago, her life was really pitious, unable to get acres two squares of meals a day. Both of them where solely depended on agricultural wage paid employment as a major source of income and thereby lead their life. She attempted to obtain loan from the banks to set up a petty shop, but she could not get due to lack of collateral security.

In 1998, she joined "Santoshi Mata Mahila Development Self-Help Group" formed by SABALA in Ainapur tanda. Her main purpose to join the group is to save some money out their earnings and gain access to credit to take up income generating activities, like petty shop. She obtained loan of Rs 10,000 to set up a kirani shop in the village and accordingly, the kirani shop was set up in the year 2005. The total investment was estimated at Rs. 20,000; of which Rs. 10,000 was borrowed from the group's revolving fund granted by the banking institution against their savings and Rs 10,000 was from their own savings. The monthly income from kirani shop was estimated to be around Rs. 1,500, estimating annually at Rs. 18,000. Similarly, the income from wage employment was estimated to be Rs. 2,000 and from craft Rs. 3,000 per annum. The annual income of the household was approximated at Rs.23, 000. The increased income of the household has contributed to acquire household assets. After joining the group, she purchased wall clock, bicycle, fan and a couple of chairs, and she also radio and tape recorder before joining the group. She felt that the expenditure towards, education, health, food and clothing has been improved significantly after joining the group. As it is opined by her, she has been honored in the house, involved in the discussion making process and invited by others to take participation in some of the community and village based activities.

Case Study 6: Lalibai

Lalibai, who belongs to the *lambani* community, is a resident of Ainapur tanda in Bijapur taluk. Kasibai lives in a semi- pucca house with her husband (50 years), two sons (20 and 14 years) and a daughter (15 years). Lalibai is not literate, whereas her husband studied up to the 4th standard. She involved in tailoring and craft works while her husband does carpentry works in the village. The household has not possessed any land. The carpentry work is their family occupation.

As it was learned that soon after her marriage with Mr. Basavaraj Rajput, the life of Lalibai was miserable, unable to lead a socially satisfied life. Before joining the SHG, she had to work as a casual labour in agriculture. There was not adequate work and income for her and hence, lots of difficulties have to be faced. She tried to approach the nearby bank, along with some body else in the village, for getting loan to take up income generating activity. But she could not get the loan due to lack of collateral security and reluctant attitude of the bank officials. On an enquiry it was learnt that the reluctant attitude of the bank officials was due to high defaulting cases from the same village.

In 1998, she joined "Santoshi Mata Self-Help Group" formed by SABALA. The main purpose of her joining was to gain access to credit and take up income generating activity and provide better education to her children and lead a better life in the society. After attending programme on tailoring activity conducted by SABALA, in the year 2006, she started a tailoring activity in her village by taking a loan of Rs. 10,000 from the group. The total investment made for this activity was estimated at Rs. 15,000. Out of which, 10,000 was from the group and Rs. 5,000 was her own source. The annual income from tailoring activity was estimated at Rs. 18,000, from craft it was Rs. 2,000 and from carpentry services rendered for the villagers, the total income was estimated at Rs. 6,000. The bulk of the income is in the form of grains. The annual household income from all the sources was estimated at Rs.26, 000.

It is evident that the income of the household increased rapidly and resulted in an acquisition of household assets and thereby leading relatively a better life. After joining the group, she purchased tape recorder, bicycle, fan, tailoring machine, and before joining the group, she had only radio and a buffalo. The expenditure towards education, health, nutritious food items and housing has increased after joining the group. She feels that her knowledge relating to importance of her children's education, health, banks and her role in the society has improved. she felt that her confident in leading a better life has improved due to her association with the group.

Conclusions and Policy Implications

The foregoing analysis on a few case studies of SHG members formed by SABALA in Aheri, Minchanal and Ainapur tandas clearly indicates that SABALA has targeted the poor belonging mainly to the *lambani* community, who are historically deprived of certain basic needs of their life. SABALA has considered organizing the poor into a plat form popularly know as "self-help group" as a challenge and provide them savings and credit services, enabling them to under take income generation activities.

It has been found from the case studies that, lack of productive assets (land), human capital (education), employment growth, poor performance of agriculture and more dependent people are the important sources of poverty. Lack of Government programme (wage and self-employment, social security schemes, etc.) and lack of opportunities to access and use common property resources are also found to be important factors keeping a large chunk of the people in poverty. The intervention made by SABALA, an NGO, has made several changes in the lives of the poor. It has been found that the savings by SHG members have increased. The members of the group have been able to access micro credit and under take certain income generating activities which give them regular employment and income. The provision of micro credit has positively contributed to an increase in the household annual income, which in turn, resulted in an improvement in the household assets such as radio, tape recorder, wall clock, TV, bicycle, table and chairs, fan and also livestock. The household endowments have improved due to the provision of micro credit. The expenditure towards education, health, food and nutrition and housing has increased significantly. There has been a greater importance in the household budgetary expenditure towards human resource development and thereby building their capabilities. It is evident that social mobility of the SHG members has been improved. The SHG members have been respected within and outside the house. Most of the SHG members were involved in major decision making activities by their husband or other family members. Most of the members felt that their confidence to lead a better life has increased due to their association with SABALA. The observation made on the basis of a few case studies of members of SHGs formed by SABALA in Bijapur district of Karnataka state, however, can't be strictly generalized. It warrants in-depth study employing different techniques of data collection and analysis.

References

Baulch, Bob (1996), 'The New Poverty Agenda: A Disputed Consensus', *IDS Bulletin*.

Biradar, R. R. (2005), *Incidence of Poverty Among Social Groups in rural India: Why do SCs/STs Experience Greater Incidence of Poverty*, a paper submitted for presentation at the Foundation-Day seminar, NIRD, Hyderabad, held during November 9-10, 2005.

Biradar, R. R. and Jayasheela (2006), *Gender and Social Inequality in Education in Rural India: What are Its Effects*, a Paper Submitted to the National Institute for Rural Development, Hyderabad.

Chamber, R. (1983), *Development, Putting the Last First*, Langman.

Deepa, Narayana, R. Chambers, M. K. Shah and Patti Petesch (2000), *Voices of the Poor: Crying out for Change*, Oxford University Press, New York.

Government of Karnataka (GoK) (2006), *Karnataka Human Development Report 2005*, Planning and Statistics Department, Government of Karnataka, Bangalore.

Namerta (1998), *Income and Employment Generation Programme of NGOs in India*, NOVIB Bangalore.

Narasimhan, Sankuntala (1999), Empowering Women: An Alternative Strategy from Rural India, Sage Publications, New Delhi.

Nussbaum, Martha C. (2000), Women and Human Development: The Capabilities Approach, Kali for Women, New Delhi.

Purushothaman, Sangeetha (1998), The Empowerment of Women in India: Grassroots Women's Networks and State, Sage Publications, New Delhi.

Rajasekhar, D. and R. R. Biradar (2004), Reluctant Partners Coming Together? People, Government and NGOs, Concept Publishing Company, New Delhi.

Rajasekhar, D. (2000a), 'Non-Government Organizations (NGOs) in India: Opportunities and Challenges', *Journal of Rural Development*, Vol. 19, No. 2.

Rajasekhar, D. (2000b), 'Micro-Finance Programme and Women's Empowerment: A Study of Two NGOs from Kerala', *Journal of Social and Economic Development*, Vol. 3, No. 1.

Rao, Geetha (1999), *Is Microfinance Enough? A Study of the Impact of Microfinance on the Empowerment of Women in Karnataka,* (Mimeo).

Sen, Amertya (2001), Development as Freedom, Oxford University Press.

Sridhar, D. M. and R. R. Biradar (2004), Interface between Government and Target Group Members of NGOs: A Case of GRAMA, in Rajasekhar and Biradar (eds.), *Reluctant Partners Coming Together? People, Government and NGOs,* Concept Publishing Company, New Delhi.

Thorat, Sukhadeo (2004), *Persistence of Poverty: Why do Scheduled Castes and Scheduled Tribes Stay Chronically Poor?* Working Paper for Centre for Chronic Poverty, London.

Viswanath, Vanita (1993), NGOs and Women's Development in Rural South India: A Comparative Analysis, Vistaar Publications, New Delhi.

World Bank (WB) (2000b), World Development Report 2000-2001:Attacking Poverty, Oxford University Press, New York.

12

AGRICULTURAL CREDIT FLOW BY PUBLIC AND PRIVATE SECTOR BANKS—AN ECONOMIC ANALYSIS

Girija Yabannavar,
Hosamani S. B. & Kulkarni B. S.

Introduction

Agricultural Credit has played a vital role in supporting farm production in India. Though the outreach and amount of agricultural credit have increased over the years, several weaknesses have crept in which have affected the viability and sustainability of these institutions. Following the shifts in consumption and dietary patterns from cereals to non-cereal products, a silent transformation is taking place in rural areas calling for diversification in agricultural production and value addition processes in order to protect employment and incomes of the rural population. In the changed scenario, strong and viable agricultural financial institutions are needed to cater to the requirements of finance for building the necessary institutional and marketing infrastructure. What is needed in agriculture now is a new mission mode similar to what was done in the 1970's with the green revolution. The difference now is that initiatives are needed in a disaggregated manner in many different segments of agriculture and agro-industry, horticulture, aquaculture, pisci-culture, dairying, sericulture, poultry, vegetables, meat, food processing, other agro-processing and the like.

The statement that agriculture plays a crucial role in the development of the Indian economy is still true. It accounts for 21 per cent of GDP and about two-thirds of the population is dependent on the sector. The importance of agricultural credit as a critical input to agriculture is reinforced by the unique role of Indian agriculture in the macroeconomic framework and its role in poverty alleviation. Recognizing the importance of the agricultural sector in India's development, the government and the Reserve Bank of India (RBI) have played a vital role in creating a broad-based institutional framework for catering to the increasing credit requirements of the sector. Agricultural policies in India have been reviewed from time to time to maintain pace with the changing requirements of the agricultural sector, which forms an important segment of the priority sector lending of scheduled commercial banks and target of 18 per cent of net bank credit has been stipulated for the sector.

Agriculture in India has always been heavily dependent on the monsoons and has hence been an inherently risky activity. At different times we have also had onerous rural tax systems under different empires, most recently under the British. Indigenous systems of credit had to develop as a consequence of seasonal needs and fluctuations in order to facilitate smoothing of the consumption pattern of farmers over the year. With intermittent failures of the monsoons and other customary vicissitudes of farming, rural indebtedness has been a serious and continuous characteristic of Indian agriculture. Because of the high risk inherent in traditional farming activity, the prevalence of high interest rates was the norm rather than the exception, and concomitant exploitation and misery often resulted.

Considering the above divergent views on the performance of the banks an overall objective and rigorous evaluation on the growth of agricultural credit was felt to identify important dimensions of performance to evolve policy options.

Specific Objectives

1. To assess the pattern & growth of credit flow in agriculture.
2. To identify the extent of instability in credit flow to agriculture.
3. To analyse the growth in profitability of commercial and public sector banks.

Methodology

The study has been based on the time series data. The entire period is divided into two phases i.e., 1990-91 to 1995-96 as Pre-WTO period and 1996-97 to 2005-06 as Post-WTO period. The technique of Compound Growth Rate analysis was used to analyse the pattern and growth of credit flow in agriculture and also to know the growth in profitability of commercial and public sector banks. The co-efficient of variation technique (Instability analysis) was employed to examine the extent of instability in growth of credit flow and profitability of banks. Simple tabular analysis was used with percentages to know the per cent increase in target and achievements by the banks in implementation and formulation of Service Area Credit Plan by pubic sector banks.

Results and Discussion

The results of the study are presented under the following important heads.

Capital Formation

The compound growth rates of gross capital formation in agriculture of public and private sector banks during pre-WTO and post-WTO period is depicted in Table 1. The table indicates that there was remarkable growth in capital formation in agriculture in both public and private sector banks during post-WTO period (1996-97 to 2005-06) when compared to pre-WTO period (1990-91 to 1995-96). The growth rate for gross capital formation for public sector banks during pre-WTO period was 6.65 per cent per annum and was found to be significant at 5 per cent level. Where as, it was 16.46 per cent per annum during post-WTO period and was significant at 1 per cent level. Similar trend was observed in the case of private sector banks wherein the compound growth rate of gross capital formation was 2.22 per cent during pre-WTO period whereas the growth rate showed a multifold increase with 20.03 per cent during post-WTO period, which was significant at 1 per cent level.

Table 1
Compound Growth Rate and Variation of Gross Capital Formation in Agriculture of Public and Private Sector Banks (1990-91 to 2005-06)

	Pre-WTO period (1990-91 to 1995-96)		*Post-WTO period (1996-97 to 2005-06)*	
Particulars	*Compound Growth Rate (Per cent/ annum)*	*Coefficient of Variation (%)*	*Compound Growth Rate (Per cent/ annum)*	*Coefficient of Variation (%)*
Public Sector Banks	6.65*	90.64	16.46**	35.31
Private Sector Banks	2.22	96.31	20.03**	27.85
Total	3.54	94.56	19.23**	29.66

Note: * indicates significant at 5 per cent level of significance.
** indicates significant at 1 per cent level of significance.

The growth rate of total (public & private) gross capital formation in agriculture was also showed a similar trend with 3.54 per cent growth during pre-WTO period and 19.23 per cent growth during post-WTO period and was found to be significant at 1 per cent level. This indicates that during post-WTO period more emphasis was given for capital formation in agriculture by both public and private sector banks.

The coefficient of variation in capital formation during the pre-WTO period for private sector banks was the highest with 96.31 per cent followed by total (Public & Private) with 94.56 per cent and public sector banks with 90.64 per cent. On the contrary, the coefficient of variation during the post-WTO period was quite less as compared to pre-WTO period with public sector banks having variation of 35.31 per cent followed by total (public & private) with 29.66 per cent and private sector banks (27.85%). The credit policies framed by the planners coupled with proper implementation by the banks might have led to the lower instability in the credit flow and then capital formation.

This tremendous increase in gross capital formation in agriculture in post-WTO period was mainly due the consequences of the green revolution and further higher rate of technology orientation, more investment in Research and Development (R&D) etc which necessitated more pumping of money into the sector for additional investment.

Flow of Institutional Credit

The credit delivery arrangements by scheduled commercial banks and that too, in terms of out standings at year-ends and not in terms of fresh annual flow of advances were furnished in the reports. NABARD provides such data on total credit flow for agriculture separately for co-operatives, RRBs and Commercial Banks. These data (Table 2) show that with the introduction of special agricultural credit plans, commercial banks and RRBs have come to play an increasing role in the supply of total agricultural credit, while co-operatives have begun to take a back seat. The share of co-operatives in total farm credit has declined steadily from about 40 per cent in 1999-2000 to 24 per cent in 2005-06; suggesting that less than one-fourth of institutional credit for agriculture comes from co-operatives. This is reflected in the increasing concern in recent years over the effectiveness, governance, and financial health of rural co-operative banks and the attention being given to rural lending by commercial banks. Just under a third of rural credit continues to be extended by the co-operative system and hence it is essential that they be revitalized and put on a sound business footing.

The compound growth rates of flow of institutional credit to agriculture by different banks for the year 1997-98 to 2002-03 is depicted in Table 3.

The growth of medium/long term credit to agriculture in all the three banks was the highest compared to short term credit. In the case of Co-operatives the growth rate for short term credit to agriculture was 18.81 per cent. Whereas, it was

Table 2
Flow of Total Institutional Credit for Agriculture by Institution

(Rs. Crore)

Years/ Agency	*Cooperatives*	*Per cent Increase*	*Scheduled Commercial Bank (4+5)*	*Per cent Increase*	*RRBs*	*Percent Increase*	*Commercial Banks*	*Per cent Increase*	*Total Institutional Credit (2+3)*	*Per cent Increase*
(1)	(2)		(3)		(4)		(5)		(6)	
1999-00	18.363 (39.7)		27,905 (60.3)		3172		24,733		46,268	
2000-01	20,800 (39.4)	13.3	32,027 (60.6)	14.8	4220	33.0	27,807	12.4	52,827	14.2
2001-02	23,604 (38.0)	13.5	38,441 (62.0)	20.0	4854	15.0	33,587	20.8	62,045	1705
2002-03	23,716 (34.1)	0.5	45,844 (65.9)	19.3	6070	25.1	39,774	18.4	69,560	12.1
2003-04	26,959 (31.0)	13.7	60,022 (69.0)	30.9	7581	24.9	52,441	31.9	86,981	52.0
2004-05	30,639 (26.6)	13.7	84,604 (73.4)	41.0	11,718	54.6	72,886	39.0	115,243	32.5
2005-06	37,272 (23.7)	21.7	120,228 (76.3)	42.1	14,076	20.1	106,152	45.6	157,500	36.7

Note: Figures in brackets are percentage to total.
Source: NABARD data quoted in GOI (2006), Economic survey 2005-06 up to 2004-05 and from NABARD for 2005-06.

30.97 per cent for medium/long term credit. Similar trend was observed in the case of Regional Rural Banks (RRBs) and Commercial Banks, wherein the growth rates of short term & medium/long term credit were 16.90 per cent and 37.82 per cent for RRBs and in the case of Commercial Banks the growth rates for short term & medium/long term credit were 15.72 per cent and 24.80 per cent respectively. The growth rates were found to be significant for all the banks and credit flows except for short-term credit of Regional Rural Banks (RRBs). The table clearly indicated that more credit is being flown to agriculture sector by the banks. However, there is a need to minimize the degree of fluctuation in the flow.

Table 3
Compound Growth Rates and Variation of Flow of Institutional Credit to Agriculture during 1997-98 to 2002-03

Particulars		*Compound Growth Rate (Per cent/annum)*	*Coefficient of Variation (%)*
Co-operatives	Short-term	18.81**	31.58
	Medium/Long term	30.97*	54.77
Regional Rural Banks	Short-term	16.90	96.12
	Medium/Long term	37.82*	62.24
Commercial Banks	Short-term	15.72**	27.28
	Medium/Long term	24.80**	42.67

Note: * indicates significant at 5 per cent level of significance.
** indicates significant at 1 per cent level of significance.

The coefficient of variation was the highest for Regional Rural Banks with 96.12 per cent for short-term credit & 62.24 per cent for medium/long term credit followed by Co-operatives with 54.77 per cent for medium/long term credit & 31.58 per cent for short-term credit and was the lowest for Commercial Banks with 42.67 per cent for medium/long term credit & 27.28 per cent for short-term credit.

Profitability of Banks

The compound growth rates and variation of profitability of scheduled commercial banks (SCBs) during pre & post-WTO periods are depicted in Table 4.

Table 4
Compound Growth Rates and Variation of Profitability of Scheduled Commercial Banks (SCBs)

	Pre-WTO period (1990-91 to 1995-96)		*Post-WTO period (1996-97 to 2005-06)*	
Particulars	*Compound Growth Rate (Per cent/ annum)*	*Coefficient of Variation (%)*	*Compound Growth Rate (Per cent/ annum)*	*Coefficient of Variation (%)*
Interest income	11.83*	24.99	11.00	28.44
Interest expenditure	10.17	22.86	8.23**	24.30
Net interest margin	16.21	32.12	16.07	40.02
Operating expenses	18.59**	32.18	12.22	31.40
Surplus from interest income	-4.58	63.49	42.22**	89.61
Other income	17.97*	37.66	19.91**	49.67
Gross surplus (Operating profit)	14.71	38.93	24.13	57.38
Provisions & Contingencies	5.35	34.67	23.41	54.16
Profitability (Net profit)	-10.90	68.22	29.42**	65.78

Note: * indicates significant at 5 per cent level of significance.
** indicates significant at 1 per cent level of significance.

The growth rate for operating expenses was the highest with 18.59 per cent during pre-WTO period (1990-91 to 1995-96) followed by other income (17.97%), net interest margin (16.21%), gross surplus (14.71%), interest income (11.83%), interest expenditure (10.17 %) and provisions & contingencies (5.35%). The growth rates for surplus from interest income (-4.58%) and profitability (-10.90%) were found to be negative. Among the indicators, interest income and other income were found to be significant at five per cent level of significance, where as, operating expenses was found to be significant at one per cent level of significance.

The growth rate for surplus from interest income was the highest with 42.22 per cent growth during post-WTO period followed by profitability (net profit) with 29.42 per cent, gross surplus (24.13%), provisions & contingencies (23.41%), other income (19.91%), net interest margin (16.07%), operating expenses (12.22%), interest income (11.00%) and it was the lowest for interest expenditure with 8.23 per cent. On the contrary, surplus from interest income and profitability (net profit) were positive in post-WTO period as against in pre-WTO period.

The net profit of all SCBs declined significantly in pre-WTO period due to the imposition of stricter disclosure norms by the RBI, higher capital losses on bank's investment in government securities and the increased cost of borrowed funds. The net profit of all SCBs increased by 360 per cent during post-WTO, which was possible on account of rise in their operating profit.

The coefficient of variation during pre-WTO period was the highest for profitability with 68.22 per cent followed by surplus from interest income (63.49%), gross surplus (38.93%), other income (37.66%), provisions & contingencies (34.67%), operating expenses (32.18%), net interest margin (32.12%), interest income (24.99%) and interest expenditure (22.86%).

The coefficient of variation during post-WTO period was the highest for surplus from interest income with 89.61 per cent followed by profitability (65.78%), gross surplus (57.38%), provisions & contingencies (54.16%), other income (49.67%), net interest margin (40.02%), operating expenses (31.40%), interest income (28.44%) and interest expenditure (24.30%).

The compound growth rates & variation of profitability of public sector banks (PSBs) during pre & post-WTO periods are depicted in Table 5.

The growth rates for public sector banks followed a similar trend as in the case of scheduled commercial banks where in the operating expenses was the highest with 17.79 per cent during pre-WTO period (1990-91 to 1995-96) followed by other income (16.84%), net interest margin (15.18%), gross surplus (12.77%), interest income (10.35%), interest expenditure (8.44%) and provisions & contingencies (6.65%). The growth rates for surplus from interest income (-19.99 %) and profitability (-14.68 %) were found to be negative. Among the indicators, interest income and interest expenditure were found to be significant at five per cent level, where as, operating expenses and other income were found to be significant at one per cent level of significance. During the pre-WTO period all commercial banks, especially Public Sector Banks (PSBs) recorded fall in operating profit and negative net profit due to the implementation of the prudential accounting standards and provisioning for Non-Performing Assets (NPAs) and lost assets.

Table 5
Compound Growth Rates and Variation of Profitability of Public Sector Banks (PSBs)

	Pre-WTO period (1990-91 to 1995-96)		*Post-WTO period (1996-97 to 2005-06)*	
Particulars	*Compound Growth Rate (Per cent/ annum)*	*Coefficient of Variation (%)*	*Compound Growth Rate (Per cent/ annum)*	*Coefficient of Variation (%)*
Interest income	10.35*	21.56	10.12	26.48
Interest expenditure	8.44*	19.42	7.28**	22.34
Net interest margin	15.18	29.81	15.24	38.01
Operating expenses	17.79**	30.16	10.22	26.89
Surplus from interest income	-19.99	91.80	48.57**	99.23
Other income	16.84**	35.15	18.95	47.66
Gross surplus (Operating profit)	12.77	36.75	25.03	59.48
Provisions & Contingencies	6.65	37.44	25.20	56.90
Profitability (Net profit)	-14.68	92.48	25.58**	64.42

Note: * indicates significant at 5 per cent level of significance.
** indicates significant at 1 per cent level of significance.

The growth rate for surplus from interest income was the highest with 48.57 per cent during post-WTO period followed by profitability (net profit) with 25.58 per cent, provisions & contingencies (25.20%), gross surplus (25.03%), other income (18.95%), net interest margin (15.24%), operating expenses (10.22%), interest income (10.12%) and it was the lowest for interest expenditure with 7.28 per cent. On the contrary, surplus from interest income and profitability (net profit) were positive in post-WTO period as against in pre-WTO period.

Among the indicators, interest expenditure, surplus from interest income and profitability were found to be significant.

The coefficient of variation during pre-WTO period was the highest for profitability with 92.48 per cent followed by surplus from interest income (91.80%), provisions & contingencies (37.44 %), gross surplus (36.75 %), other income (35.15%), operating expenses (30.16 %), net interest margin (29.81%), interest income (21.56 %) and interest expenditure (19.42%).

The coefficient of variation during post-WTO period was the highest for surplus from interest income with 99.23 per cent followed by profitability (64.42%), gross surplus (59.48%), provisions & contingencies (56.90%), other income (47.66%), net interest margin (38.01%), operating expenses (26.89%), interest income (26.48%) and interest expenditure (22.34%).

The data presented in Table 6 showed the impact of formulating and implementing the Service Area Credit Plans by Public Sector Banks. The annual growth was between 12.5 per cent and 24.0 per cent during 2000-02 to 2003-04. The growth was spectacularly high at 54.50 per cent during 2004-05 which, however, declined to 44.60 per cent in the following year. Disbursements of credit as against targets ranged from 92.10 per cent to 117.30 per cent during the six-year period. Achievements were higher than 100 per cent only in the last two years.

Public sector banks recovery to demand under direct agricultural advance was 69.30 per cent during the year 2001 which gradually increased during the following three years. It, however, phenomenally rose to 84.10 per cent in the year 2005. During the five year period, the demand, (loan amount to be recovered) and percentage of recovery to demand have progressively increased in the successive years whereas overdue amount has increased until the year 2004 and then it steeply declined by Rs. 29,620 million in the following year.

The compound growth rates & variation of Non-performing Assets (NPAs) ratios of public sector banks in India are depicted in Table 7.

The table shows that all the ratios of Non-Performing Assets (NPAs) were found to be negative which shows a remarkable achievement in reducing the growth of non-performing assets by the public sector banks for the period 1993 to 2005. The growth rate for Gross NPAs to Assets Ratio was found to be -9.53 per cent followed by Gross NPAs to Advances Ratio (-9.50%), Net NPAs to Asset Ratio (-8.74%) and Net NPAs to Net Advances Ratio with

Table 6

Targets & Achievements Under Service Area Credit Plan and Recovery of Direct Agriculture by Public Sector Banks during 2000-01 to 2000-06

Year	*Target*	*Achievement*	*Annual Growth %*	*Demand*	*Recovery*	*Overdue*
2000-01	258,930	246,540 [95.2%]	12.5	224,290	155,400 [69.3%]	68,890 [30.7%]
2000-02	308,830	293,320 [95%]	19.0	254,610	177,580 [72.3%]	68,303 [27.7%]
2000-03	368,380	339,210 [92.1%]	15.6	289,400	210,110 [72.6%]	79,300 [27.4%]
2000-04	425,760	422,110 [99.1%]	24.4	335,440	250,202 [74.5%]	85,420 [25.5%]
2000-05	556,160	652,180 [117.3%]	54.5	351,920	296,120 [84.1%]	55,800 [15.9%]
2000-06	850,240	942,780 [110.9%]	44.6	NA	NA	NA

Note: (a) Figures in brackets under Achievements indicate % achievements of targets

(b) Figures in brackets under Recovery indicate % recovery to demand & under overdue indicate % overdue to demand

Source: *Kurukshetra*, Vol. 55, No. 12, Oct. 2007.

Table 7

Compound Growth Rates and Variation of Non-Performing Assets (NPAs) Ratios of Public Sector Banks in India during (1993 to 2005)

Particulars	*Compound Growth Rate (Percent/ annum)*	*Coefficient of Variation (%)*
Gross NPAs to Advances Ratio (GNPA)	-9.50	33.02
Gross NPAs to Assets Ratio (GNPAs)	-9.53	35.87
Net NPAs to Net Advances Ratio (NPA)	-7.91**	31.42
Net NPAs to Asset Ratio (NPAs)	-8.74**	26.69

Note: ** indicates significant at 1 per cent level of significance.

-7.91 per cent. The NPAs to Net Advance Ratio and Asset Ratio were found to be significant at one per cent level of significance.

The coefficient of variation for Gross NPAs to Assets Ratio was the highest with 35.87 per cent followed by Gross NPAs to Advances Ratio (33.02%), Net NPAs to Net Advances Ratio (31.42 %) and Net NPAs to Asset Ratio (26.69%). The reduction in NPA indicates a better performance of the banks, proper identification of borrowers, assessment, follow up and recovery were the main factors that might have contributed for this phenomenon.

Policy Implications

1. The factors responsible for the low flow of credit to the agricultural sector are poor credit delivery system, attitude & behaviour of bank employees especially in the case of subsidized loans, political interference, ineffective grievance redressal system, limited powers to the manager, low public investment in agriculture sector etc. are some of the important factors that need special attention in order to boost up the flow of credit to agricultural sector.
2. Banks are now urged to price the credit to farmers based on actual assessment of individual risk rather than on a flat rate depending on category of borrower or end use while ensuring that interest rates charged are justifiable and reasonable. This policy would go a long way in improving the credit delivery system and increasing the flow of credit to agricultural sector.
3. There is a need to create an environment through regulation, to prevent collusive behaviour among banks and conglomerate relationship between banks and non-financial groups.
4. Innovative channels for credit delivery for serving new rural credit needs should be adopted. Banks will have to simultaneously put in steps to increase deposit mobilization.
5. The better way of dealing with the problem of non performing assets is to ensure the quality of loan portfolio.

Banks have to make sustained efforts to improve the quality of credit appraisal, inspection of borrowal units and monitoring the performance of assisted units.

References

R. Radhakrishna (2008), Emerging Policy Regime for Bank Credit Delivery & Tasks Ahead-A Critical Review, *India Development Report*: 112-133.

Saghir Ahmad Ansari and Nisar Ahmad Khan (2007), Banking Sector Reforms: Achievements and Future Challenges, *Banking Finance*, 20(4):13-23.

M. Mohsin Khan (2006), Challenges for the Indian Banks in New Millennium, *Banking Finance*, 21(12): 5-14

Amrit Patel (2007), Changing Face of Rural India, *Kurukshetra*, 55(12): 3-14.

13

MICROCREDIT: A POWERFUL STRATEGY FOR ATTACKING POVERTY IN DEVELOPING COUNTRIES

P. LOGANATHAN & K. SARAVANAN

Introduction

MOST of the poor in Asia's developing countries live in rural areas, and the majority of them work in Agriculture. To lift the rural poor out of poverty, improved productivity in agriculture, which results in higher per capita output, is required. Also needed is expanding employment and income-earning opportunities in agricultural related and other rural non farm activities.

Asia achieved high economic growth in the last three decades, with the gross domestic product (GDP) of cast and South-East Asia grouping by 7 to 10% per-annum and the economics of South Asia by to 6% (IFAD 2001). The simultaneous achievement of high economics growth rates and poverty reduction would seem to suggest a positive impact of growth on poverty reduction.

The objective of the First United Nations Decade for the Eradication of Poverty (1997-2006), proclaimed by the General Assembly in its resolution 50/1 07 or 20 December 1995, is to achieve the goal of eradicating absolute poverty through national action and international cooperation. Progress on the anti-poverty front was last reported to the General Assembly in the report to the Secretary-General entitled "Observance of the International Year for Eradication of Poverty (1996) and recommendations for the rest of the Decade.

The General Assembly, in its resolution 52/194 of 18 December 1997, noted that, in many countries microcredit programmes have proved to be an effective tool in freeing people from-poverty and have helped to increase their participation in the economic and political processes of society. Among other provisions, the Assembly called upon the relevant organs, organizations and bodies of the United Nations system, in particular its funds and programmes and the regional commissions, as well as relevant international and regional financial institutions and donor agencies involved in the eradication of poverty, to explore including the microcredit approach in their programmes as a tool for the eradication of poverty. The assembly requested the Secretary-General, in collaboration with relevant organizations of the United Nations system, including funds and programmes and the World Bank, to submit to it at its fifty-third session a report on the role of microcredit in the eradication of poverty.

The World Summit for Social Development, held in Copenhagen in March 1995, also underlined the importance of improving access to credit for small rural or urban producers, landless farmers and other people with low or no income, with special attention to the needs of women and disadvantaged and vulnerable groups. Governments were called upon to review national legal, regulatory and institutional frameworks that restrict the access of people living in poverty, especially women, to credit on reasonable terms; to promoting realistic targets for access to affordable credit, providing incentives for improving access to and strengthening the capacity of organized credit systems to deliver credit and related services to people living in poverty and vulnerable groups; and to expanding financial networks, building on existing networks, promoting attractive opportunities for savings and ensuring equitable access to credit at the local level.

Role of Microcredit in Poverty Eradication

This is the first time that the Secretary-General has been requested to report to the General Assembly on the subject of micro credit. In the broader context of the international fight against poverty, the paper highlights the strengths and weaknesses of the micro lending approach, from which some conclusions about the future course of action are drawn. The report, as requested by the General Assembly, provides information from United Nations funds, programmes and agencies on their actions especially in the field.

Microcredit and Poverty of Developing Countries

Since the World Summit for Social Development the priority given to poverty eradication has grown. As stated in the previous report of the Secretary-General on the eradication of poverty (N52/573), it is now broadly accepted that robust economic growth that is labour-intensive and equitable, combined with larger outlays of social expenditures, especially directed towards the poor (now estimated at 1,3 billion people), are a winning combination in the fight against poverty.

Several factors have led to increased interest in microcredit in promoting growth with greater equity. There has been a growth in the recognition of the importance of empowering all people by increasing their access to all the factors of production, including credit. In addition, the value of the role of non-Governmental organizations in development is receiving more attention.

It is in that context that microcredit has recently assumed a certain degree of prominence. It is based on the recognition that the latent capacity of the poor for entrepreneurship would be encouraged with the availability of small-scale loans and would introduce them to the small-enterprise sector. This could allow them to be more self-reliant, create employment opportunities, and, not least, engage women in economically productive activities. Currently, there are estimated to be about 3,000 microfinance institutions in developing countries. These institution also help create deeper and more widespread financial markets in those countries.

Successes Story of Microcredit Programmes

Informal and small-scale lending arrangements have long existed in many parts of the world, especially in the rural areas, and they still survive. Good examples are schemes in Ghana, Kenya, Malawi and Nigeria ("merry-go-rounds", "esusus" etc.). They provide the rural population with access to savings within the local area and with a certain cushion against economic fluctuations, and they encourage a cooperative and community feeling. The groups formed provide joint collateral and serve as instruments for spreading valuable information that is useful for economic and social progress.

All economies rely upon the financial intermediary function to transfer resources from savers investors. In market economies, this function is performed by commercial banks and the capital markets. More widespread financial intermediation, as well as increasing depth and variety, are a hallmark of advancing development. But in many developing countries, capital markets are still at a rudimentary stage, and commercial banks are reluctant to lend to the poor largely because of the lack of collateral and high transaction costs. The poor would borrow relatively small amounts, and the processing and supervision of lending to them would consume administrative costs that would be disproportionate to the amount of lending. A study by the International Fund for Agricultural Development (IF AD) has confirmed that complicated loan procedures and paperwork, combined with a lack of accounting experience, limit poor people's access to formal sources of credit. Other reports cite the fact that commercial lenders in rural areas prefer to deal mainly with large-scale farmers.

The absence of commercial banks has led to non-conventional forms of lending. The recent/prominence given to microcredit owes much to the success of a relatively few microcredit programmes and their increasing scale. The Grameen Bank of Bangladesh, the most prominent of the successes, now reaches over 2 million people, with cumulative lending of about $2.1 billion. Similar successful examples are known in Latin America (e.g., Banco Solidario in Bolivia), less so in Africa (the Kenya Rural Enterprise Programme is a good example). Progress I has also been recorded in several transition economies, mixed in some cases. Such institutions have not only achieved a degree of success, but they have also managed to attract donor support and press attention.

These schemes are characterized by relatively small loans, a few hundred dollars at most. The repayment period is relatively short, about a year or so. Women are a major beneficiary of their activities, and the destination of the funds primarily includes agriculture, distribution, trading, small craft and processing industries. The administrative structure is generally light and the entire process is participatory in nature. The impact of microcredit lending varies widely between rural areas and urban areas.

In many developing countries, overall interest rates are relatively high to begin with, so that rates charged by micro lending schemes are quite high when the risk premium is added. Many of these micro-institutions claim a high rate of repayment. This is attributable to the informal participatory structures, which create an atmosphere in which debtors respect their obligations. While this phenomenon is certainly true of the better-run institutions, it is not possible to verify whether this is a universal feature. There is little by way of "global" research in this area, even though the literature on microcredit has proliferated in recent years.

It should be noted that although a large number of studies undertaken so far on the impact of microcredit programmes on household income show that participants of such programmes usually have higher and more stable incomes than they did before they joined the programmes, some practitioners still have reservations about the findings of those studies. Moreover, not many microcredit programmes can afford to undertake impact assessments because they are generally expensive and time-consuming. There are serious disagreements among experts on the validity of methodologies used in some of the published studies. In some cases, even the more rigorous studies have produced inconclusive results. Some studies show that there are limits to the use of credit as an instrument for poverty eradication, including difficulties in identifying the poor and targeting credit to reach the poorest of the poor. Added to this is the fact that many people, especially the poorest of the poor, are usually not in a position to undertake an economic activity, partly because they lack business skills and even the motivation for business.

In many cases, microcredit programmes have been stand-alone operations. There is now considerable consensus that lending to the poor can succeed provided it is accompanied by other services, especially training, information and access to land. An OECD study, for example, emphasized that credit needs to be supplemented with access to land and appropriate technology. But such activities require strong support from the public sector. In some of the lowest-income countries, lack of access to land is the most critical single cause of rural poverty, which dominates the poverty situation in those countries. Yet, few countries have substantial land reform programmes.

Moreover, in the proliferation of micro lending institutions, non-governmental organizations and foreign donors have played an increasing role. Non-governmental organizations vary in quality and strength. The best results are produced, research shows, when developing country Governments and non-governmental organizations work hand in hand. While donor participation can be positive, it should be noted that total official development assistance (ODA) has declined in recent years.

Recent Developments in other Countries

Over the past decade, microfinance institutions have adopted innovative ways of providing credit and savings services to the entrepreneurial poor. Two approaches have been advocated on the role of credit in poverty reduction. While supporters of the income-generation approach maintain that credit should be provided mainly to the entrepreneurial poor to enable them to finance specific private income-generating activities to increase their revenues, proponents of the so-called new minimalist approach argue that credit progammes would still be helping the poor fight poverty by giving credit to any poor person who is able to repay a loan without dictating to that person how and on what the loan should be used. Some studies have pointed out that the problem of the non-productive use of credit, as advocated by the minimalist approach, lies in the fact that by consuming rather than investing their loans, the actions of such borrowers, if imitated by other poor people, could produce a negative impact on the future growth of microcredit.

Several microfinance institutions have succeeded in reaching the poorest of the poor by devising innovative strategies. These include the provision of small loans to poor people, especially in rural areas, at full-cost interest rates, without collateral, that are repayable in frequent installments. Borrowers are organized into groups, which reduces the risk of default. These are also effective mechanisms through which to disseminate valuable information on ways to improve the health, legal rights, sanitation and other relevant concerns of the poor. Above all, many microcredit programmes have targeted one of the most vulnerable groups in society -women who live in households that own little or no assets. By providing opportunities for self-employment, many studies have concluded that these programmes have significantly increased women's security, autonomy, self-confidence and status within the household.

Asia

Microlending has progressed to the greatest extent in the Asian region. An innovative approach that has been used successfully by Grameen Bank's credit-delivery system is "peer-group monitoring" to reduce lending risk, although some studies have suggested that the reason for the Grameen Bank's high repayment rates is also partly due to the practice of weekly public meetings -at which attendance is compulsory-for the repayment of loan installments and the collection of savings. It is reported that the meetings reinforce a culture of discipline, routine repayments and staff accountability. Not all microfinance institutions use peer-group monitoring. Other institutions such as the Bank Rakyat of Indonesia, which serves 2.5 million clients and 12 million small savers, rely on character references and locally recruited lending agents in place of physical collateral.

Thailand's Bank of Agriculture and Agricultural Cooperatives serves approximately 1 million microborrowers and 3.6 million micro-savers. Newcomers such as the Association for Social Advancement of Bangladesh, with half a million clients, and the People's Credit Funds of Viet Nam, with more than 200,000 members or clients, are other examples of the potential for growth in the industry. Other institutions such as the Association of Cambodia Local Economic Development Agencies, Buro- Tangail of Bangladesh, the Self-Employed Women's Association Bank of India, and Amanah Ikhtiar Malaysia are also reported to be making good progress.

Various institutions are involved in the delivery of microfinance services. They include formal commercial banks, rural banks, cooperative institutions, credit unions and non-governmental organizations. Their methods of doing business range from Grameen Bank-style solidarity groups and institutions dealing with individual clients to self-managed self-help groups. Reports indicate that some institutions have gone beyond credit to offer insurance and other financial services. Both the Grameen Bank and the Bangladesh Rural Advancement Committee offer non-financial services, such as retail outlet facilities for products of their clients.

Latin America

In Latin America, Action International, a non-profit development agency, and its affiliates was reported to have disbursed in the past five years $ 1 billion in loans to poor micro entrepreneurs. Its first-time loans are between $100 and $200, and the overall repayment rate is above 98 per cent. Its network of 19 affiliates in Latin America and North America provides $300 million a year in loans to poor entrepreneurs (56 per cent of whom are women).Since 1987, Accion's network has grown from 13,000 to more than 285,000 active borrower clients. The six largest affiliates now provide $1 million per month in loans.

Banco Solidario of Bolivia, which has grown from a credit-providing non-governmental organization to a fully licensed commercial bank, provides financial services to 67,000 people, more than one half of the total number of clients in the entire Bolivian banking system. The Association for the Development of Micro-Enterprises of the Dominican Republic and Accion Communitarian del Peru are reported to have achieved sustainability.

Africa

In West Africa, where microfinance institutions are still in their infancy, a World Bank case study of nine micro finance programmes -the Pride, Credit rural and credit mutual de Guinee; Credit mutual du Senegal and Village Banks Nganda of Senegal; Reseau des caisses populaires and Sahel Action Project de promotion du petit credit rural of Burkina Faso; and Caisses villageoises du pays dogon and Kafo Jiginew of Mali - concluded that all nine of these programmes are very much in the mainstream of best practice in the field of microfinance. In terms of sustainable lending to micro entrepreneurs, the study gave high marks to the programmes on the following basis: all nine programmes are located near their clients and in the largest catchment areas possible; they use lending technologies that are simple, well-tailored to the cultural environment and inexpensive for both lender and client; they have employed effective techniques for obtaining high repayment rates; most include savings, which meet a critical need of many people, and they price their loans far above commercial lending rates, though not at full cost recovery.

A recent study of 11 major microentreprise finance programmes -Agency de credit pour l'entreprise privee of Senegal, Asociacion Dominicana para el Desarrollo de la Mujer of the Dominican Republic, Banco Solidario of Bolivia, Badan Kredit Desa, Bank Rakyat Indonesia and Lembaga Perkreditan Desas of Indonesia, Bankin Raya Karkara of the Niger, Corporation de Accion Solidaria of Colombia, Fondacion Integral Campesina of Costa Rica, Grameen Bank of Bangladesh, and the Kenya Rural Enterprise Programme -

showed that 10 of the programmes were operationally efficient. Five institutions were fully profitable, generating inflation-adjusted positive returns on assets. It was reported that, in 1993, the Agence de credit pour enterprise private of Senegal, Banco Solidario of Bolivia and Lembaga Perkreditan Desas of Indenosia had covered 100, 103 and 137 per cent of their costs, respectively. In view of the growing popularity of microfinance institutions, .some of which now explore the possibility of deposit mobilization of leverage commercial capital, It IS reported that bank regulators In such countries as Bolivia, Ghana, Kenya and Peru, and other countries, are creating laws or special regulations for this new breed of institutions. In Bolivia, it is reported that Banco Solidario, a private commercial micro enterprise bank, is regulated by the Superintendence of Banks, with the same financial and reporting requirements as traditional banks, but with simpler loan documentation and risk classification rules. In the case of Bolivia, which seeks to encourage new microfinancial institutions, it is reported that the Government has begun licensing a new class of intermediaries, known as private financial funds, subject to the same solvency and reserve requirements as banks, but with lower minimal capital requirements.

Recent Developments of International Institutions

One of the outcomes of recent discussion has indicated that a more coodinated and concerted international effort is required if microcredit is to spread and succeed on the scale that expectations now require. It is with that perspective in mind that the World Bank has led the process of international coordination primarily by establishing the Consultative Group to Assist the Poorest (CGAP), which brings together a number of western donor countries and international agencies. The group has ancillary structures which ensure that government organizations and borrowers in general are consulted.

CGAP, which comprises 25 members, including United Nations bodies, is a multi-donor effort to address the problems facing micro financing. The most important of these are lack of access to information, the measurement of loan delinquency, setting of interest rates, designing lending procedures and developing business projects. The objective of CGAP is to foster good donor practices, including performance standards.

With regard to the level of funding to microcredit institutions, in its first two-and-a-half-years, CGAP provided about $18 million in grants to micro finance institutions and also committed $400 million in the past three years to microfinance activities. These are relatively modest amounts. Grants have been made directly to institutions and networks of practitioners. Eligibility criteria have included the following: (a) institutions must serve more than 3,000 very poor clients, of which at least 50 per cent must be women; (b) institutions must be operationally self-sufficient and on the path to financial self-sufficiency; and (c) institutions must be on the path to mobilizing domestic commercial resources.

An important positive development from the CGAP process is that success stories and their characteristics are now much better known. To spread these best microcredit practices to different parts of the world -often under vastly varying conditions -is now the central challenge facing the international community and the developing countries.

Within the international community, many United Nations organs have now started to support microcredits, especially, under the leadership of the United Nations Development Programme (UNDP). The provision of actual financial resources is rather limited; instead, United Nations bodies have emphasized capacity-building and institutional strengthening, training and consultations to spread best practices. Under the provisions of General Assembly resolution 52/194, United Nations organs were requested to provide information on their activities, this information is contained in chapter III below.

It should. be borne in mind. that total world ODA is diminishing, and resources for United Nations bodies are under special stram. Therefore, a better use of the available resources has become a more pressing imperative. It is important that resources are channelled to sectors that have potential, especially agriculture, infrastructure and education.

It would be a pity if experimentation with new forms of development activities were to lead to a squandering of aid.

Towards Stronger Support to Small Enterprises

The discussion above suggests that if microcredit is to playa strong role in development, certain requirements need to be fulfilled. The most crucial requirement is to perceive microcredit lending as part of a comprehensive programme of support to the small enterprise sector. According to CGAP estimates, the sector already employs 500 million of the poor; it constitutes an active base for strengthening the private sector in a large number of developing countries. This would entail Governments of developing countries formulating plans and programmes to support small enterprises in general, of which microcredit should be an integral part. Furthermore, the regulatory framework should be receptive to small enterprises. Many micro-borrowers have complained of this particular shortcoming in developing countries.

There are many examples of successful interventions in the OECD countries in favour of small enterprises, the foremost among them being the United States Small Business Administration is a rather remarkable organization that is fully backed by the Government, operates through the private sector and provides the small business sector with a wide array of support services, including information and training of course, commercial rates of interest prevail in the programme).

Developing countries could benefit by instituting similar comprehensive programmes, eventually involving the private sector and, where applicable, efficient non-governmental organizations. The United Nations could provide more robust technical assistance programmes in that direction. There is a delicate balance to be struck between getting the poor eventually into the market economy and commercial lending rates on the one hand, and the importance of providing low-cost assistance to them at the initial stage of their entrepreneurship.

Targeting is a particularly thorny topic. There have been allegations that in fact the very poor are so weak as not to benefit from microlending, and that it is the "better off poor" that benefit. While all the poor need to be included in the programmes, the shortage of funds impels organizers to make special efforts to reach the less well-off among the poor. Microcredit should be viewed as complementary to the provision of basic services like education, housing, health and nutrition. The latter are indispensable in the fight against poverty.

A crucial part of any future effort should be to strengthen the administrative structures of existing microcredit institutions proliferate. It is possible that economies of scale are important in microlending. Dynamic leadership and paid management staff are probably crucial. The provision of information on available services to the poor is particularly essential. This is not at present the case, even in some advanced developing countries. Information on services for the poor is rarely made readily available.

In that context, the long-term financial sustainability of micro credit operations deserves particular attention. In the more successful schemes, repayment rates are high, but this is not so with many operations that do not have a high profile. In the absence of long-term sustainability, microcredit operations become a welfare or charity operation. While the latter have their own place in development in some circumstances, they should not characterize microcredit institutions.

Probably the single most important element in ensuring long-term sustainability of these operations is to include in them the savings mobilization function. This is not always the case at the present time. The operation that lends to the poor should also cater to their savings needs. In many developing countries, savings habits are quite widespread, but the institutional structures do not usually cater to them. The possibility of combining savings and lending operations in some form of credit union organization should always be explored. Once again, the credit union movements in the OECD countries could be emulated by developing countries.

International organizations could provide technical assistance in the setting up of frameworks for credit unions and in strengthening their management.

Donor countries have a special responsibility to ensure that financial intermediation programmes are soundly based, operate through solid local entities and involve the public sector and that monitoring is an important part of the process. To some extent, the recent prominence given to those operations is donor-driven; the responsibility on the donors is subsequently heavy. It is particularly important that donor funds, whether grants or loans, not be perceived in recipient countries as simple transfers.

Coordination among the donor countries has in fact been perceived to be weak in many settings, thus giving rise to duplicative projects and fragmentation of available institutional capability in the developing countries. The CGAP process should be greatly strengthened and directed to better donor coordination. The United Nations system can help in that process, especially at the field level. The United Nations system also needs to spread a more realistic notion of the potential of microcredit approaches, and to put them in the broader perspective of the fight to eradicate poverty.

Conclusion

Since poverty in developing countries is a gigantic problem, its sustained reduction will be crucial in achieving the millennium development Goal of having poverty eliminated by the year 2015, poverty in this sub region is basically a rural problem, as the over whelming majority of the poor lives and work in rural areas. Given he geographical and social concentration of poverty among curtains areas and groups of rural poor, it can also be agreed that rural poverty reduction efforts should focus on the less-favoured areas (remote uplands and mountains, marginal coastal areas and unreliably watered dry lands) and on socially marginalized groups such as women, and indigenous peoples.

Micro credit have become increasingly popular in the new development agenda across the globe and even more so in the developing world, because such micro credit offer income and employment opportunities. In Asian countries, there fore, micro credit is one of the more viable alternatives to create employment opportunities and consequently to reduce poverty.

How ever, government should acknowledge the social contributions of developing micro-credit. There fore, government should provide a suitable regulatory environment to promote micro lending. This should include competitive wholesale borrowing, introducing microcredit insurance systems and minimizing the restrictions on entry by the small banks serving micro-credit. The banking Institutions in low income countries normally do not pay attention to potential micro-credit clients because they do not fit into the traditional perception of what constitutes a good client.

The inability to provide clear collaterals has led the financial institutions to be believe that funding micro-credit should be charity activity or a part of the government's welfare schemes. This means banks do not use appropriate credit risk assessment of micro credit. To overcome these situations the following suggestion can be fruitful : Entrepreneurs should be equipped with training, business counseling, environmental counseling, marketing and raw material regular and strong monitoring system should be provided coupled with supporting the micro credit for sustainability.

References

International Fund for Agricultural Development, The State of World Rural Poverty: An inquiry .into Its Causes and Consequences (New York, New York University Press, 1992).

United Nations Capital Development Fund, Microfinance and Anti-Poverty Strategies, A Donor Perspective (1997).

Consultative Group to Assist the Poorest and World Bank

CGAP, "The Microcredit Summit Report", Communique Issued by the Council of Heads of State and Government at the Microcredit Summit, 1997.

A policy framework for the Consultative Group to Assist the Poorest (CGAP)-A Microfinance Programme".

FOCUS notes Nos. 1,2 and 10.

"Microfinance: The New Emerging Market?", by Mohini Malhotra, Newsletter No. 3.

"Towards Creating a Poverty-free World", by Mohammad Yunus, Newsletter No. I.

"Three Innovative Institutions in Bangladesh: BRAC, ASA and Buro-Tangail", by Gregory Chen, Newsletter No. 5.

"Strengthening Asian MFIs",by Jyita Mukherjee, Newsletter No. 5.

World Bank, "Case Studies in Microfinance, Zimbabwe: ZAMBUCO Trust" (1995) (Abstract Executive Summary).

"The Informal Sector and Microfinance Institutions in West Africa", Regional and Sectoral Studies, Leila Webster and Peter Fidler, eds. (1996).

Buckley, Graeme, "Microfinance in Africa: Is it either the problem or the solution?", *World Development*, Vol. 25, No. 7, (1997).

Currie, Anthony, "Small Lenders Count too", Euromoney (July 1996).

Development Centre of the Organisation for Economic Cooperation and Development, Microfinance for the Poor, Hartmut Schneider, ed. (1997).

Johnson, Susan and Ben Rogaly, "Microfinance and Poverty Reduction", Oxfam (United Kingdom and Ireland) and ACTIONAID (1997).

MkNelly, Barbara, and Christopher Dunford, "Are credit savings Services Effective?", A Literature and Analysis, Freedom from Hunger, Research Paper No. 1.

Mosley, Paul, and David Hulme, "Microenterprise Finance: Is there a Conflict between Growth and Poverty Alleviation?", World Development, vol.26, No.5 (1998), pp. 783-790.

United States Agency for International Development, "Assessing the Impacts of Micro Enterprise Interventions: A Framework for Analysis, Managing for Results, Working Paper No. 7 (March 1995).

14

RURAL CREDIT IN INDIA: ISSUES AND PROSPECTIVES

S. K. Dhage & B. G. Lobo

Introduction

Rural finance is primarily agricultural finance and a large part of this refers to the needs of cultivators as distinguished from processing and marketing of agricultural produce. Credit has sometime s been called the handmaid of production and finance is a crucial part for the development of agriculture. Credit is required for purchase of inputs like fertilizers and seeds, for payment of farm labour charges, and for meeting domestic expenditure of cultivator's family. Credit is also required for replacement of wasting asset on the farm and also for new capital investment. The needs have to be met in the hard way by giving unified and in some cases new direction to familiar institutions, making them work. Institutional credit is the major need of the day because it frees the cultivator from the clutches of moneylenders and enables them to obtain credit that is cheaper, systematized and productive.

The significant increase in the credit flow from institutional sources brought forth a strong sense of expectation from the public sector banks. However, this expectation could not be sustained as the emphasis throughout was on achieving certain quantitative targets. As a consequence, inadequate attention was paid to the qualitative aspects of lending resulting in loan defaults and erosion of repayment ethics, to a greater or lesser extent, by all categories of borrowers. The end result was a disturbing growth in overdues, which not only hampered the recycling of scarce resources of banks, but also affected profitability and viability of financial institutions. Ultimately, financial deepening occurred but the development impact of rural finance was blunted. In 1991 that is on the eve of reforms the rural credit delivery system was in poor shape.

The basic aim of the financial sector reforms was to improve the soundness, efficiency and productivity of all credit institutions, including rural credit institutions whose financial health was far from satisfactory. The reforms sought to enhance the areas of commercial freedom, increase their outreach to the poor and stimulate additional flows.

Issues Pertaining to Rural Credit

According to Prof. M. S. Sriram there are some important issues related to need of agricultural credit. It is evident that the needs of rural credit are not being met by a single agency. The nature of relationships is quite diverse as described below:

- Borrowing from social networks based on reciprocity; there is no appraisal, paper work or collateral. Several times these loans are interest free. This is works on unorganised social capital.
- Forming SHGS and carrying out financial intermediation through them, disproves the notion that the poor cannot save. The paperwork is minimal, collateral is absent and interest margins remain within the community. This works on the organised and formalised social capital.
- Borrowing from informal money-lenders happens when the amount is larger than what social networks can offer. This attracts a high interest, but is timely, quick and flexible. Collateral is negotiated. This disproves the notion that the poor cannot service a high interest rate loan.

- Tied Credit–loans tied to complementary non-financial transactions in land, labour and commodities. The lender deals with the borrower in a 'non-lending' capacity as well, the terms are opaque and tend to be exploitative, even though the transactions costs of borrowing are low.
- Formal financial institutions on the semi-regulated space like companies, chit funds, microfinance institutions
- Formal financial institutions with state support and patronage in the regulated space like co-operatives and banks.

The question is whether it is desirable to have one dominant source of credit for the rural areas. While it might be desirable to move the financial transactions from the informal [and possibly exploitative] sources to the formal space, the argument that it should be from a single source needs to be examined. It might not be practically possible for a single source to finance the diverse needs of the rural population.

There are emergency needs at one end and asset purchase at the other. The households straddle between multiple sources for different purposes. Moneylenders seem to be cutting all across the segments, because they are accessible.

The question is whether financial services should be available from diverse sources or limited sources. From the point of view of the customer, it is desirable to have multiple sources offering the services, so that the customer has choices. For the providers it might be good to be a single provider so that any adverse usage and excessive borrowing can be avoided. Ultimately the formal sector will have to find mechanisms of occupying a significant place in each of the need segments. For that, it is extremely important to understand the product attributes of the demand side, so that credit becomes efficient ads value.

Strategy of RBI to Increase the Flow of Credit

First, the coverage of rural credit is extended to include facilities such as storage as well as credit through NBFCs. Second, procedural and transactional bottlenecks are sought to be removed, including elimination of Service Area Approach, reducing margins, redefining over dues to coincide with crop-cycles, new debt restructuring policies, one-time settlement and relief measures for farmers indebted to non-institutional lenders. Third, Kisan Card Scheme is being improved and widened in its coverage while some banks are popularizing General Credit Cards (GCCs) which is in the nature of clean overdraft for multipurpose use, including consumption. Fourth, public and private sector banks are being encouraged to enhance credit-delivery while strengthening disincentives for shortfall in priority sector lending. Fifth, the banks are urged to price the credit to farmers based on actual assessment of individual risk rather than on a flat rate depending on category of borrower or end-use while ensuring that interest-rates charged are justifiable as well as reasonable. In brief, the thrust is on enhancing credit-delivery in a regime of reasonable credit-prices within the existing legal and institutional constraints.

Reserve Bank's Initiatives Towards Rural Credit

Reserve Bank of India Act, 1934 envisaged a special developmental role for the Reserve Bank in the sphere of agricultural credit with responsibility, in particular, for financing seasonal operations and the marketing of crops.

The Rural Banking Enquiry Committee (Thakurdas Committee, 1950) stressed the importance, for an efficient system of agricultural finance, of a sound co-operative credit structure capable of developing close relations with the Bank. The Reserve Bank followed up the Rural Banking Enquiry Committee with the informal conference. Following the conference's recommendation, the Reserve Bank decided to organise a Rural Credit Survey and constitute a Standing Advisory Committee on Agricultural Credit.

The All-India Rural Credit Survey, commissioned in August 1951, covered seventy-five districts around the country. Eight villages in each were chosen for the survey, which was based on a sample of fifteen households from each of the selected villages, with a view to recommend practicable policies for the future on rural credit. The survey was completed during November 1951-July 1952, under the committee of Direction, headed by A. D. Gorwala. Dr. D. R. Gadgil was one of members of the committee. The Report was submitted in August 1954.

The survey was struck by the utter insignificance of co-operatives in providing rural credit. 'Positive and deliberate' measures rather than 'small administrative, functional or other changes' were required to ensure the success on co-operative credit institutions and enable them to become self-supporting. The State's tendency in the past had been to 'over-administer and under - finance' the co-operative movement, but the Report pointed out the need for an integrated system of co-operation and rural credit. The Report envisaged a key role for the Reserve Bank of India in coordinating the proposed network of co-operative institutions and for its Agricultural Credit Department in over seeing their functioning. The Reserve Bank would occupy a 'strategic position' in the co-operative credit sector, while other principal participants would play a major role in rural co-operation, *viz.*, co-operative economic activity and the training of co-operative personnel.

Since cooperative credit institutions depended on the banking system for a number of services, there was a need for positive State association with a defined sector of commercial banking. The Report thus recommended the creation of the State Bank of India through the statutory amalgamation of the Imperial Bank of India and the major State associated banks to undertake an expeditious programme of banking expansion, particularly in the rural areas. The Reserve Bank was expected to manage the Imperial Bank's passage to State ownership.

The Reserve Bank prepared a draft-bill, approved by the Board in February, 1955, which among other things, authorised it to make long-term loans to State Governments to subscribe to the share capital of co-operative institutions and to central land mortgage banks, and set up the proposed special funds. The bill also provided for a third Deputy Governor to have exclusive responsibility of rural credit. The bill was passed into law on May 8, 1955. The National Agricultural Credit (Long-term operations) Fund was created in 1955 and the Reserve Bank was authorised to specify from time to time, the purposes for which, it would make medium-term loans. Over the years such loans were made to finance a wide range of investments relating to the rural sector. The State Bank of India was created in July 1955 in order to give a boost to direct flow of funds of the banking system into certain neglected, but important, sectors of the economy such as agriculture and allied activities and spread banking facilities in rural areas. The flow of funds to the rural sector increased over the years. However, the demand for productive investment in the rural sector was not fully met.

In 1960, the Committee on Co-operative Credit (Vaikunth Lal Mehta Committee) advised examining the possibility of using P. L.480 funds to finance long-term productive investment in agriculture. Consequently, the Reserve Bank and the Government began to think to create a specialised agency to finance agricultural investment. It was thought that the demand for agricultural credit might require the establishment of some specialised institutions, which would ultimately relieve the Reserve Bank of its function so far as rural finance and agricultural credit was concerned. The Agricultural Refinance Corporation Bill, 1962 received the President's assent in March 1963. The Corporation under the chairmanship of D. G. Karve, the then Deputy Governor, started its operation in Bombay on July 1, 1963. The Corporation took up a wide range of activities of the rural sector for refinance/direct loans/ subscriptions to fully guaranteed debentures of eligible institutions covering central land mortgage banks, State cooperative banks, scheduled commercial banks (share holders of the corporative), and co-operative societies under the approval of the Reserve Bank.

The High-Yielding Varieties Programme (or HYVP) was launched during *Kharif* 1966-67, as part of the new agricultural strategy towards achieving self-sufficiency in food by 1970-71. The Bank, for its part, assured the State Governments that the programme would not be allowed to suffer. Special credit limits would, if necessary, is sanctioned to co-operative banks.

However, the demand for credit was poor and was found to be mainly due to cultivators' resistance to new practices, lack of proper motivation and orientation amongst extension staff, and reduced operational efficiency of central co-operative banks and primary societies.

In July 1966, the All India Rural Credit Review Committee (Venkatappiah Committee) was formed to review the progress made in the supply of credit for intensive agricultural production and marketing from all the institutional sources including commercial banks, working of the crop loans system, progress of rural branches of commercial banks and coordination between different agencies involved in rural credit. The Committee submitted its report in July 1969 and admitted that co-operatives would have to be strengthened but it had no hesitation in highlighting that they should be all the better and the farmer would be better served, if other institutions coexisted with them in healthy competition. In other words, the adoption of the multi-agency approach as the most feasible and appropriate response to the credit requirements of agriculture and allied activities was recommended.

The adoption of 'social control' as a policy measure in 1968 helped the Reserve Bank to motivate the commercial banks into the area of agriculture and rural credit on a significant scale. The National Credit Council, constituted in December 1967 recognised the importance of the commercial banks' role as complementary to co-operative initiatives.

The nationalisation of the 14 major commercial banks in July 1969 helped the orientation of commercial banks lending policies and procedures to meet the requirements of the priority sectors of the economy with due to attention to the financing needs of the small farmers. The multi-agency approach covered the Lead Bank Scheme, which provided, boost to the improved flow of funds to agriculture sector through the organised credit channels. Agriculture sector got the place of importance in the priority sector lending. Realistic targets for deposits for central cooperative banks were attempted. The borrowing needs, consequently from the Reserve Bank were met at differential rates of interest (concessional rate usually being a few basis points below the Bank rate). By mid-1977, the scheme of financing primary agricultural credit societies was in operation in 12 States, 24 commercial banks through 604 branches had taken over 343 societies for financing, however, over the years, it was found that the experience with the working of the scheme was in general not satisfactory.

In the context of the large finance gap, the commercial banks, Regional Rural Banks (RRBs) and co-operatives were deeply concerned during late 1970s. The system of district credit plans was introduced to meet the credit needs by different agencies. The commercial banks were geared up to fulfill priority sector targets and the target was raised to 40 per cent of their outstanding advances by March 1985. Another target was the attainment of 60 per cent of credit deposit ratio by the banks by March 1985 in respect of rural - semi urban branches separately.

The Reserve Bank of India appointed a Committee to Review Arrangements for Institutional Credit for Agriculture and Rural Development, chaired by B. Sivaram, former Secretary of the Ministry of Agriculture, Government of India in 1979. The report was submitted in 1981 and recommended the setting up of a National Bank for Agriculture and Rural Development (NABARD). The NABARD came into existence in July 1982. All major rural credit related works from the Reserve Bank of India were shifted to the NABARD. Works relating to the urban-cooperative banks remained with the Reserve Bank. A new Department as Rural Planning and Credit Department (RPCD) was set-up in the Reserve Bank, to look into the broad rural credit policies of the Reserve Bank as a part of over all monetary management of the economy for price stability with sustainable growth of the economy.

The Reserve Bank so, far devoted its attention to provide necessary credit to rural sector for boosting agricultural growth directly and indirectly through many institutions. It might be indicated that the Reserve Bank of India provided short-term and medium term loans to State co-operative banks, for agricultural production and marketing activities.

Post-Reform condition of Rural Credit

After peaking to over 35,000 in 1993, the number of rural bank branch offices steadily declined thereafter, coming down to around 30,000 in 2006. The share of these offices in total bank branches peaked in 1990 (58 per cent) and steadily declined thereafter to under 45 per cent in 2006. As we saw above, especially between 1977 and 1990, branch expansion exploded in unbanked regions, while declining in already banked locations. After 1990, exactly the opposite started to happen. Mergers and swapping of rural branches, rather than expansion, became the norm. The number of RRBs that rose to 196 by 1990 had fallen to 104 by 2006. A concerted effort was made to reduce the total number of loan accounts. They steadily fell from the peak figure of 659 lakh in 1991 to 524 lakh in 2001, before increasing once again. Private Banks have increased their share in both credit and deposits from around 4 per cent in each in 1990 to around 18-19 per cent in each in 2005.

The profitability of public sector banks has improved following liberalisation. Total non-performing assets (NPAs) of public sector banks as a proportion of total advances have declined. But the share of rural credit has fallen continuously from the peak of 15.3 per cent in 1987 to 8.4 per cent in 2006. The share of rural deposits has also fallen steadily from its peak of 15.5 per cent in 1990 to 10.8 per cent in 2006. The sharp rise in rural credit in 2004-06 will hopefully lead to a trend reversal in these shares. The rural credit deposit ratio of commercial banks fell from a peak of nearly 69 per cent in 1984 to just 41 per cent by the end of the 1990s. It has also risen sharply in the last two years. But it remains well below the levels in the 1980s. The incremental credit-deposit ratios have fallen even more sharply–for rural bank branches from over 60 per cent in the 1980s to under 35 per cent in the 1990s; for semi-urban branches, from nearly 49 per cent in the 1980s to 30 per cent in the 1990s.

This decline in credit-deposit ratios has been the worst in the already underdeveloped regions. The intensity of banking had historically been the lowest in these regions but they benefited greatly from the social banking period of the 1970s and 1980s. However, the post-reform period shows that public sector banks have increasingly opted for investment in risk-free returns of government securities, their share in total earning assets rising from 26 to 33 per cent during the 1990s. This trend has been reversed in the 21st century. 27 But there is no doubt that the enforcement of stringent prudential norms, capital adequacy stipulations, setting up of the Board for Financial Supervision (BFS) and pressure to reduce NPAs have made banks so risk averse that they have reduced their exposure to private loans with even a modest risk of non-recovery. The rise in interest rates in 2006-07 has been seen as showing an "utter disregard for the development needs" of the Indian economy, with "adverse repercussions for medium and small borrowers", while rendering "in a nonchalant manner, large proportions of bank credit to cash-rich corporate at below prime lending rates".

Future Prospectives

In above background, as Dr. Y V. Reddy said the agenda for future consists of five parts. First, there is a need for legal and institutional changes relating to governance, regulation and functioning of rural cooperative structure and Regional Rural Banks who have to be critical instruments for rural credit in future. In this regard, it is useful to note the nature of competition and accountability to shareholders governing the functioning of commercial banks which would make their foray into rural credit predominantly subject to commercial considerations. The changes warranted in cooperatives as well as RRBs involve deep commitment of state-governments and have significant bearing on political economy. Thus, the current thrust to improve credit–delivery may soon face limits unless the legal and institutional changes are agreed upon and acted upon in good faith in a timely fashion. It is the fervent hope of RBI that a consensus will develop soon on these fundamental changes that are essential for achieving the broad policy objectives.

Second, there are overhang problems of non-performing loans and erosion of deposits in both cooperatives and RRBs.

There is some assessment of magnitudes of losses and capital needs in RRBs while in the case of cooperatives the data are not yet firm. It may not be appropriate to continue to permit institutions that are not solvent to seek and accept public deposits and hence RBI favours early restructuring and recapitalisation. There is an inevitable fiscal impact of any scheme of recapitalisation which has to be transparent and has to bear all the costs of overhang issues as well as capital adequacy to assure continued solvency and safety of public deposits in future. Such a one-time fiscal support is justifiable, urgent and essential for several reasons, including that "There Is No Alternative" and delayed response could end up being more expensive. The current acceleration in credit-delivery can be sustained in the medium term, if such fiscal support from States and Centre is firmly put in place soon to revive or reorganize rural cooperative structure and RRBs.

Third, there is a need to foster credit culture to make enhanced rural credit a lasting phenomenon. A benign credit-culture is one which encourages appropriate credit price, credit-delivery under transparent conditions of lenders' as well as borrowers' liabilities and incentives for repayment rather than default. Measures that counter such a benign credit culture are often well-intended, but as the experience so far has shown they tend to be seriously counter productive. There is a need for a consensus in this regard, so that, rural credit system in India is compatible with our goals of higher growth and better equity. In this regard, it is necessary to recognise that expansion of credit in some of the States which have low credit-deposit ratio depends on credit culture capturing factors relating to governance and commercial viability..

Fourth, on the critical issue of risk-mitigation, it is held that experiments with crop or credit-insurance in India have not been very satisfactory so far. In fact, many farmers argue that where compulsory insurance is resorted to, it increases the burden of borrowing from institutional sources and once the transaction costs are added, the overall costs exceed the Prime Lending Rates significantly. There are several risks that a farmer faces, and of these future price and monsoon conditions are most severe and almost entirely beyond the control of the farmer. While Minimum Support Price is a mechanism that has served us well, its cost-effectiveness is subject to debate and in any case the coverage is limited to cereals like rice and wheat and in some areas cotton. The farmer faces the risks of monsoon conditions and usually the adverse climatic conditions are widespread in a geographical area, with the result severe limits are set on private-insurance. The issue of strategy to reduce risks as one of the four major areas of long-term planning (in 1993) but they covered only water conservation, venture capital and insurance promotion, where viable. Perhaps, it is necessary to recognize that if some elements of insurance are not viable, extending credit becomes more risky and hence constrained.

Finally, in the light of the above, there is merit in considering a comprehensive public policy on risk-management in Agriculture, as not only a means of relief for distressed farmers but as an ingredient for more efficient commercialized agriculture. The components of such a policy have to be worked out in detail, but illustratively, the public-policy could consider some of the elements described here. First, establishing a well articulated, objective and independent assessment of impact of adverse monsoon conditions and appropriate relief to farmers on an assured basis. Second, facilitating farmers to assure themselves of a price for all their products before harvesting, or even sowing the seed, through a well regulated network of Forward, Futures and Options markets. Third, establishing and implementing liability of suppliers for any shortfall in quality or assured supply in vital inputs such as seeds, pesticides, power and water. Fourth, gradually eliminating and replacing price-subsidies with outlays on risk mitigation for farmers in the broadest sense and Fifth, positioning flexibility in extending rural credit within a broad framework of such a comprehensive public policy on risk-management in Agriculture.

Conclusion

In spite of the commendable expansion of branch network and progressive policy initiatives, large number of rural population continue to remain outside the formal banking system for a variety of demand and supply side reasons and constraints. From the experiences gained from the success of the SHG-Bank linkage programme and other micro finance initiatives in India and abroad, it has been established that interfacing NGOs and other socially conscious organizations/persons between the banks and the ultimate customers would prove rewarding in the philosophy of "Financial Inclusion".

The arrangements suggested are expected to be substantially beneficial to both the demand and supply sides. The rural customers shall benefit by increased access to composite financial services in a relatively hassle free manner, inclusion of those in remote and resource scarce regions/ areas into formal system, significant reduction in borrower level transaction costs in view of doorstep/near doorstep availability of services, and better understanding of their needs by empathetic functionaries of outreach entities engaged by banks. The difficulties involved in bringing large numbers of amorphous entities under an expensive central regulatory framework, its impracticality and cost involved in effective supervision and follow-up also weighed in favour of this recommendation. In the meantime, the Group considered it desirable that the non-deposit taking MFIs may attempt self regulation by forming State level associations to evolve code of ethics, uniform standards of accounting practices and disclosures, empanel and train auditors, etc. with the assistance of NABARD and SIDBI.

Several support systems such as institution and use of funds from the Micro finance Development and Equity Fund, the National Micro Finance Information Bureau, the Rural Banking Technology Development Fund, and policy options and regulatory relaxations in regard to permission to engage Business Correspondents, FDI norms, promotion and development of MFIs harnessing the capabilities of apex level organizations like NABARD, SIDBI, and associations of MFIs have been recommended.

References

Chandrashekhar, C. P. and S. K. Ray (2005), 'Financial Sector Reform and the Transformation of Banking' in V. K. Ramachandran and M. Swaminathan (eds).

Chakrabarty Tapas Kumar (2004), Paper Presented at the National Seminar on "Markets and Institutions–An Indian Experience in Nineties" at the Planning Commission's Centre for Research in Planning and Development, Department of Economics, M.S. University, Baroda, in February.

EPW Research Foundation (2007), 'Need for Calibrated Policy in Interest Rates and Credit', *Economic and Political Weekly,* February 24.

Mohan Rakesh (2006), Agricultural Credit in India–Status, Issues and Future Agenda. *Economic and Political Weekly,* Vol. 41, No. 12, pp. 1013-1021.

Reddy Y. V., Governor (2004), Reserve Bank of India at a Seminar on "India's Economic and Social Development-National and International Perspective" at ASCI, Hyderabad on November 16.

Reserve Bank of India (2006), Quarterly Statistics on Deposits and Credit of Scheduled Commercial Banks: March.

Sarkar, J and P Agarwal (1996), 'Banking: The Challenges of Deregulation', India Development Report, IGIDR, Mumbai.

Shetty, S. L. (2005), 'Regional, Sectoral and Functional Distribution of Bank Credit' in V. K. Ramachandran and M Swaminathan (eds).

Sriram M. S. (2007), The Paper Presented at the National Symposium on Farm Credit for Inclusive Growth, College of Agricultural Banking, Reserve Bank of India. Pune: January 12-13.

15

CHANGING SCENARIO OF RURAL CREDIT IN INDIA

S. K. DHAGE & B. G. LOBO

Introduction

THERE are several concerns in relation to rural credit which are generally expressed in terms of inadequacy, constraints on timely availability, high cost, neglect of small and marginal farmers, low credit-deposit ratios in several States and continued presence of informal markets. It is held that while the commercial banks are more focused in improving efficiency and profitability, they have tended to give comparatively less priority to rural credit. Regional Rural Banks (RRBs) and Co-operatives appear to face serious problems of governance as well as operational efficiency. It is argued that most part of the Co-operative Credit structure is multi-layered, under capitalized, over-staffed and under-skilled, often with mounting non-performing assets while in a few cases resulting in erosion of public deposits as well. Many of the RRBs also appear to share most of these problems, though there are some vibrant and viable institutions in this category. These problems relating to rural credit have been well documented and several policy-approaches were made to remedy the situation. However, there is some element of dissatisfaction that overall situation in regard to rural credit is not improving to the desired level inspite of such a series of actions. It is a matter of concern that cognizable success is eluding the policy-makers, at a time when increasing commercialization warrants a big thrust in institutional credit to agriculture. There is thus a discernible widespread intellectual recognition that while immediate measures are undertaken to increase the flow of credit to agriculture, there is a need to review the policy of rural credit in a comprehensive and thorough manner.

Need of Rural Credit

It is well known that the burden of indebtedness in rural India is very great, and that despite major structural changes in credit institutions and forms of rural credit in the post-Independence period, the exploitation of the rural masses in the credit market is one of the most pervasive and persistent features of rural life in India. Rural households need credit for a variety of reasons.

They need credit to meet short-term requirements of working capital and for long-term investment in agriculture and other income-bearing activities. Agricultural and non-agricultural activities in rural areas typically are seasonal, and households need credit to smoothen out seasonal fluctuations in earnings and expenditure. Rural households, particularly those vulnerable to what appear to others to be minor shocks with respect to income and expenditure, need credit as an insurance against risk. In a society that has no law of free, compulsory and universal school education, no arrangements for free and universal preventive and curative health care, a weak system for the public distribution of food and very few general social security programmes, rural households need credit for different types of consumption.

These include expenditure on food, housing, health and education. In the Indian context, another important purpose of borrowing is to meet expenses on a variety of social obligations and rituals. If these credit needs of the poor are to be met, rural households need access to credit institutions that provide them a range of financial services, provide credit at reasonable rates of interest and provide loans that are unencumbered by extra-economic provisions and obligations.

Historically, there have been four major problems with respect to the supply of credit to the Indian countryside. First, the supply of formal sector credit to the countryside as a whole has been inadequate. Secondly, rural credit markets in India themselves have been very imperfect and fragmented. Thirdly, as the foregoing suggests, the distribution of formal sector credit has been unequal, particularly with respect to region and class, caste and gender in the countryside. Formal sector credit needs specially to reach backward areas, income-poor households, people of the oppressed castes and tribes, and women. Fourthly, the major source of credit to rural households, particularly income-poor working households, has been the informal sector. Informal sector loans typically are advanced at very high rates of interest. Further, the terms and conditions attached to these loans have given rise to an elaborate structure of coercion–economic and extra-economic–in the countryside.

That these constitute what may be called the "problem of rural credit" has been well recognized; recognized, in fact, in official evaluations and scholarship since the end of the nineteenth century. Given the issues involved, the declared objectives of public policy with regard to rural credit in the post-Independence period were, in the words of a former Governor of the Reserve Bank of India, "to ensure that sufficient and timely credit, at reasonable rates of interest, is made available to as large a segment of the rural population as possible" The policy instruments to achieve these objectives were to be, first, the expansion of the institutional structure of formal-sector lending institutions; secondly, directed lending, and thirdly, concessional or subsidized credit. Public policy was thus aimed not only at meeting rural credit needs but also at pushing out the informal sector and the exploitation to which it subjected borrowers. Rural credit policy in India envisaged the provision of a range of credit services, including long-term and short-term credit and large-scale and small-scale loans to rural households.

Main Problems of Rural Credit System

There is considerable unmet demand for rural credit. Local money-lenders continue to provide credit to the rural families, as the reach of institutional agencies to weaker sections has remained poor. Meeting the credit needs of 25 million nonfarm informal sector enterprises continues to be a challenge to the rural financial institutions (RFIs). Though the coverage of micro-finance scheme has expanded, still around 70% of the poor are out of this network. The micro-finance sub-sector of institutional credit has not explicitly targeted the agricultural sector. RFIs have bypassed tenants and sharecroppers. More than 60% of the farm families are yet to receive the Kisan Credit Cards.

The rate of interest charged by RFIs from farmers is considerably higher than that charged by financial institutions from urban marginal farms, which are nonviable or viable at the margin, and the self-employed in the informal sector. Despite an understanding reached between the Indian Banks. Association and the government in the presence of the Reserve Bank of India (RBI) that crop loans will carry single-digit interest; banks were reportedly charging 12% to 14% interest.

On the supply side, RFIs are under stress, particularly since the financial sector reforms of 1992-93. Commercial banks view rural financing as costly and cumbersome. Their transaction costs are high at an estimated 6% to 7% of loans advanced. One reason for these high transaction costs is the corporate culture of these banks. To bring down costs, they are focusing on selected clientele of large borrowers. The bank staff is not motivated to go to rural branches. Many commercial banks have closed nonviable rural branches because of rising nonpaying assets and the high cost of rural lending. . Up to the middle of the 1980s, regional rural banks (RRBs) enjoyed a cost advantage vis-à-vis the commercial banks but by the late 1980s they lost this advantage. Their transaction costs have also now gone up to 6% or 7% of advances. They are too strongly tied to their sponsor banks and have little freedom of operation.

Cooperatives, though their scale of lending and reach to rural areas is outstanding, work more as channels of credit than banks. Their efforts to mobilize deposits are inadequate. Even otherwise, the depositors in cooperative banks have no safeguards. There are three main problems with cooperative RFIs. First, their financial position is precarious. Some time ago, the government had sanctioned Rs. 15,000 crore for recapitalization of cooperative banks but on second thought the matter was referred to another committee (A. Vaidyanathan). Second, a three-tier hierarchy and absence of de-layering comes in the way of rural lending. Third, excessive bureaucratic control and politicization has compromised their democratic character and efficient functioning.

This apart, widening of the scope of the priority sector has affected agricultural lending. The RFIs linkages with input supply or output marketing institutions have remained weak. With the scheme, commercial banks have tended to park funds under RIDF rather than direct lending for agricultural purposes. There is also a problem of inter-regional differences in the reach of RFIs. In the north-eastern states, the network of RFIs is relatively weak. The micro-finance program is also concentrated in a few states.

Another problem is of delays in processing loan applications, particularly by commercial banks. It has been reported that during 2003-04, the commercial banks received 746,696 loan applications, sanctioned only 451,458, and made actual disbursement to only 419,995 applicants. Matters were reported to be even worse during 2004-05.

Rural Credit Facility during the Reform Era

Prior to the banking sector reforms rural banking and rural credit supply were mandatory on financial institutions. The rural banking sector suffered from severe non-payment of debts, which deteriorated the financial viability of the institution. The banking sector reforms, to correct the anomalies in the system, have substantially changed the institutional arrangement for rural credit. The organised financial sector in

India is either unable or unwilling to finance a range of activities that are of crucial importance both for growth and development. Agriculture, unorganised manufacturing and many types of infrastructure are instances of such sectors. Recent financial sector reforms have naturally focused primarily on improving the viability and stability of financial institutions. New institutions such as rural based micro-credit agencies are fast replacing the traditional credit providers.

Credit availability being a key factor in helping the poor to escape poverty it is of vital importance to explore the possibilities of reaching credit to the poor, especially to the rural poor. One of the fundamental problems faced by the poor is the inability to provide collaterals for credit accessibility.

Success of Institutional Credit

After the creation of NABARD, attempts were diverted effectively to consolidate the multi-agency flows of funds to the rural sector for generating effective use of funds to the growth of the agricultural sector It would be useful to indicate the dynamics of the gross domestic product contributed by the agriculture and allied activities over a long period. Rural income in nominal terms increased significantly over the years of latest three decades.

National Rural Credit (Stabilisation) Fund and National Rural Credit (LTO) Fund were earlier designated as National Agricultural Credit (Stabilisation) Fund and National Agricultural Credit (LTO) Fund, respectively, and were maintained by the Reserve Bank of India prior to the formation of NABARD on July 12, 1982. These Funds were transferred to NABARD on September 10, 1982. Balance as on August 14, 1981 was Rs. 1025 crore in NRC (LTO) Fund and Rs. 365 crore in NRC (stabilisation) Fund. However, NABARD's resources are augmented by the line of credit from the Reserve Bank of India–the facility which was enjoyed by the Agricultural Refinance and Development Corporation (ARDC), before the creation of NABARD.

The Reserve Bank's assets in the form of loans and advances to State co-operative banks were Rs. 306 crore in 1971 and raised to Rs. 891 crore in 1982. After the creation of NABARD, financial needs of State co-operative banks were mainly attended by the NABARD. Some flow of credit to the state co-operative banks from the Reserve Bank of India however, continues. In 1983, loans and advances outstanding to the State co-operative banks were only Rs. 57 crore and over the years, the amount declined to nil in 1998 before rising further to Rs. 35 crore in 2002.

RBI's loans and advances outstanding to ARDC/ NABARD were Rs. 95 crore in 1976 and increased significantly to Rs. 1,152 crore in 1983. The outstanding loans and advances of NABARD increased to Rs. 6,500 crore in 2002.

Institutional credit (direct and indirect credits from co-operatives, Scheduled Commercial banks, RRBs and Rural Electrification Corporation) for agriculture and allied activities increased many folds during the last three decades. Loans outstanding (short-term and long-term) were around Rs. 2,235 crore at the end of 1971-72 and increased to Rs. 8,252 crore at the end of 1979-80. During this period, institutional credit to rural sector increased by around Rs. 4,580 crore on an annual basis. At the end of 1980-81, loans outstanding were around Rs. 10123 crore and increased to Rs. 35,353 crore at the end of 1989-90. On an annual average, loans outstanding increased by Rs. 21,156 crore. At the end of 1990-91, loans outstanding were around Rs. 37,408 crore and increased to Rs. 10, 9816 crore at the end of 1999-2000. On an annual average basis, loans outstanding increased by Rs. 69,777 crore. On annual average basis, loans outstanding increased by 15 times during 1971-72 to 1999-2000 (Table 1).

It is observed that till 1970-71, cooperatives had virtually a monopoly in meeting agricultural credit needs of the farmers in India. From the data plotted for years 1997-98 to 2003- 04, it is seen that the total institutional credit for the 1997-98 was Rs.31,956 crores and this figure for 2003-2004 year was Rs.80,000 crores. This gives an average increase of more than Rs.8000 crore per annum. It is also marked that due to advent of commercial and rural banks into the credit market, the overall percentages of credit supply through cooperatives were decreasing from 44 per cent (1997-96) to 37 per cent (2003- 04). Accordingly, the rate of credit supply by commercial banks are increasing from 50 per cent (1997-98) to 55 per cent (2003-04).The share of RRBs in credit supply is limited to 6% (1997-98) to 8 per cent (2003-04). As per the credit requirement estimates, the short term credit supply is always more in comparison to medium term and long term supply. It is nearly 70:30 per cent for cooperatives, 55:45 for commercial Banks and it is 3:1 in RRBs.

Table 1
Institutional Credit For Agriculture and Allied Activities (Rs.crore) (Rounded figures)

Year	*Loans outstanding*
1971-72	2,235
1974-75	3,539
1979-80	8,252
1980-81	10,123
1984-85	19,035
1989-90	35,353
1990-91	37,408
1994-95	66,346
1999-2000	1,09,816

Note: *Institutions cover co-operatives, scheduled commercial banks, Regional Rural Banks and Rural Electrification Corporation Ltd. Loans outstanding cover short-term and long-term credit direct as well as indirect.*

Source: *Handbook of Statistics on the Indian Economy, RBI, 2002-03.*

Success of Microfinance

It is into this vacuum created by the withdrawal of the state in rural credit that microfinance has entered. Both the NABARD and RBI define microfinance as the "provision of thrift, credit and other financial services and products of very small amounts to the poor enabling them to raise their income levels and improve living standards". Two broad approaches characterise the microfinance sector in India self-help group (SHG)-bank linkage and microfinance institutions. The SBL is the larger model and is unique to India but the internationally more established MFI model is the one that appears to be the increasingly favoured route.28 The SBL approach dates from the NABARD initiated pilot of 500 SHGs in 1992. NABARD has had a key role to play in initiating and nurturing India's unique SBL programme. It was largely responsible for the RBI including Linkage Banking as a mainstream activity of banks under "priority sector" lending in 1996. NABARD's work with its partner NGOs also led to the government according "national priority" to the programme in the union budget of 1999. Beginning as a pilot in 1992 with 500 SHGs, by March 2006, over 22 lakh SHGs had been provided with bank loans. They covered over 3 crore households and had disbursed Rs 11,398 crore to their members 29 In comparison, the loans outstanding of 162 MFIs in India were estimated to be around Rs. 1,600 crore in March 2006.

Observations about Rural Credit in India after Reforms

The slower growth in institutional finances through commercial banks, credit cooperatives, RRBs and LDBs, particularly during the decade of 1991-2000, and poor performance thereafter is mainly due to adverse environment created by the financial sector reforms. As pointed out by Mujumdar (1999), the new policy regime of financial sector reforms has grossly neglected the rural credit delivery system. Due to unfavourable policy framework, the entire rural credit delivery system encompassing rural branches of commercial banks, cooperative credit institutions and RRBs is reduced to a moribund state, while lauding the financial sector reforms also felt that the exaggerated importance given to developing institutions has resulted in "putting the core issues of the financial system, like improving the rural credit delivery system, on the back- burner". He criticized the blind dependency on market forces, irrespective of their macro-economic implications. He has also shown concern for the shrinking flow of financial resources to agriculture, both in terms of investment and working capital. In fact, the public investment in agriculture is reported to be declining. Between 1992 and 1997, only 8 per cent of the total public investment went to agriculture, and the actual investment in this sector fell about 40 per cent short of the planned level.

With a view to revive the agricultural credit delivery system, there is need to tackle twin problems facing the system, viz., growing NPAs with falling CD ratios and poor recovery performance of RFIs, aside from adopting innovative approaches like linking of Self-Help Groups (SHGs) and Non-Government Organizations (NGOs) with mainstream financial institutions. Such linkages are reported to have not only reduced transaction costs but also ensured better repayment performance. One of the recent studies conducted in Maharashtra has shown cent per cent recovery of loans through SHGs despite having excessively high rates of interest (24-36 per cent per annum) on their loan advances (Kshirsagar and Shah, 2002).

Since the new generation lending institutions like SHGs have shown lower transaction cost and higher rate of recovery despite excessively high rates of interest on their loan advances, it is imperative for credit cooperatives and commercial banks to study the mechanism of new generation lending institutions in terms of their pattern of loan recovery and interest rate structure. These groups are also reported to have favourably impacted the social and economic status of their members.

As for the rural credit scenario, one of the recent welcome developments has been the establishment of the Rural Infrastructure Development Fund (RIDF) instituted by NABARD with the objective of advancing loans to state governments and state-owned corporations for hastening ongoing projects, mainly those related to medium and minor irrigation, soil conservation, watershed management.

Conclusion

The philosophical base for financial sector reforms is derived fro macro economic perspective along ignoring the macroeconomics of development which is at the heart of rural credit. the investigation in macroeconomics of development is led in the recent years the elaboration of what is called institutional economics which takes a bottom up approach of economic development and reform.

The new generation lending institutions like SHGs show high rate of recovery despite excessively high rates of interest on their loan advances. They also show lower transaction cost as compared to other lending institutions. This makes it necessary for credit cooperatives and commercial banks to study the mechanism of new generation lending institutions in terms of their pattern of loan recovery and interest rate structure. The in-house studies conducted earlier have clearly shown lower transaction costs and higher recovery performance of SHGs. These groups are also reported to have favourably impacted the social and economic status of their members.

Further, the RFIs of Maharashtra are also seen to be beset with high levels of NPAs or overdues. There is, therefore, a need to take more stringent and cohesive measures for recovery of loans from chronic and heavy defaulters. In brief, in order to rejuvenate rural credit delivery system, the twin problems facing the system, viz., high transaction costs and poor repayment performance, need to be tackled with more fiscal jurisprudence reserving exemplary punishment for willful defaults, especially by large farmers. In fact, insofar as the rural credit delivery system is concerned, the focus should be on strategies that are required for tackling issues such as sustainability and viability, operational efficiency, recovery performance, small farmer coverage and balanced sectoral development.

References

Bardhan, Pranab (2001), "Social Justice in the Global Economy", *Economic and Political Weekly*, Feb. 3-10.

Gulati, Ashok and Seema Bathla (2002), 'Institutional Credit to Indian Agriculture: Defaults and Policy Options', *Occasional Paper-23*, NABARD, Mumbai.

Mujumdar, N. A. (1999), 'Reviving Rural Credit', *EPW*, June 19-25, p. 1577.

NABARD (2000), Task Force on Supportive Policy and Regulatory Framework for Micro Finance in India.

Puhazhendhi, V. and B. Jayaraman (1999), 'Rural Credit Delivery: Performance and Challenges Before Banks', *EPW*, January 16, pp. 175-182.

Ramchandran V. K. & Swaminathan Madhura (2004), Paper to be presented at the International Conference on 'The Agrarian Constraint and Poverty Reduction' organised by the International Development Economics Associates (IDEAs), Ethiopian Economic Association (EEA), and CODESRIA Addis Ababa, December 17 to 19.

Rangarajan, C. (1996), 'Rural India, The Role of Credit', Reserve Bank of India Bulletin, May: Bombay: Reserve Bank of India.

Reddy Y.V. (2006), The first Smarajit Ray Memorial Lecture delivered by, Governor, Reserve Bank of India, organised by the Andhra Pradesh Mahila Abhivruddhi Society, Hyderabad on December 16, 2006 at Hyderabad.

Reserve Bank of India (1999), Report on Micro Credit, Micro Credit Special Cell.

Reserve Bank of India (2002-03), Handbook of Statistics on the Indian Economy.

Thamarajakshi, R. (1999), 'Agriculture and Economic Reforms', *Economic and Political Weekly*, Vol. XXXIV, August 14-20, p. 2293.

16

IMPACT OF INSTITUTIONAL CREDIT ON THE RURAL ECONOMY OF KARNATAKA: A CASE STUDY OF KOLAR GRAMEENA BANK

V. Muniraju & V. Ramakrishnappa

Introduction

India is a land of villages with nearly 65 per cent of the population live in rural areas. Rural economy is backbone of Indian economy and agriculture is the main occupation of the rural families. However, modern agriculture is requires farm technology includes the use of improved seeds, fertilizers, pesticides, insecticides, irrigation and intensive use of agricultural inputs. These inputs, though facilitate higher yields require heavy investment, which the majority of the farmers cannot afford because of their poor economic base. The farmers in under developed countries cannot expect their capital needs to come from savings, because their income from farm operations is barely sufficient to provide minimum necessities of life. On the other hand, rural households are also engaged in non-farm activities for their livelihood. Hence, the farmers have to depend to a large extent on institutional and non-institutional agencies for external finance to perform farm and non-farm activities. Under these circumstances, rural credit assumes greater importance in the rural economy of India.

Various credit cooperatives, commercial banks and rural banks are by far the major financial institutions engaged in meeting the capital requirements for diversified activities and developing the rural economy of the country. The rural credit system comprises of about 30 state cooperative banks and 369 district central cooperative banks (DCCBs) with 13,635 branches, one lakh primary agricultural credit societies (PACS) and 196 regional rural banks (RRBs) with more than 12,000 branches spread throughout rural India. In addition to these exclusive rural bank networks, about 30,000 rural and 14,000 semi-urban branches of commercial bank branches form institutional credit (Reddy, 2006; GoI, 2008). Non-institutional credit agencies like traditional moneylenders, shopkeepers, input dealers, agents and relatives etc. The historic all India rural credit survey (AIRCS) carried out in 1954 confirmed that formal credit institutions provided less than 9 per cent of rural credit needs in India. Moneylenders, traders and rich landlords accounted for more than 75 per cent of rural credit. However, the NSSO report (59th Round) on Situation Assessment Survey of Farmers during 2003 reveals that of the 89.33 million farmer households, 48.6 per cent were indebted. Total debt of farmer households was estimated at Rs.1.13 lakh, of which Rs.65,000 crore was from institutional agencies and Rs.48,000 crore from non-institutional agencies. The institutional credit accounts for about 57.5 per cent of total rural credit needs and the remaining 40 per cent of rural credit gets taken care of by non-institutional sources like traditional moneylenders, shopkeepers and relatives.

Evolution of an effective institutional credit structure, which can meet the credit needs of the rural economy, has been one of the objectives of the credit policy in India. The Reserve Bank of India as the central bank of the country has been following a policy of encouraging the development of institutional credit structure in rural areas. With the adoption of the multi-agency approach for institutional rural credit, co-operatives, commercial banks and regional rural banks (RRBs) have been functioning simultaneously in rural credit dispensation. The RRBs have become the third component of the multi-agency credit system for agriculture and rural development in the country. The main objective of these is to strengthen the rural economy by providing credit for the development of agriculture, trade, commerce, industry and other productive activities in the rural areas. Credit is essential for small and marginal farmers, agricultural labourers, artisans, small entrepreneurs and other weaker sections for productive purposes at their door-steps with lower rate of interest. The experience of Grameen Bank in Bangladesh shows that rural credit has an effective in helping poor people to use their own efforts and creativity to meet their basic needs (Yunus, 2004). In this background, the case study attempts to assess the impact of regional rural bank of Kolar Grameen bank (KGB) on rural economy with special reference to Kolar district of Karnataka.

Objectives and Methodological Framework

The objectives of this paper are to: (i) to examine the pattern of distribution of credit by Kolar Grameen Bank across different sections of the rural poor.; (ii) to evaluate the impact of institutional credit on different economic status of borrowers; (iii) to analyse the repayment performance among borrowers.

The study was conducted during 2001-02 and is confined to three taluks from Kolar District. A multi-stage stratified random sampling procedure was adopted to select samples for evaluating the objectives of the study. In the first stage, Kolar Grameena Bank was purposely selected for an in-depth analysis. The six branches from Kolar Grameena Bank have been selected based on backward and forward criteria at second stage. Finally, 200 beneficiaries from different branches were selected. A simple random sampling technique was adapted in the selection of beneficiaries in order to provide equal opportunity to all beneficiaries. A complete list of the beneficiaries who borrowed credit from respective branches of Kolar Grameena Bank has prepared separately and was classified into four groups viz., (a) Those availing crop loan, (b) Agricultural labourers, (c) Artisans and small scale industries and (d) Trade and business. The study is largely based on primary data and pre-tested interview schedule was employed to collect the information and data. Simple statistical techniques such as mean, cross tabs were utilsed and a linear regression model was fitted in order to find out the factor influencing the repayment of loans.

Kolar district, popularly known as the land of 'silk and milk' is located in the southern region of the State of Karnataka. It belongs to the semi-arid drought-prone region of the state and lies between 77° 21' to 78° 35' east longitude and 120 46' to 130 58' north latitude, extending over an area of 8,225 km². The district is bounded by the districts of *Bangalore Rural* and *Tumkur* on the west; on the north, by *Anantapur District,* on the east by *Chittoor District* of *Andhra Pradesh* and on the south by *Krishnagiri* and *Vellore* of *Tamil Nadu*. Total population of the district according to 2001 census was 25.36 lakh of which 75 per cent were lived in rural areas. The major sources of employment are *agriculture, dairy* farming, *sericulture* and coolie. Farmers in the district are totally dependent upon bore well water for *irrigation* and *drinking*. There are 216 rural bank branches in the district. Canara Bank is the major term lending institution and has 11 banks of Primary Agricultural & Rural Development Bank. Kolar Grameena Bank is having a network of 50 branches in rural, 10 branches in semi-urban and one satellite branch in Kolar district. These institutional agencies are engaged in delivering the credit for farm and non-farm activities in the district.

Distribution of Respondents by Social Groups

The two hundred sample households of the KGB have been classified into different groups on the basis of their socio-economic characteristics like caste, occupation, land ownership, value of assets owned and income. The sample households were classified into 4 major caste groups viz., forward castes, backward castes, scheduled castes and schedules tribes. The groupings were done in such a way as to represent the status of a household in the social hierarchy. The shares of different caste groups in the total loans obtained from KGB are given in Table 1. It can be seen that both forward and backward caste groups have received more than proportionate share in the total loans borrowed from KGB. The forward and backward caste households which constitute nearly 72 per cent of the total sample and remaining 28 per cent were belongs to ST and SC groups. The results clearly indicate that the loans of KGB have gone mainly to those households who are in the higher social hierarchy.

Table 1

Classification of Borrowers According to Caste Groups

Caste Groups	*No of households*	*Percentage*
Forward caste	70 (35.00)	43.08
Backward caste	74 (37.00)	46.09
Scheduled caste	48 (24.00)	8.85
ScheduledTribe	8 (4.00)	1.98
Total	200 (100.00)	100.00

Note: Figures in brackets are percentages to total.

Occupation of the Sample Households and Amount Borrowed:

The sample households were classified into four groups on the basis of their occupation. The main occupation here is defined as one which contributes the major share of family's annual income. The four major groups of occupation are: cultivators, agricultural labourers, artisans and industry and trade and business. The distribution of loans from KGB across households classified by their main occupation is given in Table 2. It may be seen that 43 per cent of the total loans of KGB has gone to households who are cultivators and who belong to the landed category.

Table 2

Share of Different Occupation Groups in the Loans of KGB

		KGB loan	
Occupation	*No of house-holds (per cent)*	*Percentage share*	*Average in Rupees*
Cultivators	84(42.00)	43.03	48,178
Agricultural labourers	48(24.00)	5.39	10,566
Artisans & industry	20(10.00)	12.41	58,375
Trade&Business	48(24.00)	39.16	76,736
Total	200 (100.00)	100.00	47,025

Note: Figures in brackets are percentages to total.

Among different occupational groups, the cultivator households constituting about 42 per cent of the total sample have received 43 per cent of total loans. The households having trade and business as their main occupation have received 39.16 per cent of loans which is more of their proportion (24.00 per cent) in the total number. The artisans and industry households have received 12.4 per cent of loans which is more or less equal to their proportion (10 per cent) in the total number. For the agricultural labour group, the proportion of loan received (5.39 per cent) is far below their proportion (24 per cent) in the total number of households. When one looks at the average loan received from KGB by different occupation groups of households, those belonging to the category of trade and business could draw a highest average loan amount (Rs. 76,736), followed by artisans and industry owners (Rs. 58,375) but the cultivator category stood third, with average loan amounting to Rs. 48,178 (Table 2). The category of agricultural labour stood last in this respect also and drew a far lower average loan amount as compared to other three groups.

Purpose-wise Distribution of KGB Loans Across Sample Households

The sample households were borrowed credit from KGBs for farm and non-farm activities, which help to promote a particular type of economic activity and improve their economic conditions. The purpose wise utilization pattern of KGB's loans is shown in Table 3. The cultivators were utilised the credit for overall development of agriculture with respect

Table 3
Proposes of Credit Across Occupation Groups

Occupational group	*No. of Borrowers*	*Purpose*
Cultivators	84	a. Crop loans
		b. Irrigation loans
		c. Cart & Bullocks
Agricultural labourers	48	a. Animal Husbandry
Artisans (small scale industry)	20	a. Small scale industry
Artisans (Trade & Business)	48	a. Trade & Business
Total	200	

to irrigation facility, seeds, fertilizers, pesticides and cart and bullocks which make more profitable. The agricultural landless labourers are preferred animal husbandry activities and artisans were chosen business and service sector.

Impact of KGB Credit on Different Economic Status of Borrowers

The main objective behind providing credit is to improve economic conditions of the borrowers in their income, employment and consumption. Here, we assessed the impact of KGB's credit on the sample households.

Impact of KGBs Finance on Incomes

The bank finance has brought out changes in the incomes of farmers, agricultural labourers, artisans and trade and business persons which in turn would lead to higher consumption, employment and asset levels. Incomes generated in pre-loan period and post-loan periods by different categories of sample beneficiaries, are presented in Table 4. The table shows that the annual average income per household in the pre-loan period was the highest at Rs. 56,402 for farmer beneficiaries followed by trade and business (Rs. 54,305), artisans and industrialists (Rs. 46,950), while it was and lowest at Rs. 8,999 for agricultural category beneficiaries. Similarly, the annual average income per household in the post- loan period was the highest at Rs. 71,394 for trade and business followed by Rs. 59,449, for farmers Rs.55101 for artisans while it was again the lowest at Rs.9647 for agricultural labourers.

Table 4

Impact of KGB Loan on Income of the Borrowers Across Occupation

(Rs/per family/year)

Occupational group	*Before loan*	*After loan*	*Difference*	*Percentage increase*
Cultivators/Farmers	56402	59449	3047	5.40
Agricultural labourers	8999	9647	648	7.20
Artisans & Industry	46950	55101	8151	17.36
Trade & Business	54305	71394	17089	31.47
Total	166656	195591	28935	61.43

The annual average income difference between pre- loan and post-loan periods was the highest in the trade and business category with an amount of Rs. 17,089 followed by artisans (Rs. 8151), farmers (Rs. 3047) and it was the lowest for agricultural labourers (Rs. 648). The percentage of increase in income in the post-loan period was the highest (31.47 per cent) for trade and business, followed by artisans and industry (17.36 per cent), agricultural labourers (7.20 per cent) and the lowest (5.40 per cent) for the farmer, category beneficiaries.

It can be concluded that the trade and business category got highest benefit through finance provided by KGB. The main reasons behind the success of the trade and business is proper utilization of the loan. The farmer beneficiaries got the minimum benefit from the finance provided by KGB. The main reason for the low performance as revealed by the beneficiaries were insufficient irrigation facilities and lack of working capital for cultivation.

Impact of KGB Loan on Employment of Sample Households

An attempt is made to analyze the impact of the KGB loans on employment generation by different categories of beneficiaries. Since poverty and unemployment in rural areas go side by side additional employment will lead to higher income and consumption among the rural people who are living on or below poverty line. The details of employment generated after the utilization of the loan amount are shown in the Table 5. It showed that the employment after availing the loan from the KGB has increased. The highest number (760 man days) of man days with 12.47 per cent increase was observed in the case of artisans and industry, followed by 11.58 per cent in respect of agricultural labourers, 7.88 per cent in the case of farmers and 6.14 per cent with regard to trade and business. Artisans and industries category got more employment due to more efficient use of the loan in enlarging the working base and thereby generating more output. This lead to the demand for more labor and hence there was an increase in the mandays generated in this category. The employment generated was the lowest in the case of beneficiaries who availed credit under trade and business category.

Table 5
Impact of KGB Loan on Employment Generation Across Sample Households

(man days/family/year)

Occupational group	*Before loan*	*After loan*	*Difference*	*Increase (Per cent)*
Cultivators/Farmers	3818	4119	301	7.88
Agricultural labourers	4285	4781	496	11.58
Artisans & Industry	6095	6855	760	12.47
Trade & Business	12098	12841	743	6.14
Total	26296	28596	2300	38.07

Impact of KGB loans on Consumption of Sample Households

The levels of consumption during pre-loan and post-loan periods by different categories of sample beneficiaries were examined. Table 6 clearly indicates that the annual average consumption per household in the pre-loan period was highest at Rs. 18,332, for farmer beneficiaries followed by agricultural labourers (Rs. 15,323), artisans (Rs. 11,953) and it was lowest at Rs. 11,802 for trade and business beneficiaries. The annual average income per household in the post loan period was the highest at Rs. 26184 for farmer beneficiaries followed by agricultural labourers (Rs. 26,183), artisans (Rs. 15,646) and it was the lowest at Rs. 15598 for trade and business. However, the annual average difference between pre-loan and post-loan period consumption was the highest for the agricultural labourers category with an amount of Rs. 10860 followed by farmers Rs. 7853, trade and business Rs. 3796 and the lowest was for artisans with an amount of Rs. 3693.

Table 6
Impact of KGB Loan on Consumption

(Rs./family/year)

Occupation group	*Before loan*	*After loan*	*Difference*	*Increase (Per cent)*
Farmers/Cultivators	18332	26184	7853	42.84
Agri. Labourers	15323	26184	10861	70.88
Artisans &Industry	11953	15646	3693	30.89
Trade &Business	11802	15598	3796	32.17
Total	57410	141022	83612	145.64

It can be concluded from the foregoing analysis that among the beneficiaries who have availed KGB credit, agricultural labourers achieved the highest increase in consumption. The main reason for this was perhaps lack of precautionary savings on their part and their extremely low per capita consumption prior to raising loans.

Repayment Performances of KGBs Credit Borrowers

One of the main indicators of the success of an institution's credit programme in terms of quality of service provided and the extent of its economic impact, is the loan repayment performance of its borrowers. Indian rural credit system has been plagued for long by the problem of overdues. All credit institutions, irrespective of their organizational nature, be it cooperatives or commercial banks or RRBs, are facing this problem. The repayment performance is measured here mainly in terms of the percentage of loan repaid to the actual amount due at the time of field work under. The amount due includes the principal and the interest on it. The data on loan amount due and the actual amount paid by the borrowers were collected from the KGB branch's ledgers and the same were cross checked with the borrowers of the sample households at the time of field work.

Repayment Performance by Different Socio-economic Groups

An attempt was made to analyze the repayment performance and behavior of sample households belonging to different socio-economic groups. For this purpose the socio-economic classification of sample borrowers on the basis of caste, occupation, value of durable assets owned, and income is adopted here.

The repayment performance and behavior of the sample households belonging to different groups under each of the socio-economic categories is measured here in two ways:

1. The percentage of repayment to the principal amount borrowed from KGB by each group and
2. The percentage of households under each group having regular repayments over the years.

All households were considered as a regular repayers if they had been repaying loans borrowed from KGB regularly over the years. All the households who have borrowed from KGB for the first time and whose loan had not yet become due for repayment were excluded for this purpose. The repayment performances of borrowers across caste and occupational groups have been shown in Table 7 and Table 8.

Table 7
Repayment Performance of Different Caste Groups

Caste Groups	*Percentage of repayment to principal amount*	*Percentage of households having regular repayments*
Forward Caste	46.48	81.42
Backward Caste	38.83	85.13
Scheduled Caste	37.65	75.00
Scheduled tribe	60.62	87.50
Average	42.09	81.50

Table 8
Repayment Performance of Different Occupational Groups

Occupational group	*Percentage of repayment to principal amount*	*Percentage of households having regular repayments*
Farmers	72.00	71.43
Agricultural labourers	71.78	89.58
Artisans & Industry	45.79	98.00
Trade & Business	40.48	85.42
Average	42.09	81.50

Regarding the caste-wise repayment (Table 7), the repayment performance (as measured in terms of percentage of principal dues repaid and percentage having regular repayment), declines as one moves from the highest to lowest group. Of course, the ST caste groups' repayment performance was far better than all other caste groups as well as average repayment. The forward caste households showed a higher repayment performance in terms of percentage of principal amount dues paid (46.48 per cent), Backward caste, stood first in regular repayment (85.13 per cent). On the other hand scheduled caste households showed a very low repayment as well as regular repayment performance (37.65 per cent and 75.00 per cent respectively).

Occupational-wise analysis indicates that (Table 8), the farmers and agricultural labourers showed a higher repayment performance then others. The repayment performance of artisan constituted about 45.79 per cent, followed by trade and business (40.48 per cent). While the artisan households have made highest 98 per cent of regular repayment, farmer households, made only 71.43 per cent.

Factors Influencing the Repayment of Loans

In order to understand the factors which influence the repayment of loans borrowed from KGB, a multiple linear regression model was used. The model basically tries to find the extent of influence of various economic and non-economic factors on the repayment of loans. The model specification and the explanation of the variables included are given below,

$$Y = a + b_1X_1 + b_2X_2 + b_3X_3 + b_4X_4$$

where

Y = proportion of amount repaid to the actual amount due

X_1 = Proportion of loan diverted for non-productive purposes

X_2 = Delinquency of loan repayment. If yes, then value is 1, otherwise 0

X_3 = amount borrowed

X_4 = private borrowings. If yes then value is 1, otherwise 0

The results of the multiple linear regression are given in Table 9. All the explanatory variables except the delinquency of loan repayment have the expected signs. The coefficient of determination (R^2) was found to be very low (0.156) but it was statistically significant. The individual coefficients were also statistically significant. The proportion, of loan deviation was found to have negative influence on the proportion of loan repayment and was statistically significant, one unit increase in the proportion of loan deviation would reduce the proportion of loan repayment by 28.04 units. This is quite possible because, with an increase in deviation of loan amount, the actual loan amount used for productive purpose will be reduced, thereby having negative effect on the returns generated, thus the borrower has a very little amount to repay the loan.

Table 9
Factors Influencing Repayment of KGB Loans

Factors	*Coefficients*	*Standard error*
Constant	43.77*	3.003
X_1	-28.04*	6.955
X_2	+16.63*	4.984
X_3	-0.000074*	0.0000001
X_4	11.98**	4.828
R^2	0.156*	-

* significant at one per cent level.
** significant at five per cent level.

The delinquency of loan repayment has positive effect on the repayment of loans, this relationship is rather puzzling and is not found to be of usual relationship. The actual amount borrowed had a very little effect on proportion of amount repaid. This is quite possible since the repayment of loan is generally independent of the magnitude of the loan amount borrowed.

From the foregoing analysis of the repayment performance of sample households by the socio-economic characteristics it is possible to infer that the households in the higher socio-economic groups had repayment performance than those at lower levels.

Conclusions and Policy Issues

Based on the analysis of the study the following conclusions drawn regarding the credit borrowed by the households from RRB of Kolar Grameena Bank. The households in the upper strata have received the major share of KGB's loans as compared to those in the lower strata. It may therefore be inferred that the success of the RRB selected for the study as a reform in the field of institutional credit was found to be limited, as its functioning has benefited mainly the well-off borrowers as compared to the rural poor for whom it is basically meant.

There is no doubt that Grameen Bank has had a very positive impact on rural economy. The bank loans have made a positive, though impact on the borrowers' income, employment and consumption. Across different socio-economic groups, it is the households at the lower levels of such groupings who were having relatively low or poor repayment performance. The observed low economic impact of the loans borrowed mainly under government sponsored schemes coupled with the negative attitude was found responsible for low repayment performance of these households, whereas the households in the higher socio-economic strata showed relatively better repayment performance. This was mainly due to their understanding of the need for regular and prompt repayment in order to have regular access to a cheap source of credit.

The rural credit system should strive for greater people's participation in the rural development process from the stage of credit planning to the stage of recovery of loans. This would enable proper identification of credit needs and establish viability of credit program. In addition, banks should also associate themselves with reputed non-governmental organisations and self-help groups in the process and utilise their services for successfully implementing the credit programme. Besides, these banks should also participate in the extension of education programmes for the rural people as to provide them information about the new technology and the banking facilities offered by them.

Comprehensive animal and crop insurance schemes are necessary for the effective deployment of institutional credit. Effective supervision and monitoring of credit are necessary for ensuring optimum utilization of loans.

References

GoI (2008), Economic Survey 2007-08, Ministry of Finance and Economic Division, New Delhi.

NSSO (2005), Situation Assessment Survey of Farmers Indebtedness of Farmer Households NSS 59th Round (January–December 2003), National Sample Survey Organisation, Government of India, Report No 498 (59/33/1).

Reserve Bank of India, (1954), *All India Rural Credit Survey*, Reserve Bank of India, Mumbai.

Reddy, A . Amarender (2006), "Productivity Growth in Regional Rural Banks", *Economic and Political Weekly*, March 18, 2006, pp. 1079-1086.

Yunus, Muhammad (2004). "Grameen Bank, Microcredit and Millennium Development Goals", *Economic and Political Weekly*, 39(36): 4077-4080.

17

MICRO CREDIT— A RAY OF HOPE FOR POVERTY ALLEVIATION IN INDIA

Pushpa Sinha & Ratna Mitra

Credit is a term, which has, became the key word of the modern capitalist economy. It has changed the whole outlook of the modern business and even the life of the rural India. The developing countries like India is also in need of credit.

Development is a process, which is always accompanied by change aiming at the socio-economic transformation of the present society into a modern one, which is greatly influenced by human beings. Development is generally followed by the socio-economic change. When a country is passing from one stage of development to another stage than the whole structure of the economy undergoes a change so the rural development is an important dimension of these change. Without it the objectives of the government in relation to development cannot be achieved.

India lives in her villages and India could develop only when her village could more forward. Indian villages are dependent upon agriculture even after more than six decades majority of the labour force earns their livelihood from agriculture and are fully depended upon it with the increasing population the burden on the land is also increasing. The poor farmers are becoming poorer because of sub-division of the already small parts of land. As a result of it there is problem of credit which forces them to borrow money from the non-institutional sources who use to change from them exorbitant rate of interest, but they had no way out because it provide them with ready availability of cash without any formalities, apart from it they do not use to get loans for consumption purpose from the banks.

Rural indebtedness goes on increasing and it is one of the major handicaps in the way of bringing about required improvements in the process of economic development of India. Another important reason for rural indebtedness is due to the ancestral debts, which usually pass on from father to the son, and the process goes on continuing.

Rural development is a broader concept, which includes various parameters right from social welfare to removal of rural poverty. Rural development has emerged as a strategy designed to improve the economic and social life of a specific group of people, the rural poor. It involves extending the benefits of development of the poorest among those who seek a livelihood in the rural areas. It includes optimum utilization of the natural and human resources of a given rural area for the enrichment of the quality of its population. Rural development is a process through which collective efforts, aimed at improving the well-being and self realization of people living outside the urbanised areas.

Rural development however is a very difficult task in a state like Bihar. The socio-economic profile of the people in the state is very low. Various facilities like irrigation; electrification, transport, communication, health and education, which are all necessary infrastructure, are not adequate. There are very less opportunities for other alternative sources of employment.

For many Indian farmers, it is incuetable to incur debt within every stage of the agricultural process. In order to help the agricultural industry in India, the government has enforced a minimum support price for helping the farmers but they being the most lowest income group to meet their desperate need of immediate cash, most farmers resort to and selling their output to the middlemen, who buy it below the MSP.

In India, access to credit remains another significant challenge for low-income households. Typically the poor access credit through the informal sector where monopolistic practices frequently occur and interest rates are exorbitant. In addition to the outright discrimination poorer households live in remote regions have hardly any assets and are viewed as being 'unprofitable' by formal institutions.

Presently NABARD, Commercial, Cooperative Development and Regional Rural Banks as well as number of Primary Agricultural Credit Societies represent India's banking system. The main source of institutional credit for farmers is agricultural co-operative societies, which charges lower interest rate but the loan recovery rate within these societies is low. This had led to a decrease in the number of loans provided and stricter collateral requirements for approval such as a steady stream of cash flow for borrowers and a minimum level of assets. As access to formal credit gets more difficult, the farmers choose private lenders or what we call non-institutional sources of credit due to quick cash transactions and minimal conditionality of those who can get formal credit for every Rs. 100 borrowed, Rs 80 goes towards servicing old loans. The National Sample Survey Organization (NSSO) found in its recent survey that 48.6 per cent of rural farm households were indebted which could be higher for districts facing the crisis. Roughly 80 per cent of the farmers are previous defaulters and thus ineligible to apply for fresh loans. A fact-finding team from India's Planning Commission found that the current outflow of credit was insufficient and the gap between need and availability was filled by private moneylenders who completely sized all profits.

Poverty is a well-known socio-economic problem in most of the developing countries. What is needed is to develop mechanisms to access knowledge about the financial services by reaching the people of the grassroots level. They need financial help for permanent solution of their problem. Finance perse is not the solution. Such information and guidance can best be delivered by appropriate mechanisms. If such effective mechanisms are put in place they in turn reinforce the demand for credit while attempting to reach the hitherto excluded sections through a campaign mode is a laudable initiative. The reality of Indian banking still remains on one hand there is a high skewedness in financial assets in favour of urban households. The RBI figures also indicate that 85 commercial banks concentrated in urban centers account for 78 per cent of India's financial assets which co-operative banks and regional rural banks account for only nine per cent and three per cent respectively. This explàins to some extent the rural retrogression in phenomena such as farmers' suicide.

Here is the role of that micro credit is suppose to play in the developing economies where in reality their is great need of credit. Micro is the extension of very small loans (micro loans) given to the unemployed, to the poor entrepreneurs and to others living in poverty who are not considered bankable. These individuals lacks collateral steady employment and verifiable credit history and therefore cannot meet even the most minimal qualifications to gain access to traditional credit.

Micro credit is a part of microfinance, which is the provision of a wider range of financial services to the very poor. Micro credit is a financial innovation which originated in Bangladesh where it has successfully enabled extremely impoverished people to engage in self employment projects that allow them to generate an income and in many cases begin to build wealth and exit poverty.

The credit of introducing and innovating the concept of micro loans goes to the Nobel prize winner of Bangladesh Muhammad Yunus who changed the life of millions of Bangladeshis. Grameen Bank started is today lending about $ 800 million a year with average loan size of almost $ 130, the bank has 7 million borrowers 97 per cent of them women and an unmatched 98 per cent loan repayment rate. The father of micro-credit Yunus says that the target clients of micro finance are those who has less, small loans are granted to the small entrepreneurs, to whom the normal banks never grant loans to the poorest of the poor who have no collateral. What so ever ninety seven per cent of the borrowers are women. There is no banking secrecy at Grameen Bank. All banking transactions are conducted in public. All our borrowers are the owners of this Bank. The Grameen Bank has to date lent more than 7 million loans to clients, people without any collateral and has a 98 per cent repayment rate. Muhammad Yunus states that they ever give loan to the beggars. He said that they are going from house to house to beg in the same manner. They can also go from house to house offering something, a product and the result was incredible, they have lot of ideas.

What is Micro Credit

Thus we can define micro-credit as provision of thrift, credit and other financial services and product of very small amount to the poor in rural, semi urban and urban areas for enabling them to raise their income levels and improve living standards. Micro credit institutions are those, which provide these facilities.

The reform of the interest rate regime has constituted an integral part of the financial sector reforms initiated in our country in 1991. In consonance with their reform process, interest rates applicable to loans given by banks to the micro credit organizations or by the micro credit organizations to the Self-Help groups/member beneficiaries has been left to their discretion. The interest rate ceiling applicable to direct small loans given by banks to individual borrowers however continues to remain in force. Banks have been given freedom to formulate their own lending norms keeping in view the ground realities. They have been asked to devise appropriate loan and savings products and the related terms and conditions including size of loan, unit cost, unit size, maturity period, margins etc. Such credit covers not only consumption and production loans for various farm and nonfarm activities of poor but also include their other credit needs such as housing and shelter improvements.

Micro credit is based on a separate set of principles, which are distinguished from general financing or credit. Micro-credit emphasizes building capacity of micro entrepreneurs employment generation, trust building and help to the micro entrepreneur on initiation and during difficult times. Micro-credit is a root for socio-economic development. For Indian economy Micro-credit is of great importance Micro credit is extended by the SHGs that to Self-Help groups and the co-operative linkages.

Self-Help Group

A Self-Help Group (SHG) is a registered or unregistered group of micro entrepreneurs having homogenous, social and economic background, voluntarily coming together to save small amounts regularly. They mutually agree to contribute to a common fund and to meet their emergency needs on mutual help basis. The group members use collective wisdom and peer pressure to ensured proper end use of credit and timely repayment thereof. Infact peer pressure had been recognized as an effective substitute for collaterals.

An economically poor individual gains strength as part of a group besides financing through SHGs reduce transaction costs for both lenders and borrowers. While lenders have to handle only a single SHGs account intends of a large number of small sized individual accounts, borrowers as a part of a SHG cut down expenses on travel (to and from the branch and other places) for completing paper work and on the loss of workdays incanvassing for loans.

NGO

Non-governmental organization (NGO) is a voluntary organization established to undertake social intermediation like organizing SHGs of micro entrepreneurs and entrusting them to banks for credit linkage or financial intermediation like bulk funds from banks for on lending to SHGs.

The government policy in India has further strengthened these public movements. NABARD an apex development bank cum agency focusing on rural and agricultural development has been a great focus to promote micro credit through these linkages. Government of India vide their notification dated August 29,2000 have included Micro-credit/Rural credit in the list of permitted non-banking financial company (NISFC) activities for being considered for Foreign Direct Investment (FDI)/Overseas Corporate Bodies (OCB)/Non-Residents Indians Investment to encourage foreign participation in micro credit projects. This covers credit facility at micro level for providing finance to small producers and small micro enterprises in rural and urban areas.

Micro finance providers in India can be classified under three broad categories, formal, semiformal and informal. The formal banking sector constitutes the first category while the semi-formal group consists of a variety of MFIs and SHGs. Informal providers on the other hand are not legal entities and include moneylenders and various social net works. Presently semiformal and informal lenders dominate the sector.

The Target Group

Micro lenders are not established merely through the need of poor people but by the decision making of donors who first identify a social or developmental objective such an objective usually makes reference to the need of credit amongst a specific group of people. On broad terms we all think of the beneficiaries of micro credit as 'poor' or 'dis-advantage'. However there are important sub-divisions, and there may be problems in reaching the target group.

Some lenders specifically target micro credit at women. Women are usually seen as economically less independents than men in the same social group and benefits from their economic empowerment are argued to extend more directly to their children. Therefore women are often seen as more desirable lenders from a social equity point of view than men and there is a large number of micro lenders who explicitly aim at women empowerment.

Another important group at which micro-credit is sometimes targeted are young people with high youth unemployment and insufficient job creation by the formal sector. Hence creating a perspective along with income earning opportunities is seen by some lenders and donors as a priority. Alternative target groups may comprise rural people because they are seen as unable to benefit from development and employment creation in cities and town. Much of the debate about micro credit takes place under the title of rural finance, although the two are not necessarily the same.

Targeting specific sections of the population has not only social but also economic implications. There are two sides of it, first different groups may be variably efficient in utilizing micro loans in creating viable enterprise and second different groups typically have different repayment pattern. Thus impacting on the sustainability of micro lenders. Therefore the social desirability of lending to a specific group of people does not imply financial sustainability of lending to them.

In most credit schemes it is found that women are better repayers. They pay more punctually and they default less often than men. Hence the targeting of women is not only socially desirable but also makes economic sense.

Reaching the rural poor is difficult; it is expensive to maintain outreach structures in rural settings with poor infrastructure and low population density. Some researchers agreed that the higher social stability in rural communities aids the reliability of financial relationship. Similar considerations must be applied to any other potential target group that may be identified.

But the most important part is that the lender must decide how to reach a target group. Some lenders restrict their service to women or youth or to the rural communities. Others structure a programme so that it primarily appeals to their intended target group but does not exclude other. Men should not be excluded, it will lessen the viability of such schemes.

Micro-credit is often associated with small business development. However money is fungible and small business are often practically parts of private house holds. Therefore micro credit may find its way into financing projects that the lender is acute unaware of. However the question should be considered whether credit should be targeted at all specific activities. Some credit schemes do not seek to target their loans to any specific use. They assume that poor people themselves know best how to better themselves and that some apparently consumptive expenditures may well have investment properties.

Why Micro Credit

The multiplier theory occupies are important place in modern economic theory. The basic concept of multiplier says that the effect of investment on income, output or employment is manifold than the original increase in investment. The same can be distinctly demonstrated in a credit programme for the rural poor through the continuous expansion of their economic base. Income also rises if borrowings from banks are being channelised for productive purpose i.e. the borrowings are invested for further addition to be made in the process of production. The vicious cycle of low-income low savings low investment- Low income- Can be broken with the injection of credit in the cycle. "Credit intended for more investment- More income- more savings- more investment- More income" is the result that is sought through the credit intervention. It is assumed that those who save and those who borrow are two different groups of people. Savers put away deposits in bank while borrowers go to the bank and borrow the savings of others at price. However a saver can himself be on investor as is usual case of the poor.

The impact of micro-finance on the different sectors of the economy can be under stood with the help of following diagram.

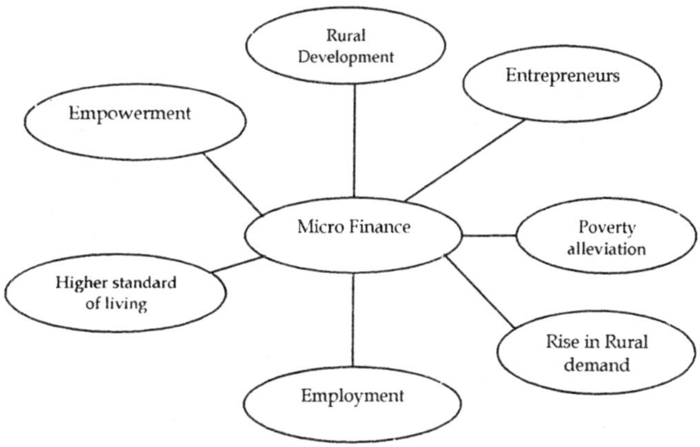

It is evident that micro-finance can improve the livelihoods of poor and low income people and helps the poor people to have access to savings, credit, insurance and other financial services so that they are able to cope up with everyday demands more resiliently and confidently. Besides with the help of micro credit poor people can set up their over micro-enterprises and thereby help in eradicating poverty by providing a regular source of livelihood creating jobs, allowing children to go to school, enabling families to obtain health and sanitation facility and empowering people to make their choices that best serve their needs. Since more than 90 per cent of micro finance beneficiaries are women, empowering the lady of the house does more miracles in uplifting the standard of living of poor and enables them to the integrated with overall economic development of the nation and this will be one step forward in the direction of empowerment of women.

SHG Bank Linkage

SHG are the real grass root level set up for micro credit growth They reach the poorest settings as well as are empowering lakhs of women entrepreneurs all around India. The various models like poor group bank linked SHs, Nuo-linked SHGs help in creating a social infrastructure with which the rural population is comfortable, Which helps in making roads for spreading credit.

There is a concentration of SHGs in the Southern states mainly on account of proactive role played by the state governments. However, NABARD has taken up intensification of the SHG bank linkage program in 13 identified priority states which account for about 70 per cent of the rural poor population viz U.P, Orissa, West Bengal, M.P, Maharastra, Gujrat, Rajasthan, Jharkhand, Bihar, Assam, H.P Below is the table showing the cumulative growth in SHG Bank linkage in priority.

Graduation of SHG members to take up micro enterprises requires intensive training on various aspects of management including understanding of the market structure. Significant progress was made during the 2005-06 that witnessed sustained

Table 1
Cumulative Growth in SHG-Bank Linkage in Priority States

State/Year	*2002*	*2003*	*2004*	*2005*	*2006*
Assam	1024	3477	10706	31234	56449
Bihar	3957	8161	16246	28015	46221
Chhatisgarh	3763	6763	9796	18569	31291
Gujrat	9496	13875	15974	24712	34160
Himachal pradesh	5069	8875	13228	17798	22920
Jharkhand	4198	7765	12647	21531	30819
Maharashtra	19619	28065	38535	71146	131470
Madhya Pradesh	7981	15271	27095	45105	57125
Orissa	20553	42272	77588	123256	180896
Rajasthan	12564	22742	33846	60006	98171
Uttar Pradesh	33114	53696	79210	119648	161911
Uttranchal	3323	5853	10908	14043	17588
West Bengal	17143	32647	51685	92698	136251
Total Priority States	141804	249462	397464	667761	1005272
	(31)	(35)	(37)	(41)	(45)

Figure in the parentheses indicate percentage share of priority states in total No. of SHGs credit linked.

Source: NABARD.

expansion of the programme with credit linkage of 0.6 million new SHGs from 1.6 million SHG as on 31 March 2005 to 2-2 million on 31 March 2006. Banks extended loans of Rs. 4,499 crore during 2005-06 registering growth of 50.3 per cent over the previous year as showing in Table 2.

Table 2
SGH-Bank Linkage Programme (Amount in Rs. Crores)

Total	*SHGs financed by banks (Nos. in '000)*		*Bank Loans*		*Refinance*	
Year	*During the year*	*Cumula-tive*	*During the year*	*Cumula-tive*	*During the year*	*Cumula-tive*
1992-99	33	33	57	57	52	52
1999-00	82 (147.9)	115 (247-9)	136 (138.1)	193 (238.1)	98 (88.4)	150 (188.4)
2000-01	149 (82.3)	264 (129.9)	288 (111.8)	481 (149.2)	245 (150)	395 (163.3)
2001-02	198 (32.6)	461 (74.9)	545 (89.5)	1026 (113.4)	395 (61.4)	790 (100)
2002-03	256 (29.5)	717 (55.4)	1022 (87.4)	2049 (99.6)	622 (57.5)	1413 (78.8)
2003-04	362 (41.1)	1079 (50.4)	1856 (81.5)	3904 (90.6)	705 (13.3)	2118 (49.9)
2004-05	539 (49.1)	1618 (50)	2994 (61.4)	6898 (76.7)	968 (37.2)	3086 (45.7)
2005-06	620 (15)	2239 (38.3)	4499 (50.3)	11398 (65.2)	1068 (10.3)	4154 (34.6)

Figures in the parentheses indicate annual percentage growth.

Source: NABARDs.

The SHG bank linkage programme is now considered by the banking system as a commercial proposition with advantages of lower transaction costs and higher coverage of rural clients by the bank branches. The linkage position by banks are shown below.

Table 3
Linkage Position-Model-Wise

	As on March 31, 2005		*As on March 31, 2006*	
Model	*No. of SHGs ('000)*	*Bank Loan (Rs. crore)*	*No. of SHGs ('000)*	*Bank Loan (Rs. crore)*
SHGs promoted, guided and financed by banks	343 (21.2)	1013 (14.7)	449 (20.1)	1637 (14.4)
SHGs promoted by NGOs/Govt. agencies and financed by banks	1158 (71.6)	5529 (80.2)	1646 (73.5)	9200 (80.7)
SHGs promoted by NGOs and financed by banks using NGOs/ formal agencies as financial intermediaries	117 (7.2)	356 (5.2)	143 (6.4)	561 (4.9)
Total	1618	6898	2239	11398

SHG through Micro-Finance have the potential to fight against poverty and can be an important access to credit (Micro-Credit) also allows poor and the marginalized people to take advantage of the economic opportunities while increased employment and earnings are by no means automatic members of SHGs have over whelming demonstrated the reliable sources of micro-credit provide a fundamental basis for planning and expanding economic activities or micro entrepreneurs. Many studies show that women members of SHGs who joined and stayed in micro-credit programme have better economic conditions than non-members suggesting that micro credit programmers contribute to these improvements. It is also evident from the study as showed table.

Micro Credit and Poverty Alleviation

Poverty is complex in nature and has multiple dimensional effects. Poverty is often as the consequence of unemployment which being gender related to feminization of poverty. To eliminate poverty, particularly that affects women; they should be empowered by providing credit facilities by banks and other financial bodies.

Micro-finance is playing a vital role in poverty alleviation in the country. Financial services enable the rural poor to leverage their initiative, accelerating the process of generating incomes and economic security. Conventional financial institutions seldom lend down market to serve the needs of low-income families especially to women lead families.

Micro-finance is required to meet large unmet demands of rural poor. Perhaps the micro-finance institutions are small and insignificant, yet the larger point is about policy space for innovation and diversity of approaches to meet larger unmet demands. The strategy of poverty alleviation has been modified keeping in view of the experience. The new strategy (Micro-finance) has had its own merit. The basic weakness of this approach is that still it is remain unorganized in nature. Micro-finance implies providing with savings, credit and insurance facilities to expend income-generating activities in rural areas and to increase household income security.

Suggestions

There is urgent need for bringing changes in the nature of institutional finances services, from being supply driven to demand driven and market oriented. Our purpose is to strengthen the practice of micro-finance. Since the demand side is represented by the vulnerable SHGs, this side requires greater thrust along with flexibility. In order to enforce effectiveness of micro credit for better sustainability and continuity it is suggested.

1. It is essential to explore in detail the demands or requirements of the poor and envisage purposeful approach and methodology of initiating this project. Since the micro-financing is already in swing, most of its prerequisites are familiar, hence appropriate policy making should be easier considering all its aspects.
2. There is the necessity of undergoing training of both the beneficiaries or the participants of the SHGs and

the financers separately emphasizing the role of each person. Proper method of imparting one's duties should be mentioned. Result-oriented motivation should be envisaged.

3. The hiring and recruitment policy that MFIs pursue is another aspect that exerts influence on productivity and efficiency of micro credit. The MFIs must themselves be equipped with clear policy and facilities while reaching the poor.
4. The MFIs must establish performance standards for each level from loan officers at the entry point to the senior level. Incentive should be provided for good performance and staff training and retention.
5. In order to ensure efficiency in terms of our reach and delivery of services, the MFIs should establish a decentralized code of operation. In addition to providing standard guidelines on staff function, it is essential to place ceiling on branch expenses.
6. Several times the cost of operation of the MFIs is much higher than the size of the loan. This problem is inevitable in the teething stage, hence it cannot be rejected on the ground of high establishment cost. The system of micro-credit should be carried on at any cost as the benefits will be reaped in the long run on very vast spectrum in updating the poor.
7. The MFIs should never get boxed into fixed rules of business and should constantly evaluate the productivity and efficiency of its functions. However the poor should not be victimized for overhead costs of the NGOs and the MFIs in the name of financial sustainability.
8. Within the financial self- financial paradigm there is some disagreement about the degree to which the loans should be directed towards particular purposes. Although the general directive is that the loans be used for direct or productive purposes only, our experiences show that many attempts by programmers fail on account of rigidity.

9. As per the general system of micro-finance, they do not cover the insurance risk. Sooner this scheme is launched greater will be the magnitude of micro-finance.

Given the need for streamlining micro-finance and promoting it as an effective tool for poverty alleviation, ADB (2000) has made the following proactive recommendations to be adopted by the Reserve Bank of India (RBI).

(i) RBI should promote understanding that higher interest rates provide increased access to finance for the poor rather than exploiting them;

(ii) RBI should initiate action to bring the needed legal framework for MFIs;

(iii) RBI should establish prudential regulation and supervision structures for MFIs; which are appropriate to their size.

(iv) RBI should develop prudential norms and reporting standards for MFIs.

Conclusion

In India, Economic Reforms with a human face have been accepted as the guiding principle of sustainable development. Keeping the Poor at centre, the Policies need to be reoriented so as to develop and optimize the potential of such a large segment of the Population and enable them to contribute in the growth process significantly in terms of output, income, employment and consumption. After the pioneering efforts of the last ten years, the Micro-finance Scene in India has reached a take- off point. With some efforts substantial progress can be made in taking MFIs to the next orbit of significance and sustainability. This needs innovative and forward- looking policies, based on the ground realities of successful MFIs. This, combined with a commercial approach form the MFIs in making Micro-finance Financially Sustainable, will make this Sector vibrant and help to achieve its single-minded mission providing Financial Services to the Rural Poor.

It is necessary to recognize that we, in India, have to focus on extending financial services in both rural and urban areas for ensuring financial inclusion of all segments of the population. At the same time, one should avoid the temptation of creating one set of banking and financial institutions to cater to the poor or the unorganized, and another for the rest. The medium to long-term objective should be to ensure inclusion of all segments in the mainstream institutions while taking advantage of the flexibility of multiplicity of models of delivering a wide range of financial services. In this light, a comprehensive framework to revive the cooperative credit system, revitalize the Regional Rural Banks and reorient commercial banking system needs to get a high priority while simultaneously encouraging and enabling the growth of micro-finance movement in India, which has been very successful. We need to build on its strengths and extend it to vast areas, which are inadequately covered by both banking and micro-credit entities. Micro-finance, broadly defined, needs to be explored in the light of the new paradigm described. RBI and NABARD recognize the growing importance of micro-finance and are committed to enable its healthy growth

References

"Micro Finance Productive Linkages", *Economic and Political Weekly*, March 6, 2004.

Micro Finance: Reserve Banks Approach Address by Dr. Y.V. Reddy. Governor, RBI at Micro Finance conference Organised by the Indian school of Business Hyderabad on August 6, 2005.

Dwarakavaths H. D. (2002), "Rural Credit and Woman Self-help Groups", *Kurukshetra,* p. 9.

Reddy Micro Finance RBI Approach Aug. 2006.

The Indian Economic Association 90th Annual Conference.

Yojna January 2008 Special Issue Micro Finance.

Micro-finance in India Sectoral Issues and Challenges (Nov. 2004): Y. S. P. Thorat, Managing Director, NABARD.

Various Issues of NABARD Bulletin Mumbai.

18

RURAL LENDING IN THE REFORM ERA

Pushpa S. Abbigeri

Introduction

Agriculture is the backbone of the Indian economy. It provides employment to more than 55 per cent of the countrys workforce along with livelihood support to about 2/3rd of the countrys population. Priority sector credit is one of the strategic inputs for the successful implementation of the rural development scheme. In the wake of liberalization, privatization and globalization extraordinary development is taking place all over the world. To meet the challenges of globalization an intervention is required to uplift the less advantaged people of the country. Leading financial institution National Bank for Agriculture and Rural development (NABARD) has played significant role in rural development.

The banking scenario in the country in the post liberalized era has witnessed sweeping changes. A changing environment due to globalization and innovation is forcing the banks to change their focus. RBI launched major reforms in 1992 following the recommendations of Narasimhan Committee to create a more profitable, efficient and sound banking system. The paradigm shift in the banking structure has made the rural banking sector more customer centric. In the pre-reforms period there was a regime of directed credit delivery system to the priority sector. The rationale behind the government was to serve this sector on priority basis. Unfortunately, commercial banks did not take adequate interest in advancing credit to this sector until there was a directed system of credit delivery by the government before the nationalization of the banks. The government directed that banks should advance 40% of their total credit to the priority sector among which direct advance to agriculture would be 18% per annum. The Narasimhan Committee report on financial sector reforms pointed out that directed lending had reduced the income of banks which had high administrative costs and interest rate was far below the commercial rate of credit. The committee recommended a gradual phasing out of directed credit and to reduce it 10% from 40%.

The government did not accept the recommendations, instead continued with the 40% of bank credit as far as allocation of credit was concerned. Banking policy reforms envisaged a decline in rate of interest and interest on agricultural credit has been reduced. To serve agriculture and agro-based activities Regional Rural banks were established and National Bank for Agricultural and Rural Development (NABARD) was created to supervise the credit delivery system. Banks were asked to open more branches in rural areas. Another objective of increasing the rural presence of commercial banks was to protect the cultivators from the exploitation of private money lenders. Many rural programs like IRDP, FFDP, crop loans were launched to help agriculturist with credit as a major input and every commercial bank was given suitable target. Today, the rural development is an important issue and the banks are playing important role in the same.

Objectives of the Study

1. To find out the impact of Micro Finance Program.
2. To analyze the impact of Kisan Credit Card Scheme.

Methodology of the Study

The present study is based on the secondary data. It was collected through a review of related literature on the topic and annual report of NABARD.

Rural Credit Needs and its Institutional Structure

Imperial bank was nationalized in 1956 and renamed as State bank of India in 1956 to serve the credit needs of neglected sectors of the economy. Co-operative credit societies were formed to provide loans to agricultural sector. Regional Rural Banks (RRBs) were established in 1975 to cater to the financial needs of the rural sector, particularly agricultural and agro-based activities. Major banks were nationalized in 1969 and RRBs were created in 1975. National Bank for Agricultural and Rural Development (NABARD) was created in early 1980s. It took over the functions of ARDC and refinancing activities of Reserve bank with respect to Co-operatives and RRBs as well as Commercial banks. More branches were opened in rural areas. The ratio of bank branches in rural areas to urban areas became 3:1 in mid 1980s. Net credit flow to agriculture increased steadily up to 1992.

India has extensive banking infrastructure comprising co-operative credit structure, public and private sector commercial banks and regional rural banks. The co-operatives have over 1, 09,000 retail outlets to provide rural families easy access to institutional credit in all villages. Moreover, extensive network of around 47,265 rural and semi urban branches of public sector commercial banks and RRBs have been allocated a specific number of 5 to 10 villages in order to mobilize savings and credit in a planned way through formulation of Service Area Credit Plan for each branch.

Rural Lending Schemes

Banks are now concentrating more on the rural areas than before. Conductive policies of the government have increased the bank finance in rural areas. Banks have identified the emerging areas to address the credit needs of the rural masses and to meet the challenges of the new era. Microfinance program and Kisan Credit card scheme has been introduced for the rural development.

Micro Finance

Rural India is in the process of transforming itself into a vibrant economy due to the Micro finance program. NABARD has launched the pilot project of SHG-bank linkage program in 1992 and the RBI evolved a supportive policy framework for the growth of microfinance sector. Micro finance provides an opportunity for the banks to reach rural poor in groups for extending various financial services and ensure financial inclusion.

Micro finance means providing small loans to very poor families to help them in engaging in productive activities or promote their tiny business. According to Robinson, Economist, "microfinance refers to small scale financial services for both credits and deposits, that are provided to people who farm, fish or herd, operate small or micro enterprises where goods are produced, recycled, repaired or traded, provide services, work for wages or commissions gain income from renting out small size of land, vehicles, drought animals or machinery and tools to other individuals and local groups in developing countries both in rural and urban areas." Micro finance is the strategy to reduce poverty by means of credit support to the poor, equitable gains from development on a sustainable basis. Micro finance is emerging as a poverty reduction and empowerment tool which has made impact in the lives of the poor members of the SHGs in rural India. One of the successful ways through which microfinance services are provided to the people is through SHG. The poor are provided the hassle free finance at proper time through the formation of Self Help Group. Micro finance includes broader range of services such as credit, savings, insurance etc. Drawing lessons from the experiments carried out in various parts of the world, particularly by the well known Grameena bank of Bangaladesh an attempt was made to build financial relationship between informal groups of people and formal agencies like banks for catering to the financial service requirements of the poor, especially downtrodden women. SHG is a great revolution in India. Microfinance program covered the entire country, more intensively rural areas, through three types of models viz, (i) SHG bank linkage model (ii) Individual banking model (iii) Grameen model. In order to reduce regional imbalances in the spread of SHG bank linkage program NABARD specified 13 states which have a large population of the poor, for focused attention. During the last 15 years MFIs including SHG bank linkage program have contributed modestly to serve around 10 per cent poor in India out of 70 million poor families. These branches have been providing microfinance through linking SHGs. The NGOs have played a commendable role in promoting SHGs and linking them with banks.

The program of linking SHGs with the banking system continues to be the major micro finance program in the country, and is being implemented by commercial banks, RRB's and Co-operative banks. The progress of the SHG-bank linkage program since its inception is shown in the following table.

Table 1
No. of SHGs Linked to Banks in India (1992-93 to 2006-2007)

Year	*Cumulative No. of SHGs*	*Bank Loan (Rs. Mn)*
1992-93	255	2.9
1993-94	620	6.5
1994-95	2122	24.5
1995-96	4757	60.6
1996-97	8598	118.4
1997-98	14317	237.6
1998-99	32995	570.7
1999-00	114775	1929.8
2000-01	263825	4809.0
2001-02	461478	10263.0
2002-03	717360	20487.0
2003-04	1079091	39042.0
2004-05	1628476	68984.6
2005-06	2238565	113980.0
2006-07	2924973	180410.0

Source: NABARD website

The table shows that there has been a rapid growth of SHGs linked with the Commercial banks, RRBs and Co-operative banks. In the first year 1992-93 the program started by linking 255 groups with a loan disbursement of Rs. 2.9 mn. The average loan per SHG was about Rs. 11.37 thousand in 1992-93 whereas it has increased to Rs. 61.68 thousand in the year 2006-07. Particularly after 2000, the number of SHGs linked to the banks has grown exponentially. More than 29.2 lakh SHGs were linked to bank credit till March 2007 registering a growth of 24.2 per cent over the previous year.

SHGs Regional Spread

Growth in Credit linkage of SHGs regional spread is shown in the following table.

Table 2
Number of SHGs Credit Linked

Region	*2001-02*	*Cumulative*	*2006-07*	*Cumulative*
Northern	4,221	9,012	48,921	1,82,018
Northeastern	160	477	29,237	91,754
Eastern	11,057	22,252	1,31,530	5,25,881
Central	8,631	28,851	64,814	3,32729
Western	6,911	15,543	1,04,193	2,70,447
Southern	1,09,218	1,87,690	3,07,713	15,22,144
Total	1,40,198	2,63,825	6,86,408	29,24,973

Source: NABARD.

Micro finance program was concentrated in southern region in 2001-02. The year 2006-07 has witnessed spread of micro finance in other regions also. The regional spread of the program reveals that the share of non-southern regions improved from 29% as on 31st March 2001 to 48% as on 31st March 2007.

Kisan Credit Card Scheme

Kisan Credit Card is another successful product launched for the rural development. In order to rationalize the credit delivery system NABARD came out with the idea of Kisan Credit Card. The card is issued to the farmers who have some land. Kisan Credit Card emerged as an innovative credit delivery mechanism for meeting the production credit requirements of the farmers in a timely and adequate manner. The Kisan Credit Card was launched in August 1998 to provide adequate and timely support from the banking system to farmers for their cultivation needs including all purchases in a flexible and cost effective manner. KCC provides revolving credit facility involving any number of withdrawals and repayments within the limit. Limit is fixed on the basis of operational land holding, cropping pattern and scale of finance applicable in the respective area. KCCs have emerged as highly successful credit delivery mechanism to the farm sector. The product which was initially targeted at borrowers requiring short-term crop loans has been expanded to allied and non farm activities. The loan disbursed under KCC facility were also brought under insurance scheme.

Smart Cards–It is proposed that the smart card be issued as kisan credit cards. Plastic cards with chips embedded on them have been globally accepted as the most effective and secured data storage and payment mechanisms. These cards have the capability to store data and transact using this data. Since data is stored in the card, it can work in an offline mode and does not rely on a back end or networking for transactions. The card will carry personnel details about the farmer, his land holding, credit worthiness, loan details, repayment details etc. The bank branches will be provided with smart card readers to do transactions on these cards.

The introduction of Kisan Credit Card offers various benefits to the farmer as well as to the banker such as–

- Minimum paper work
- Simplification of documentation for withdrawal of funds from the bank
- Easy availability of credit any time enabling reduced interest burden for the farmer, sanction of the facility for three years subject to satisfactory operations.
- Flexibility of withdrawals from a branch other than the issuing branch at the discretion of the bank.

- Reduction in workload for branch staff by avoidance of repeat appraisal and processing of loan papers.
- Improvement in recycling of funds and better recovery of loans.
- Reduction in transaction cost to the banks.
- Better banker client relationship.

The Kisan Credit Card has been under implementation in all states and UTs by all Public Sector Commercial Banks, Regional Rural Banks and Co-operative Banks facilitating smooth flow of crop loans.

The details of the cards issued by co-operative banks, commercial banks and regional banks up to 2007 is tabled below.

Table 3
No. of Cards Issued (in lakhs)

Year	*Co-operative Banks*	*RRBs*	*Commercial Banks*	*Total*
1998-99	1.55	0.06	4.45	6.07
1999-00	35.95	1.73	13.66	51.34
2000-01	56.14	6.48	23.90	86.52
2001-02	54.36	8.34	30.70	93.41
2002-03	45.79	9.64	27.00	82.43
2003-04	48.78	12.75	30.94	92.47
2004-05	35.56	17.29	43.95	96.80
2005-06	25.98	12.49	41.65	80.12
2006-07	22.97	14.06	37.67	74.70
Total	327. 08	82. 84	253. 92	663. 86

Source: NABARD.

Of the 663.86 cards issued by the banking system since its inception of the scheme, Co-operative banks accounted for the largest share of 49.27% followed by commercial banks 38.25% and Regional Rural Banks (RRBs) 12.48%. The growing popularity of KCC scheme reflects hassle free and timely operations and easy availability of credit.

Concluding Observations

NABARD is trying to free the small rural borrowers from the clutches of local money lenders by providing loans at affordable rates through SHGs. Nabards micro finance scheme have been hailed as very innovative and effective. Micro finance is emerging as a poverty reduction and empowerment tool which has made impact in the lives of the poor members of the SHGs in rural India. Women empowerment is taking place through these groups as about 90 per cent SHGs that are linked to the banks are reported to be of women. But still they have a long way to go. Problems are faced in the process formation of group. The group sustainability depends on the preparedness of the members of SHG. NGOs play a pivotal role in developing, promoting and motivating these groups. Promoters should mould the mind set of the members of the groups by counseling and educating them about lucrative business proposals. Rural areas are bestowed with plenty of natural resources and a group can start a cottage industry if members are trained in the right direction.

The public sector banks have strong roots in the rural areas. Banks should help in spreading awareness by educating people about benefits of the programs and encouraging to form SHGs and get them credit linked. Training may be provided to the members on various vocational courses so as to enable them to utilize their potential. Need based management training to SHGs before recommending them loan to group activities will reduce the risk. Hence, banks can act as a driving force in utilizing the huge untapped manpower for the empowerment of the rural people.

Kisan Credit Card Scheme has achieved significant success. It has streamlined the credit delivery mechanism and simplified the existing systems, procedures and documentation relating to sanction and disbursement of credit to the farmers. There has been spectacular growth in institutional credit flow for agriculture. Banks have been issuing ATM enabled Kisan Credit Cards for the benefit of the farmers.

Rural Development is a delicate issue. It requires changing mind set of rural masses. Sufficient attention must be given to educate rural population so that they can avail the opportunities and reap the benefits of rural lending schemes.

References

Anil Makhija (2006), "Managing Rural Financing", Indian Banker, Volume 1, No. 3, p. 135-137.

B. K. Swain (2007), "Financial Inclusion Through Microfinance", Professional Banker, p. 64-72.

B. N. Kumar (2004), "The Kisan Credit Card", ICFAI Publication.

Chinmoy Kumar (2005), "Rural Banking", Professional Banker, p. 50-57.

Dr. Kishore C. Pandhy (2008), "Microfinance", Professional Banker, p. 53-56.

D. Ramani (2007), "Micro Credit 'or' Self Help Groups in India-Emerging Issues and Challenges", *Indian Banker*, Volume II, No. 1, p. 38-43.

K. C. Sharma (2007), "Microfinance Through Self-help Groups", Professional Banker, p. 29-36.

P. Sreelakshmi (2008), "Empowerment Through Microfinance", Professional Banker, p. 51-53.

R. Subramanian (2007), "Microfinance A Promoting Instrument for SHGs", Professional Banker, p. 17-20.

Saroj Upadhyay (2006), "Banking Reforms and Agricultural Credit", Professional Banker, p. 33-39.

Srujona Vari (2008), Changing Face of Rural Banking, Professional Banker, p. 40-42.

19

CONTOURS OF CO-OPERATIVE DEVELOPMENT IN KARNATAKA-ISSUES FOR THE NEW MILLENNIA

S. Mahendra Kumar

Introduction

Karnataka has a widespread network of about 29,930 Co-operative Societies serving various sectors of the state's economy, particularly in the fields of agriculture, industry, trade, and services. This sector also plays a very important role in the implementation of socio-economic programs. In the field of agriculture and allied services, co-operative institutions shoulder the task of providing term-loans, seeds, fertilizers and insecticides to the farming community, and marketing of agricultural produce to consumers. They play a crucial role in the public distribution system as well as in holding the prices. The collection, procurement and distribution of milk and milk products by about 8,253 co-operatives in the state deserve special mention.

The State has a very strong and stable network of Apex co-operative financial institution extending developmental and promotional services to the population in general and the farming community in particular. The State Apex Bank, the Karnataka State Agriculture and Rural Development Bank, and District Central Co-operative Bank play a pivotal role in extending finance for agricultural production. More than 4409 primary agricultural credit societies cater to the needs at the village level. With the growing importance of procurement and distribution, storage has become crucial and Karnataka has 6321 go-downs with a capacity of over 13.34 lakh tonnes.

Karnataka has the distinction of being Pioneer State in the formation of the first co-operative credit society at Kanaginahal of the erstwhile Dharwad District in 1905. Siddanagowda Sanna Ramanagowda Patil was the founder of this co-operative credit society and was registered by Robert Mecniel, Registrar of former Bombay Presidency.

The State of Karnataka has many firsts to its credit in co-operatives. The first Consumers' Co-operative Society was started in 1905 at Bangalore, the first Urban Co-operative Bank in 1907 at Bangalore, the first Marketing Co-operative Society in Hubli in 1915, and the first Land Mortgage Bank in 1929, at Dharwad. Besides, the State Co-operative Land Mortgage Bank was started in 1929 at Bangalore.

The State has witnessed a tremendous growth in the organization of co-operative societies, i.e., from mere 3000 societies in 1947, to 29,930 societies in the year 2001 registering a ten-fold increase (Table 1), and from a working capital of Rs. 3.71 crores to Rs. 2,21,9,867 crores during the same period. This is a remarkable progress in the field of co-operatives.

Co-operatives in Karnataka, have been classified into nine types, viz., Agricultural co-operatives constituting milk co-operatives (33 per cent) Non-agricultural co-operatives (12 per cent), Marketing and Producers co-operatives (2 per cent), Consumers' co-operatives (7 per cent), Housing co-operatives (5 per cent), Industrial co-operatives (8 per cent), Women co-operatives (4 per cent), water uses and irrigation societies (5 per cent) and others (7 per cent). All these co-operatives meet the requirements of different categories of the people in the state.

Data Source and Methodology

The Data for the study is based on the secondary source of information published by Government of Karnataka,

Department of Co-operation, Bangalore. The Methodology adopted for the study is Simple Growth Rate and Trend Analysis (time series data) to know the performance growth of co-operatives in Karnataka during the study period.

Globalization and Co-operatives

Globalization implies integration of the economy of the country with the rest of the world economy and opening up of the economy for foreign direct investment by liberalizing the rules and regulations and by creating favorable socio-economic and political climate for global process. Whereas, Co-operatives are viewed as institutions meant for the globalize world to bring socio-economic improvements and not as business enterprises. The winds of free trade blow stronger than ever. Co-operatives cannot be isolated from this change. They face tough competition from the private sector. To survive and grow amidst these fast changes, our co-operatives are required to reorient themselves, by improving their efficiency, effectiveness and adaptability. They will have to develop professionalism sharpen their core competencies and devise market driven business strategies.

However, co-operatives all over the world faced "both survive and thrive" in the era of economic reforms. New investment opportunities are getting created, old business models are under very pressure. Inputs of science and technology and information technology have to be used in co-operatives. The Ninth Five Year Plan stated that co-operatives shall be encouraged to grow as self-esteemed grass-root institutions, to inculcate the habit of thrift and self-help among viable groups to meet effectively the local credit and development needs. The success of co-operatives in taking advantages of globalization will totally depend upon how the State and the members of the co-operative strive to reap the economic benefits.

Until recent times co-operatives have never faced any real competition either in production and sales nor services and dispensation of credit from other sectors of the economy. This is due to protection given by the state. Under the liberalization, privatization and globalization policy of the states, all leading multinational corporations have entered in all fields of economic activity, which has compelled the co-operatives to reshape their policies and practices. These, more so in the agricultural sector and banking sector where co-operatives play a significant role in the provision of credit and service. The working efficiency and effective functioning of co-operatives are basically controlled by bye-laws.

Growth of Co-operative Movement in Karnataka

Co-operative movement in Karnataka is as old as the First Co-operative Societies Act itself. It was in 1905, the first co-operative credit society was registered in Dharwad that sowed the seeds of co-operation. Table 1 depict the trends in growth of co-operative movement in Karnataka. If we look at the Table 1 we witness only 5 societies in 1905 with 386 members, with a share capital of Rs. 0.11 lakhs and with a working capital of Rs 0.14 lakhs. Later in the years 1915-16 the number of societies rose to 800 with a members of 64, 857, share capital of Rs. 20.26 lakhs and a working capita of Rs. 44.21 lakhs. Subsequently, during the years 1925-26 the number of societies increased to 1603(i.e., by 6.86 per cent against the years 1920-21), with a membership of 92,292, share capital of Rs. 35.52 lakhs and working capital of Rs 112.38 lakhs. Later during 1935-36 the number of societies was place at 1906, with a membership of 1,44,499, share capita of Rs 52.60 lakhs and working capital Rs. 226.05 lakhs. During 1945-46 the number of societies rose 2526, membership to 2,26,595, share capital to Rs. 75.80 lakhs and Rs. 363.88 lakhs of working capital. The years 1955-56 witnesses a change in the growth of societies it rose to 6008 societies with a membership of 7,84,432, share capital Rs 278.52 lakhs and working capital Rs. 1,299.30 lakhs.

Later in the years 1965-66, the number of societies stood at 18,303, membership of 34,15,000, with a share capital of Rs. 2,892 lakhs and with a working capital of Rs. 16,931 lakhs. Again in the year 1975-76 the number of societies was place at

Table 1
Growth of Co-operative Societies in Karnataka

Year	No. of societies	Growth Rate	Membership	Growth Rate	Share Capital	Growth Rate	Working Capital	Growth Rate
1905	5		386		0.11		0.14	
1911	111	2120	9043	2242.75	2.31	2000	3.71	2550
1921	800	620.72	92121	918.7	34.34	1386.58	81.97	2109.43
1931	1500	87.5	13761	-85.06	48.88	42.34	189.32	130.96
1941	2213	47.53	14347	4.26	53.08	8.59	271.77	43.55
1951	1956	-11.61	50128	249.4	138.74	161.38	690.9	154.22
1961	5190	165.34	243300	385.36	1738.3	1152.92	10340.91	1396.73
1971	14871	186.53	434500	78.59	8235	373.74	52366	406.4
1981	19437	30.7	828900	90.77	17570	113.36	126128	140.86
1991	23159	19.15	1180000	42.36	43108	145.35	315833	150.41
2001	29930	29.24	16167000	1270.08	197316	357.72	2219867	602.86

22,713, with a membership of 55,45,000, with a share capital Rs. 12,543 lakhs, and a working capital of Rs. 91,637 lakhs. During 1985-86 the societies were 24,059,with a membership of 99,31,000, a share capital of Rs. 26, 95,300 and a working capital Rs. 224,879.000 lakhs. In 1995-96 the number of societies rose to 26,411 with a membership of 1,35,58,48, a share capita of Rs. 76,565,76 lakhs and with a working capital of Rs 10,26,550.86 lakhs. During the years 2000-01 the number of societies is placed at 29930 with a membership of 1,61,67,000, with a share capital of Rs. 1,97,316 lakhs and with a working capital of Rs. 22,19,867.65 lakhs.

The analysis in the table -I depicts that since its origin in 1905 in Karnataka till 2000-01,that the number of societies and membership has shown an increasing trend. In case of share capital and working capital also we wittiness tremendous change in their operations. The table also depicts the per cent change from 1905 to 2001 in respect of number, membership, share capita and working capital against previous year reference.

In case of Number of societies it is found that in the year 1911 there was tremendous increase in the organization, excepting in the years 1961 and 1971 where it shows a higher growth rate, but between 1991 and 2001 the growth in the societies shows an increasing trend. In case of Membership also, it was found that membership showed an increasing trend, between 1991 and 2001 it is found to be positive, In respect of Share Capital also it is found to be an increasing trend especially during 1991 and 2001, In respect of Working Capital it appears to an increasing trend but during 1991 and 2001 also it is found to be positive.

Table 2 depicts the Decadal growth of co-operative societies in Karnataka between 1961 and 2001. Here in this table it has to be noted that only few selected types (which are in limelight) of societies have taken into consideration. The Primary cooperative agricultural and rural development Banks (PCARDBS) appears to be steady excepting between 1991 and 2001, where it appears negative. In case of Primary agricultural credit Societies (PACS) it is found that there is negative growth

Table 2

Decadal Growth of Co-operative Societies in Karnataka

Societies	*1961*	*1971*	*Growth Rate*	*1981*	*Growth Rate*	*1991*	*Growth Rate*	*2001*	*Growth Rate*
PCARDBS	118	170	28.88	177	3.95	177	0	173	-2.25
PACS	9107	8675	-4.97	4871	-78.09	4350	-11.97	4388	0.86
Urban Banks	154	210	26.66	259	18.91	223	-16.14	313	28.75
Farming Societies	144	499	71.14	595	16.13	240	-147.91	108	-122.22
Milk Societies	70	617	88.65	2577	76.05	6291	59.03	8253	23.77
Consumer's Societies	395	1302	69.66	1541	15.5	1650	6.6	1502	-9.85
Housing Societies	350	920	61.95	1309	29.71	1606	18.49	1274	-26.05
Industrial Societies	1064	1835	42.01	1892	3.01	1001	-89.01	891	-12.45
Other Societies	1388	1355	-2.4	1368	0.95	1439	4.93	3309	56.51
Societies under Liquidation	277	2175	87.26	4408	50.65	4158	-6.01	3823	-8.76
Grand Total	14954	19437	23.06	23159	16.07	25083	7.6	29930	16.19

between 1971 and 1991 but it has improved its growth in 2001, the Urban Banks have shown an positive trend excepting in the year 1991 where it is negative. Farming Societies which had positive trend up to 1981 have dropped down between 1991 and 2001, Milk Societies which occupies 33 per cent of the total societies in the State at present seems to be very progressive during the period of reference and also between 1991 and 2001. Consumers Societies up to 1991 shows an positive trend but it has become negative during 2001,Housing Societies also signifies the same trend. Industrial societies which had shown positive trend up to 1981 seems to appear to be negative during 1991 and 2001, other Societies category depicts a rosy picture till 1991 but during 2001 it shows a positive sign. The total number of liquidated societies in the State showed a negative growth till 1991 has improved in 2001 (this is a positive trend for improvement), the total number of societies the growth rate seems to be positive but during 2001 it seems to be highly positive.

Summary and Conclusions

The above analysis in the larger context of globalization shows that there is an impressive performance of Co-operatives in Karnataka in respect of number of societies, membership share capital working capital. As regards individual societies is concerned it is witnessed that Urban Banks, Milk Co-operatives, and other types of Co-operatives have made an impressive performance. But Farming Societies, Housing Societies, Consumers' Societies, Industrial Societies and Primary co-operative agricultural and rural development Banks have a negative Growth rate during Year 2001.

From the above discussions it may be suggested that Co-operatives are still under the mercy of the State and to over come this trauma it has to be more competitive, financially sound, better managed and autonomous in their functioning. Let us hope that in the years to come Co-operatives will be in position to face any challenge and show the World that they survive and thrive and can suit any Economy independently.

References

Government of Karnataka, Gazzetter, 1995.

Government of Karnataka, Co-operatives At A Glance-2001.

Proceedings of the State Level Seminar on Co-operatives and Globalization-Creating Opportunities For All -19th and 20th August 2005, Porayar, Tamil Nadu.

Mathur B. S., Co-operation in India (1999), Sahitya Bhavan, New Delhi.

20

SELF HELP GROUPS AND POVERTY ALLEVIATION

R. RAMAKRISHNA, N. SUBBA RAO & D. TATA RAO

Introducion

POVERTY reduction in the nineties is slower than the pre-reform period. The national elasticity of poverty with respect to mean consumption is 0.8 per cent points in the nineties as against 1.6 per cent points in the pre-reform period. The main reason for the slow decline in poverty is the pattern of growth that was promoted following the policies of liberalization, privativzation, and globalization. Policies of globalization have helped the already industrialized states much more as compared with the less industrialized states and the neglect of agriculture has been responsible for the skewed pattern of distribution in the post-reform period.

A number of rural development schemes and programs have been formulated and implemented from time to time as measures to attack rural poverty. But it was realized that these programmes could not deliver the desired results and suffered from a number of defects. There is also evidence to the act. good macro-economic policies resulting in sustained growth is likely to have short-lived success at best (UNDP, 1999). Hence, it is felt that the poverty alleviation programmes should contribute for economic growth (Rao, 1992).

That the poverty has declined due to the target oriented poverty Alleviation programmes (PAPs) in the late 1980s, despite deceleration in agriculture growth (Parthasrathy, 1995; Kannan, 1995). On the other hand, there is an argument that an exclusive focus on poverty eradication programmes, in the absence of good macro-economic policies resulting in sustained growth is likely to have short-lived success at best (UNDP, 1999). Hence, it is felt that the poverty alleviation programmes should contribute for economic growth (Rao 1992).

Providing the poor with access to financial services is one of many ways to help increase their incomes and productivity. In many countries including India, however, traditional financial institutions have failed to provide this service. Policy makers and the non-governmental organizations (NGOs) recognized that both the human capital and the productive capacity of the poor needed to be improved in order to reduce poverty. To address these needs self-help groups (SHGs) were introduced in 1992 following the example of Bangladesh Grameena Bank. Their purpose is to help the poor become self-employed and thus escape poverty. Many of these programmes provide credit using social mechanisms, such as group-based lending to reach the poor and other clients, including women, who lack access to formal financial institutions. With increasing assistance from the World Bank and other donors, micro finance is emerging as an instrument for reducing poverty and improving the poor's access to financial services in low icome countries.

To formalize the mechanism further, the Reserve Bank of India (RBI) constituted a working group in November 1994 to review the functioning of the NGOs and the SHGs and made suitable recommendations for expanding their activities in the rural areas. Accepting the recommendations, the RBI advised the lending banks that the SHGs should be considered as an additional segment under the priority sector advances and integrated them with the main stream of credit operations. The Government of India bestowed national priority to the Programme through its recognition in the Union Budget, 1999.

Progress and Performance of SHGs

Though the promotion of the SHGs is by external intervention there appears to be a fairly good progress in this regard in India. About 29, 24,973 SHGs (cumulative) spread allover India which have been linked with banks by the end of March 2007(NABARD, 2006). Model-wise analysis shows that up to March 2007 Model-II SHGs (SHGs formed by NGOs and formal agencies, but directly financed by banks) continued to have a major share of about 73 per cent of the total number of SHGs financed. Further, the spread of SHGs shows that the Southern Region occupied the first place in the Programme. Among the states of the Southern Region, Andhra Pradesh occupied the leading role. Agency wise analysis shows that at the National level, commercial banks are the major partners followed by the RRBs and the cooperatives' role is rather minimum in the programme. (Tables 1 and 2 & Figures 1 and 2).

A major feature of the performance of SHGs is coverage of poor sections. This is possible mainly due to the emphasis of the NGOs promoting SHGs to work mainly for the development of tribals, land-less labour and especially the women from these categories. Secondly, most of the SHGs have been able to successfully promote regular savings habits even among these poor households. These savings appeared to be working towards making the SHGs self-reliant besides increasing the members' stake in their functioning. Thirdly with funds mobilized through savings and borrowings from banks, the SHGs are able to meet loan demands of the members for both production and household purposes. In contrast the formal agencies, the diversity in loan purpose appears be their striking feature. Their autonomy as well as easy access to information over members' activities seems to have enabled the SHGs to meet such diversed loan demands of the members. Fourthly, despite not following collateral-based lending, like formal agencies, the SHGs have been able to register high loan recoveries. A combination of factors like peer monitoring (Wydick Bruce, 1999), easy and flexible loaning procedure, higher interest rates, effective screening (Wenner, 1995), flexible repayment schedules (Besely, T. and Coate S, 1995 & Paxton

Table 1
SHG-bank Linkage–Highlights March 2001 to March 2007

Items	*March 2001*	*March 2002*	*March 2003*	*March 2004*	*March 2005*	*March 2006*	*March 2007*
No of new SHGs provided with bank loan during the year	1,49,050	1,97,653	2,55,882	3,61,731	5,39,365	6,20,109	6,86,408
No of SHGs provided with bank loan (cumulative)	2,63,825	4,61,478	7,17,360	10,79,091	1618456	2238565	2,924,973
% of women groups	90	90	90	90	90	90	90
No. of participating banks	314	444	505	560	545	545	498
(i) Commercial Banks	43	44	48	48	47	47	50
(ii) Regional Rural Banks	17	191	192	196	158	158	96
(iii) Co-operative Banks	794	209	265	316	340	340	352
No. of States / Uts	27	30	30	31	31	31	31
No. district covered	412	488	502	563	N.A	583	587
No. of NGOs	1,030	2,155	2,800	3,024	N.A	4896	-
Bank Loan (cumulative)	4,809	10,263	20,487	39,042	68985	113.98	180.41
Refinance (Cumulative)	4,007	7,965	14,188	21,247	N.A	41.60	54.59
No. of families assisted (in million)	4.5	7.8	11.6	16.7	N.A	32.98	40.95
Average Loan/SHG (Rs)	18,227	22,240	28,559	36,179	N.A	50917	78693
Model–wise linkage (cumulative)							
(i) SHGs formed and financed by banks	13%	16%	20%	20%	20	20	17
(ii) SHGs formed by formal agencies and NGOs but directly finance by banks	76%	75%	72%	72%	74	74	75
(iii) SHGs financed by banks throughNGOs	11%	9%	8%	8%	6	6	08

Source: Progress of SHG-Bank Linkage in India 2005-06, MICD, NABARD, New Delhi, 2006.

Table 2
Model-Wise Per cent Distribution of SHGs and SHG Credit in 2006

States	*Model I SHG (no.)*	*Model II SHG (no.)*	*Model III SHG (no.)*	*Model I SHG Credit (Amnt.)*	*Model II SHG Credit (Amnt.)*	*Model III SHG Credit (Amnt.)*
Haryana	12.5	87.5	0	9.6	90.4	0
Himachal Pradesh	2.5	96.9	0.6	2.6	97.3	0.1
Punjab	12.9	86.6	0.5	12.8	86.4	0.8
Jammu & Kashmir	0.8	99.2	0	0.3	99.7	0
Rajastan	10.2	89.8	0	9	91	0
Assam	79.4	11.9	8.7	89.4	7.3	3.3
Bihar	1.9	97.6	0.5	1.2	98.4	0.4
Orissa	37.1	51.7	11.2	37.7	54.8	7.5
West Bengal	33.5	34.5	7.2	65.4	25.3	9.1
Madhya Pradesh	30.1	68.8	1.1	28.6	70.5	0.9
Uttar Pradesh	17.6	79.7	2.7	15.7	82.8	1.5
Gujarat	6.9	66.9	26.2	7.4	61.1	31.5
Maharashtra	38.1	61.7	0.2	38.0	61.9	0.1
Goa	29.9	70.1	0	32.8	67.2	0
Andhra Pradesh	0.3	98.4	1.3	0.1	98.7	1.2
Karnataka	55.3	32.7	12	62.8	29.4	7.8
Kerala	16.8	51.6	31.6	16.9	54.7	28.4
Tamil Nadu & UTP	4.4	87.8	7.8	4	89.9	6.1
Region						
North	8.8	91.1	0.1	7.6	92.3	0.1
North-east	75.8	16.1	8.1	83.2	13.7	3.1
East	32.9	58	9.1	36.5	56.5	7.0
Central	19.6	0	1.9	17.4	81.5	1.1
West	31.7	62.8	5.5	30.7	61.8	7.5
South	12.7	80.2	7.1	9.6	85.3	5.1
All-India	21.0	72.7	6.3	14.3	80.8	4.9

Note: *(Amnt. = Amount)*
Source: Same as Table 1.

2000), etc, seem to have positively influenced the loan recovery performance of the SHGs. Finally the studies on SHGs also reveal that the SHGs promoted by the NGOs appear to be, from inception, dependent upon the NGOs for their various managerial and other requirements (Ramakrishna, 2004).

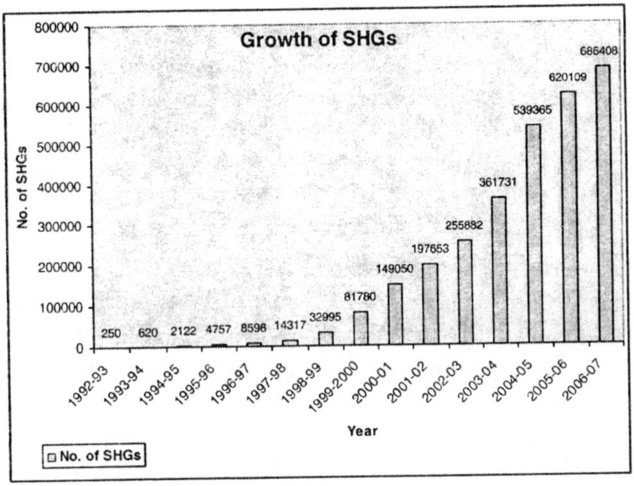

Figure 1

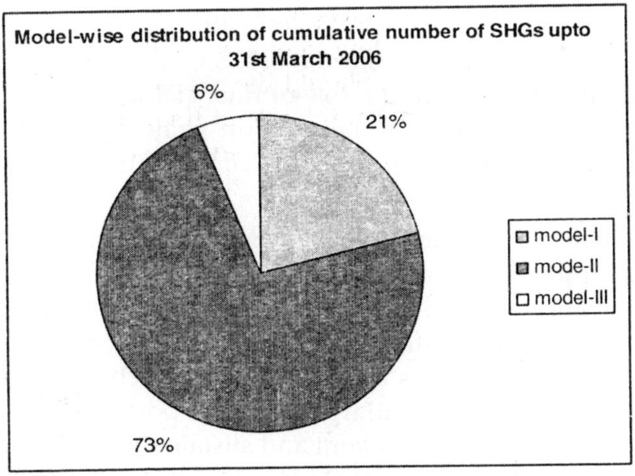

Figure 2

Conclusions and Recommendations

The above review, therefore, reveals that though the progress of the SHGs is limited in terms of spread, they certainly seem to hold a good potential in the field of credit for the poor. Precisely, based on such an assessment, the NABARD has an ambitious plan of expanding the SHGs all over the country and promote them as instruments, which can supplement the institutional agencies in effectively reaching the rural poor. However, there are certain questions, spelt below need to be answered before one can think of the SHGs assuming the above role visualized from them.

1. The experience so far suggests that in India, the SHGs have come up only in those areas where the NGOs have taken the initiative. Though under the new policy, financial institutions can also promote the SHGs, they have for many reasons shown reluctance, leaving the task of organizing the SHGs and NGOs. Then what is the best way of promoting SHGs on a wider scale?
2. While the SHGs as financial intermediaries have the goal of providing easy access to savings and credit for the poor, the NGOs may have many supplementary goals like creating people's institutions and gender empowerment. Should the SHGs confine themselves to nearly perform the role of financial intermediaries or should they also help attain some of the above objectives? Then how is the SHG-Bank Linkage is helpful in this direction?
3. There are also questions like size of SHGs, nature of composition, membership, operational structure, reliance on own funds or on external sources, nature of lending and decisions on rates of interest on both members' savings and credit etc., which need to be understood particularly from the point of view of making SHGs self-relaint and sustainable and deliver the goods expected of them.

References

Besely, T. and Coate, S. (1995), "Group Lending, Repayment Incentives and Social Collateral", *Journal of Development Economics*, Vol. 46, No. 1, pp. 1-18.

Hanumantha Rao, C.H. (1992), "Integrating poverty Alleviation Programmes with Development Strategies–Indian Experience" *Economic and Political Weekly*, Vol. 27, No. 48, pp. 2603 to 2607.

3. Kannan, K. P. (1995), "Declining of Incidence of Rural Poverty in Kerala", *Economci and Political Weekly,* Vol. XXX, No. 41 & 42, Oct. 15-21.

NABARD (2006), "*NABARD and Micro Finance,* 2005-2006, Mumbai.

Parthasarathy, G. (1995), "Public Intervention and Rural Poverty: Case of Non Sustainable reduction in Andhra Pradesh", *Economic and Political Weekly,* Vol. XXX, No. 41 & 42, Oct. 14-21.

Paxton, *et. al* (2000), "Modeling Group Loan Repayment Behaviour: New Insights from Burkiner Faso", *Economic Development and Cultural Change,* Vol. 48, No. 3, April, p. 639-655.

Rama Krishna R. (2004), "*Developing Gross Root Organisations for Sustainability of Self Help Groups*", Indira Devi M. (Ed), Strategies for Sustainability of Self Help Groups, Andhra University Press and Publications, Visakhapatnam, p. 71-76.

UNDP (1999), "*Reflector Paper on Diversities and Disparities in Human Development*", UNDP, New Delhi.

Wenner, M. W. (1995), "Group Credit: A Means to Improve Information Transfer and Loan Repayment Performance", *Journal of Development Studies,* Vol. 32, No. 2, December.

Wydick Bruce (1999), "Can Social Cohesion be Harnessed to Repair Mrket Failures? Evidence from Group Lending in Guatemala", *The Economic Journal,* Vol. 109, No. 457.

21

KISAN CREDIT CARD SCHEME: AN OVERVIEW WITH A FOCUS ON ANDHRA PRADESH

N. Subba Rao

The 'Kisan Credit Card', (KCC) Scheme operationalised since 1998-99 all over the country aimed at accelerating institutional credit flow to the farm sector. It was also expected to usher in qualitative improvement in institutional credit delivery for agriculture and allied activities. The Scheme, a major policy initiative and a landmark of significance in the annals of rural credit in India, envisages flexible and hassle-free credit flow to farm households, arresting misutilisation and conferring higher recovery benefits among others to the lending agencies.

In this paper an attempt is made to take stock of the progress of the Scheme in Andhra Pradesh in the light of the situation obtaining at the National level. To provide a better perspective this is being attempted against the background of the salient features of the Scheme and major findings of the studies on KCC Scheme undertaken by the National Bank.

Salient Features of the KCC Scheme

The salient features of the Scheme succinctly put forth by the National Banks in its Annual Report 1998-99 are presented below:

- Farmers eligible for production credit of Rs. 5000/- and above to be provided with a Kisan Credit and a pass book or a card-cum-pass book.
- Revolving cash credit facility involving any number of drawals and repayments within the credit limits.
- Entire production credit needs for the full year plus ancillary activities related to crop production are considered while fixing credit limit. In due course allied activities and non-farm credit needs also to be covered.
- Limit fixed on the basis of operational land holding, cropping patter and scale of finance.
- Each drawal to be repaid within twelve months.
- Card valid for 3 years subject to annual review
- As incentive for good performance, credit limits to be enhanced to take care of increase in costs, change in cropping pattern, etc.
- Conversion/ re-schedulement due to natural calamity is also permissible where warranted.
- Security margin, rate of interest as per the RBI norms.
- Operations, issuing branch or at the discretion of the bank, through other designated branches or PACS in the case of cooperatives.
- Cash withdrawals through slips/ cheques accompanied by card and pass book.
- Envisages improvement in the loan disbursement procedure making it less cumbersome.

As could be seen the Scheme not only provides for a broad-based assessment of production and related credit needs of the farm households, but confers greater flexibility in operating the loan accounts, putting an end to the cumbersome procedural delays of the by-gone era. Provision of personal accident insurance to KCC holders is another notable feature. The salient features of the Personal Accident Insurance Scheme are:

- Maximum amount insured is Rs. 50,000/- against death and permanent disability and Rs. 25,000/- for partial disability.
- Insurance Company is to nominate a nodal office for coordinating the implementation of the Scheme in each district.
- Master Insurance Policy will be issued by this nominated office of the insurance company to each DCCB/RRB covering all the KCC holders in the district.
- Nominal premium is Rs. 15/- for a one year policy and Rs. 45/- for a three year policy.
- Sharing of premium is in the ratio of 1:2 between the card holder and the bank.
- Simplified claim settlement procedure under the Scheme.

Major Findings of NABARD's Studies on KCC Scheme

As part of monitoring the implementation of the Scheme, the NABARD has conducted several evaluation studies to assess the ground level impact of the Scheme. These studies carried on in 17 major states covering 54 districts in all, have brought to the fore both positive impact of the Scheme as well as constraints in its implementation. These findings provide the desired perspective for the present study.

The Positive Impact

- Wide acceptability of the Scheme among farmers and bankers.
- Timely and adequate provision of credit.
- Simplification of loaning procedure and documentation.
- Elimination of repeated processing of loan proposals
- Flexibility to borrowers for purchase of inputs from any source of their choice
- Convenience to borrowers for withdrawals and repayments at any time.

- Treatment of the card as a symbol of prestige in the farmers' community.
- Assured availability of credit for three years with provision for enhancement in credit limit at the time of renewal.
- Improved recovery of loans through more frequent banker-borrower contacts.
- Transparency in operations of accounts.

Constraints in Implementation

- Selective approach being adopted in identifying beneficiaries.
- Reluctance on the part of some banks to extend KCC facility in mono crop areas.
- Disbursement of kind component also in cash under KCC perceived as a serious threat to the existing cooperative marketing structure.
- Cash disbursements done only at the DCCB branch level in some states involving travel of long distances for drawal of cash.
- Levy of costly service charges by some of the commercial banks / RRBs for issue of KC Cards to farmers (Rs. 25/- to Rs. 250/- in some states).
- Levy of stamp duty by some of the state governments for issuing loans under KCCs, which is otherwise not being levied for normal crop loans.

Progress of KCC Scheme

As per the Annual Report 2001-2002 of the National Bank, (2002, p. 51) around 378, SCBs/DCCBs 194 RRBs and 29 Commercial Banks are involved in the implementation of the Scheme. Of the total number of 232 lakhs cards issued since the inception of the Scheme in 1998-99, as many as 87.76 lakhs were issued during 2001-2002. In the total cards issued during 2001-2002, cooperatives accounted for the highest number of 54.36 lakhs, followed by commercial banks, (26.06 lakhs) and RRBs (8.43 lakhs).

State-wise position of KC cards issued at the end of March 2001 is shown in Table 1.

Table 1
Progress of Kisan Credit Cards Issued in India 2000-2001

(Amount Rs. in lakhs)

State	*No. of Cards*	*Share of KCC Issued to Total*
Andhra Pradesh	3460487	25.68
Maharashtra	1761511	13.30
Rajasthan	1513697	11.43
Uttar Pradesh	1478813	11.17
Orissa	889932	6.72
Tamil Nadu	807874	6.10
Karnataka	748433	5.65
Gujarat	523435	3.95
Punajab	463463	3.50
Haryana	439604	3.32
Kerala	428278	3.23
Mahdya Pradesh	342971	2.59
Bihar	291107	2.20
West Bengal	95806	0.72
Himachal Pradesh	30280	0.23
Jammu and Kashmir	13555	0.10
Others	15450	0.11
Total	13244396	100.00

Source: Agenda & Background Notes 150th SLBC Meetings, Hyderabad, p. 43.

Of the 232 lakhs KCC issued in the country around 220 lakhs are issued in the last two years only. There are marked variations in this regard also even among major states. During 2000-2001 Andhra Pradesh occupied the first position among the states accounting for around 26 per cent of the KCC issued in the country.

District-wise Progress of KCC in Andhra Pradesh

The relative share of various districts in the KCC's issued in the State by all the banking institutions are shown in Table 2.

Table 2
Kisan Credit Cards Issued by all Banks in the State as on 31.8.2001

District	*No. of Cards*	*Percentage to Total*	*Amount (Rs. lacs)*	*Percentage to Total*
1	2	3	4	5
Srikakulam	72102	2.04	4247.21	1.49
Vizianagaram	102194	2.90	3866.84	1.35
Visakhapatnam	159623	4.53	6583.41	2.30
East Godavari	206706	5.86	25047.42	8.76
West Godavari	211326	6.00	25316.43	8.86
Krishna	263730	7.48	26508.02	9.27
Guntur	315498	8.95	23783.03	8.32
Prakasam	142747	4.05	12551.71	4.39
Nellore	105605	3.00	14195.36	4.97
Cuddapah	138813	3.94	12482.52	4.37
Chittoor	136702	3.88	11873.49	4.15
Kurnool	165206	4.68	16904.68	5.91
Ananthapur	218720	6.21	12872.01	4.50
Khammam	231467	6.57	9408.31	3.29
Warangal	104863	2.98	7622.68	2.67
Nalgonda	200395	5.68	12405.58	4.34
Karimnagar	156101	4.43	8371.21	8.82
Nizamabad	212128	6.02	25215.12	8.82
Adilabad	119246	3.38	7932.05	2.77
Medak	103967	2.95	5502.35	1.92
Mahabubnagar	109079	3.10	8540.15	2.99
Rangareddy	48117	1.37	4663.21	1.63

Source: Andhra Pradesh State Focus Paper 2002-03, p. 114, NABARD Regional Office, Hyderabad.

In terms of number of KCC's issued in the State by all banking institutions upto the end of August 2001, Guntur District occupied the first place accounting for the highest number of cards distributed, followed by Krishna and Khammam.

Among district with the lowest number of cards issued, Ranga Reddy, Srikakulam and Vizianagaram occupied the three places in orders.

However, in terms of the amounts advanced through the KCC, Krishna occupied first place followed by West and East Godavari districts.. At the bottom end are Vizianagaram, Srikakulam and Ranga Reddy with less than two per cent of share in the advances under the KCC.

District-wise Coverage of Borrowers through KCC.

The progress in converge of borrowers by cooperatives through Cooperative Kisan Credit Cards (CKCC) upto March 2002 is presented in Table 3.

Table 3
Cooperative Kisan Credit Cards: Progress Report
(Position as on 31.3.2002)

Name of the DCCB	*Total No. of Borrowers*	*Total No. of Cards as on 31.3.2002*	*% of Achieve-ment*	*Total Amount disb. upto 31.3.2002*
1	2	3	4	5
Adilabad	128593	118773	92.36	5573.45
Anantapur	159638	152453	95.50	4299.54
Chittoor	97018	95846	98.79	3661.76
Cuddapah	74736	69336	92.77	2325.18
Eluru (West Godavari)	263048	256365	97.46	19586.84
Guntur	243442	226021	92.84	21910.92
Hyderabad (Rangareddy)	97642	84734	86.78	4814.54
Kakinada	280951	271540	96.65	15888.73
Karimnagar	146621	116092	79.18	3069.53
Khammam	216558	209976	96.96	4784.70
Krishna	247543	243312	98.29	22816.79
Kurnool	119568	109033	91.19	3915.20
Mahabubnagar	78602	73416	93.40	3704.82
Medak	99258	79178	79.77	5325.13
Nalgonda	223957	176738	78.92	5428.17
Nellore	70851	70089	98.92	2564.28
Nizamabad	171172	151379	88.44	13173.26
Prakasam	120392	112544	93.48	7145.80
Srikakulam	81958	65720	80.19	346.35
Visakhapatnam	188595	149458	79.25	6071.18
Vizianagaram	114722	80142	69.86	965.40
Warangal	179486	148926	82.97	6661.89
Total	3404346	6061071	89.92	164033.46

Source: KCC Monthly & Qtrly. 123 sp.

At the state level, cooperatives have issued 30.61 lakh credit cards covering around 90 per cent of the 34.04 lakh borrowing members. In 13 among the 22 districts the coverage was more than 90 per cent. Among the various districts, the coverage was as high as 99 per cent in Chittoor. Next to Chittoor stood Krishna with coverage of 98 per cent, followed by West Godavari (Eluru

DCCB) (97 per cent). At the other end, with relatively low coverage are the north coastal districts of Vizianagaram (70 per cent), Visakhapatnam (79 per cent) and Srikakulam (80 per cent).

In terms of total disbursement through CKCC, Krishna District stood first, followed by Guntur and West Godavari. In Srikakulam, Vizianagaram and Cuddapah the disbursements under CKCC are the lowest compared to other districts. The marked differences in coverage and particularly disbursement through CKCC are largely due to strengths and weaknesses of PACS's and DCCBs in the districts.

District-wise Coverage of Area and Claim Settlement under National Agricultural Insurance Scheme

The National Agricultural Insurance Scheme is being implemented in Andhra Pradesh since Kharif 2000. The Scheme is applicable to crop loans issued under KCC scheme also. For loans issued under KCC the banks should pass on the premium to GIC as well as claims settled by the GIC to the concerned farmers promptly. The 150th State Level Bankers Committee Andhra Pradesh (Andhra Bank 2002) which reviewed the Scheme noted below:

(i) Farmers are representing that the Crop Insurance Premium is very high, and some farmers are not coming forward to take crop loans while some are clearing the existing crop loan balances leaving the Crop Insurance Premium in the balance accounts.

(ii) While setting claims the GIC is taking the average yield for the last three years to calculate the threshold yield. In case of draught/flood affected districts where crop failed continuously for two to three years even the average for three years may be very less (Andhra Bank, H.O. 2002, 47).

As these problems are applicable to crop loans issued under KCC Scheme also, an attempt is being made to look into available data both district wise and season wise pertaining to the Agricultural Insurance Scheme. Details on the farmers and area covered, sum-insured, premium and subsidy and claims for the Rabi season 2000-01 and Kharif 2001 are shown in Table 4 & 5.

Table 4

National Agricultural Insurance Scheme District-wise Details of Coverage and Claim Settlement

District	*Farmers*	*Area (Ha.)*	*Sum insured*	*Premium*	*Subsidy*	*Claim*	*% of Insurance covered area to cropped area*
Adilabad	87	209	690500	13673	2936		0.12
Anantapur	3244	3224	39643500	754465	129251	4240095	6.15
Chittoor	3512	5385	43165040	814873	291046	2331384	4.17
Cuddapah	6378	10323	79170635	1453901	288218	11487109	5.87
East Godavari	5043	7725	57818438	867277	270568		2.42
Guntur	1630	3664	27642448	414810	90824		1.38
Karimnagar	6577	9431	61247052	933426	337233		6.24
Khammam	818	1658	11759870	237913	55166	3108	1.73
Krishna	4013	4980	49686870	754670	26554	85686	1.90
Kurnool	5383	11399	71793161	1340355	139806	108100	3.06
Mahabubnagar	5545	64264	488694154	8201899	2498713	8714	34.88
Medak	14769	22617	119809013	1805823	681043		13.96
Nalgonda	21320	34194	25845316	3812019	1254793	2941522	26.00
Nellore	28468	47252	423217609	6850443	1945447	23046830	18.74
Nizamabad	11742	13300	118972083	1867973	696605		13.00
Prakasam	19528	35217	2723700924	5515160	1136324	377535	12.60

Contd...

District	*Farmers*	*Area (Ha.)*	*Sum insured*	*Premium*	*Subsidy*	*Claim*	*% of Insurance covered area to cropped area*
Ranga Reddy	4569	9993	47418083	717527	263038		14.62
Srikakulam	3075	3378	23139565	426294	172797	2766247	3.60
Visakhapatnam	2141	1404	8758336	144041	69939	1946661	1.69
Vizianagaram	4775	4018	24887890	455243	197712	6591894	3.72
West Godavari	7848	14204	119899142	2154380	631357	1168	5.04
Warangal	4422	5440	44379169	697987	256653		3.80
State Total	214887	319279	2391338798	40234149	11673023	54942655	8.02

Source: Agenda &Background Notes 150th SLBC Meeting, Andhra Bank, Hyderabad, 2002.

Table 5

National Agricultural Insurance Scheme District-wise Details of Coverage and Claim Settlement

State: Andhra Pradesh — *Season: Kharif 2001* — *Amount in Rupees*

District	Farmers	Area (Ha.)	Sum insured	Premium	Subsidy	% of Insurance covered area to cropped area
1	2	3	4	5	6	7
Adilabad	52204	96924	408387676	19798779	4747778	26.40
Anantapur	177280	417210	2060560565	71907366	13790659	50.88
Chittoor	64309	75161	951696056	15258863	5158899	19.06
Cuddapah	84527	131092	1060588333	38433078	7632918	59.05
East Godavari	133783	185068	1521942547	33219986	11562162	46.72
Guntur	42937	53223	593304216	26058068	7316707	9.20
Karimnagar	41183	45780	365099170	11257789	3343730	14.01
Khammam	25445	38657	308898877	14197395	4279547	11.10
Krishna	109616	133090	1407996710	38328792	11851918	30.27
Kurnool	75723	192951	847512220	31042349	4621406	35.10
Mahabubnagar	109966	135725	974477975	32231722	8922386	26.46
Medak	70146	73078	738042575	11761426	3606698	24.73
Nalgonda	65856	87116	656557245	19420339	5822591	19.58
Nellore	20126	34186	334427498	8097137	2082218	31.34
Nizamabad	76026	80973	808004398	18054634	6164752	38.28

Contd...

State: Andhra Pradesh		*Season: Kharif 2001*			*Amount in Rupees*	
District	*Farmers*	*Area (Ha.)*	*Sum insured*	*Premium*	*Subsidy*	*% of Insurance covered area to cropped area*
1	2	3	4	5	6	7
Prakasam	26511	41496	337682068	13509800	3710761	16.69
Ranga Reddy	46701	60458	318349083	11005738	3503027	28.00
Srikakulam	49151	65284	472053207	11874076	3730424	21.18
Visakhapatnam	71545	65768	573968107	7350321	2841502	20.04
Vizianagaram	26165	26718	183217816	3527300	1196808	7.64
West Godavari	467310	245473	2213039840	47126110	13992095	63.56
Warangal	84171	94433	1099097833	24131397	N.A.	31.17
Total	1600000	2300000	17562200000	504400000	N.A.	28.20

Source: As ex Ante.

During Rabi 2000-2001 more than two lakh farmers were insured covering an area of 3 lakh ha., for an amount of Rs.239.13 crores. The Gross premium was Rs. 4.02 crores. The claim to a tune of Rs. 5.49 crores are payable. There are marked inter-district variations in the percentage of cropped area covered by the Insurance scheme. The area covered was the highest of around 35 per cent of Mahabubnagar while it was as low as 0.12 per cent in Adilabad.

In Kharif 2001, 16 lakh farmers have insured covering an area of around 25 lakh ha., for an amount of Rs. 1756.22 crores. The Gross Premium of Rs. 50.44 crores. Details on the claims are not available. The proportion of area covered by Insurance to cropped area is higher in Kharif 2001. As in Rabi 2000-01 there are marked inter district variations in the proportion of area covered under crop insurance. It was high as around 64 per cent in West Godavari while the lowest coverage is noted in Guntur.

The marked inter district variations in the proportion of area covered under Crop Insurance is largely due to variations in farmer's perceptions about risks and fears about the likelihood of getting adequate coverage in case of risk. Partly this is due to the nature of crop grown and related problems.

Conclusion

To sum up, the KCC Scheme has made considerable progress in the country for the last two years. In this process the role played by cooperatives is considerable as they accounted for a lion's share of KCC's issued in the country. During 2000-2001, Andhra Pradesh occupied first position among States in issuing Kisan Credit Cards in the Country. However, the coverage continues to be less than half in terms of number and amount of crop loans disbursed. Marked inter-state and inter district variations existed in the progress of this Scheme. Guntur District stood first in Andhra Pradesh for the highest number of KCC in the state at the end of March, 2003. In13 out of the 22 districts the coverage with the KCC was more than 90 per cent. There are marked inter district differences in the coverage of borrowers with the KCC.

The KCC Crop Insurance is not as smooth as expected. This is reflected in low proportion of cropped area covered resentment among farmers that the premia are high, and claim settlements are not timely and rewarding.

References

Andhra Bank, H.O. (2002), Agenda & Background Notes 150th SLBC Meting, Hyderabad.

NABARD, H.O. (2002), Annual Report 2001-2002, Mumbai.

NABARD, R.O. (2002), Andhra Pradesh State Focus Paper 2001-2002, Hyderabad.

22

UPLIFTMENT OF SHGs THROUGH MICRO FINANCE INSTITUTIONS IN RURAL INDIA

B. Vijaya & Veerendrakumar

Introduction

Micro finance has emerged as one of the most sustainable and effective tools for enabling the poor and disadvantaged sections of the society to access institutional credit. The Indian banking system, on its part, has shown a willingness and residence to experiment and join the micro finance movement in a way that has no parallel any where in the world. The micro finance agencies are providing credit facilities to the SHGs for the sake of upliftment of SHGs and rural economy with reducing poverty, eradicating unemployment problem and increasing areas people's income. According to J. P. Lewis "The low outreach of banks, coupled with collateral vacuum in their new expectations and left the underprivileged and the poor dependent on the non-institutional channels, mainly the moneylenders for meeting their growing production oriented credit needs".

Micro Finance in India

India has not been a leading country in micro finance despite of a massive poverty. Until recent reforms, it was a prime example of a country that aggressively pursued the directed-credit approach. With a limited success, the Government began to drift away from the directed credit to liberalise the financial sector and strengthen it by reorienting banks and other financial institutions towards a market based financial system. Micro Finance programmes began on a large scale in 1990s.[1]

Micro finance is being practiced as a tool to attack poverty the world over. The term "Micro Finance" could be defined as "Provision of thrift, credit and other financial services and products of very small amounts to the poor in rural, semi urban areas, for enabling them to raise their income levels and improve living standards "National Bank for Agricultural and Rural Development" (NABARD).

Objectives of the Study

The following specific objectives have been set to carry out the present study.

1. To know the operational aspects of the Self Help Group.
2. To know the performance of Bank Linkage Programme in India.
3. To study the role of SHGs.
4. To make suggestions to improve the SHGs.

Operational Aspects of Self Help Group

Credit is important in the lives of the rural poor in a developing economy. As the distribution of land in the countryside remains skewed, the majority of the rural population is left with an inadequate resource base for production. Faced with a weak social security system to fall back upon, this section of landless or near land-less rural population is forced to depend upon credit for its livelihood. It was this understanding that led various developing countries to make credit as an integral part of their poverty alleviation programmes. The conception and implementation of such programmes were often based on the broad principles of social banking in several developing countries including India. [2]

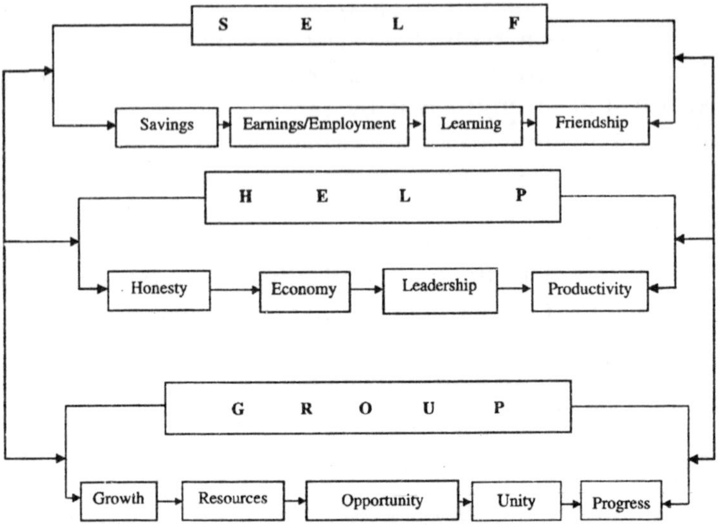

Chart 1: Operational Aspects of Self Help Group

It is evident from the above chart, that the Self Help Groups are usually informal groups whose members have a common perception of need and importance towards collective action. These groups promote savings among members and use the pooled resources to meet the emergent needs of their members including the consumption needs. The number of members in SHGs is normally ranges from 10 to 20. It is expected that within the groups, there should be true democratic culture in which all the members must participate actively in the debate rather than discussion. Through the cohesiveness among the members would be increased due to homogeneity of the groups in terms of education, occupation, income distribution, sex composition. But in the long term, stability of the SHGs depends on their members loyalty to it and adequacy of the SHGs to meet the growing needs of the members. The basic objectives of the Self Help Groups is to develop savings capability among the poorest sections of the society, which in turn reduce dependence on financial institutions and develop self reliance. Earlier, ever poverty alleviation programme initiated by the Government of India has failed in capacity building of the financial support. At this movement, Government must realise that it would provide basic minimum facilities to the people particularly marginalised sections with primary education to all women, men and children, primary health, rural roads, safe drinking water, sanitation and strong public discrimination system. [3]

SHG Bank Linkage in India

The SBL (Self Help Group Bank Linkage) approach involves the formation of the SHGs (mainly of women). These women regularly save money that is placed in a local (generally public sector) bank account. The SHG has a set of bye-laws devised and agreed by the members themselves. These include rules for monthly savings, lending procedures, periodically and timing of meetings, penalties for default etc. Meticulous accounts and records are maintained. [4]

The banking system would be attributed to the promotional efforts made by the Regional Rural Banks (RRBs), Co-operative Banks and Commercial Banks coupled with this NABARD took specific steps to accelerate the pace of enlargement of the programme.

Table 1
SHGs Linked Bank Loans and Refinance From Banks as on 31-03-2006

Year / *Agency*	*2002*	*2003*	*2004*	*2005*	*2006*
Commercial Banks					
No. of SHGs Credit Linked	14425	20987	35912	54814	78520
Bank Loans (Rs. Lakh)	2426.24	4539.58	10227.4	20210.4	36420.9
Refinance (Rs. Lakh)	1171.22	1206.97	1215.97	1402.03	2110.74
Percentage of Refinance	48.27%	26.58%	11.88%	6.93%	5.79%
Regional Rural Banks					
No. of SHGs Credit Linked	13279	23473	38631	62732	83383
Bank Loans (Rs. Lakh)	3021.7	6048.29	10947.3	21973.3	38413.4
Refinance (Rs. Lakh)	2509.49	4954.27	8923.99	14789	30635.1
Percentage of Refinance	83.04%	81.91%	81.51%	67.30%	79.75%
Co-operative Banks					
No. of SHGs Credit Linked	9328	17718	29323	45652	63025
Bank Loans (Rs. Lakh)	1951.7	3973.05	7346.63	12991.2	24600.6
Refinance (Rs. Lakh)	1638.58	3231.6	5343.84	9245.86	14175.5
Percentage of Refinance	83.95%	81.33%	72.73%	71.17%	57.62%

Source: Status of SHGS–BLP by NABARD Regional Office, Banglore-2006.

The above table shows that the SHG Bank Linkage Programme, the Regional Rural Banks, Co-operative Banks and Commercial Banks has grown up rapidly over a period from 2002 to 2006.The refinance capacity is slowly decreased over a period from 2002 to 2006 i.e., 48.27% to 5.79% in Commercial Banks. In the Regional Rural Banks the percentage of refinances reduced marginally over a period from 2002 to 2006 i.e., 83.04% to 79.75%. So also in Co-operative Banks the refinance percentage reduced over a period from 2002 to 2006 i.e., 83.95% to 57.62%. It is clear from the above table that refinance performance is more in Regional Rural Banks, but in Commercial Banks and Co-operative Banks the percentage of refinance is very less.

Table 2
SHG-Bank Linkage in Karnataka as on 31-03-2006

Particulars	*Cumulative as on 31-03-2005*	*During 2005-06*	*Cumulative as on 31-03-2006*
No. of SHG Promoted	236886	66805	303671
No. of Groups Credit Linked	163198	61730	224928
No. of Groups Refinance Linked	94635	20150	114785
Bank Loan (Rs. Crore)	551.74	442.60	994.34
Refinance (Rs. Crore)	254.84	66.43	321.27
Families covered* (in Lakhs)	24.48	9.26	33.74
No. of poor people assisted*(in Lakhs)	122.40	46.30	168.70

*Estimated

Source: Status of SHGS –BLP by NABARD Regional Office, Banglore-2006

It is evident from the above table that the performance of various participating banks in linkage of SHGs with the formal banking system scaled enviable heights during the year 2005-2006. The banks have extended credit to the SHGs to the extent of Rs. 442.60 crore during the year and cumulative ground level credit dispensation to the SHGs stood at Rs. 994.34 crore as on March 2006. While the families covered under the programme during 2005-06 were 9.26 lakh, the number of poor people assisted stood at 46.30 lakh.

Role of SHGS in Rural Sector

Credit plays very important role in the lives of the rural poor in a developing economy. The majority of the rural population is left with an inadequate resources base for production. In the rural areas activities like weaving, handlooms, fiber cutting etc., are undertaken. Through these activities standard of living increases and it generates the employment opportunities.

The Micro Finance builds mutual trust and confidence between bankers and the rural poor. Poor people appreciate Micro Credit because they don't, have any need to pledge something to lenders. It is the very nature of micro credit that no collateral security is required to be put off with the lender in the avenge of getting monetary assistance. Moreover, this facility is quite convenient to unreached poor who are not having access to financial services in desired manner. Another important thing is that the amount of loan is disbursed to whole group which means each and every member of SHG shares the risks and burden of loan in result of which everyone enjoys the loan facility and keeps itself limited liable.[5]

Micro Financing to the Self Help Group, not only creates a good marketing facilities in the rural areas but also helps the women folk in creating self confidence in the matters of financial bargaining and monetary gains in other developmental schemes.

Financing of economic activities is a prerequisite for the rural economy to develop. The eradication of rural poverty depends largely upon the availability of credit. Agriculturist, rural artisans self employed persons and retail traders are heavily dependent on additional monetary resources to get their income levels raised. Hence the credit plays a pivotal role in the development of the rural sector.[6]

Bankers, basically, have problems in dealing efficiently and economically with a large number of small borrowers. The group approach can ensure wider coverage of poor families through bank credit, also the members of group learn to independently approach the bank for bigger loan due to direct interaction and guidance from the bank.

The Government duty is to organise village survey to identify members, motivate them to form groups and render training guidance for management of funds and maintenance of accounts. The NGOs and voluntary organizations playing a significant role and their contributions is unique in identifying the problems of the people in general and weaker section in particular. The groups evolve system of operations, often with the help of Non -Governmental Organizations and manage the common pooled resources in legal way. While combining the group and Non-Governmental Organizations the Micro Financing Institutions ensures that the tribal dependence on the money-lenders will decrease easily.

The NGOs are actively involved in promoting, nurturing and linking the groups with banks. They play two different roles, one as the promoter of SHGs, another as the financial intermediaries channalise to the bank assistance to the SHGs. Most SHGs have come up due to the catalytic role played by the NGOs. They have a future role to play in big way.[7]

Suggestions

Self Help Groups contribute to the rural economy in a big way. To make them more active the following suggestions are made.

1. The banks must provide proper training for skill and entrepreneurship development. The group members would be able to diversify into income generating activities, thus improving their credit absorption capacity.
2. Most of the Self Help Groups members are facing illiteracy problem. Due to this problem every member of the group is unable to know the certain activities, financial transactions, different incentives from Government etc. Therefore it is necessary to take keen interest by the Government NGOs and other institutions to educate rural peoples specially of Self Help Group members through Saksharatha.
3. It is a good opportunity for both men and women for empowering in rural areas. The active role of Government Banks and other Financial Institutions extending loans to groups with attractive low rate of interest rates and simplified procedure will help lot.
4. Particularly in rural areas after formation of the groups really women's are empowered socially and economically.

Hence it is the duty of Government to assist the women in starting many more SHGs covering the all rural areas in the country. Women have the potential and will to establish and manage income generating activities of their own, need is encouragement, support from family members, Government and the society.

5. Under the group the committee members should change every year. It gives twice benefits to groups, one benefit for committee members to take relaxation and second it gives chance to other members to give experience in handling group.
6. The Self Help groups is not a static institutions, it grows on the resources and management skills of its members and their increasing confidence to get involved in the issues and programmes that require their involvement in public and private spheres.
7. Micro finance will not succeed unless we give external support like training, accounting skills and networking them.
8. The proper Management Information System is to be ensured for regular flow of informal on the functioning of the unit financial through micro finance so as to have close supervision/monitoring.
9. The Self Help Groups audit their books of account every year, which helps to know the economic conditions of groups and make a final report to present during the meeting.
10. The members have to take initiative in improving their socio-economic status by participation in Government programmes such as family welfare, promoting their nutritional and educational status, awareness on environmental public wealth through sanitation and clean drinking water etc.

Conclusion

The "SHG-Bank Linkage Programme" and observed a significant development which has witnessed for- reaching impact on the rural economy of the country since from two decades. Through this programme the credit requirement of such poor families was mostly for meeting the consumption needs or in a very small way for petty trade and retail activities are met. Particularly in rural areas the informal agencies, like moneylenders, traders, relatives, neighbours and friends played important role as financial intermediaries in the rural areas for fulfilling credit needs of the poor. These aspects are not stagnant for future purposes, it is a good opportunity poor people through Self Help Group to develop in a systematic manner.

Notes and References

1. Nadiya Yusuf (2005), "Micro Finance: SHGS Impact on Sustainable development In Rural India". 'Sustainable Development Opportunities and Challenges' R Dayanandan Serials Publications New Delhi, pp-363.
2. Chavan Pallavi and R. Ramkumar (2002), "Micro Finance Credit and Rural Poverty An Analysis of Empirical Evidence". *'Economic and Political Weekly'* Vol. 37, No. 10, 09-03-2002, p. 316.
3. Bisoy Deepak (2005), "Micro Finance Through SHGs Empowerment of Weeker Section" 'Sustainable Development Opportunities and Challenges' R. Dayandan Serials Publications New Delhi, p. 316.
4. Shah Mihir, Rao Ragu and Vijay P. S. Shankar (2007), "Rural Credit in 20th Century India Overview of History and Perspectives" *'Economic and Political Weekly'* Vol. 42, No. 15 April 14-20-2007, p. 135.
5. Tushir Monika Chadda Sumita and Ahlawat. "Role of Micro Finance to Uplift the Economic Conditions of Women Households in Harayana Through SHG. 'Southern Economist' Vol.19. No.1 March-2005, p-190.
6. Kunjukunju 2005, "Role of Institutional Finance in Rural Development of Kerala". *'Finance India'*, Vol. XIX, No. 1 March 2005, p. 190.
7. Anita, H. S., Ashok, D. and Revankar (2007), "Micro Credit Through Self Help Groups for Rural Development" *Southern Economists*, Vol. 46, No. 8, Aug. 15, 2007, p. 19.

23

AN AGENDA FOR NEW INSTITUTIONAL ORDER IN THE GLOBAL ERA

S. V. Padmini

There are a number of major obstacles that will have to be surmounted in order to build a new global order. The first is the absence of a set of shared principles that are embraced by all the major players. The second is that, given the asymmetrical power relations found in global society, the various actors differ in their ability to influence this process. The third is the difficulty of forming international coalitions capable of offsetting those inequalities, whether through developing-country partnerships or international alliances of social sectors which feel that their interests are being harmed by the globalization process. In addition to all the above, there is the central paradox of the world of today, the gap between global issues and what continue to be essentially national and local political processes. The challenges involved in building a new institutional order are therefore enormous. The article sets out four basic principles for the creation of a better world order: shared objectives; rules and institutions that respect diversity; complementarity of national, regional and international spheres of activity; and equitable participation coupled with appropriate rules to uphold international governance. Further the article draws together the elements of various proposals regarding national strategies for dealing with globalization: macroeconomic stability in abroad sense, the attainment of systemic competitiveness. In addition the article focused the crucial role played by regional actors in a globalized world and some of the main issues that ECLAC feels should figure on the global agenda: the provision of public goods; the correction of the global order's asymmetries in the areas of finance and macroeconomics, production, technology and factor mobility; and the consolidation of a rights-based international social agenda, Building systemic competitiveness In addition to providing complementary analyses that refer specifically to Latin America and the Caribbean.

I

Fundamental Principles for the Construction of a Better Global Order

Three Key Objectives: Supply Global Public Goods, Correct International Asymmetries and Firmly Establish a Rights-based Global Social Agenda

The globalization process has highlighted the need to provide certain "global public goods," such as the defence of democracy (and, hence, of civil and political rights), peace, security (including the war on terrorism), disarmament, international justice, the struggle to do away with internationally organized crime and corruption, environmental sustainability, the effort to combat and eventually eradicate pandemics and to increase cooperation in the field of health and sanitation in general, the worldwide war on drugs, the accumulation of human knowledge, cultural diversity, the defence of public spaces held in common by all, global macroeconomic and financial stability, and, more generally, the development of an appropriate institutional structure for the management of economic interdependence (Kaul, Grunberg and Stern, 1999).1 There is a huge gap, however, between the recognition of this fact, on the one hand, and, on the other, the weakness of the existing international supply structures for these goods and the amount of resources allocated for this purpose.

The dividing line between "public goods" in the traditional sense of the term (goods whose consumption is non-exclusive) and those with strong externalities is somewhat blurred, and this list therefore includes some goods (e.g., public spaces, many forms of cultural expression and human knowledge) which do not fit the classic definition of public goods.

Support for the international organizations needed to supply or coordinate the provision of global public goods is therefore essential. The emphasis here should be on the coordination of supply rather than on supply functions as such, since in many cases the regional level may be the most appropriate one for the provision of public goods. Another reason for focusing on the regional level is because the concerted efforts of non-governmental organizations and the private sector must be brought to bear on this task. This is why, as a general rule, the provision of global public goods is accomplished through the efficient operation of *networks* of various types of organizations rather than being carried out by individual agencies. The need to provide sufficient financing for the supply of global public goods has been underscored by a number of recent reports (United Nations, 2000b; Zedillo and others, 2001a). It is important here to differentiate between these kinds of contributions and official development assistance (ODA), since all countries should play a part in financing global public goods based on the principle of "common yet differentiated responsibilities", as formulated in the Rio Declaration on Environment and Development issued at the United Nations Conference on Environment and Development (also known as the Earth Summit) in 1992. The supply of public goods is not the only item on the international agenda, of course. It must be backed up by the accomplishment of two complementary tasks: overcoming the asymmetries of the global order, and formulating a rights-based international social agenda. These tasks could be included on the public-goods agenda, but doing so would create confusion, because, in the final analysis, they have to do with the equitable distribution of essentially *private* goods. Indeed, the provision of public goods and redistribution are classic, but quite different, duties of the State. Moreover, the elimination of international asymmetries and the formulation of a rights-based social agenda involve different spheres of activity, since the former focuses on rectifying disparities between *countries* whereas the latter focuses directly on individuals. In order to surmount asymmetries at the global level, it is important to realize that, in the presence of widely differing positions such as those found in a hierarchical international system, attempts to apply equal terms in order to set up a level playing field will only serve to heighten existing inequalities. In the light of the considerations discussed in the preceding chapter, it becomes clear that the global agenda must include action on three different fronts. The first is to enhance the transmission of growth impulses from developed to developing countries via international trade and technology transfer. The second is to work through international lending agencies to give developing countries more breathing space for the adoption of countercyclical macroeconomic policies, help reverse the international concentration of credit and expedite the financial development of these countries. The third is to make sure that the global agenda places just as much emphasis on the international mobility of labour as it does on the international mobility of capital. If an international social agenda is to be established, every member of the global society must be acknowledged as a citizen of the world and, hence, as possessing certain *rights*. The most cogent expressions of these rights are found in international declarations on civil, political, economic,social, cultural and labour rights, on the rights of women, children and different ethnic groups, and on the right to development.2 The commitments made by countries at world summits, some of which are accorded special recognition in the United Nations Millennium Declaration, complement those instruments to a great extent. These instruments also reflect a recognition of the fact that the responsibility for fulfilling their provisions is primarily borne at the national level. It is to be responsibility for fulfilling their provisions is primarily borne at the national level.

The right to development was enshrined in United Nations General Assembly resolution 41/128 of 4 December 1986. This resolution defines the right to development as "a comprehensive economic, social, cultural and political process, which aims at the constant improvement of the well-being of the entire population and of all individuals on the basis of their active, free and meaningful participation in development and in the fair distribution of benefits resulting therefrom, ..." Sengupta (2001) focuses on the components of justice and equity inherent in this concept and on the importance of making sure that countries' growth rates are not only reasonable but also sustainable and are not achieved at the cost of human rights or a decline in opportunities for personal fulfilment. See, in this regard, Artigas (2001).

It is to be expected, however, that compliance with international commitments will be a gradual process, since this is the only way that it can contribute to the construction of a true world citizenry. The tensions existing between cultural identity and globalization will inevitably affect this process, and a way therefore has to be found to reconcile the principles of equality on which human rights declarations are based with the "right to be different". These three central objectives of the global agenda reflect the fact that, in an interdependent world, the rights of all depend, in the final analysis, on the existence of a "global social covenant". Embracing this widely accepted principle of nation-building implies an awareness of the fact that economic affairs cannot be separated from the social and political fabric and that, therefore, if nations are to survive and prosper, market forces must function within the framework of an institutional order based on broader, more inclusive social values and aims. The existing international order suffers from serious shortcomings in terms of its capacity to achieve these three objectives. The United Nations is the appropriate institutional framework for a dialogue about ways of ensuring the global coherence of the system and of filling the voids that exist in relation to international cooperation. Decision-making authority and executive capacity in certain fields are, however, held by a wide range of specialized agencies that work not only at the global level but in the regional and national arenas as well.

Global Rules and Institutions that Respect Diversity

The essentially national and local nature of policy making has profound implications for the international order. The globalization process notwithstanding, the primary setting for the exercise of democracy will continue to be nations and local communities for a long time to come. The focus for global institutions should therefore be on acknowledging interdependence and managing it proactively. Ultimately, however, these institutions rely on national responsibilities and policies, as One of these principles' implications is that it is futile to promote democracy unless national representative and participatory processes give the people a say in the formulation of economic and social development strategies (Ocampo, 2001). This is why respect for diversity—within the bounds of interdependence and, thus, of the common good of "cosmopolitan society"—is a crucial element of any democratic international order. 3

This view fits in with the idea that institution-building (institutional capital), social consensus (social capital), the development of human capital and technological capacity (knowledge capital) are .essentially endogenous processes. It also reflects the belief that there is not just one "right" path to development and integration into the global economy. There are a range of different options depending on the political and institutional history of each country and the differing challenges and This principle is embodied in the more recent thinking on cooperation for development, which emphasizes that its effectiveness will depend on there being a sense of national policy ownership. In fact, this principle has won acceptance as a basic guideline for the design of ODA conditionality, IMF, 2001). However, quite frequently, it is ignored in practice. Indeed, an effort is often made to "compel" ownership of the policies that international agencies feel are appropriate (Helleiner, 2001). Even so, the importance of ownership is one of the overarching rules governing the operations of international agencies. Their role is to support national decision-making, not take its place.

The reader will recall Kant's call for the formation – based on a covenant among States – of a cosmopolitan society. Kant was one of the first philosophers to propose that the social contract be extended to include States, provided that they complied with the "republican clause", i.e., guarantee individual rights and freedoms, the division of power, the supremacy of the law, and a representative system of government.

Complementarity of Global, Regional and National Institution Building

In the absence of suitable institutions, globalization is proving to be a disintegrative force. At the national level, some regions, production sectors and social groups are coming out as"winners" and others as "losers" in the intense Schumpeterian process of creative destruction now being witnessed worldwide (ECLAC, 2000a). This process is not only increasing each country's internal heterogeneity but, at the same time, is also undermining the State's ability to ensure its cohesiveness. The powerful centripetal forces which the global economy has been generating for several centuries now (Prebisch, 1987) impel developing countries to focus on carving out a foothold in industrialized markets and competing among themselves to attract footloose investments. Under these circumstances, integration efforts aimed at forming larger economic units are relegated to a position of secondary importance. A virtuous circle of complementary global, regional and national institution-building is needed in order to cope with these forces.

International debate has gradually given rise to a broad consensus as to the fundamental role of national strategies in determining how successful a country will be in forming linkages with the world economy. Such strategies are also essential in order to handle the disintegrative forces being generated by globalization within each nation. Moreover, as noted earlier, they continue to be the main vehicle for democracy in the global era. inevitably be insufficient and this, in turn, will hinder national development. What is more, unless a frontal attack is launched against the strong tendency towards inequality at the international level which has been in evidence for the past two centuries, national efforts may prove relatively prospects continue to be a source of dissatisfaction, the heterogeneity existing across countries and Action at the regional and subregional levels plays a critical role as a midway point between the global and national orders. This arena for what ECLAC has termed "open regionalism" (1994) proposals being made regarding international economic and social reform. There are, however, at least four arguments that attest to the importance of this intermediate sphere. The first is the complementarity existing between global and regional institutions in a heterogeneous international community. The advocacy of democracy, peace and disarmament are all examples of instances in which, given the existing degree of international heterogeneity, it is best to base the provision of the corresponding public goods on a combination of world and regional organizations. The protection of strategic ecosystems and many spheres of economic activity—such as macroeconomic policy coordination and others that will be touched upon later—are other cases in point. processes. In political terms, this means that, within the global order, the smaller countries will be able to make their voice heard (or heard much more clearly) only if it takes the form of a regional voice. This has to do not only with the development of rules and standards, but also with the defense of their interests under existing rules and standards. In fact, the paradox of the global system is that global rules are most important for small countries, which are, however, precisely the ones that have the least influence over their formulation and defence. Meanwhile, the most influential actors try to avoid making commitments or to compel other actors to accept their rules. These problems can only be solved if the smaller countries organize themselves. The third argument, which is closely tied in with the first two, is that regional and subregional institutions enjoy a greater sense of ownership. There are opponents to this view as well, of course, who contend that regional and subregional institutions are less powerful than their individual members. The validity of these arguments will therefore depend on the depth of the corresponding regional agreements, which is what ultimately determines their effectiveness.

As the world becomes increasingly interdependent, the scope of autonomy has shifted to subregional or regional levels in some areas. This is what has been happening in the case of macroeconomic policy. It is also the case with the regulation of competition and of public utilities when transnational corporations enter the market. In all these fields, the regional arena is becoming the crucial one for the exercise of some degree of true autonomy, and it is possible that this will increasingly be the case as time goes on. The main conclusion to be drawn from this analysis is that global public goods should be provided by a network of world and regional institutions, rather than by one or a few international institutions. A system of this type can be made to function efficiently and may prove to be more balanced in terms of power relations. In fact, this is the most advantageous system for the less powerful countries within the global order.

The construction of a truly new international architecture is founded upon the overall effect of global and regional institutional reforms. Unfortunately, many of the proposals put forward in recent years regarding the financial and, above all, social aspects of the international architecture focus almost entirely on adapting national structures to the global era. In other words, these proposals are looking at the *national* rather than the international architecture, and this is precisely their main weakness.

Equitable participation and appropriate governance

The insufficient degree to which developing countries participate in international economic institutions has been a controversial issue in recent years. In some cases—as in the formulation of financial rules and standards—they play little or no role at all. In others, the role they play is not commensurate with the size of their economies, much less that of their populations; this point has been raised, in particular, in connection with their voting power in some institutions. In still other instances, even though decisions are made by consensus, agreements are reached on a different addition, a number of experts have pointed out that the cost of active participation in a complex world order may be prohibitive for the poorest and smallest countries. decision-making at the international level. Achieving this will require positive discrimination in favour of poor and small countries on the part of the international community. As discussed in the preceding section, it will also require an effort on the part of the smaller countries to organize themselves at the regional or subregional level. Another point to be made here is that preference should be given to institutional schemes having the largest possible number of active participants. Although groups formed by countries that share a particular interest or specific purpose may contribute to consensus-building, such groups should channel their views through established mechanisms rather than taking their place. 4 The adoption of appropriate rules of governance is another essential element. Principles developed at the national level in relation to democratic and corporate governance can serve as the foundations and improving international institutions (Marfán, 2002). 4 See, for example, Culpeper (2000) regarding the proliferation of groups or associations dealing with financial issuesfor building There is no single formula for accomplishing this, since constitutions, laws, rules and regulations, and traditions differ in each historical context and evolve over time. It can be said, however, that the most effective and legitimate forms of governance are based on shared principles. These principles do not, moreover, develop spontaneously, and an explicit effort must therefore be made to institutionalize them. Four principles of good governance can be outlined here. The first is for governmental functions to be carried out by a body with executive powers rather than by an assembly. The second is that the civil rights of the governed take precedence over rules and regulations established by the various levels of government. Consequently, the rights of minorities should be clearly established, while bearing in mind that their identification and recognition as fundamental rights are the end result of a learning process. The third principle is that the authorities should regularly give an accounting of what they have done to safeguard the interests of the community and uphold the rights of all its members. Transparency, timely disclosure and, more generally, accountability are essential components of this community process. The fourth principle is that the authorities should submit to the scrutiny of independent bodies and to outside audits that will provide confidence among minority groups. These groups do not govern, but they do have the right to oversee the actions of those who do hold power. Furthermore, the bodies in charge of enforcing individual rights should have the power to penalize wrongdoing. A good example of the application of these principles is provided by political governance in a representative democracy, where executive power is exercised by representatives who have been elected by the majority. It is the duty of this branch of government to uphold the fundamental rights of citizens as set down in the Constitution and other laws that apply equally to all citizens and to provide a regular accounting of the ends and means by which the government functions. Oversight of its acts and its enforcement of citizens' rights and of the law are carried out by independent agencies. An important part of this function is the auditing performed by the principal parliamentary minority (the opposition). Another example can be found in corporate governance. In this case, majority shareholders control the firm's board of directors and management. The dispersion and varying interests of effectively. Good corporate governance seeks to prevent the shareholders that hold a controlling interest from obtaining a disproportionate share of profits or other benefits relative to the size of their stake. To achieve this, executives and members of the board are required to comply with certain rules concerning transparency and timely disclosure and with regulations that set out their responsibilities. In addition, there are independent oversight agencies (including outside auditors) and in-house auditing committees (usually formed by members of the board elected by minority shareholders). These bodies complement the work of regulatory agencies and the judiciary, which have the power to penalize wrongdoing. The governance of the globalization process could be substantially improved by adherence to these same principles. The large nations are obviously the leaders of the globalization process and hold a dominant position in the major international financial institutions, in which voting power is based on capital contributions. The resemblance ends there, however, since the other principles of governance are not clearly established. For example, it is not certain that the major nations' control over the process is legitimized by their respect for the rights of all countries. Nor is there a universally accepted institutional structure for upholding the rights of less powerful nations. In fact, quite often there is not even a clear idea of what those rights are. The application of these principles to improve the governance of the globalization process will therefore entail according priority to the fundamental rights of developing countries (especially the smaller ones), institutionalizing accountability and increasing oversight by bodies that will inspire the confidence of all the parties concerned. This approach involves placing certain limits on the power of the most influential countries, since this is the only way to improve the governance of the globalization process. It will also lead to a greater commitment to the global institutional structure on the part of developing countries by increasing their sense of ownership.

II

National Strategies for Dealing with Globalization

The Role and Basic Components of National Strategies

As has been discussed at length in the literature on institution-building in recent years, in today's global era, any development strategy must be found upon a solid, democratic social covenant to ensure its political stability; non-discretionary local systems and modes of behavior that provide security as to contract performance; and the formation of an impartial, relatively efficient State bureaucracy. These are also, of course, basic components of a pro-investment environment as well. These general sorts of institutional elements are not sufficient in themselves, however. They are the backdrop for the development process, but they do not account for the specific forces that drive growth in developing countries or, in many cases, that lead to the depletion of growth impulses. 5 National strategies for today's global era should incorporate at least four core elements:

(a) macroeconomic policies designed to reduce vulnerability and facilitate productive investment;
(b) strategies for developing systemic competitiveness;
(c) a keen awareness of the priorities of the environmental agenda, which, by its very nature, is essentially global in scope; and
(d) highly active social policies, especially in the fields of education, employment and social protection (ECLAC, 2000a, 2000b 2001b; ECLAC/UNEP, 2001).

There are no universally valid models in any of these areas. Thus, the institutional learning process and, most importantly, democracy have a broad sphere of action in which to function. One of the most serious mistakes made in the last quarter of the twentieth century was the promotion of a single "solution" in each of these fields based on the principle of full market liberalization. The tendency to equate successful integration into the globalized world with economic liberalization overlooks the fact that many equally successful strategies have *not* been based on all-out market liberalization but instead on various ways of forming "virtuous-circle" linkages between the State and the market. It would be just as mistaken, however, to take the opposite approach and try to resuscitate models which were successful when the world economy was less integrated but which thus correspond to stages in the development of the world economy that are now clearly a thing of the past.

Macroeconomic Strategy

The experiences of Latin America and the Caribbean during the final quarter of the twentieth century demonstrate that all forms of macroeconomic disequilibrium are economically and socially costly. A number of lessons can be drawn from these experiences. First, macroeconomic discipline economic discourse in recent decades, which has focused attention on fiscal balances and low inflation. This narrower view overlooks many important dimensions of macroeconomic stability, such as balanceof-payments sustainability, the soundness of national financial systems, and the stability of real variables such as economic growth and employment. Macroeconomic management should be directed towards avoiding unsustainable public or private deficits, guarding against financial imbalances in flows or in the way balances are structured, controlling inflation and curbing any instability in real economic variables. To use the terms employed by Maddison (1991), these factors are associated with the "ultimate causality" rather than with the "proximate causality" of economic growth. See also Ocampo (2002a). In order to achieve all these objectives, some important policy choices will have to be made and, for these purposes, there is no simple way of defining stability or any universally valid system flexibility in macroeconomic management has to be combined with suitable regulations. Recent events leave no doubt as to the fact that, in the long run, macroeconomic authorities' credibility can be strengthened more effectively through prudently managed flexibility than through the adoption of overly rigid rules.6 Within this framework, one of the authorities' key objectives should be to lengthen the time horizon for macroeconomic management in order to take in the whole of the business cycle and support dynamic long-term growth. Encompassing the entire cycle will provide the necessary scope for the adoption of countercyclical macroeconomic policies that can help forestall unsustainable booms and afford sufficient flexibility in dealing with external crises. The option of employing countercyclical policies is quite limited without the support of international institutions, however, and this has consequently become one of these institutions' basic functions in the current phase great extent, complementary—since more stable economic growth is one of the strongest incentives for fixed capital investment—but they can also confront policy makers with some difficult choices. Based on these principles, fiscal policy should be designed using a pluriannual horizon. It should also be based on long-term guidelines for ensuring a structural fiscal balance that allow moderate, temporary surpluses or deficits for countercyclical purposes or, alternatively, set an explicit target for the ratio between the public debt and GDP. The active use of stabilization funds (or equivalent instruments) can be the most effective way to build up surpluses during booms that can then be used to contend with crisis situations. The desirable level and structure of public revenues and expenditures will, in the long run, depend on what kind of demands each society's fiscal covenant places on the State (ECLAC, 1998c). In countries with very low tax burdens (as is true of a number of Latin American nations), taxes can be increased to finance the core functions of the State, especially in social sectors. In fact, as recently stated by the World Bank (2002a), the tax burden and levels of public expenditure in the developing world tend to be low in comparison to those of developed countries. Monetary and exchange-rate management are, of course, closely related. Some degree of flexibility in the exchange regime is essential for countercyclical monetary management (i.e., for the application of restrictive policies during booms and expansionary ones during the downswing in the cycle). The desirable degree of flexibility will be greater in the larger economies that have well developed capital and exchange markets. It may be wise to allow the exchange rate to appreciate in order to soak up excess foreign exchange during booms, while a depreciation may be needed to spur the production of tradables during crises and to provide enough breathing room for reactivationoriented fiscal and monetary policies. In financially open economies, the prudential regulation of capital flows, either through the use of reserve requirements or taxes on external borrowing or by means of direct regulation, is an extremely useful supplementary tool for avoiding excessive external borrowing during booms and to prevent liability structures from becoming skewed towards short-term obligations. In more closed economies, caution should be used in opening up the capital account. In fact, if a country does not have a solid financial system, there is really no convincing argument for opening it up at all. policy, since its core function is to prevent unsustainable financial structures from being spawned during economic booms. 6 This may, in fact, be the major lesson to be learned from Argentina's experiences over the past decade. Direct regulatory tools include rules on borrowing by public-sector agencies at all levels, direct restrictions on certain types of private flows (short-term borrowing, portfolio flows or external borrowing by non-tradable sectors). In the long run, economic growth hinges on a combination of sound fiscal systems that provide the necessary resources for the public sector to do its job, a competitive exchange rate, moderate real interest rates and the development of a deep financial market. Macroeconomic policy should be focused on ensuring the first three elements. The last is a complementary process. The key objective of financial deepening is to provide suitably priced investment finance with sufficiently long maturities. In the absence of a well developed financial market, many investors (particularly the larger ones) will turn to international lenders, thereby substituting exchange risk for maturity risk. Use of this escape valve therefore entails serious hazards, as well being beyond the reach of smaller firms. The liberalization of financial systems in Latin America and the Caribbean has not deepened financial markets or reduced the region's high intermediation costs as much as had been expected. Consequently, the public sector still has an important role to and investment funds, bond and mortgage markets, and hedging systems) or in arranging for the direct provision of such facilities by well-run development banks. The existence of this unsatisfied demand for investment finance is compounded by the absence of suitable financial services for micro- and small enterprises and for the poorer households. This situation creates a greater demand for direct or indirect public intervention. Low national savings rates are another constraint on investment financing in Latin America and the Caribbean. Efforts to increase public-sector saving, the creation of corporate savings incentives (especially to encourage firms to retain profits) and special mechanisms to foster household saving (for retirement, in particular) may be useful means of raising national savings rates (ECLAC, 2001b, Chap. 4).

Building Systemic Competitiveness

A dynamic transformation of production structures should not be viewed as a reactive phenomenon that automatically follows from good macroeconomic management, but rather as an active and essential component of any development strategy, even at this juncture in the globalization process (Rodrik, 1999a; ECLAC, 2000a). The core objective of these strategies should done by ECLAC over a decade ago (ECLAC, 1990; Fajnzylber, 1990), 8 is based on three main elements. The first is the role of knowledge as the foundation for competitiveness, since it is the only factor that enables countries to produce goods and services capable of "making the grade" on international markets while protecting and increasing their citizens' real incomes. The second is the idea that competitiveness depends less on individual firms than on the performance of each sector as a whole, its interaction with input-supplying sectors and, ultimately, the smooth operation of the entire economic system. The third is that, given the serious imperfections existing in technology markets and strong externalities among economic agents associated with the systemic nature of competitiveness, the development of sound technology markets and production linkages is in large part the outcome of the deliberate efforts of the State, business associations and, particularly, of collaborative initiatives undertaken by the State and private sector to create a virtuous circle that will bolster the system's competitiveness. The three basic components of this strategy are:

(i) the creation of innovation systems to speed up the accumulation of technological capacity;

(ii) support for changes in production structures and the formation of production linkages; and

(iii) provision of quality infrastructure services. The creation of adequate social safety nets and sustainable environmental management are however, and will be considered later on in this document. 8 These concepts also contain elements developed concurrently by other authors: see, in particular, Porter (1990).

Given the key role of knowledge, any competitiveness strategy must be based on increased investment in education, vocational and business training, and science and technology. This process, whose aim is the creation of dynamic innovation systems, should be led by the State, but the private sector should also be actively involved. These efforts should focus on increasing the capacity of all actors to absorb knowledge and on developing appropriate mechanisms for the transfer and adaptation of technology and business skills, especially to medium-sized and small firms. Business associations and incentives for various forms of collaboration between these associations and providers of educational and vocational training play a fundamental role in this effort. Innovation systems should be strengthened at all (i.e., local, national and, to a growing extent, regional) levels. In view of the intrinsic importance and cross-cutting nature of new information andcommunication technologies, efforts to promote their active use throughout the economic, social and even political (e-government) systems are of vital importance. Access to a quality telecommunications network and to competitively priced information and communications equipment is one of the pillars of this endeavour. Other mainstays include the production of software, incorporation of technology into production and trade, and the formation of business networks that make effective use of new technologies. The incorporation of new technologies into the educational and health-care systems requires special State support and community mechanisms produced by disparities between different social sectors' access to new technologies) is a much more serious Economic growth necessarily entails an ongoing process of changing production patterns in which some branches of production lead growth while others lag behind. This process is not necessarily automatic or harmonious, since the expansion of new sectors involves the development of a complementary set of activities based on a technological learning process, the establishment of commercial networks and significant coordination costs (Hirschman, 1958; Chang, 1994; Ocampo, 2002a). The diversification of the production structure must therefore be an explicit priority of any competitiveness strategy. This idea has been expressly recognized in the industrialized world, where It also enjoyed wide acceptance in the past as a component of State-driven industrialization strategies in developing countries, and it is an essential element of the most successful developing economies, especially those in East Asia. Diversification strategies have been discarded in most countries of the region, however. Within the context of the globalization process, the diversification of production has three priorities. The first is the diversification of the export base and of target markets. This calls for a very active form of commercial diplomacy aimed at securing stable access to external markets, as well as the development of a competitive, high-quality service infrastructure—in the areas of finance, insurance, promotion and certification—to back up exports of goods and services. The second priority is to develop programmes to broaden the linkages of activities oriented towards the international market or dominated by transnational corporations. The weakening of such linkages is one of the most problematic aspects of recent trends in the region. For this reason, "linkage policies" designed to increase the value added in export sectors and/or sectors with a high proportion of FDI should be adopted as a forward-looking priority. Among these linkages, those associated with the provision of technology-intensive services are of special importance. These policies would, in practice, amount to a shift away from a policy aimed at maximizing the quantity of exports and FDI to a policy aimed at improving their quality.

The third priority is to support the formation of production clusters in particular locations. This process is a response to the growing dynamism of local spheres of economic activity in the global era. It is particularly important for steering small and medium-sized enterprises towards production for the international market or linkage with export sectors (ECLAC, 2000a, vol. III, chap. 3). The other core aspect of competitiveness policy is the provision of *quality infrastructure services.* In a number of countries, various public-private partnerships have succeeded in making significant progress in this regard, particularly in telecommunications, port services and maritime transport, and – to a lesser extent and with wider discrepancies from one country to another – in energy services (electricity and gas) (ECLAC, 2001a, Chap. 5). It must be acknowledged, however, that private participation in these sectors has been accompanied by serious regulatory gaps and, in some cases, has burdened the State with contingent liabilities that do not always have a sound rationale (ECLAC, 1998; 2000a, vol. III, chap. 5). The main problems in terms of infrastructure continue to be found in land transport, including both railways and roads. Shortcomings in both the quantity and the quality of road networks are particularly severe. Accordingly, substantial improvements in road infrastructure, the correction of regulatory gaps and the rationalization of the management of contingent liabilities should be given priority, as should improvement of the efficiency of State enterprises in areas where the State continues to provide services directly. Progress on all these fronts will require major institutional and organizational efforts to formulate and implement active competitiveness policies, since the pre-existing systems of government intervention in productive development were dismantled or severely curtailed in most of the countries of the region during the economic liberalization phase. Such systems would, in any case, be ill-suited to the new environment. In this area, as in others, it is necessary to "invent" new institutions, whose management will no doubt require an intensive learning process. The possible models for these institutions are certainly not uniform, since they depend on the specific characteristics of each situation. A public-private partnership is essential to fill the information gaps found in each of these sectors (i.e., the former's limited microeconomic information and the latter's insufficient familiarity with global and cross-sectoral processes). In other words, institutional design must take into account both the "forest" and the "trees".

The instruments to be developed for this purpose should be based on checks and balances that establish a clear link between incentives and results (Amsden, 2001) and thereby preclude rent-seeking behaviour on the part of beneficiary firms. This endeavour should comprise various combinations of horizontal and selective instruments, depending on each country's institutional context, to be chosen on the basis of shared strategic visions of the directions to be emphasized in joint public-private efforts. This is less an exercise in "picking winners", as it is commonly called, than an effort to identify opportunities and direct the actions needed to ensure that some of them bear fruit. This type of strategic exercise is one in which all private investors engage on a regular basis. It is hard to understand why some schools of economic thought consider it illegitimate to carry out such an exercise in relation to a particular territory, whether it be a town, a country or even a subregion or region.

References

John Bach McMaster, *The Life and Times of Stephen Girard [Microform] Mariner and Merchant*, 2 Vols., *Library of American Civilization 20034* (Philadelphia: Lippincott, 1918), p. 388.

The Canton Register, Vol. 8, No. 10 Reproduced a Special Edict of the Hoppo to reduce this Discount to a Just One. Cited in KS Latourette, *The History of Early Relations between the United States and China, 1784-1844* p 71.

"The Foreign Merchant Stands, with His Crying Need for Fixity of Exchange between Gold and Silver, which Required for its Establishment a Fixed Unit of Currency, which in Turn can be Obtained by Coinage" HB. Morse, Trade and Administration of China (London, 1920) p. 187.

24

MICROFINANCE IN INDIA– FROM FINANCIAL TO SOCIAL INTERMEDIATION

V. Basil Hans

"Much remains unknown in microfinance" – ***Karlan and Sendhil***

Introduction

Microfinance is the buzzword, a product of new developmental thinking and policy- making in the globalisation era. It is a unique amalgamation of industrial (including financial) and institutional reforms in the present scenario of development economics. As a major tool of development, it is fast developing as an international industry (Fisher and Sriram, 2002). For the developing countries it has come as a breakthrough in the philosophy and practices of poverty eradication, economic empowerment and inclusive growth. Yet given the enormity of economic compulsions and complexities in agrarian economies like India, microfinance is an unfinished agenda.

While the contributions of microfinance institutions (MFIs)[1] to monetary liquidity and financial sustainability is cognizable, it is unclear whether microfinance in its present structure contributes to reduction in poverty (Hermes and Lensink, 2007) or is the best route to rural development. The MFIs as financial intermediaries have been doing a commendable job, particularly for financial rejuvenation in the countryside. But they need to graduate into agents of social intermediation thereby bringing social capital and microfinance together. The social intermediation processes of microfinance initiatives are necessary to extend their outreach to and within poorer segments of the population, particularly women, and have a separate value in and of themselves by positively enhancing the social capital of the participants (Szabo, S., 1999). MFI by releasing the true potential of its members through social intermediation ensures building an inclusive society.

Microfinance movement is nothing short of a revolution in developmental finance. It is easy to be complacent about the origin and growth of MFIs in the agrarian-developing economies like India where there is a fertile soil for such institutions, where credit has been a binding force for the populace, and where the history of institutions such as cooperative societies has been almost parallel with the history of freedom movement. That is why group-based financial activities get easily rooted here. They have had done credible job in mobilising people and their resources for productive investments. Development practitioners in social development have also noted their apparent capacity to empower the most vulnerable, especially women; to allow the not-yet-economically-active to become so; and to create community-based structures that build mutual support and trust.

The "group" element of microfinance has become a central aspect of practice and it has been recognised by some as a methodological component equal in weight to the actual exchange of finance. Labelled "social intermediation," to reflect a parallel concept to financial intermediation, the organisation of groups to mediate financial and social services to members is seen as an essential part of the microfinance process enabling the poor to bridge a daunting series of barriers that have kept them outside the financial system - barriers that are at once physical, economic, and social. Social intermediation achieves this by creating social capital that compensates for their lack of material assets. In turn, this investment in social capital creates creditworthy borrowers where none existed before, and supports financial investments in their economic activities (Edgecomb, 1998). In this sense MFIs become not only agents of change but also avenues of unity and solidarity. They have the potential of developing social capital. Yet not all is well with MFIs with regards to their forms and functions. They are facing criticisms and are also receiving suggestions for alternative strategies for achieving more, intensively and extensively. For instance the question of "regulation" is currently in vogue. Although much research has been done regarding the role and reach of the MFIs as "financial" intermediaries, studies regarding the "social" perspective are limited. Therefore, it is necessary to understand this perspective contextually, both in theory and practice, with reference to the Indian economy. We also need to examine how the MFIs can and should graduate from financial intermediaries to social intermediaries in order to enhance their quality.

Defining Microfinance

To most, microfinance and microcredit mean the same, i.e. providing very small loans to very poor families, to help them in the economic activities. But specifically, microfinance refers to loans, savings, insurance, transfer services and other financial products targeted at low-income clients whereas microcredit refers to a small loan to a client made by a bank or other institution. Microcredit can be offered, often without collateral, to an individual or through group lending. The typical microfinance clients are low-income persons that do not have access to formal financial institutions.

Microfinance clients are typically self-employed, often household-based entrepreneurs. In rural areas, they are usually small farmers and others who are engaged in small income-generating activities such as food processing and petty trade. In urban areas, microfinance activities are more diverse and include shopkeepers, service providers, artisans, street vendors, etc. Microfinance clients are poor and vulnerable non-poor who have a relatively stable source of income (the Microfinance Gateway).

In the most simple terms, microfinance is "banking for the poor" and covers microcredit, micro savings, micro insurance and remittances (Kandelwala, 2007). Microfinance services are financial services that poor people desire and demand (i.e. they are willing to pay) for. The term also refers to the practice of delivering those services in a sustainable manner. Christen *et.al.* (1984) have viewed the microfinance movement as "a world in which as many poor and near-poor households as possible have permanent access to an appropriate range of high quality financial services, including not just credit but also savings, insurance, and fund transfers." Even the World Bank feels that the poor, i.e. the target clients of microfinance, need and use more financial services than just microloans.[2] In this sense microfinance is microcredit *plus*, the additional features of the former being:

- Deposit services (savings facilities)
- Insurance
- Money transfer (remittance) services
- Micro leasing

In this regard the definition of microfinance given by the World Bank is noteworthy:

> "Microfinance refers to small-scale financial services–primarily credit and savings–to people who farm or fish or herd and who operate small enterprises or micro enterprises...; who provide services; who work for wages or commissions; who gain income from renting out small amounts of land, vehicles, draft animals, or machinery or tools; and to other individuals and groups at the local levels of developing countries, both rural and urban. Many such households have multiple sources of income" (Robinson, 2000).[3]

In India the recent Task Force on Microfinance has defined microfinance as the "provision of thrift, credit and other financial services and products of very small amounts to the poor in rural, semi-urban or urban areas for enabling them to raise their income levels and improve living standards. In the Indian context terms like "small and marginal farmers", "rural artisans" and "economically weaker sections" have been used to broadly define micro-finance customers (Basix, 2000; Khandelwal, 2007). These target groups need to be given both economic and social support for development. It is now widely recognised that widening and deepening reach of the poor with microfinance have both social and commercial dimensions. How to balance the social objectives with the financial objectives of microfinance is therefore, an important challenge (DHAN Foundation, 2003).

Microfinance in the Saga of Credit (The Evolution)

Microcredit, in the sense of small loans to the poor, is of ancient origins in India. Traders and moneylenders have traditionally provided credit to the rural poor. But such loans were usually made at exorbitant rates of interest leading to considerable hardship and impoverishment of borrowers, including undesirable and illegal practices like 'begar' (bonded labour). What we refer to as microfinance today does not include such exploitative practices, but rather lending to the poor at reasonable but sustainable rates. The pioneer and mainstream institutions involved in providing microfinance in India have been the cooperatives, the Regional Rural Banks (RRBs), the National Bank for Agriculture and Rural Development (NABARD), the Small Industries Development Bank of India (SIDBI), and the Housing Development Finance Corporation (HDFC). Then came the alternative micro financial institutions viz. the NGOs such as self-help groups (SHGs) and the Non Banking Finance Companies (NBFCs) (Prasad, 2007) The poster boys among the Indian microfinance NGOs–SHARE, BASIX, SEWA, MYRADA and PRADAN, for instance–have deservingly received attention from academicians, media-persons as well as the government (Chakrabarti).

The idea of micro finance was originally developed as a survival strategy for the poor. Then it became a part of development finance. In India, Ela Bhatt established the Self-Employed Women's Association (SEWA) in 1972. It was to bring poor women together and give them ways to fight for their rights and earn better livings. Its membership grew to

7000 members in 1975 and to over now 700,000 now. Mohammed Yunus founded the Grameen Bank project in Bangladesh in 1976.[4] It operates very differently from mainstream banks. Most of its clients are women. The bank encourages them to form a small group of five borrowers. The group members guarantee each other's loan. These loans are used for self-employment activities like raising cows, seasonal crop trading, weaving, sewing, operating grocery shops. Over the years more than one third of these groups have crossed the poverty line, and another third are close to crossing it.

There are over 7000 micro finance institutions worldwide, serving over 16 million poor people. They provide poor people with access to small loans at more manageable interest rates, and lead to self-sufficiency and poverty alleviation. Today there are many models of microcredit. Through the 1980s and 1990s, microcredit programs throughout the world improved showing that poor people, especially women, had excellent repayment rates. Some of these rates were better than the formal financial sectors of most developing countries. For instance the Grameen Bank of Bangladesh has loans currently in the hands of borrowers totalling over US$300 million, with deposits of a similar amount. Over 95 per cent of the Grameen Bank's 3.8 million members are women. It has reversed conventional banking practice by removing the need for collateral and created a banking system based on mutual trust, accountability, participation and creativity. Likewise the SEWA Cooperative Bank has $1.5 million in working capital and more than 30,000 depositors with a loan return rate of 94 per cent. SEWA's efforts to increase the bargaining power, economic opportunities, health security, legal representation, and organisational abilities of Indian women have brought dramatic improvements to hundreds of thousands of lives and influenced similar initiatives around the globe (Ramakrishnan, 2007).

In India we notice two strands of microfinance, *one*, the 'mutual' strand–where microfinance is organised around the concept of mutuality as in the case of SHGs, and *two*, the 'providers' wherein an external agency called microfinance institution (MFI) offers the financial services without opening up its own governance structure to the clients (Sriram and Radha, 2007). India is brimming with SHGs who are part of a bank linkage programme supported by the NABARD. This programme, involving banks, NGOs and Government agencies throughout the country, is now the largest microfinance movement in the world, with 2 million Self Help Groups and over 25 million members. SHGs represent a unique approach to financial intermediation that combines access to low-cost financial services with a process of self-management and development for the women who are SHG members.[5] SHGs are formed and supported usually by NGOs or by Government agencies. Linked to banks and also to wider development programmes, SHGs are seen to confer many benefits, both economic and social. SHGs enable women to grow their savings and to access the credit which banks are increasingly willing to lend. SHGs can also be community platforms from which women become active in village affairs, contest in local election or take action to address social or community issues like the abuse of women, alcohol, the dowry system, schools, water supply etc (EDA).

Microfinance *Plus* (The Revolution)

The microfinance revolution started in the 1970s with independent initiatives in Latin America and South Asia. Thus far, it has allowed 65 million poor people around the world to receive small loans without collateral in order to build up assets, and buy insurance. The emphasis is on increasing economic productivity (Someshwar, 2008). Over the last decade or so microfinance has gained momentum in India. India now occupies a niche in global microfinance through promotion of self-help groups (SHGs)[5] and the typically Indian SHG-Bank Linkage model (Vasimalai and Narender, 2007). Many of those connected with microfinance–providers and borrowers–have come to accept today that it is a good tool to fight poverty. While in case of technology, "small is beautiful" was an accepted philosophy since the Gandhian era, in case of credit it might have taken cue from the small savings schemes in

India, including the conventional pigmy scheme by banks. Providers feel that they now have a potential weapon to do something within their means to help people of small means. For Chandra Shekar Ghosh of 'Bandan' a popular MFI in India, the most attractive factor in microfinance is simplicity. He says that remaining "simple, transparent and focussed" is more important than dreaming big (Chakravarty, 2007).

The microfinance movement–lending as much as a few hundred dollars to poor entrepreneurs to set up businesses such as a small grocery store, family farm, or tailoring shop–has been around for decades. What is new is that India's biggest commercial lenders, such as HDFC and UTI banks, as well as the State Bank of India, have started to focus in on this sector in a serious way. Even multinational banks with operations in India like ABN Amro, Standard Chartered, HSBC, and Citigroup are moving into the microfinance sector. They are striking up partnerships with other microlending specialists in India, and there is even talk of creating a secondary market for these loans. Microloans could be bundled together into larger bond issues and sold to Indian and global investors. If that happens, it could create the kind of liquidity that might take microlending in India into a higher realm (Lakshman, 2006).

Revolution in terms of reach and diversity of products/ services is a unique feature and contribution of microfinance. It has revolutionised the face and phases of rural credit and credit to the poor. It is credit not just to poor but to poor who are economically active but have inadequate finance for viable activities. Similarly it is much more than provision of credit. So today we hear of the call for "going beyond microcredit" or "new frontiers for microfinance" or new products or services in a limited sense. They include social security plans such as health and life insurances, pension etc. Many MFIs have recognised the need to be socially relevant and active in order to be commercially viable and useful. They have found appropriate ways of revenue enhancement, loss reduction and demand side management. The Kalinjiam success story is a case in the point (see Box 1).

Box 1

The Kalanjiam Initiative

- Kalinjiam in Tamil means 'prosperity' and also 'granary'.
- Kalanjiam Community Banking Programme (KCBP) is promoted by DHAN Foundation.
- DHAN Foundation (Development of Humane Action) is a professional development institution, incorporated as a Public Trust.
- KCBP was started in the year 1990, with groups, clusters and federations as "nested institutions".
- It has promoted 47 federations of women.
- Federations existing for more than three years have initiated many social development programmes–housing, infrastructure, health, education, sanitation, drinking water, skill building, insurance and business promotion.
- These federations have established linkages and entered Memorandum of Understanding (MoU) with local, district administration, municipalities, apex banks, CAPART, HDFC SIDBI, NABARD and industrial houses.
- The notable initiatives include comprehensive health programmes offered by federation with health insurance, group housing programme for evicted urban poor (of Madurai city), remedial education centres and decentralised libraries, collaboration with business houses for providing employment and income for members and facilitating rural-urban linkages.
- Six federations have initiated special programmes of health and education and propose to upscale over next three years.
- Many federations actively participate in promoting philanthropy in each location by way of supporting education of children through scholarships, donations to people affected by fire accidents, floods and other calamities, and for meeting major health expenses.
- Federations provide awards to meritorious students and people from various walks of life who have higher sense of social responsibility and involved in service.
- The KCBP is supported by the Sir Ratan Tata Trust since 1997.
- As on Sept. 2006 KCBP has an outreach of 3,47955 poor women spread over 139 locations in 6605 villages/slums of Tamil Nadu, Andhra Pradesh, Karnataka, Pondicherry, Maharashtra, MP, Rajasthan and Orissa.
- It has mobilised more than Rs. 75 crore of savings.
- Its achievements in accessibility of credit and basic infrastructure, (computer aided)-education, (online)-resource consultancy, employment assistance, gender issues, leadership development etc., has been commendable.
- One of the Kalanjiam leaders, Ms. Chinnapalli has been honoured with the Stree Shakti Puraskar, a national award.

Source: Sir Ratan Tata Trust (2005); Khalanjiam Foundation; DHAN Foundation (2006); and Vasimalai and Narender (2007).

Having less means or low income is only one aspect of poverty; the other aspects are uncertainties and irregularities in income streams available and low accessibility to credit and investments. The speciality of microfinance in this regard is that it is meant for those have dire need of credit and yet find it most difficult to get it from the traditional sources. In these days of globalisation, liberalisation and 'reforms', where profitability and 'viability' of operations are the only considerations, microfinance is proving itself to be a successful phenomenon. And as Mr. Udaia Kumar, Managing Director of Share Microfin, says "Bankers are now realising that poor people are bankable". How else would one explain the case of private commercial banks willingness to support micro-credit operations of NBFCs such as Share Microfin and Basix among others? Diversity and viability are now the "added criteria" for profitability, financially and otherwise.

Diversification is reflected in the fact that more than 15 organisations registered as NBFCs are into this activity, including Share Microfin and Basix. On the other hand, estimates put the NGOs nationwide at over 900, who are also into microcredit. The DWCRA has set an example in Andhra Pradesh, with the likes of Mr. Bill Clinton and Mr. Kofi Annan appreciating the concept.[6] The suggestion/prediction by some that Microfinance might see an IPO in the near term came true when Compartamos, the Mexican microfinance bank, went public on Friday, April 20th, 2007 raising $407 mm in a secondary share sale that offered up roughly 30 per cent of the company (Compartomos, 2007).

Micro financing has been revolutionising the rural economy through the SHGs. The success of the concept of microcredit through SHGs has encouraged the government to use as an instrument to address the issues of poverty and unemployment (Ramakrishnan, op. cit), with emphasis of local participation and decision-making. That way the bottom of the pyramid is being addressed through innovative strategies. Democratisation and decentralisation of finance for women empowerment is a revolution. Introduction of smart cards is a technological revolution. From financial management to environmental management and disaster management (e.g. rehabilitation during Tsunami); from Kisan cards to Smart cards; and from economic security to social security, the MFIs have travelled a long distance and the journey was worth it. They have moved with the times and moved along with the locals.

Vikram Akula who started the SKS Microfinance in 1998 and who is now on Time's list of people who shape our world, says, "There is already an MF revolution emerging in the villages and slums. It could be more powerful than the green revolution" (Shastri, 2006). Thus, microfinance has sweeping changes in the financial activities; the revolution engulfing both macro and micro enterprises.

Social Intermediation and Microfinance

Microfinance is a very powerful tool that can be used effectively to address poverty, empower the socially marginalised poor and strengthen the social fabric. Especially when directed at women, the benefits of microfinance multiply many folds. The use of microfinance to enhance income-generating opportunities of the poor is a popular tool for governmental as well as non-governmental organisations working to raise standards of living in developing countries. As evidence has shown women, in particular, have high repayment rates and benefit extensively from local microfinance initiatives. Increasing attention in recent years has been paid to the ways in which microfinance fosters social capital formation among the poor (ABN-AMRO; World Bank, 1999). Social intermediation ensures a certain minimum of social capital in the first phase of economic growth, and enhances its quantity and quality subsequently and sequentially.

Lynn Bennett calls social intermediation as the process "which combines the functions of social organisation and financial linkage... carried out through an NGO, or local government organisation, though self-help groups or through individuals, as locally appropriate" (Hulme and Paul, 1996). He further defines it as "the process of creating social capital as a support to sustainable financial intermediation with poor and disadvantaged groups or individuals" (Ledgerwood, 2000).[7] Social intermediation, thus, is the process of building human and social capital required by sustainable financial intermediation for the poor. It may require subsidies for a longer period than financial intermediation, but the subsidies must eventually be done away with (*ibid*).

One of the formulations of social capital–a concept that is still evolving–is that it refers to the willingness of individuals to cooperate with other individuals and with institutions for a common purpose. The World Bank Social Capital Initiative considers social capital as the internal social and cultural coherence of society, the norms and values those interactions among people and the institutions in which they are embedded.[8] Therefore, sustainable growth requires not only physical, natural and human capital, but also social capital.

Credit needs of poor sections of the society are determined in a complex socio-economic milieu (Veerashekharappa, 2007). While for borrowers microfinance becomes economically helpful and socially progressive for lenders also it must become economically lucrative and socially progressive. This is what societal welfare intermediation (through financial or otherwise) is all about. This is the new ethics of microfinance.[9]

Social is in-built in microfinance–in the relationship between borrowers and between borrowers and the institution, peer supervision, social collateral, sweat collateral (ala Gandhian bread labour)–where the recipient has to work to earn cash to enable repayment (Someshwar, *op. cit*). Microfinance institutions could also serve as intermediaries between borrowers and the formal financial sector and on-lend funds backed by a public sector guarantee (Phelps, 1995). It is now being accepted that certain intangible human values can be used as collaterals for supporting investment in economic endeavours as in case of human capital formation, for example. This can be measured tangibly in terms of higher leverage labour productivity, abysmally low in India (Khadria, 2007). The aspects of social intermediation that MFIs can count upon are trust, sharing, interaction, educating and empowering, confidence and capacity (including skills) building, gathering experiences from ex-clientele and dormant groups outreach to the neediest and so on. There is a theoretical logic here that justifies the operationalisation of social capital like trust, commitment, loyalty etc in societal relationships within the micro level institutions and also between micro level and macro level institutions[10] (ibid). Where neither traditional systems nor modern institutions provide a basis for trust, MFIs are capable of doing this through social intermediation (Ledgerwood, *op. cit)*.

An important subject of current debate is that overcoming the many barriers that have prevented large potentially productive segments of the population from access to formal financial institutions may require more than conventional financial intermediation. It is not simply availability of credit from the financial market that has to be ensured but also some measure of up-front investment to develop the human resources–in terms of confidence, knowledge, skills and information–among the clients, and often to build local structures that help them link with financial institutions. It also involves investing in changing the skill mix and operating procedures of the financial institution seeking to expand its outreach. This process of developing new markets among the working poor is thought of as social intermediation (Bennett and Cuevas, 1996). Social intermediation, in other words, is a process of integrating the poor and marginalised people into the formal financial markets by socio-cultural mechanism. However, social intermediation is distinct from the provision of social welfare services in that social intermediation enables 'beneficiaries' to become clients able to enter into a contract involving reciprocal obligations. The level, nature and time horizon of the investment required for social intermediation varies with the barriers facing a given client/target group. It is also likely to depend on the level of responsibility in financial intermediation that the client group is required or willing to acquire (*ibid*).

Thus, in social intermediation institutions now have a tool other than financial intermediation to engage in and lend support to microfinance. It is an acknowledgement of the fact that that many poor clients of microfinance are simply not in a position to use loans productively. Social intermediation through a range of activities and capacity-building prepares people to become good borrowers and savers, better manage their own finances or their own financial groups and help them to put whatever 'social capital' they have to more productive use. Networking develops group cohesiveness and group cohesiveness leads to empowerment. That is the beauty of microfinancing. Because such interventions imply interacting closely with people at the grass roots, they are a good fit with the classic characteristics of NGOs. The trade-off, of course, is that such interventions are not likely to be financially self-sustainable. They need instead to be seen more as human capital investments. The banker must accept that this is a role which the NGO, as a committed social engineer, is better suited to execute. Social engineering is a full-time activity which has no substitute for the limited community contacts that a committed banker might indulge in. Moreover, the calling of retail banking has its own demands while credit plus initiatives are the forte of NGOs (Padhi; Ledgerwood, *op. cit.*). The benefits of networking also include low cost marketing, knowledge diffusion, easy access to timely health care etc.

The Microfinancial Sector (Development and Regulation) Bill, 2007 with all its legal aspects aims to ensure that NGOs use their social mediation skills to ensure financial intermediation (Shylendra, 2007). What is needed, however, is to explore the two-way relationship between financial intermediation and social intermediation before making any alterations to the prevailing structure of microfinance. This is of utmost importance in the developing countries keeping in view the need for developing social and economic infrastructure, together.

Some Lacunae

Microfinancing in general and social intermediation in particular is not an easy task. In a developing country with a long tradition of pecuniary and social economies and diseconomies, MFIs are facing certain shortcomings at present. MFIs have to be more careful in social engineering.

For instance there is a view that gender specific strategies, for instance, are not possible in the initial stages of designing. But in the basic SHG model shared problems of poverty, oppression and gender-based discrimination are used as entry points after which credit and savings are introduced (Ramamurti, 2007; Pandey, 2005). At one extreme there are still instances where women are given supportive roles rather than professional roles and at the other indifferent attitude of men when women assume professional role. Lack of real participatory management is a major stumbling block for empowerment of people. Lack of skills and data on intermediation parameters are the other obstacles. As a result even though MFIs succeed in replacing physical collateral with social collateral, quality assessment is lagging behind.

In India the self-help group (SHG) movement is seeking to provide social intermediation through the Rashtriya Mahila Kosh (RMK) and Women's Development Corporations, though they are still small compared to the erstwhile IRDP, says the Planning Commission.

Members of the MFI movement need to be sensitized about the relevant social issues and imperatives like population control, overcoming communal disharmony, child labour, drink evil, promoting ecological balance etc. Future MFIs need to develop composite microfinance that encompasses financial, technical, legal and social intermediation. Diversification of activities would be appositive a gain not only for the MFIs but also for the economy.

For the sake of financial inclusion, Dr. Rangarajan calls for improvements in absorptive capacity of the borrowers, which banks and other intuitions can make, and also an attitudinal change (Rangarajan, 2007). So we need to concentrate on three 'A's in microfinance: Access, Absorption, and Attitude. These should be included in future reforms in the MFI sector.

To be complete and successful intermediaries the MFIs must have the capacity to meet high performance standards. Basically the test of performance lies on the range and quality of services they provide, and the volume of domestic resources they generate. They must achieve excellent repayments and provide access to clients. And they must build up operational and financial self-sufficiency, and expanding client reach. In order to do so, MFIs need to find ways to cut down on their administrative costs and also to broaden their resource base. Cost reductions can be achieved through simplified and decentralised loan application, approval and collection processes, for instance, through group loans subsuming borrowers' responsibilities (Otero *et al.* 1994).

Conclusion

Microfinance is an intervention which has emerged in response to the need to address the challenge of financial inclusion. The entry of NGOs in financial intermediation has to be seen from this angle. Using strengths of social intermediation, NGOs so far have shown considerable potential in contributing to the cause. Formal institutions have failed, and therefore, it has become necessary that NGOs are helped in overcoming their constraints (Shylendra, *op. cit*). But while raising questions about the potential, reach and transparency of MFIs from the financial side, we need to ask questions from the social side also. For example, what does it take for SHGs to mobilise for social or community action? How effective are such actions? On both sides, financial and social, who is really benefiting? Do the poorest benefit, do they not join at all or if they do join, are they more likely to drop out? Have they/how have they overcome all the social barriers (including that of caste) in their intervention strategies? Studies exploring these and more questions, based on field research in all the regions of India would present a reality check of 'what is really happening', uniquely exploring both social and financial performance in the MFI sector in general and SHG movement in particular (EDA, *op. cit.*). Answers to these questions will help decide how effective is microfinance not only as a tool of financial inclusion but also as a test of sustainable development.

Notes

1. A microfinance institution is an organisation that offers financial services to low income populations. Almost all of these offer

microcredit and only take back small amounts of savings from their own borrowers, not from the general public. Within the microfinance industry, the term microfinance institution has come to refer to a wide range of organizations dedicated to providing these services: NGOs, credit unions, cooperatives, private commercial banks and non-bank financial institutions (some that have transformed from NGOs into regulated institutions) and parts of state-owned banks, for example (the Microfinance gateway).

2. World Bank, *Microfinance in South Asia–Towards Financial Inclusion for the Poor*, Report, July 2007. See particularly Chapter 5.
3. Marguerite Robinson is an Institute Fellow at Harvard University's Institute for International Development (HIID) and also works as an independent consultant. Ms. Robinson has written extensively on microfinance. She has also advised numerous governments, banks and financial institutions on microfinance. She has authored a number of books including *The microfinance revolution: Sustainable finance for the poor* (in 4 volumes) published by the World Bank in 2001.
4. Prof. Mohammed Yunus organised the poorest of the poor into SHGs and made them realise the very basic theory of survival (Naithani, 2001).
5. The SHG is a 'not-for-profit' civil society organisation which is like a mini deposit institution. For more on this refer More and Ananth (2007).
6. Though a national programme, Andhra Pradesh has drawn attention because, the scheme which was started with 15 women with each contributing one rupee a day, has grown to a corpus of $180 million in a short time. These groups produce as many as 400 products, and the then Chief Minister, Mr. N. Chandrababu Naidu, had gone to the extent of suggesting that they adopt sophisticated technology such as Internet to sell the products, which include wooden toys, pickles, garments, among others (Reddy 2001).
7. For details see L. Bennett, "Developing sustainable financial systems for the poor: where subsidies can help and whey they can hurt", World Bank Asia Technical Department, unpublished paper, 1993; and L. Bennett, A Systems Approach to Social and Financial Intermediation with the Poor". Paper presented at the banking with the Poor Network/World Bank Asia Regional

Conference on Sustainable Banking with the Poor, November 3-7, Bangkok.

8. See foreword to Working Paper No. 1: The Initiative on Defining, Monitoring and Measuring Social Capital.
9. Add to this the "ethics of repayment", microfinance would be panacea for rural poverty and backwardness. No need for unnecessary loan waivers. Productive and progressive farmers and entrepreneurs would be seen in the countryside. NABARD's Vikas Voulnteer Vahini (propagating the ethics of repayment) would come in handy here.
10. See A. Shales, "The Phelps Vision", *The Straits Times*, Singapore, October 12, 2006, p. 27.

References

ABN-AMRO (year not mentioned). 'Micro Finance'. Available at: *http://www.abnamro.co.in/ProductsnServices/MicroFinance/mf.html*. Accessed April 1, 2008.

Basix (2000), 'Equity for Equity'. Available at: *http://www.basixindia.com/micro_finance_in_inda.asp*. Accessed March 21, 2008.

Bennett Lynn and Carlos E. Cuevas (1996). 'Sustainable Banking with the Poor', *Journal of International Development*, Vol. 8, No. 2, March-April Available at: *http://www.worldbank.org/mdf/mdf1/poor.htm*. Accessed March 17, 2008).

Chakrabarti, Rajesh (2004), 'The Indian Microfinance Experience–Accomplishments and Challenges'. Available at: *http://creditwatch.googlepages.com/Microfinance_in_India.doc*. Accessed March 19, 2008.

Chakravarty, Saswati (2007), "Celebrating the Bandhan of Micro-loans", *The Economic Times*, Tuesday, 25 December, pages 1 & 3.

Christen, Robert Peck, Fisher Thomas and M. S. Sriram (2002), *Beyond Microcredit*, London: New Economics Foundation.

Compartomos (2007), 'If You Build It, They Will Come: Compartomos Goes Public', *BankerIndia*, March-May. Available *at: http://bankerinindia.typepad.com/my_weblog/2007/04/index.html*. Accessed March 23, 2007.

DHAN Foundation, Madurai (2003), Seminar on Future of Microfinance. Available at: *http://www.maduraisymposium.in/docs/microfinance_conference.pdf*. Accessed March 28, 2008.

——(2006), 'Micro Financing to Enable Rural Communities'. Available *at: http://www.i4donline.net/May06/673.pdf.* Accessed April 1, 2008.

EDA Rural Systems (Year not mentioned),'*The Lights and Shades of SHGs in India*'. Available at: *http://www.edarural.com/imar.html.* Accessed March 30, 2008.

Elaine Edgcomb (1998), 'Social Intermediation and Microfinance Programs', The SEEP Network c/o PACT. Available at: *http://www.microfinancegateway.org/files/1242_01242.pdf.* Accessed March 23, 2008.

Fisher Thomas and M. S. Sriram (2002), *Beyond Micro-Credit: Putting Development Back into Micro-Finance,* New Deli, Vistaar Publications.

Hulme, David and Paul Mosley (1996), *Finance Against Poverty,* Volume 1, London and New York: Routledge.

Kalanjiam Foundation (year not mentioned), "Beyond Microfinance' Available at: *http://www.dhan.org/kcbp/frames.html.* Accessed March 2008.

Khadria, Binod (2007), "Social Collateral and Human Capital", *Economic and Political Weekly,* Vol. XLII, No. 13, March 31-April 6, pp. 1087-88.

Khandelwala, Anil K. (2007), "Microfinance Development Strategy for India", *Economic and Political Weekly,* Vol. XLII, No. 13, March 31-April 6, pp. 1127-35.

Kharlan Dean and Sendhil Mullainathan (2006), 'Is Microfinance Too Rigid?', *Eye on Microfinance,* Issue # 2, August. Available at: *http://ifmr.ac.in/cmf/newsletter/CMF-EOMF-02-(Final)-w.pdf.* Accessed March 19, 2008.

Lakshman, Nandini (2006), 'India's BIG Microfinance Revolution', *Business Week Online,* September 25. Available at: *http://www.rediff.com/money/2006/sep/25bweek.htm.* Accessed on March 24, 2008).

Mor Nachiket and Bindu Ananth (2007), "Inclusive Financial Systems–Some Design Principles and a Case Study", *Economic and Political Weekly,* Vol. XL11, No. 13, March 31-April 6, pp. 1121-26.

Naithani (2001), "Micro Finance the Self Employment Activities–A Seesaw of Ideas", *Kurukshetra,* Vol. 49, No. 10, July, cited in Prasad, Anita Prasad (2007), "Role of Nationalised Banks in the Development of Micro Finance", *Participative Development,* Vol. 6, No. 1, Jan.-June, 2007, pp. 26-33.

Otero, M. and Rhyne, E. (1994), The New World of Micro-enterprise Finance-Building Healthy Financial Institutions for the Poor, Kumarian Press, West Harford, Connecticut. Cited in Piyush Tiwari and S.M. Fahad, 'Microfinance Institutions in India', Concept Paper. Available at: *http://www.gdrc.org/icm/conceptpaper-india.html.* Accessed February 3, 2008.

Padhi Bibhudutt (2003), 'Mainstreaming Microfinance: Bridging the NGO-Banker Divide', *Economic and Political Weekly*, Vol. 38, No. 46, November 15-21, pp. 4832-36. Available at: *http://www.gdrc.org/icm/country/shg-padhi.html. Accessed February 2, 2008)* and *http://www.epw.org.in/uploads/articles/3466.pdf.* Accessed on April 4, 2008).

Pandey, B. K. (ed.) (2005), *Rural Development: Towards Sustainability*, Volume 2, Rural Sustainable Development, Delhi, Isha Books.

Phelps, P. (1995). "Building Linkages between the Microenterprise and Shelter Sectors: An Issues Paper," GEMINI, Betuesda, Maryland. Cited in Piyush Tiwari and S.M. Fahad, *op. cit.*

Ramakrishnan, R. (2007), 'Micro Finance–Emerging Trends in Financial Management', April 17. Available at: *http://www.indianmba.com/Faculty_Column/FC557/fc557.html.* Accessed March 24, 2008.

Ramamurti, Shantha (2007), "Banks and Microfinance–Indian Experience", *Professional Banker*, Vol. VII, Issue 2, February, pp. 67-76.

Rangarajan C. (2007). "Financial Inclusion: Some Key Issues", Lecture delivered at Corporation Bank Chair in Bank Management, Mangalore University, Mangalagangothri, Karnataka, August 10.

Reddy, P. Vikram (2001), 'Microfinance Catching up among Rural Poor', *The Hindu*, Monday, April 02. Available at *http://www.hindu.com/thehindu/2001/04/02/stories/06020008.htm.* Accessed March 23, 2008.

Robinson, Marguerite (2000), 'The Microfinance Revolution'. Available at: *http://www1.worldbank.org/finance/assets/images/mfp_robinppt.pdf.* Accessed March 24, 2008).

S. Szabo (1999), "Social Intermediation Study: Field Research Guide: Exploring the Relationship between Social Capital and Microfinance", World Bank Paper, The Microfinance Gateway. Available at: *http://www.microfinancegateway.org/content/article/detail/2437.* Accessed February 03, 2008.

Shastri, Paromita (2006), '10 Questions', *Outlook India,* 15 May. Available at: *http://www.outlookindia.com/10question.asp?secname=Society&fodname=20060515*. Accessed March 24, 2008.

Shylendra H. S. (2007), 'Microfinance Bill: Missing the Forest for the Trees', *Economic and Political Weekly,* July 14. Available at: *http://www.epw.org.in/uploads/articles/10807.pdf*. Accessed March 30, 2009.

Sir Ratan Tata Trust (2005), 'Micro Finance-Kalinjiam Foundation's Collaboration with the Trust: Significant achievements'. Available at: *http://www.srtt.org/prog-edu-micro-kalanjiam.html.* Accessed April 1, 2008.

Someshwar, Manreet Sodhi (2008), 'Fizzling Subprime and Fizzy Microcredit', Sify, Thursday, 06. Available at: *http://sify.com/finance/fullstory.php?id=14617901*. Accessed March 24, 2008.

Sriram M.S. and Radha Kumar (2007), "Conditions in Which Microfinance Has Emerged in Certain Regions", *Economic and Political Weekly,* Vol. XLII, No. 49, 8-14 December, pp. 67-72.

The Microfinance Gateway. 'What is Microfinance?' Available at: *http://www.microfinancegateway.org/section/faq.* Accessed February 03, 2008.

Vasimalai M. P. and K. Narender (2007), "Microfinance for Poverty Reduction: The Khanjiam Way", *Economic and Political Weekly,* Vol. XL11, No. 13, March 31-April 6, pp. 1190-95.

Veerashekharappa (2007), "Credit Accessibility To Vulnerable Sections: Management Perspective", *Ushus,* Vol. 6, No. 1, January-June, pp. 86-101.

World Bank (1999), '*Social Intermediation Study Field Research Guide–Exploring the Relationship between Social Capital and Microfinance*', Manual for Pre-Testing, September 9. Available at: *http://siteresources.worldbank.org/INTSOCIALCAPITAL/Resources/400219-1150464137254/fieldguide.pdf.* Accessed March 23, 2008.

World Bank (2008), *Microfinance in South Asia–Towards Financial Inclusion for the Poor,* (Report). Available at: *http://web.worldbank.org.* Accessed March 17, 2008.

Other

http://planningcommission.nic.in/plans/mta/mta-9702/mta-ch6.pdf (April 2, 2008).

http://www1.worldbank.org/finance/html/mfp_1.html (April 3, 2008).

25

MICRO-FINANCE AS A TOOL OF EMPOWERMENT: A CRITICAL REVIEW

N. S. Mugadur & H. H. Uliveppa

Introduction

The micro-finance has been defined by Micro-Finance Summit 1997 as "programmes that provide credit for self-employment and other financial and business services (including savings and technical assistance) to very poor persons". It is also stated that the "finance is provided to the people, who work in agriculture, fishing, herding, who operate small or micro enterprises, who provide services; who work for wages or commission; and other individuals and groups at the local levels of developing countries both rural and urban".

In this paper an attempt has been made to covers wide spectrum of areas in micro-finance through self-help groups. SHGs as a provider of micro-finance have been examined. The living conditions of the people and their status of women micro-finance in India and employment has also been examined in detail. The study highlights growing of micro-finance for several reasons and the role of NABARD.

Nature of the Problem

In India, it is still worse because of the sex segregated character of society, the conditions of poverty and the traditional value system. Gender discrimination is equally an economic issue having serious implications on sustainable development of societies.

A Study revealed that nearly 85 per cent of the female population in the country was not able to participate adequately in economic reconstruction of the nation (Sharma, 1985).

In rural area, participation of men is relatively easier than that of women. The problems in women's participation are listed as below:

1. Some of the farm women may feel inhibited to participate for reasons such as lack of confidence, family pressure, customs, etc.
2. Most of the women may not to take up job though they remained unemployed due male domination their husbands were not interested in sending their wives to venture in such new occupations.
3. As wage-earning agricultural labourers, women suffer other kinds of disadvantages also. A woman is not mobile like a man as she is bound by her home and family responsibilities. Thus, while the male agricultural labourer may move from place to place in search of work for better wages, the woman sticks to the house picking up the work in the vicinity of her house and accepting whatever wage is given.
4. At the village level women's participation depends upon the social structure of the community, the class composition, social stratification and status hierarchy of groups, the distribution of power and authority and traditionally determined decision making patterns.
5. While men can attend farmer's camps to learn about the use of new implements, fertilizers, pesticides and crop rotation, etc., women remain at home and will be ignorant and thus become unfit to handle jobs

where scientific methods or new technologies are involved.

6. Employment for women is restricted by:
   (a) Increase in landless households and female labour.
   (b) Impact of farm technology and mechanization.
   (c) Inadequate educational opportunities for them.
   (d) Lack of access to career guidance and
   (e) Lack of situational support.

On account of the problems mentioned above, participation of rural women may not be easily forthcoming.

Reasons for Growing of Micro-Finance

Micro-finance is distinctly different from other populist Poverty Alleviation Schemes. It must be understood that all small loans are not micro-finance (Kulshatra 2000).

Micro-finance has gained recognition world wide and is growing for several reasons:

1. *The promise of reaching the Poor:* Micro finance activities can support income generation for enterprises operated by low-income households
2. *The promise of financial sustainability:* Micro finance activities can help to build financially self-sufficient, subsidy-free, often locally managed institutions.
3. *The potential to build on traditional system:* Micro finance activities some times mimic traditional systems (such as rotating savings and credit associations). They provide the same services in similar ways, but with greater flexibility, at a more affordable price to micro enterprises and on a more sustainable basis. This can make micro-finance services very attractive to a large number of low-income clients.
4. *The contribution of micro finance to strengthening and expending existing formal financial system:* Micro finance activities can strengthen existing formal financial institutions. Such as savings and loan co-operative

banks, and even state run financial institutions, by expanding their markets for both savings and credit and potentially, their profitability.

5. *The growing number of success stories:* There is an increasing number of well-documented, innovative success stories in settings as diverse as rural Bangladesh, urban Bolivia, and rural Mali. This is in stark contrast to the records of state-run specialized financial institutions, which have received large amounts of funding cover the past few decades but have failed in terms of both financial sustainability and outreach to the poor.
6. *The availability of better products as a result of experimentation and innovation*: The innovations that have shown the most promise are solving the problem of lack of collateral by using group based and character based approaches; solving problems of repayment discipline through high frequency of repayment collection. The use of social and peer pressure and the pros of higher repeat loans; solving problems of transaction costs by moving some of these costs down by the group level and by increasing outreach; designing staff incentives to achieve greater outreach and high loan repayments; and providing savings services that meet the needs of small savers.

Growth of Micro-Finance in India

It has to be supported by time series data in respect of growth of micro-finance in India, that it would be nice. Viewed from a historical perspective, the origins of micro-finance could be traced to the beginning of the co-operative movement in Germany where the movement was started in the filed of credit, the Raiffeiseen Societies. The peasant at that time was perpetually dependent on the merchant usurer and could not arise out of poverty and squalor because of continuously living on the border (of poverty) and facing risks of agricultural production. The objective of the society was to improve the situation of its members both morally and materially. This was sought to be achieved through obtaining the necessary capital for granting loans to members for the development of their business and household. The fundamental concept is, these, common guarantee, which was based on mutual knowledge and confidence of neighbours. Loans, short or medium term, were given for specific purposes, which had to be productive. All loans were granted on the basis of two securities. No long-term loans were issued nor mortgage of assets as collateral was allowed. Societies, based on the principles of co-operation, were also established in finance for producer-workers, in Sweden for industrial production and in Denmark and Norway for the agricultural sector. (Gadgil, 1960).

Most poor people manage to mobilise resources to develop their enterprises and their dwellings slowly overtime. Financial services could enable the poor to leverage their initiative, accelerating the process of building incomes, assets and economic security. However, conventional finance institutions seldom lend down-market to serve the needs of low-income families and women-headed households. They are very often denied access to credit for any purpose, making the discussion of the level of interest rate and other terms of finance irrelevant. Therefore, the fundamental problem is not so much of unaffordable terms of loan as the lack of access to credit itself (Kim Kyung Hwan, 1995).

Over the last ten years, however, successful experiences in providing finance to small entrepreneur and producers demonstrate that poor people, when given access to responsive and timely financial services and use the proceeds to increase their income and assets. This is not surprising since the only realistic alternative for them is to borrow from informal market at an interest much hither than market rates. Community banks, NGOs and grassroots savings and credit groups around the world have shown that these micro enterprise loans can be profitable for borrowers and for the lenders, making micro finance one of the most effective poverty reducing strategies (Tiwari and Fahad, 2002).

To the extent that micro finance institutions become financially viable, self-sustaining, and integral to the communities in which they operate, they have the potential to attract more resources and expand services to clients. Despite the success of microfinance institutions, only about 2 per cent of world's roughly 500 million small entrepreneurs are estimated to have access to financial services (Barry et al. 1996). Although, there is demand for credit by poor and women at market interest rates, the volume of financial transaction of microfinance institution must reach a certain level before their financial operation becomes self-sustaining. In other words, although microfinance offers a promising institutional structure to provide access to credit to the poor, the scale problem needs to be resolved so that it can reach the vast majority of potential customers who demand access to credit at market rates.

Informal sector micro finance institutions have comparative advantage in terms of small transaction costs achieved through adaptability and flexibility of operations (Ghate *et al.* 1992). They are better equipped to deal with credit assessment of the urban poor and hence to absorb the transaction costs associated with loan processing. On the other hand, formal sector institutions have access to broader resource-base and high leverage through deposit mobilization (Chirsten *et al.* 1994).

Micro finance institutions could also serve as intermediaries between borrowers and the formal financial sector and on-lend funds backed by a public sector guarantee (Phelps 1995). Business-like NGOs can offer commercial banks ways of funding micro entrepreneurs at low cost and risk, for example, through leveraged bank-NGO-client credit lines. Under this arrangement, banks make one bulk bank to NGOs and the NGOs package it into large number of small loans at market rates and recover. (Women's World Banking 1994).

Indian Micro-Finance Context

Micro-finance has been present in India in one form or another since the 1970s and is now widely accepted as an effective poverty alleviation strategy. Over the last five years, the micro-finance industry has achieved significant growth in part due to the participation of commercial banks. Despite this growth, the poverty situation in India continues to be challenging. India is said to be the home of one third of the world's poor; official estimates range from 26 to 50 per cent of the more than one billion population. About 87 per cent of the poorest households do not have access to credit. The demand for micro-credit has been estimated at up to $30 billion; the supply is less than $2.2 billion combined by all involved in the sector.

Indian public policy for rural finance from 1950s to till date mirrors the patterns observed worldwide. Increasing access to credit for the poor has always remained at the core of Indian planning in fight against poverty. The assumption behind expanding outreach of financial services, mainly credit was that the welfare costs of exclusion from the banking sector, especially for rural poor are very high. Starting late 1960s, India was home to one of largest state intervention in rural credit market and has been euphemistically referred to as 'Social banking' phase. It saw nationalisation of existing private commercial banks, massive expansion of branch network in rural areas, mandatory directed credit to priority sectors of the economy, subsidised rates of interest and creation of a new set of rural banks at district level and an Apex Bank for Agriculture and Rural Development (NABARD) at national level. These measures resulted in impressive gains in rural outreach and volume of credit. As a result, between 1961 and 2000 the average population per bank branch fell tenfold from about 140 thousand to 14000 (Burgess & Pande, 2005) and the share of institutional agencies in rural credit increased from 7.3 per cent 1951 to 66 per cent in 1991.

Micro-credit emergence in India has to be seen in this backdrop for a better appreciation of current paradigm. Successful micro-finance interventions across the world especially in Asia and in parts of India by NGOs provided further impetus. In this backdrop, NABARD's search for alternative models of reaching the rural poor brought the existence of informal groups of poor to the fore. It was realised that the poor tended to come together in a variety of informal ways for pooling their savings and dispensing small and unsecured loans at varying costs to group members on the basis of need. This concept of self-help was discovered by social-development NGOs in 1980s. Realising that the only constraining factor in unleashing the potential of these groups was meagerness of their financial resources, NABARD designed the concept of linking these groups with banks to overcome the financial constraint. The programme has come a long way since 1992 passing through stages of pilot (1992-1995), mainstreaming (1995-1998) and expansion phase (1998 onwards) and emerged as the world's biggest micro-finance programme in terms of outreach, covering 1.6 million groups as on March, 2005. It occupies a pre-eminent position in the sector accounting for nearly 80 per cent market share in India.

Under the programme, popularly known as SHG-Bank Linkage programme there are broadly three models of credit linkage of SHGs with banks. However, the underlying design feature in all remains the same i.e. identification, formation and nurturing of groups either by NGOs/other development agencies or banks, handholding and initial period of inculcating habit of thrift followed by collateral free credit from bank in proportion to the group's savings. In accordance with the flexible approach, the decision to borrow, internal lending and rate of interest are left at the discretion of group members. Its design is built on combining the "collective wisdom of the poor, the organizational capabilities of the social intermediary and the financial strength of the Banks".

The programme has received strong public policy support from both Government of India and Reserve Bank of India. The importance attached to it by Government is exemplified by mention of yearly targets by Finance Minister in his annual budget speech as well as introduction of similar group based lending approach in government's poverty alleviation programme. The success of the programme in reaching financial services to the poor has won international admiration. World Bank policy paper hails the programme and states that it is particularly suited to India because the model capitalises on country's vast network of rural bank branches that are otherwise unable to reach the rural poor.

SHG as Provider of Micro-Finance

A Self-Help Group (SHGs) is a small, economically homogeneous and cohesive group of rural poor voluntarily coming together.

- To save small amounts regularly.
- To mutually agree to contribute to a common fund.
- To meet their emergency needs on mutual help basis.
- To have collective decision-making.
- To solve conflicts through collective leadership.
- To provide collateral-free loans with terms and conditions decided by the group.

SHGs is a homogeneous group of rural poor, voluntarily formed to save whatever amount they can conveniently save out of their earnings and mutually agree to contribute to a common fund of the group to be lent to the members for meeting their production and credit needs. The Self-Help Groups are informal groups where members have an impulse towards collective action for a common cause. The common need here is meeting their emergent economic needs without being dependent on outside help. The members pool their savings and re-lend it among themselves on a rotational basis. The contribution by each member is not saving in true economic sense, but it is their sacrifice from present consumption for meeting their future contingency.

The self-help group comprises of people living in proximity, who cooperate to improve their individual lives by sharing their own resources and using their combined leverage for better effect.

The concept has been effective in enabling poor women to share financial resources, namely their savings, and utilizing the find created to take loans at interest rates that are substantially lower compared to alternative sources of credit.

The self-help group or the thrift and credit group, as it is interchangeably referred to in this report, offers tangible as well as intangible benefits to the clients, i.e., poor women. An avenue for cash saving, otherwise difficult to retain. Income on their savings through interest earning loans to members.

Loans without collateral, at lower interest rates. The possibility of sourcing loans from external agencies if the need for credit is greater than the saving fund generated by the members. A forum for discussing and tackling common issues.

The ideal SHGs is democratic unit in which all members participate equitably in the decision-making processes. To achieve this objective, homogeneous SHGs are usually promoted with minimal difference between members in terms of caste and class.

The success of the SHG requires that members to decide upon the objective parameters, policies and systems through internal consensus. This will ensure that the decision reflects the needs and capacities of group members.

Role of APEX Level Institutions in India

The level of financial institutions, which are promoting, supporting and financing micro-finance programmes in the country, there is main role of NABARD.

NABARD's involvement in promoting micro-finance through the concept of SHG, started in 1987, with a sanction of Rs.10 lakh as grant assistance from its R & D Fund to MYRADA for providing seed money to the Credit Management Groups (CMGs) promoted by it. The object of providing grant assistance was to facilitate building up a thrift fund and aiding the members of the CMGs with margin money to borrow from the Formal Credit System. The success of this experiment was the Precursor to the launching of the Pilot Project in 1992 for linking 500 SHGs with banks. The linkage programme promoted by NABARD is unique as it facilitates "relationship banking" as compared to "Paralleled Banking" practiced in other countries. Under the "relationship banking", improvements in the existing relationship between the poor and the banks are attempted with intermediation by the NGOs, who either play the role of the promoters of SHGs or financial intermediaries. The basic philosophy of the "linkage models" promoted by NABARD is to establish synergy between the banks, who have the financial strength and the NGOs who have the ability to mobilize the poor and build-up their capacity to avail loans from the banks. This is expected to facilitate the poor to graduate to a level from where they can access larger amounts of loan directly from the banks without the intervention of NGOs. A special feature of the linkage model is that the banks also directly act as SHPI (Linkage Model III). By the end of March 2001, 17 per cent of the total groups linked were promoted and nurtured by bank branches without the involvement of the NGOs. As many as 2002 banks (comprising 38 Commercial Banks, 129 RRBs and 25 Co-operative Banks) and 550 NGOs are participating in the linkage programme. Woman SHGs were linked with banks by March 2001. The cumulative disbursement of bank loans was Rs. 4808.8 million and refinance assistance of Rs. 4010.0 million (Table 1). The linkage programme is estimated to have benefited 5,60,000 rural poor families in about 280 districts of the country.

Table 1
Cumulative Progress in SHG Linkage Programme (Rs. in Million)

Year	*No. of SHGs Linked*	*Bank Loan*	*Refinance Assistance*
1992-93	255	2.9	2.7
1993-94	620	6.5	4.6
1994-95	2,122	24.4	23.0
1995-96	4,757	60.6	51.6
1996-97	8,598	118.4	106.5
1997-98	14,317	237.6	213.9
1998-99	32,995	570.7	520.6
1999-2000	94,645	1929.8	1501.3
2000-2001	2,63,825	4808.8	4010.0

Source: Annual Report, 2000-01, NABARD, Mumbai.

SHGs and Women Empowerment in Karnataka

Self-Help Groups of women in India have been identified as an effective strategy for the empowerment of tribal women in rural area as well as women in urban areas: bringing women together from all spheres of life to fight for their rights or a cause. Women through these SHGs work on a range of issues such as health, nutrition, agriculture, forestry; social awareness, etc besides income generation activities and seeking micro credit. In this regard the Government Karnataka has launched the Stree Shakti Scheme for setting up one lakh self-help groups to empower 20 lakh women. Village level Anganawadies and NGOs have been involved for setting up SHGs at the grass root level. As on August last, 75,026 SHGs had been formed. The SHGs had 2,31,103 members from the Scheduled Castes, 90,708 from the Scheduled Tribes, 70,766 from the minorities and 7,03,393 members from other communities (The Hindu 17/10/2002). Abhivruddi also organized and mobilized women in Gubbi Taluk and helped to form self-help groups. It has helped them to get financial assistance from the local credit institutions. The members of the SHG have been meeting regularly and discussing many problems regarding their financial support and other matters with the director Abhivruddi has been other officials of the concerned department. Abhivruddi has been usefully conducting and organizing different skill oriented training programmes for self-help groups with the help of taluk and district level officials. The participation of self help groups from the beginning encouraged them to take active involvement in income generation activities. The members these groups are motivated and encourage by the Abhivruddi to start small savings. The women have started coming together with a meager contribution of ten rupee per week. After 5 months they have started lending within a group for nominal rate of interest to their own group members to meet their emergency needs. The formation of SHGs has provided a platform for women's group action and solidarity at village level for the first time in the taluk. The poor tribal women organized by Abhivriddi and attempts have been made to empower then through capacity building.

Conclusion

The present study has elucidated some interesting information about the growing of micro-finance for several reasons. The micro-finance has gained recognition world wide. It is distinctly from other populist poverty alleviation schemes. Micro-finance is one of the most effective poverty reducing strategies. SHGs is a economically homogeneous groups of rural poor, voluntarily formed to save out of their earnings. The success of SHGs required that members decide upon the objective parameters, policies and systems through internal consensus. NABARD involvement is promoting Micro-finance through the concept of SHGs. Women SHGs were linked with banks by March 2002. the creation of income generating assets/ activities through loans availed from banks has made significant impact on the overall economic status of the group members.

References

Annual Report 2000-2001 and 2004-2005, NABARD, Mumbai.

Barry, Nancy, Armacost, Nicola and Kawas Celina (1996), "Putting Poor people's Economics at the Center of Urban Strategics", *Women's World Banking, New York.*

Basu, P. & Srivastava, P. (2005) Scaling up Micro-finance for India's Rural poor, *World Bank Policy research working paper 3646.*

Burgess, R. & Pande, R. (2005), Do Rural Banks Matter? Evidence from the Indian Social Banking Experiment, *American Economic Review,* Vol. 95 (3), pp. 780-795

Chriseten, R. Peck Rhyne, Elisabeth and Vogel, Rebort C. (1994), *"Maximizing the Outreach of Micro enterprise Finance: The Emerging Lessons of Successful Programms"*, September IMCC, Arlington, Virginia.

Gadgil D. R. (1960), *"Origin and Spread of Co-operative"* Lecture Delivered at the University of Punjab, Chandigarth, *"Writings and Speeches of D.R. Gadgil on Co-operation"*, Gokhale Institute of Politics and Economics, Pune, 1975.

Ghate, P. *et. al.* (1992), *"Informal Finance: Some Findings from Asia"*, Oxford University Press, Hongkong.

Kim Kyung Hwan (1995), "Access to Credit, Term of Housing Finance and Affordability of Housing", *Housing Finance International* 9(4), June, 22-27.

Kulshrestha, L. R. (2000), "Micro-Finance", the New Development Paradigm for Poor Rural Women, *Kurukshetra,* Vol. 45, No. 5, November, pp. 24-25.

Micro-Credit Summit, Washington DC, February, 1997.

Phelps, P. (1995), "Building Linkages Between the Micro Enterprise and Shelter Sectors: An Issues, Paper", *GEMINI*, Betuesda, Maryland.

Seibel, H. D. and Dave, H. R. (2002), Commercial Aspects of SHG-Bank Linkage Programme in India, *NABARD*, Mumbai.

Tiwari Piyush and S. M. Fehad (2002), "*Micro Finance Institutions in India*", Housing Development Finance Cooperation, Ramon House, Mumbai.

Women's World Banking (1994), "*United Nations Expert Group on Women and Finance*" New York.

——(2002) SHGs Through Empower, *The Hindu*, Dated: 17-10-2002, p. 4.

26

GLOBALIZATION AND CO-OPERATIVE BANKING REFORMS IN INDIA WITH SPECIAL REFERENCE TO RURAL CREDIT ON AGRICULTURE

A. Marimuthu, A. Bose & D. Bose

Globalization is most commonly understood as a unitary process inclusive of many sub-processes that are increasingly binding people and the biosphere more tightly into one global system. The Globalization process in India has brought about damaging impact to the priority sector comprising agriculture and small scale units. The advent of multinations into our frontiers has practically wrecked these sectors, which were already in the grip of inefficient credit and inefficient management resulting in negative productivity. So, agriculture development bears a close positive correlation with credit and finance.

In this context, this paper an attempt is made to discuss co-operative rural credit in the context of globalization.

Globalization and Co-operative Movement in India

The origin of Co-operative goes back to 1800-the early of European's Industrial revolution. In India institutionalization of rural credit started with the establishment of Co-operative following the enactment of Co-operative Societies Act in 1904.

For a long time, the major source of agricultural credit was the private money lenders. This source of credit was inadequate and highly expensive and exploitative. Since, independence, a multi-agency approach consisting of co-operatives, commercial banks and regional rural banks known as institutional credit has been adopted to provide cheaper and adequate credit to farmers.

According to H. Calvert, Co-operation is a form of organization wherein persons voluntarily associate together as human beings, on the basis of equity, for the promotion of economic interest of themselves. Globalization refers to the increased openers of economics to international trade, financial flows and foreign direct investments. Hence, it is interesting to known the status, position, direction and impact of globalization on co-operative movement in India.

Revival of Co-operative Credit Structure in the Era of Globalization

In the context of globalization, Indian farmers are facing crisis due to several factors. Debt burden increased, Prices of agricultural products are not remunerative, farmers incomes decreased, costs of agriculture increased. N.S.S.O. who have conducted survey on the conditions of farmers in the country stated that 50 percent of the farmers are in the deep debts.

On the recommendation of the All India Rural Credit Review committee (1969) a multi-agency approach to rural credit was adopted with the commercial banks supplementing the efforts of the co-operative banks at the end of March 1997 these co-operatives constituted 41 percent of the total outstanding direct agricultural finance of all institutional agencies. The committee recognized the existence of co-operative structure and its reach and recommended state financial support for its strengthening. It also recommended to establishment of large sized multipurpose credit societies and Nationalization of the imperial Bank of India for extending banking services in rural areas.

Though these steps helped in augmenting the flow of agriculture credit to some extent, credit supply from the co-operatives did not match the demand for credit. Followed this, 1969 commercial banks were introduced and nationalized, the establishment of RRBs in 1975, & NABARD in 1982 and the on going financial sector reforms since 1992. And then recently the concept of local area bank was introduced in 1996-97. All are initiatives and contributed to strengthening the rural credit structure and initiate qualitative changes in credit delivery overtime.

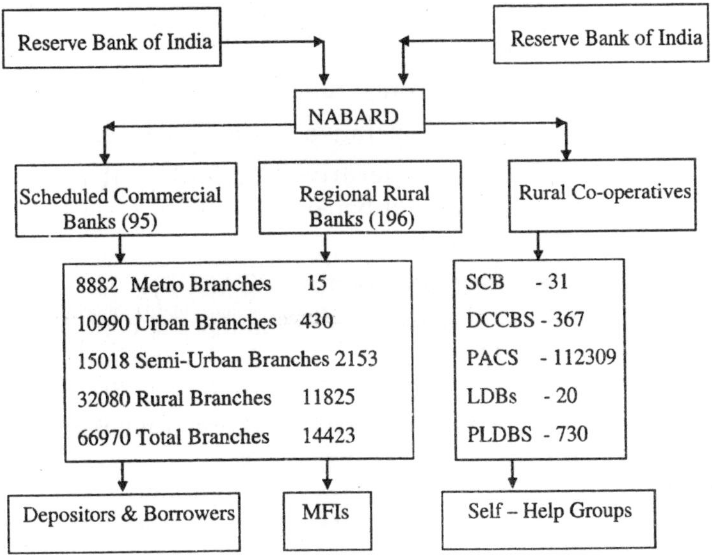

Institutional Arrangements For Rural Credit

The Short-term wing of co-operative credit societies at the Village level dispensing credit. The SCARDBs / PCACARDBs have in all 1573 branches spread over the country specializing in dispensation of term credit. Thus, in all 174958, rural outlets existed by March 2005, engaged in providing credit to agriculturists and thereby improving immensely access to rural credit. Indian financial system consists of two broad segments namely urban and rural co-operatives. The structure of the co-operative banking over 55 years can be divided into two broad segments.

The Urban Co-operative Banks

It has single tier, Primary co-operative Bank commonly known as Urban Co-operative Banks.

The Rural Co-operative Banks

It is divided into two segments:

(a) Short-term co-operative Credit structure: It has 3 tier structure.

  (i) State co-operative Banks.

  (ii) Central Co-operative Banks.

  (iii) Primary Agricultural credit societies.

(b) Long-term Co-operative credit structure:-

  (i) State Co-operative Agricultural and Rural Development Banks (SCARDB)

  (ii) Primary Co-operative Agricultural and Rural Development Banks. (PCARDB).

Presently the co-operatives are under the control of State Government in all matters varying from registration to loan recovery and audit. However, the RBI regulates and supervises certain banking activities for Urban co-operative Banks, While NABARD for the Rural Co-operatives.

Trends in Flow of Co-operative Credit to Agriculture in the Globalization Era

Co-operatives and commercial banks had almost equal share in total credit disbursement in 1997 at around 45 per cent. However, the share of commercial banks has increased to 65 percent in 2004-2005. While the share of co-operatives in total disbursement dropped to 25 per cent.

The co-operative credit structure is weak in most of the states except the states of Punjab, Haryana, Himachal Pradesh, Kerala and Uttranchal.

As on March 2004, nearly half the retail outlets of co-operataive credit institutions at the ground level were making losses, six state co-operataive banks and 133 District Central Co-operative Banks had negative net worth. The ground level credit flow for agriculture and Allied Activities in presented in Table 1.

Table 1
Level of Credit Flow for Agriculture and Allied Activities

(Rs. in Crores)

Year Institutions	*1999-2000*	*2000-2001*	*2001-2002*	*2002-2003*	*2003-2004*	*2004-2005*
Co-operative Banks	18260	20718	23524	23636	26875	31231
Regional Rural Banks	3172	4220	4854	6070	7581	12404
Commercial Banks	24733	27807	33587	39774	52441	81481
Others	103	82	80	80	84	193
Total	46165	52745	61965	69480	86981	125309

Source: NABARD and IBA Bulletin, Oct. 2005.

Table 1 discloses agricultural credit flow from various institutions. It is ascertained that the percentage share of institutional credit by Co-operative Banks declined from 62 per cent in 1992-93 to 34 per cent in 2002-03. On the source, it is found that amount of Institutional Credit to agricultural increased from Rs.46,165 Crores in 1990-2000 to Rs.125309 Crores in 2004-2005.

Impact of Globalization on Co-operative Credit to Agriculture

Co-operative movement provides opportunities for the growth and development of socio-economically weaker sections of the community, and ensure for them better living conditions. In liberalization and globalization economy, those who have major market shares can influence the market forces. Hence, co-operative sectors under the epoch of liberalization, privatization and globalization refers to evolving viable strategies and policy aiming to bring the operations of co-operative business organization within the subject of market forces. Thus, there must be a new paradigm shift from public domain to the market Umbrella.

Need for Sustainable Co-operatives

Co-operative sector must eventually become self-reliant and possess quality of self sufficiency in terms of human resources, capital and other essential resources. It is the only instrument to help the small and medium scale farmer during slack and lean seasons. By providing adequate financial assistance to New Generation Co-operatives and the rural youth, they can be made as new generation rural entrepreneurs who can solve the problem of unemployment and create rural industrial base for rural industrialization.

Co-operative Credit in India and Economic Reforms in the Globalization Era

In India, most of the co-operatives are under the control of political leaders and functioning under their direct guidance and controls. The respective state Governments have not conducted elections in the Co-operatives, which leads to Co-operatives as not being considered as member-driven organizations.

The mounting over dues of the co-operative institutions have severally restricted their capability of recycling funds for promoting facts agricultural growth. In this context, the second Narasimham Committee on Banking Sector Reforms (1998) urged that consideration be given to delayering of the co-operative credit system with a view to reducing the intermediation costs and providing the benefit of cheaper, NABARD credit to the Ultimate borrowers.

Union Minister for Agriculture has stated that reforms in the co-operative sector is the need of the hour, which should be addressed in right earnest by control and state Governments, During the year 2004-2005 Government entrusted the Co-operative to provide credit for agriculture for about Rs. 3900 Crores.

The co-operatives credit structure occupies a formidable and almost indispensable place in the rural credit scenario of the country. It consists of a short term structure with 30 state co-operative banks with 861 branches 367 District Central Co-operative Bank with 12600 branches and 1.12 Lakh Primary Agriculture Credit Societies.

The Total work force is about 3.5 Lakhs. The Structure serves a large membership of nearly 12 crores. As at the end of

March 2003, the short-term structure (excluding PACS) had a deposit base of more than Rs.1,13,000 crore loans outstanding Rs. 97,345 Crore and had during the year 2002-2003 issued loans to the tune of Rs. 90,000 Crores.

During the same period, long term structure reported a deposit base of Rs. 725 crore and loan outstanding of Rs. 14,500 Crore PACS are incurring losses every year. Out of 20 SCARDBs, 12 are incurring losses and have huge baggage of accumulated losses of the financial position of more than 500 PCARDBs is not better.

Vaidyanathan Committee

Concerning the deteriorating state of health of the co-operative credit structure in the country, Government of India have constituted a Task force under the chairmanship of Prof. A. Vaidyanathan to examine various aspects relating to the functioning of structure The committees is asked to make recommendation from the revival of co-operatives, suggest appropriate legal frame work assess the financial assistance required for revivals made of sharing and phasing, suggestions for the efficiency and viability.

Challenges before Indian Co-operatives under Globalization Era

In the new economic environment co-operatives are forced to directly and indirectly face those threats and challenges brought out by liberalization and globalization.

- Lack of operational linkages in the co-operative movement.
- The corporate governance and internal and external accountability is inadequate and less practiced in most of the cooperative business organizations
- Lack of involvement of members in co-operative business activities of difference co-operative sectors has led to the accelerated dwindling of the business turn over.
- Co-operative banks and credit societies have not attracted sizeable deposits from the public as well as members as it was expected.

- So, co-operatives are unable to generated internal resources to sustain themselves and seem to have developed a tendency of dependency syndrome of government

Strategies to Face Challenges by the Co-operatives

- The co-operatives must make efficient and effective arrangements for adopting proper management development programmes and offer training facilities to their employees, education programmes for members, and its future leaders.
- Co-operative leaders should commit themselves in the co-operative values and principles.
- Co-operatives should be developed as a dynamic and efficient instrument for over all social and economic growth and development.
- Election should be conducted by the respective State Government once in every five years which would eventually ensure democracy at gross roots level.
- In the globalized environment, co-operative have to facilitate absorption, adoption, transfer of technology and develop their own modern technology and good governance systems in their operations and business actives.
- The government and co-operatives themselves should take suitable measures to initiate development propaganda and publicity measure to bring about co-operatives nature, principles and values to people.
- There is an imperative need to retrain, veterans and motivate all the co-operative employees and those who are involved in co-operative affairs, so that they can manage them efficiently and effectively in order to over come the problems emerging out of the current liberalization and globalization scenario.
- In order to enable the co-operatives to face global competition and open market scenario, the government

should set up a separate international marketing business organization for the sale of co-operative products and goods to boost the growth the co-operative sectors.

Conclusion

To sum-up, among the institutional credit, co-operative are the single largest agency providing credit since their inception. Co-operatives as purveyors of rural credit have come to occupy a predominate place among the institutional agencies. It is heartening that the government still recognizes co-operatives as appropriate vehicle for sustainable social and economic development and can bring positive charges to people, especially at the gross roots economy. The "Co-operative must success if the poor and the farmer have to be prosperous In years to come, co-operatives in India will grow not only in size but also in the range of activities" quoted by Dr. Manmohan Singh, Prime Minister of India.

References

Kamala Kannan K. and Namasivayam, N. (2007), "Institutional Agricultural Credit in Post Reform Period", *Southern Economist,* Vol. 46, No. 2, pp. 13-14.

Lopoyetum, S. K. and Selvamani, P. (2006), "Globalization and Co-operative Movement in India", *Third Concept,* Vol. 20, No. 237, pp. 15-21.

Narasimhulu, M. (2006), "Globalization and Agricultural Sustainability in India", *Southern Economist,* Vo. 45, No. 9 pp. 11-14.

Ramesh, T. (2007), "Structural Reforms in Co-operative Banking", *The Management Accountant,* Vol. 42, No. 2, pp. 146-150.

Thorat, Y. S. P. (2006), "Revival of Co-operative Credit Structure", *Yojana,* Vo. 50, pp. 39-42.

Valasamma Antony (2007), "Towards Sustainable Development of the Agricultural Sector", *Southern Economist,* No. 46, No. 10, pp. 32-34.

Vasudevelu Naidu C. and Rukmini Reddy, M. (2007), "Agricultural Credit in India. An Analysis", *Southern Economist,* Vol. 45, No. 20, pp. 11-14.

27

CREATING A SAFETY NET THROUGH CREDIT

Sherly Kurien

Globalisation is the new buzzword that has come to dominate the world since the nineties of the last century. Globalisation has brought in new opportunities to developing countries. Greater access to developed country markets and technology transfer hold out promise improved productivity and higher living standard. But globalization has also thrown up new challenges like growing inequality across and within nations, volatility in financial market and environmental deteriorations. Another negative aspect of globalization is that a great majority of developing countries remain economy was constrained by the barriers to trade and investment liberalization of trade, investment and financial flows initiated in the nineties has progressively lowered the barriers to competition and hastened the pace of globalization.

There is a growing awareness of the importance of agriculture in this era of globalization. In the field of agriculture we have made commendable progress in terms of food production. India not only became self sufficient in food production but a net exporter of food grains in the past decade. But the situation did not continue for a long period and agricultural production become stagnant in the recent past which is a great concern for the whole country.

A special feature of the Indian economy is that an overwhelming proportion of Indian population lives in rural areas. According to 2001 census, 72.2 per cent of the population of the country lives in rural area. (Vyas 2007). The census further reveals that 73.3 per cent are employed in agriculture. But the unsavory phenomenon is the co-existence of food producers living in abject poverty. There is growing hunger amongst the poorer section of the population. With well over 400 million hungry people, India alone has more undernourished human being than all of sub-saharan Africa conbined. The FAO's state of food insecurity in the world report 2003 was happy to note that the number of those in chronic hunger fell by 80 million in 19 countries. Yet, it had risen by 19 million in India since 1996-97. Nineteen million is almost the population of the continent of Australia. It is further reported that a child dies of hunger every five seconds in the world. The largest numbers of such kids are Indians.

Indian agriculture is facing an unparallel crisis, which is rapidly pushing rural India towards impoverishment, food shortages and hunger. The per capita availability of food grains has fallen to levels that were seen last during the worst years of colonial rule and famines, The declining growth rate of productivity and production in agriculture is just one reason for this; equally important is the fall in purchasing power due to the deflationary macro economic policies and consequent contraction of the public works Programmes and employment generation activities of the state. Farm incomes have fallen due to rising input costs and a simultaneous fall in farm prices as well as with-drawl of the state farm credit, extension services, procurement, price support and infrastructure, Indebtedness and land alienation is growing.

The current hunger and starvation in rural areas is not because of drought, but because of the deflationary government policy resulting in the loss of purchasing power or effective demand in the hands of a majority of the rural population. (Utsa Patnaik). It could be observed that the absorption of food grains per head has come down from 177 kg , to 155 kg (Smitha Gupta 2005). Such low absorption levels were last seen in the initial years of worldwar II-form where they had fallen further still.

The fall in per capita production ought to be compensated by release of buffer stocks through the PDS, release of food stocks by increase in food for work programmers, food Programmes like mid-day meals programmes, etc. opines, Smith Gupta. This could protect per capita availability of food and its absorption by the people and thus prevent starvation and hunger.

This to a great extend could be attributed to the low purchasing power. The poor are very badly affected now because of the sky rocketing of food prices. It is at this juncture the PDS should function more effectively and all the needy and poor should be covered.

The fall in reserves of food grains from 60 million tones to 48 million tones was on account of exports of food grains at lower than BPL prices in the worst drought year since the mild-1980s. Around 33 million tones of grain was procured from framers in this bad drought year and Utsa Patnaik rightly maintains that these reflect distress sales. The farmers are so poor that what ever price they get they are ready to sell it off to the buyer who takes their produce. Over the years, the FCI has become the preferred buyer for the farmers. This is clear from the mounting stocks of rice and wheat since 2000 in relation to the required buffer stocks of 16.8 million tones (rice and wheat).

While the rice stocks have doubled from 11.7 million tones in 1999 to 25.6 *million* tones in 2002, wheat stocks grew four-fold from 6.8 million tones to 32.4 million tones in 2002. The steep rise in rice and wheat stocks has also meant a steep rise in the government's food subsidy bill. The subsidy on food rose from Rs. 2,450 crores in 1990-91 to Rs. 17,499 crores in 2001-02.

The recommendations of the Narasimhan committee Report on the financial system caused a fall in the credit deposit ratio of rural branches of commercial banks. The ratio fell from 69 % in 1991 to 40% in 2001 resulting in poor capital formation in rural *India*. Shetty (2002) shows that commercial bank credit has moved out of rural areas, backward regions, agriculture and small scale enterprises and in favour of urban areas, advanced regions, and the organized non-farm sector. This along with trade liberalization and changing cropping and investment patterns based on heightened expectations, resulted in growing indebtedness of the peasantry and rural poor. But thanks to the fiance minister who waved off the farmers debt and thereby giving a great relief to them.

The issue of access to credit to the agriculture sector has been found to be a major problem faring an overwhelming proportion of farmers. Science farmers as such are poor they have no alternative but to look to government as the best source of credit. Therefore credit facilities should be increased and strengthened. The loans need to be increased in terms of both volume and outreach. Easy accessibility to all who require credit, should be provided through government organization. It is always the poor who are often affected. The rural credit crisis is on the rise. In these years of globalization the rich could get a loan at six per cent interest to buy a Mercedes Benz. A farmer paid more than twice, perhaps even thrice that rate if he wished to buy a tractor. Not only has the flow of credit to rural area misdirected even the sources had been curtailed. Between 1969 and 1990 the number of rural branch banks had trebled. Once the 'reforms" began, branches began to close. As Dr. P.S.M. Rao points out, in 1990 there were nearly 35,000 branches in rural regions, that is over 58 per cent of total branches. By 2003, rural branches were down. Both in absolute numbers and percentage. New, they account for under half of the total branches. The more the banks wiggle out, the more moneylenders thrive. (*Outlook* 2005). How can the poor rural farmers do anything without money in their hands. In this giobalised era economies should open new avenues for credit facilities. Offering financial support to farmers to expand their holdings will encourage the agriculturist to carry on their business on a large scale.

Credit agencies should be encouraged to advance credit to farmers for the purchase of land. This has been done in the past, and is being done even today in some selected regions. Provisions for financing Land purchases by the Land. Development Banks and re-financing of these advances by

NABARD already exist. These have to be made more effective. The position of landless laborers are vulnerable and their dire need is to acquire or hold land as their own. This will create an interest in them and as Amartya Sen points out this entitlement or an ownership of an asset would go a long way in improving and enhancing their economic status.

The government had embarked upon several programmes to improve the well being of the farming section. The co-operative movement was imitated to provide credit to the weaker section. But they had to face series of problems like high level over dues, high level non-performing assets, large landowners cornering greater benefits, regional disparities in the distribution of credit, domination of the government over the co-operatives, poor management, lack of enthusiasm and dedication among members and poor services to the members. Other than the co-operative credit societies we had to our credit launched several rural credit agencies/schemes like Regional Rural Banks, NABARD Kisan credit scheme, Credit Monitoring. Arrangement etc: Despite making efforts, the benefits has not trickled down to the needy and down trodden. Achieving rural development is mandatory and all efforts should be continued. It should be combined efforts of the government at all levels, NGO's, local leaders and the local community. The need of the hour is to build effective, mutually beneficial and pro poor programmes to create and redirect credit to the farming section.

References

Sheila Shalla (2005), " Rural Economy, Issues and Evidence" , Working Paper Series 25, Institute for Human Development, New Delhi.

Shetty, S. L. (2002), Paper Presented to the IAMR Seminar on the Rural Non-farm Sector.

Utsa Patnaik (2004), "Republic of Hunger, Safdar Hashmi Memorial Lecture", New Delhi.

Vyas, V. S. (2007), "Marginalized Sections of Indian Agriculture: The Forgotten Millions", *The Indian Journal of Labour Economics,* Vol. 50, No. 1.

Business Line (2004), January 28

Outlook, October 17, 2005.

28

RURAL FINANCE IN CONTEMPORARY INDIA

CHANNABASAVANAGOUDA P.

Introduction

THERE has been growing interest around the developing world, including India, in the promotion of rural financial deepening, wherein the attention is gradually shifting from the earlier exclusive emphasis on credit, towards the realization of the importance of different types of financial services including deposit facilities. The successful promotion of the deepening of rural financial markets will require systematic rather than isolated efforts, with related actions being undertaken on several fronts. In India, though there have been concerns about insufficient supply of agricultural credit, there have been only a few isolated interventions to improve the policy and the institutional environment for the emergence of a robust rural financial system. On the contrary, the financial sector liberalization has lead to a reduction of credit available to the agricultural sector. The share of agriculture in gross bank credit, which had gone up steadily from 8 per cent in 1972 to 8.9 per cent in 1980, to 16 per cent in 1985 and 16.2 per cent in 1990, came down steadily to 13.5 per cent in 1994, 11.7 per cent in 1996 and 11.1 per cent in 2001. To address these concerns, the present government embarked on a programme of doubling agricultural credit in a period of 3 years. Further it has introduced the scheme of short-term agricultural credit at an interest rate of 7 per cent.

However these are piecemeal steps within an overall policy vacuum as far as rural financial system is concerned. The discourse on the suitable architecture for Rural Financial Institutions (RFIs) is conspicuous by its absence. Though the Task Force on Revival of Short Term Co-operative Credit Structure had submitted its report and the report had found acceptance with the Government of India, the operationalisation of the major recommendations of the report is yet to see the light of the day. The other part of the cooperative credit system, i.e., the long-term structure has also been studied by the same Task Force and its final recommendations are awaited. The other structure created for rural financial services, i.e., Regional Rural Banks is being tampered about in an ad-hoc manner with amalgamations at state level, sponsor-bank wise. This process of amalgamation is being carried out without a road map for expansion of rural credit and has negativated the mandate for their creation.

Trends in Rural Finance

An examination of the trend in the sector-wise and institution-wise growth in agricultural credit since the entry of commercial banks in the rural finance after nationalisation reveals two aspects clearly; the increasing share of commercial banks in rural credit and the gradual decline in the share of cooperative banks. However even in this trend of increasing share of commercial banks, till the introduction of Kisan Credit Card in 1998-99, the cooperatives continued to maintain their major share in short term credit and the commercial banks, because of their involvement in financing areas like Farm Mechanisation, Horticulture, Poultry etc. had maintained a predominant position in investment credit.

Farm credit disbursements progressively increased from Rs. 620,450 million in 2001-02 to Rs. 1,574,800 million in the year 2005-06 reflecting rise by 153.8%. Commercial banks & RRBs recorded phenomenal rise by 216% & 189% respectively

Table 1
Farm Credit Disbursements by Cooperative, Commercial and Regional Rural Banks

Rs. in Million

Year	*Co-op. Banks*	*Com. Banks*	*RRBs*	*Others*	*Total*
2001-02	235,240	335,870	48,540	800	620,450
	[37.91]	[54.13]	[7.82]	[0.14]	[100]
2002-03	236,360	397,740	60,700	800	695,600
	[34.00]	[57.18]	[8.72]	[0.10]	[100]
2003-04	268,750	524,410	75,810	840	869,810
	[30.91]	[60.29]	[8.71]	[0.09]	[100]
2004-05	312,310	814,810	124,040	1,930	1,253,090
	[24.92]	[65.02]	[9.91]	[0.15]	[100]
20005-06	372,520	1,061,520	140,760	NA	1,574,800
	[23.65]	[67.41]	[8.94]		[100]
Total	1,425,180	3,134,350	449,850	4,370	5,013,750
	[28.42]	[62.52]	[8.97]	[0.09]	[100]

Figures in bracket indicate % share to total.

as compared to 58% by cooperatives. While there has been progressive rise in each successive year in case of cooperatives, commercial & regional rural banks, there has been spectacular increase during 2004-05 & 2005-06 in respect of commercial banks & RRBs. The share of cooperatives in the total disbursements of short-term & long-term credit progressively declined from 37.9 per cent in 2001-02 to 23.65 per cent in 2005-06 whereas that of commercial banks recorded progressive increase from 54.13 per cent to 67.41 per cent during the corresponding years. RRBs accounted for 7.82 per cent in 2001-02 which progressively rose to 9.91 per cent in 2004-05 but declined by one percentage point in the following year. Agriculture credit flow for the banking system as a whole during 2005-06 has surged to Rs. 1,804,860 million, reflecting 128 per cent of the target of Rs. 1,410,000 million that was set for that year.

Agriculture credit flow target for 2006-07 had been pegged at Rs. 1,750,000 million. However, for the fiscal year 2006-07, agriculture credit up to December 2006 stood at Rs. 1,493,430 million which represented a 25.38 per cent increase over the achievement of Rs. 1,191,150 million

Table 2
Flow of Farm Credit

(Rs. in Million)

Period	*Public sector Banks*	*Private sector Banks*	*Cooperative Banks*	*Regional rural Banks*	*Total*
April-December'05	Rs. 689,910 [57.92%]	Rs.100,310 [8.42%]	Rs. 289,470 [24.30%]	Rs. 111,460 [9.36%]	Rs. 1,191,150 [100.%]
April-December'06	Rs. 868,650 [58.16%] [25.91%]*	Rs.141,340 [9.46%] [40.90%]*	Rs. 331,740 [22.22%] [14.60%]*	Rs. 151,700 [10.16%] [36.10%]*	Rs.1,493,430 [100.%] [25.38%]*

Figures in brackets indicate percentage share in the total.
Figures in bracket with *indicate percentage increase during April-December'06 over April-December'05.

recorded in the same nine-month period in the previous year. Agriculture credit flow during April to December 2006 from public sector banks grew by 25.91 per cent to Rs. 868,650 milion from Rs. 689,910 million during the corresponding period in the previous year. In case of private sector banks, it increased by 40.90 per cent to Rs. 141,340 million from Rs 100,310 million. While cooperative banks recorded increase by 14.60 per cent from Rs. 289,470 million to Rs. 331,740 million during the period, the RRBs showed increase by 36.10 per cent from Rs. 111,460 million to Rs. 151,700 million. Share of public sector banks in the total disbursement during April-December'06 accounted for as high as 58 per cent folowed by cooperative banks at 22 per cent where as RRBs & private sector banks had almost equal share of 10 and 9 per cent respectively.

During the seven year period from 2000-2006 public sector banks' outstanding credit to priority sectors increased by 221.9% from Rs. 1,274,780 million as on 31st March, 2000 to Rs. 4,103,790 million as on 31st March'06, whereas that of private sector banks shot up by 480.2% from Rs. 183,680 million to Rs. 1,065,660 million during the corresponding period. Priority sector advances of public sector banks as group accounted for over 43% of net bank credit in four years as against the target of 40% which, however, declined from 42.8%

to 40.3% in three years. In this respect, private sector banks as a group had less than that of targeted 40% during initial three years but they showed impressive performance [42.8% to 47.3%] in the following four years.

Table 3
Priority sectors & Agriculture Outstanding Credit by Public Sector & Private Sector Banks

(Rs. in Million)

Year	*Priority Sectors Public sector banks*	*Agriculture Public sector banks*	*Priority Sectors Private banks*	*Agriculture Private banks*
2000	1,274,780	452,960	183,680	40,230
	[43.3%]	[14.3%]	[38.0%]	[8.3%]
2001	1,491,160	523,710	215,670	56,340
	[43.7%]	[15.7%]	[36.7%]	[9.6%]
2002	1,714,840	581,420	241,840	65,810
	[43.5%]	[14.8%]	[38.4%]	[8.5%]
2003	1,997,860	705,010	366,480	99,240
	[41.2%]	[14.5%]	[44.1%]	[10.9%]
2004	2,444,560	844,350	489,200	147,300
	[43.6%]	[15.1%]	[47.3%]	[14.2%]
2005	3,070,460	1,099,170	698,860	216,360
	[42.8%]	[15.3%]	[43.6%]	[12.3%]
2006	4,103,790	1,549,000	1,065,660	361,850
	[40.3%]	[15.2%]	[42.8%]	[13.5%]

Figures in bracket indicates % to Net Bank Credit.

Agricultural advances of public sector banks during the period rose by 242% from Rs. 452,960 million to Rs. 1,549,000 million whereas that of private sector banks increased significantly by 799% from Rs. 40,230 million to Rs. 361,850 million during the period. Share of agricultural advances in the net bank credit by public sector banks ranged between 14.3% & 15.7% whereas that of private sector banks varied from 8.3% to 14.2% during the period. Neither public sector banks nor private sector banks as a group could achieve targeted agricultural credit of 18% of net bank credit. During 2005-06, all public sector banks [except State Bank of India (SBI) and State Bank of Patiala] were able to meet the priority sector target of 40 % of net bank credit in 2005-06 & only 10 public sector banks met the 18% sub-target for agriculture. None of the private sector banks could meet sub-target for lending to agriculture.

Table 4
Banks' Outstanding Loan to Weaker Sections and NPA Status

(Rs. in Million)

	Public sector banks [9]	*Nationalized banks [19]*	*Old Private sector Banks [8]*	*New private sector banks [20]*
Total B/O	Rs. 594,710.2	Rs. 398,074.3	Rs. 23,661	Rs. 29,323.4
NPA	Rs. 5,022.2	Rs. 32,505.9	Rs. 2,672.6	Rs. 2,761.9
NPA % of B/O	8.45%	8.17%	11.3%	9.43%

All banks' outstanding loan to weaker sections of the society as on 31st March'06 amounted to Rs. 1,045,768.9 million with NPA amount of Rs. 88,172.6 million accounting for 8.43 per cent of outstanding loan. Only eight banks in the public & nationalized sector could achieve the stipulated target of 10% of net bank credit, whereas none of the old & new private sector banks could meet the target. While 19 nationalized & nine public sector banks as a group had 8.17% & 8.45% NPAs, respectively, eight old & 20 new private sector banks as a group had higher percentage of NPAs at 11.3% & 9.43% respectively.

Rural & Semi-Urban branches of each of the public sector banks have been alloted Service Area comprising specified number of villages, since April, 1989. Each branch is expected to formulate Service Area Credit Plan every year for the purpose of providing credit to the rural households. This micro level credit planning exercise should help the bank to progressively bring within its fold all eligible house holds for providing credit & related services. In the ultimate process this exercise should prove to improve quality & productivity of lending. RBI has since the year 1994-95 has advised public sector banks to ensure 25% annual growth rate in the matter of disbursement of credit in their Service Area. Accordingly, the data presented in the above Table showed that annual growth was between 12.5% and 24.% during 2000-2001 to

Table 5
Targets & Achievements under Service Area Credit Plan &Recovery of Direct Agriculture by Public Sector Banks

(Rs. in Million)

Year	*Target*	*Achievements*	*Annual Growth %*	*Demand*	*Recovery*	*Overdue*
2000-01	258,930	246,540 [95.2%]	12.5	224,290	155,400 [69.3%]	68,890 [30.7%]
2001-02	308,830	293,320 [95%]	19.0	245,610	177,580 [72.3%]	68,030 [27.7%]
2002-03	368,380	339,210 [92.1%]	15.6	289,400	210,110 [72.6%]	79,300 [27.4%]
2003-04	425,760	422,110 [99.1%]	24.4	335,440	250,020 [74.5%]	85,420 [25.5%]
2004-05	556,160	652,180 [117.3%]	54.5	351,920	296,120 [84.1%]	55,800 [15.9%]
2005-06	850,240	942,780 [110.9%]	44.6	NA	NA	NA

Figures in brackets under Achievements indicate % achievements of targets. Figures in brackets under Recovery indicate % recovery to demand & under overdue indicate % overdue to demand.

2003-04. The growth was spectacularly high at 54.5 during 2004-05 which, however, declined to 44.6% in the following year. Disbursements of credit as against targets ranged from 92.1% to 117.3% during the six year period. Achievements were higher than 100% only in the last two years. This is attributed to Finance Minister's directives to double the farm credit disbursement in three years effective from April, 2004.

Public sector banks recovery to demand under direct agricultural advance was 69.3% during the year 2001 which gradually increased during following three years. It, however, phenomenally rose to 84.1% in the year 2005. During the five year period the demand, loan amount to be recovered & percentage of recovery to demand have progressively increased in the successive years whereas over due amount has increased until the year 2004 & then it steeply declined by Rs. 29,620 million in the following year.

Table 6
Number of Self-Help-Groups and Credit Disbursed

(Rs. in Million)

Banks	*2004 No. of SHGs*	*2005 No. of SHGs*	*2006 No. of SHGs*	*2004 Credit Rs.*	*2005 Credit Rs.*	*2006 Credit Rs.*
Commercial	538,422 [50]	843,473 [52]	118,807 [53]	22,548.3 [58]	41,590.2 [60]	69,877.0 [61]
RRBs	405,998 [38]	5638,46 [35]	740,024 [32]	12,782.5 [33]	20,995.5 [31]	38,221.5 [29]
Cooperative	134,671 [12]	211,137 [13]	310,194 [14]	3,711.2 [9]	6,398.9 [9]	10,871.8 [10]
Others	00	00	271	00	00	5.2
Total	1,079,091 [100]	1,618,456 [100]	2238565 [100]	39,042.0 [100]	68,984.6 [100]	113,975.5 [100]

Figures in brackets indicate % share in the total.

As reported under the NABARD-GTZ Rural Finance Program, at around 98 % on time repayment to the SHGs is reported to be very high. As on March'06 the number of SHGs stood at just over two & quarter million , of which over one & a half million had outstanding bank loans. Even with this huge number of SHGs it is estimated by the Committee on Financial Inclusion that the number of SHGs will have to be doubled to cover all the 50 million poor households in the country.

Other Programs

- Under Differential Interest Rate scheme [at 4%] loan outstanding as on 31st March'05 was of the order of Rs. 4,900 million outstanding with 389,000 borrowers accounting for 0.07% as of previous year's outstanding credit as against stipulation of one per cent.
- During the year 2005-06 banks have lent Rs. 6,440 million accompanied with Government's subsidy of Rs. 2,380 million to 755,969 beneficiaries of Swarna Jayanti Gram Rozgar Yojana & under Prime Minister's Rozgar Yojana sum of Rs. 7,610 million was provided to 131,290 beneficiaries.
- During the period from 2001-02 to 2005-06 banks provided 59,093,000 kisan credit cards to farmers to facilitate them

to purchase farm inputs & other requirements. Share of commercial banks was 37% as against cooperatives & RRBs at 51%&12% respectively.

- Commercial banks, RRBs & Cooperative banks have disbursed sum of Rs. 221.4 million, Rs. 22.2 million & Rs. 70.5 million to 5,173 farmers, 283 farmers & 2,826 farmers respectively to redeem their past debt with informal sources. during the year 2005-06.
- As on 31st March'06 commercial banks provided to NABARD sum of Rs. 313,373.4 in 11 tranches under
- Rural Infrastructure Development Fund for financing 244,651 projects in respect of creating irrigation facilities, constructing rural bridges & roads, assisting social sector & power generation etc.

Table 7
NPA Status of Public Sector Banks in 2004-05 and 2005-06

(Rs. in Million)

Year	*[A] Priority Sectors*	*[A.1] Agri-culture*	*[A.2] Small scale industries*	*[A.3] Other Priority*	*[B] Public sectors*	*[C] Non-priority*	*Total [A+B+C]*
2004-05	233,970	72,540	78,350	83,080	4,500	238,490	476,960
	[49.1%]	72,540	[16.4%	[17.4%]	[0.9%]	[50%]	[100%]
		[31.0%]*	[33.5%]*	[33.5%]*			
2005-06	223,740	62,030	69,170	92,540	3,500	186,540	413,780
	[54.1%]	[15%]	[16.7%]	[22.4%]	[0.8%]	[45.1%]	[100%]
		[27.7%]*	[30.9%]*	[41.4%]*			
B/O as	3,331,660	1,099,090	761,140	NA		6,269,600*	9,601,260
on 31st	[34.7%]	[11.45%]	1,471,430			[63.5%]	[100%]
Mar'05	[7.02%]**	[6.6%]**	[15.32%]			[3.87%]**	[4.96%]**
& NPA		[7.93%]	[5.64%]**				
% of B/O		[10.29%]**					

Figures in bracket indicate percentage share in the total NPA amount.
Figures in bracket with *indicate percentage share in the NPA amount of priority sectors.
Figures in brackets with **indicate NPA % of Balance Outstanding as on 31st March'05.

NPA status of public sector banks revealed that during the year 2005-06 though amount of NPA under priority sector advances declined to Rs. 223,740 million from Rs. 233,970 million in 2004-05 share of NPA in the total NPA increased to 54.1% from 49.1%. In respect of agricultural advances NPA amount declined by Rs. 10,510 million & its share in the total NPA amount also declined by 0.2 per centage points, whereas its share in the priority sectors NPA amount declined significantly from 31% to 27.7% during the period. As of 31st March 2005, total NPAs constituted 4.96% of total loan outstanding. NPAs under priority sectors were as high as 7.02% of its outstanding loans as against 3.87% in respect of all other loans. Within priority sectors, agriculture NPAs accounted for 6.6% of its outstanding loans which were significantly lower than that of small scale industries [10.29%] but marginally higher than that of other priority sectors [5.64%].

Priority sector loan outstanding accounted for 34.7% of total loan outstanding where as share of priotity sector NPAs in the total NPAs was as high as 49.05%. NPAs under agriculture were 15.21% of total NPAs as against share of agricultural advances at 11.45% of total outstanding loans. There was wide difference in respect of small scale advances with regard to its share of NPAs in the total NPAs [16.43%] as compared to 7.93% share in the total outstanding loans. Other priority sector advances had also higher percentage share of NPAs [17.42%] in the total NPAs when compared with its share [15.32%] in the total loan outstanding. Public sector banks were able to clean their balance sheets by writing off NPAs built over a period of time in financing Government sponsored programs viz, IRDP, Agro-Service-Centers & high tech projects viz, Floriculture, Aquaculture, Mushroom Farming, Tissue Culture etc.

In case of private sector banks while NPA amount under priority sectors has increased by Rs. 950 million in the year 2005-06 its share in the total NPA amount has significantly increased to 29.2% from 24.9% in the previous year. NPA amount under agriculture as well as its share in the total NPA amount & in the priority sectors also increased marginally. As on 31st March'05 NPA status of 196 RRBs was Rs. 28,043.5 million & that of 20 SCARDBs at Rs. 54,373.8 million, 727 PCARDBs at Rs. 40,559.1 million, 31 SCBs at Rs. 60,716 million & 367 DCCBs at Rs. 145,196 million accounting for 8.5%;

31.27%; 31.9%; 16.25% & 19.87% respectively of the loan outstanding.

Enabling Environment

In order to encourage Rural Financial Institutions to play catalytic role in lubricating the process of both fam sector development & rural rejuvenation at a time when the country has launched its 11th Five Year Plan[2007-08 to 2011-12], enabling environment needs to be created specifically in the areas of removal of urban-biased policies, sound agricultural & rural development policies, promotion of broad-based rural financial sector reforms & development of effective legal system to enforce contracts, sound interest rate policies, & appropriate legal status & prudential regulation of Rural Financial Intermediaries etc.

Financial Sectors

- Encourage & facilitate RFIs expand their outreach in rural areas, especially in remote locations in a cost-effective way & achieve sustainability of their methodologies. Different types of RFIs can have comparable advantages in terms of sustainability, quality,& scope of products & services being offered.
- RFIs can incorporate operational solutions to reduce transaction costs & mitigate portfolio risk, such as using remote operating models & outsourcing services [mobile banking, ATMs, mobile phone & internet banking, correspondent retail outlets & agents]; accepting alternative collateral [warehouse receipts, assured contracts, third party guarantees]; and employing portfolio securitizations & loan guarantees.
- Changing rural economic scenario has opened several opportunities for investment & development and has impacted the demand for new financial products & services among rural population.
- Needs of rural clients for financial services now extend much beyond traditional, short-tern credit products. RFIs

need to develop & experiment with different new products which include term loans for agriculture& investment, leasing products, credit & debit cards & overdraft lines, flexible saving products, insurance [agriculture, life, health& property], cash transaction/remittances etc.

Investment in Agriculture

Investment pattern both in public & private sector during the period from 1999-2000 to 2004-05 has been irratic as total investment was as low as Rs. 381,760 million in 2001-02 which increased to the highest level at Rs. 478,330 million in 2003-04 but declined to Rs. 431,230 million in the following year. Average annual investment during the six year period was Rs. 442,027 million reflecting share of public & private sector at 21.32% & 78.68% respectively. Gross Capital Formation as percentage of total GDP ranged from 1.7 to 2.2 & that of Agricultural GDP from 8.4 to 10.2 respectively with average value of 2.0 & 9.3 respectively.

Investment, more importantly in public sector, supported by well intentioned public policy is both essential & desirable in specific areas such as, [I] development of irrigation [exploiting potential surface irrigation & ground water resources, generation of electricity/power to draw ground water] [ii] intensifying soil & moisture conservation measures, [iii] land development & reclamation [iv] improving drainage system [iv] strengthening flood control measures [v] all weather road to facilitate transport [vi] storage/warehousing facilities & cold chains [vii] marketing infrastructure [viii] developing sound information, communication & market intelligence system [ix] building integrated agricultural research, extension & education system and [x] effective soil & water testing facilities and quality control & pricing system to facilitate competitively &timely supply of farm inputs [seeds, fertilizers, pesticides, water, fuel, farm equipment & machinery etc]. Public investment has potential to substantially improve credit absorption capacity of farmers & geographical areas and ultimately stimulates private sector investment & facilitates smooth flow of bank credit for undertaking seasonal agricultural operations & investment purpose which in the ultimate process lays strong foundation of sustainable agriculture.

Creation of rural infrastructure to integrate rural development with banking & finance, particularly is a must in respect of upgrading literacy & education level & providing all weather roads, electricity which have direct impact on information & communication technology.

Table 8

Public & Private Sector Investment & Share of Agriculture in GDP & Gross Capital Formation as Percentage of GDP at 1990 Prices

(Rs. in Million)

Year	*% share of Agri in GDP*	*Investment Public in Rs. m*	*Investment Private in Rs. m*	*Investment Total in Rs. m*	*GCF % of Agri. GDP*	*GCF % of Total GDP*
1999-2000	NA	77,540 [17.8]	357190 [82.2]	434730 [100]	9.6	2.2
2000-01	24.2	70,180 [18.4]	311580 [81.6]	381760 [100]	8.4	1.9
2001-02	24,4	85,290 [18.2]	382150 [81.8]	467440 [100]	9.7	2.2
2002-03	21.9	78,490 [17.1]	380180 [82.9]	458670 [100]	10.2	2.1
2003-04	22.2	128,090 [26.8]	350240 [73.2]	478330 [100]	9.7	2.0
2004-05	20.8	125,910 [29.2]	305320 [70.8]	431230 [100]	8.7	1.7
2005-06	19.9	NA	NA	NA	NA	NA
Total		565500 [21.3]	2086660 [78.7]	2652160 [100]	9.3	2.0

Figures in bracket indicate % share of public & private sector investment to total.

Rural Banking

The concept of agricultural banking & credit should be replaced by rural banking & finance for total integrated rural development & not farm sector or for that matter any other sector in isolation. Rural house-holds expect a variety of financial services, not only credit, Government may consider doing away with stipulation of targets & sub-targets. Let RFIs concentrate on their Service Area to bring every household within the fold of banking & finance during 11th Five Year Plan. Financial sustainability [not alone operational viability] of RFIs is a must. Government may therefore need to reimburse the loss incurred by RFIs while providing credit at concessional interest rate when Government is committed to the principle of social equity & removing regional imbalances. Code of ethics not to vitiate climate of recovery of bank credit through interest waiver & loan write offs need to be evolved & meticulously implemented. It is for RFIs to consider this on its merits.

Conclusion

The spatial spread of cooperatives across the country, especially in more remote & economically deprived areas has already identified itself with the rural households. Every sixth village has a cooperative; cooperative membership touches the lives of 480 million rural households, more than half the aggregate rural population. Seventy per cent of rural cooperative clients are marginal & sub-marginal farmers. This sharply focuses the need for its revival, restructuring & reforming through greater involvement & commitment by State Governments. Subsidy linked Credit programs sponsored by Government agencies should have clear demarcation of role, functions & accountability between sponsorers & RFIs and should help targeted beneficiaries to fully achieve the enshrined objectives.

References

Agricultural Credit and Indebtedness in India: Some Issues, R. S. Sidhu and Sucheta Singh Gill (2006), *Indian Journal of Agricultural Economics*, Vol. 61, January-March.

Annual Report, NABARD, Various Issues.

Annual Report, RBI, Various Issues.

Economic Growth, Financial Deepening and Financial Inclusion, Rakesh Mohan, Address at the Annual Bankers' Conference 2006, at Hyderabad on November 3, 2006.

Financial Sector Reforms in India, Rakesh Mohan, *Economic and Political Weekly*, Vol. XL, No. 12, March 19, 2005.

Productivity of Rural Credit: A Review of Issues and Some Recent Literature, M. S. Sriram, Working Paper No. 2007, Indian Institute of Management, Ahmedabad.

Report of the Expert Group on Agricultural Indebtedness, Banking Division, Department of Economic Affairs, Ministry of Finance, Government of India, 2007.

Report of the Sub-Group on Agricultural Credit Flow to Disadvantaged Sector.

Report of the Sub-Group on Cooperative Reforms.

Report of the Sub-Group on Flow of Institutional Finance.

Report of the Sub-Group on Indebtedness of Farmers.

Report of the Sub-Group on Loan Recoveries.

Report of the Sub-Group on Simplification of Lending Procedures.

Rural Banking: Problems of Localised Banking Institutions, Balasaheb Vikhe Patil, *Economic and Political Weekly*, Vol. XL, No. 12, March 19, 2005.

Rural Credit and Co-operatives in India, S. K. Sinha, Suneja Publishers, New Delhi, 1998.

Rural Credit, Role of Informal Sector, Dinesh Chandra, Segment Books, New Delhi, 1993.

Rural Economy, An Intelligence Group Report, *The Economic Times*, 2002-03.

State of the Indian Farmer, A Millennium Study, Various Volumes, Surjit Singh and Vidya Sagar, Department of Agriculture and Cooperation, Ministry of Agriculture, Government of India, 2004.

29

INCLUSIVENESS OF BANKING SYSTEM IN INDIA—IN RETROSPECT AND PROSPECT

Anjali Jain & Mona Khare

Introduction

In the 11th Five Year Plan, so much has been talked about making economic growth process more inclusive, with the objective of reducing poverty and unemployment. In this process, finance has to play a crucial role, particularly for meeting the requirements of the unorganised sector. We have created a huge financial structure in terms of banking and non-banking institutions but our experience shows that this structure has not been deployed adequately to make finance inclusive in the sense that banking services are provided at affordable cost to the poor and backward sections of the society. Whatever little we have achieved in this respect in the post-bank nationalisation period, evidenced by branch expansion in rural areas, delivery of credit to the weaker sections, credit-deposit ratio in rural and semi-urban areas, could not be sustained in the post-economic reform period.

The structure is there but it needs to be geared in the right directions. The moot question is should we create some new institutional framework for making finance more inclusive or we utilize effectively the existing structure for achieving our objective? This paper is intended to provide answer to the question and also discuss the related issues.

Concept of Financial Inclusion

Financial inclusion has been officially defined in India as the "provision of affordable financial services" to those who have been left unattended or under attended by the formal agencies of the financial system. "By F1 we mean the provision of affordable financial services, viz, access to payments and remittance facilities, savings, loans and insurance services by the formal financial system to those who tend to be excluded"- (Usha Thorat, Deputy Governor RBI, 2006).

In fact, financial inclusion has been discussed in recent years with the main objective of providing banking services at an affordable cost to the poor and weaker sections of society. In India, the recent policy statements on financial inclusion have focused on the access to at least a saving bank (no-frills) deposit account for all. (V. Leeladhar 2005).

Table 1
Percentage Share of Different Sources in Aggregate Credit-Rural and Urban Households

(in Per cent)

	Rural Households						*Urban Households*		
	1951	*1961*	*1971*	*1981*	*1991*	*2002*	*1981*	*1991*	*2002*
Institutional	7.1	17.3	29.2	61.2	64.0	57.1	59.9	70.0	75.1
Of which cooperatives	2.9	10.4	20.1	28.6	21.6	27.3	17.5	17.2	20.5
Commercial banks	-	0.3	2.2	28.0	33.7	24.5	22.5	21.6	29.7
Non-institutional	92.9	82.7	70.8	38.8	36.0	42.9	40.1	30.0	24.9
Of which money lenders	68.6	60.8	36.9	16.9	17.5	29.6	12.5	10.2	14.1

Source: Compiled from various publications of RBI

Banking System in India and the Extent of Inclusiveness in the Post-Reform Period

It was realised that the way in which the banking sector has evolved after Independence in India, has not been truly inclusive. How inclusive the commercial banks have been in the past decades should be viewed with reference to different time phases viz. (i) pre-nationalisation phase (1951-69),

(ii) post-nationalization phase 1969-1990-91 and (iii) 1991-92 onwards i.e. post-reform period. In the first phase of the development of commercial banks (1951-69), the bulk of commercial bank credit had gone to finance the corporate sector and the share of commercial banks in the dispensation of rural credit was almost negligible, only 0-3 per cent of the total in 1961. The pre-dominance of non-institutional credit is evident from the table-I, as it accounted for 92.9 per cent of the total rural credit in 1951 though declining to 82.7 per cent in 1961. It is also clear that among the non-institutional agencies, money-lenders dominated the scene. In fact the negligible role of institutional credit, prompted the government to the revolutionary step in the direction of nationalisation of commercial banks in 1969.

The nationalisation of banks in 1969 which marks the beginning of the second phase of banking development, was inspired by the concept of social banking. This period is marked by infrastructural and institutional changes in terms of spread of bank-branches to the rural and semi-urban areas, increase in the credit-deposit ratio, dispensation of bank credit to weaker sections and the less developed areas.

The number of offices of commercial banks showed a phenomenal rise from more 8,000 in 1969 to mere than 60,000 in 1991. The average population per branch of 64,000 in 1969 improved to 14,000 in 1991. The spare of rural and semi-urban branches, which constituted 63 per cent of the total number of branches in 1969, increased to 77 per cent by 1991. (Table 2).

The branch expansion of commercial banks, which showed considerable expansion in the first two phases, more particularly during the second phase, did not show similar trends in the third phase of the time period. The share of branches in the rural and semi-urban categories declined over a period of time, with an increase in the share of urban and metropolitan branches. The share of priority sector advances was in the range of 37-39 per cent whereas the credit deposit ratio ranged between 50-60 per cent during this period in the neo-liberal regime. Though the commercial banking system had attained new heights in the post-economic reform period,

Table 2
Performance of Scheduled Commercial Banks in India (1969–2005)

	1969	*1981*	*1982*	*1991*	*1995*	*2000*	*2001*	*2002*	*2003*	*2004*	*2005*
No. of Offices of which	8262	35707	51385	60220	62367	65412	65919	66190	66535	67188	68355
rural and semi urban	5175	26127	40001	46500	46345	47141	47159	47127	162	47212	47485
Percentage	(62.6)	(73.2)	(77.9)	(77.3)	(74.3)	(72.1)	(71.5)	(71.2)	(70.9)	(70.3)	(69.5)
Population per office	64000	19000	15000	14000	15000	15000	15000	16000	16000	16000	16000
Share of priority sector advances (%)	15.0	35.6	39.9	39.2	35.8	37.4	38.5	38.2	37.1	38.8	38.1
Deposits as % of national Income	15.5	34.4	39.4	48.1	51.7	53.5	58.9	60.7	65.3	68.5	68.3
Credit-deposit Ratio	77.5	65.5	66.1	60.6	54.7	53.3	53.5	53.8	56.9	56.1	64.9
Investment Deposit Ratio	29.3	35.1	35.4	37.7	38.6	36.6	37.1	38.7	41.3	43.8	41.6

Source: Compiled from various issues of Report on Currency and Finance Reserve Bank of India.

yet the process of inclusiveness, howsoever little it was, initiated in the post nationalization period, has received a set-back. Profitability has been the major consideration underlying banking operations. It is a period of mergers and consolidation of banks to face competition and to meet the requirements of globalization. These developments have reduced their involvement in social banking, evidenced by reduction in the pace of expansion of rural branches, slackening of the flow of rural credit to weaker sections and less developed regions.

There has been a significant increase in the access of rural households to institutional credit and the role of informal agencies including money-lenders as a source of credit has declined. The All India Debt and Investment Survey 1991-92 showed that the relative shares of institutional agencies in the total debt of rural households increased from 29.2 per cent in 1971 to 61.2 per cent in 1981 and further to 64 per cent in 1991 but declined to 57.1 per cent in 2002 (see Table 1). The share of money lenders in the total non institutional credit which was declining till 1981, started picking up from the 1990s and reached almost 29.6 per cent in 2002, as shown in the most recent survey of farmer indebtedness in 2002 conducted by the National Sample Survey Organisation (NSSO). A comparison of the share of institutional agencies in outstanding cash debt in 1991 (NSSO 48th round) with that in 2002 (NSS 59th round) brings out the most disturbing feature of the post-reform period i.e. the return of the rural money-lender.

Financial Exclusion Widespread in the Post-reform Period

The incidence of financial exclusion has been fairly well documented by the NSSO and other field surveys. Financial exclusion is widespread. Of the 148 million rural households more than 60 per cent received no loans from institutional or non-institutional agencies, of the 80 million farmer households, more than 50 per cent do not enjoy any loan facilities. Among the indebted rural households, about 43 per cent are served by money-lenders and other by non-institutional agencies. It is very distressing to note that about 48 per cent of all rural households, 51 per cent of farmer households and 78 per cent of rural non-farmers households do not have access to banking services. To add to this is the fact that as on March 2007 a number of unorganized outer prices are functioning without institutional credit support.

As regards urban households, the share of institutional sources, showed a progressive increase from about 60 per cent in 1971 to 75 per cent in 2002. It is also interesting to note that the share of institutional sources was relatively high for urban households in 1991 and 2002, when compared to rural households (Table 1). These trends show that urban households relied relatively less on non-institutional sources (particularly money lenders) when compared to rural households.

The survey of indebtedness carried out by the NSSO reported that in 2002, three out of four rural households and four out of five urban households do not have a bank loan. In the eleven years from 1991 to 2002, the banking system added only 4 per cent of rural households as its customers. Financial inclusion of the poor continues to be a major challenge in the post-economic reform period. The recent All India Debt and Investment Survey has revealed that only about 13.4 per cent of the rural households had access to institutional credit. Similarly, the Rural Finance Access Survey (RFAS) conducted by NCAER had also revealed the acuteness of the financial exclusion of the poor. The RFAS has found that nearly 87 per cent of the poor households were without access to any formal credit and about 70.4 per cent of the poor did not have any deposit account.

Besides this, there are many financially excluded households such as unorganised workers, self-employed, artisans and other vulnerable groups in both rural and urban areas. Finance for housing is another area where many poor are excluded.

Since it is difficult to sustain the growth momentum unless the marginalised masses are brought into the mainstream economy, the RBI has initiated action to promote "Financial inclusion" at all levels because the financial consequences of exclusion will vary depending upon the nature and extent of services denied. It may lead to increased travel requirements, higher incidence of crime, general decline in investment, difficulties in gaining access to credit or getting credit from informal sources at exorbitant rates, and increased unemployment, etc. The small business may suffer due to loss of access to middle class and higher-income consumers, higher cash handling costs, delays in remittances of money. In fact, financial exclusion can lead to social exclusion.

Financial Inclusion in Madhya Pradesh and Chhattisgarh

Madhya Pradesh and Chhattisgarh the two states in Central India, fall short of the national average–both in terms of inclusion and outreach of the banking services at a time when financial inclusion is the buzzword in Indian banking industry. The RBI in a recently published report shows Madhya Pradesh and Chhattisgarh to be much behind the newly formed states of Uttarakhand, Jharkhand in terms of number of accounts per 100 of adult population. While, MP and CG have 39 and 32 accounts, Uttarakhand and Jharkhand have 78 and 44 respectively States like Delhi, Rajasthan, Punjab etc are much ahead with 166, 45, 105 accounts respectively. Chandigarh ranks the highest with 221.

Similarly on the parameter of percentage of exclusion in Credit-Gap for rural & semi-urban category, MP and CG stands at 94 and 95, whereas all India figure stands at 90. In the category of Deposit-Gap for rural & semi-urban population, the percentage of exclusion in MP and CG are 74 and 76 respectively in comparison to all India figure of 59 (Table 3). The bank account density in MP and CG respectively to be 20 and 17–are far behind national average of 59 and are marginally

Table 3
Financial Exclusion in Central India

Parameter	*Madhya Pradesh*	*Chhattisgarh*	*All-india Avg.*
Bank Account Density	20	17	59
Credit-Gap (% of exclusion)	94	95	90
Deposit-Gap (% of exclusion)	74	76	59
No. of Account per 100	39	32	62

Source: Hindustan Times, Sep. 8, 2007.

ahead of Bihar (16) and Mizoram (15). State Lever Banking Committee of M.P. observed that financial inclusion, in real terms, is yet to take place, as the focus till now was on Kisan Credit Card (KCC), since more than 70 per cent population in M.P. consists of farmers.

An Overview of Institutional Framework

In the multi-agency approach apart from the commercial banks, financial services are provided to the rural sector by the cooperatives and RRBs. The cooperative banking system with state cooperative banks (SCBs), district central cooperative banks (DCCBs), primary agricultural cooperative credit societies (PACs), state cooperative agriculture and rural development banks (SCARDBs) and primary cooperative agriculture and rural development banks (PCARDB) is a major purveyor of financial services to the rural sector. The share of cooperatives in total institutional credit to agriculture has gradually declined from 100 per cent in 1970-71 to 49 per cent in 1990-91 and further to 30.9 per cent in 2003-04 (Table 4).

Table 4
Institutional Credit to Agriculture

	Share in Total (Per cent)		
Year	*Scheduled Commercial Banks*	*Regional Rural Banks*	*Cooperatives*
1970-71	-	-	100
1980-81	38.4	-	61.6
1990-91	47.6	3.4	49.0
2001-02	45.0	11.0	44.0
2002-03	57.2	8.7	34.0
2003-04	60.3	8.7	30.9

Source: Handbook of Statistics on the Indian Economy, Reserve Bank of India.

Regional Rural Banks (RRBs) were inducted into the banking scene in 1975 with a view to further enhance the flow of credit to rural areas. The RRB Act stated that such banks were set up to develop the rural economy by providing "Credit and other facilities, particularly to small and marginal farmers, agricultural labourers, artisans and small entrepreneurs". By the end of the 1990s, these institutions were in a stage to take off, to expand and take on a greater role in rural credit delivery, especially in the areas where the cooperatives become moribund. But the RRBs needed structural changes, including freeing themselves from the strings of their sponsor banks. The share of RRBs in total institutional credit to agricultural remained less than ten per cent except in 2001-02. Table 5 also reveals that there is almost stagnation in branch expansion as well as recruitment which ultimately crippled those banks, rendering them incapable of fulfilling their original mandate.

Table 5
RRBs: Position of Branches and Staff Strength

Year	*Number of Branches*	*Staff Strength*
1990-91	14,527	67,161
1991-92	14,539	69,379
1992-93	14,543	70,170
1993-94	14,542	70,604
1994-95	14,509	70,848
1995-96	14,497	70,975
1996-97	14,461	70,785
1997-98	14,459	70,487
1998-99	14,499	70,484
1999-2000	14,301	70,294
2000-01	14,313	70,141
2001-02	14,390	69,876
2002-03	14,433	69,547
2003-04	14,446	69,249
2004-05	14,484	68,912
2005-06	14,494	68,629

Source: Statistics on Regional Rural Banks, published by NABARD, various years.

The establishment of National Bank for Agriculture and Rural Developmetn (NABARD) in 1982 was another landmark in the area of rural credit. Infact, NABARD was set up as an apex development bank with a mandate for facilitating the flow of credit to agriculture, rural industries and other allied economic activities in rural areas. The NABARD has been playing a catalytic role in micro-credit through the conduit of self-help groups (SHGs). Several initiatives and strategies have been adopted by NABARD to fine tune the working of the system and further widen the reach of micro-finance to the poor. The SHGs financed by the banks accounted for hardly 1-2 per cent of the total number of SBAs in recent years, with a share of hardly 1-4 per cent of the total outstanding credit against SBAs, though the average amount per SHG progressively increased from Rs. 16,815 in 1999-2000 to Rs. 42,626 in 2004-05 (Table 6).

Table 6
SHG-Bank Linkage Programme

Year	*Total SHG Financed by Banks (cumulative)*	*Bank Loan (cumulative) (Rs. Crore)*	*Average Amount per SHG*
1999-00	114.78	193	16815
2000-01	263.83	481	18231
2001-02	461.48	1026	22233
2002-03	717.36	2049	28563
2003-04	1079.09	3904	36179
2004-05	1618.48	6899	42626

Source: Trend and Progress of Banking in India, RBI, 2004-05.

Rural Branch Network of Commercial Banks

The financial sector liberalisation has led to a debilitation of institutional framework for rural credit. There was tremendous expansion of rural branch network in the post-bank nationalisation period (i.e. after 1969) and the percentage of rural branches of commercial banks which was 17.6 per cent in 1969 steadily increased to 58.2 per cent in 1990 (Table 7).

Thereafter, it is a story of progressive decline, and mergers and swapping of rural branches, rather than expansion, became the norm as the RBI liberalised the policy for closure of rural branches on grounds of unavailability and lack of profitability. As is evident from the table VII that after peaking over to 35, 396 in 1993-94, declined to 33,017 in 1994-95 and further to 30,750 in 2005-06. Similarly, in percentage terms it declined from 58.2 in 1989-90 to 50.2 per cent in 1996-97 and it remained below 50 per cent till 2005-06 when it was 44.48 per cent.

Table 7
Number and Percentage of Rural Branches of Commercial Banks

Year	*Number of Branches*	*Percentage*
1969-70	1,443	17.6
1989-90	34,867	58.2
1990-91	35,134	56.9
1991-92	35,254	56.8
1992-93	35,360	56.3
1993-94	35,396	55.9
1994-95	33,017	51.7
1995-96	32,981	51.2
1996-97	32,909	50.6
1997-98	32,854	49.9
1998-99	32,840	49.3
1999-2000	32,673	48.7
2000-01	32,640	48.3
2001-02	32,443	47.8
2002-03	32,303	48.55
2003-04	32,121	47.80
2004-05	32,082	46.93
2005-06	30,750	44.48

Source: Basic Statistical Returns, RBI various issues.

Recent Legislative Measures

Recently, the government of India has introduced a bill in the Parliament to regulate micro finance institutions in the country for ensuring financial inclusion of poor who continue to face difficulties in accessing the formal banking system. The bill titled "The Micro Financial Sector (Development and Regulation) Bill, 2007" aims at developing the microfinance sector which is faced with many constraints including absence of legal framework for its growth.

The bill tries to cover broadly two category of institutions, namely, NGOs and cooperatives. The NGOs proposed to be regulated include both societies and trusts established under central and state enactments and cooperatives include all thrift and credit cooperatives except urban cooperative banks. The bill's ambit is very narrow as it does not include in its purview other institutions like NBFCs, section 25 companies and scheduled banks including RRBs. The proposed regulation therefore is more institution-based rather than activity-based.

Unless it widens its scope to include other MFIs the broader objectives may not be realised because according to one study, leading MFIs in the country are either in the form of NBFC or section 25 companies and account for nearly 90 per cent of the total clients served by MFIs in the country. By focusing only on NGOs and cooperatives, the bill attempts to shift the burden of social banking away from commercial banks to civil society institutions.

The bill has designated NABARD as the regulatory agency for MFIs with the responsibility of formulating policies for the development of micro finance sector. Many doubts have been raised over this issue. As a promoter of SHG-Bank linkage programme (SBLP), NABARD might face difficulties in promoting the alternate micro finance sector. Another basic conflict of interest relates to NABARD's role as lender v/s regulator. NABARD has launched direct financing of NGOs/MFIs recently. So, the question has been raised, whether NABARD an apex lender, would be able to look after the developmental concerns of MFIs. It is also argued that NABARD's supervisory and institutional development role with regard to RRBs and cooperatives has not been fully satisfactory. The government should constitute a new regulatory authority which is devoid of such conflicts.

Moreover, the bill fails to recognise the reality that NGOs can play only a supplementary role and that formal institutions especially commercial banks need to contribute in a big way for ensuring financial inclusion of the poor.

Role of Market Intermediaries

Financial inclusion of the unorganised sector still remains a major issue as it is extremely difficult to cover, the volume of business offered by the sector is commercially insignificant, the economic value addition by the sector is not right and hence loans given would turn into non-performing assets (NPAs) on account of high default rates. The dominant paradigm of the banking sector till now is borne out of the conventional banking mindset which pursues big volumes and large clients. A large part of the population is therefore excluded from the business of banks under such a paradigm.

Banks are being called upon to provide financial services to all types and manners of clients on lines similar to post-office under "Universal Services Obligation". Sustained growth of a nation and its continued prosperity depend critically on universal financial services coverage of all people. The country cannot afford to have an elite minority enjoying services with banks and a large unorganized majority in the cash and barter mode.

There are a variety of government sponsored, funded and subsidized programmes under which banks have lent a lot of money although reluctantly. Then are also initiatives like SHG linkage programme under which banks have lent large sums voluntarily. These have proved that the unorganised sector is a commercial proposition for the banks, what is needed are product and process innovations that could effectively meet the financial requirement of the marginalised masses.

The unorganised sector has been financed for a long time by traditional players–like village money lender, landlord, petty trader, commission agent, input supplier, commodity procurer and a host of others successfully for a long time. The reason behind the success story of these market intermediaries is their wide and deep knowledge of the local area, local economy and local people. So the task of servicing the unorganised sector could be outsourced to market intermediaries.

The RBI's internal working group on microfinance has already spawned a few new ideas including use of franchisees, facilitators, and banking correspondent for improving outreach of financial services to marginalised people. With its recent focus on financial inclusion, RBI should find ways of changing the current banking paradigm for unorganised sector. But taking into account, the past history of the role of market intermediaries as exploiters of the rural people, the RBI has to be very careful while outsourcing services of intermediaries to the money lenders for providing credit to the weaker sections.

Conclusion and Suggestions

It is necessary to recognise that in India, we have to focus on extending financial services in both rural and urban areas for ensuring financial inclusion of all segments of the population. The reorientation of commercial banking system needs to get a high priority while simultaneously encouraging and enabling the growth of micro-finance movement in India, which is gaining success recently. It should be strengthened and extended to areas which are not adequately covered by both banking and micro-credit institutions. RBI and NABARD have recognised the growing importance of micro-finance and are committed to enable its healthy growth. However, the development of the MFIs need to be considered and must be comprehensively addressed. There is a need of a very well crafted balance between the regulation and growth objectives in the formulating a regulatory regime, keeping in view the big challenge of financial inclusion of a large segment of the Indian population.

Among all the institutional credit agencies available in the country, the commercial banks constitute the most suitable agency for micro credit, but for this role they require a more broad based institutional structure, reasonably well spread regionally and functionally. In fact, commercial banks can actively take part in the scheme of promoting and developing micro finance for the purpose of making bank credit more inclusive.

Banks have many advantages over private micro-credit organisations as providers of small scale loans. They have advantages of scale, the banking system in India has a reach and spread that NGO–controlled micro-credit cannot begin to match, banks can cross subsidise loans, banks are better placed to appoint employees in developing banking and to provide specialised training to their employees and coordinate banking activities with development administration, local governments and SHGs, and banks are able to offer a wide range of financial services to borrowers than private micro-credit organisations.

Hence, the commercial banks should be involved in microfinance both directly or indirectly. The micro finance portfolio would enable commercial banks to diversify their operations considerably. The 'coordinated and collaborative approach' alone would be the right approach to bring marginalised rural households into the mainstream of the national economy. So, the prime task for our commercial banks is to examine and identify the target groups for microfinance operations. They have to create special cells to study the total requirements of these groups and come out with tailor made products and services for them. They must also understand that these groups are heterogeneous in nature and, hence, the banking products/services developed for them have to be highly diversified and target specific. Besides this, they can offer operational banking support to microfinance institutions or NGOs, or refinance a microfinance institution, or participate in the equity of such institutions.

To sum up, the banks would have to evolve sepecific strategies to expand the outreach of their services in order to promote financial inclusion of low income groups, treating it both a business opportunity as well as a corporate social responsibility. They have to make use of all available resources including technology and expertise available with them as well as with the MFIs and NGOs. Financial inclusion as a policy measure should be followed up by building up a suitable database which could serve as a guide to asses the impact of credit policies from time to time and reorient schemes of financial assistance to the targeted groups. It may appear in the first instance that taking banking to the sections constituting the 'bottom of the pyramid' may not be profitable but it should always be remembered that even relatively low margins on high volumes, can be a very profitable proposition. Financial inclusion, therefore, can emerge as commercial profitable business.

It is suggested that we may set up a mandatory system of reporting by the banks to the Parliament and the state legislatures, of the performance and progress on the social banking front once in a year and also institute a system of reward and penalty for social banking performance. Professionalised management does not mean a myopic view of short term profitability. It is expected that the NABARD, the RBI and the Central government would re-orient their policies accordingly *vis-a-vis* micro credit in the country.

References

Dev, S. Mahendra (2006), 'Financial Inclusion: Issues and Challenges', *Economic and Political Weekly,* Vol. 51, No. 41, Oct. 14-20, pp. 4313.

Leeladhar, V. (2006), 'Taking Banking Services to the Common Man-Financial Inclusion', *RBI Bulletin,* Vol. 50, No. 1, Jan. pp. 76-7.

Khandelwal, Anil K. (2007), 'Micro Finance Development Strategy for India', *Economic and Political Weekly,* Vol. 52, No. 13, March 31, pp. 1129-35.

Mohan, Rakesh (2006), 'Agricultural Credit in India-Status, Issues and Future Agenda', *Economic and Political Weekly,* Vol. 51, No. 11, March 18, pp. 1013-23.

NSSO (2005), 'Indebtedness of Farmer Households 2003, NSS Report No. 498, Central Statistical Organization, Government of India, New Delhi.

Rao, K.G.K. Subba (2007), 'Financial Inclusion: An Introspection', *Economic and Political Weekly,* Vol. 52, No. 5, Feb. 3-9, pp. 355-60.

RBI (2005a), 'Report on Trend and Progress of Banking in India–2004-05', Reserve Bank of India, Mumbai.

Reddy, Y. V. (2005), 'Micro Finance : Reserve Bank's Approach', *RBI Bulletin,* Vol. 49, No. 9, Sep. pp. 845-6.

Satish, P. (2007), 'Agricultural Credit in Post Reform Era', *Economic and Political Weekly,* Vol. 52, No. 25, June 30, pp. 2567-75.

Shah, M. Rao, R. Shankar, P. S. Vijay (2007), 'Rural Credit in 20th Century India- Overview of History and Perspectives', *Economic and Political Weekly,* Vol. 52, No. 15, April 14-20, pp. 1553-8.

Shrinivasan, N. (2007), 'Policy Issues and Role of Banking System in Financial Inclusion', *Economic and Political Weekly,* Vol. 52, No. 30, July 28, pp. 3091-95.

Shylendra, H. S. (2007), 'Micro Finance Bill: Missing the Forest for the Trees', *Economic and Political Weekly,* Vol. 52, No. 27&28, July 14, pp. 2910-14.

Swaminathan, M. (2007), 'The Micro-credit Alternative', *Economic and Political Weekly,* Vol. 52, No. 13, March 31, pp. 1171-5.

Thorat, Usha (2006), Financial Inclusion and Millennium Development Goals', *RBI Bulletin,* Vol. 50, No. 2, Feb. pp. 239-43.

30

EMPOWERMENT OF RURAL POOR THROUGH SHGs FORMED BY DRDA AND NGO IN BIHAR

C. S. Singhal

Self Help Groups (SHGs) are voluntary associations of people formed to attain certain collective goals. It has been recognized all over the developing nations that through promotion of SHGs poor people can be linked with formal credit institutions. Hence SHGs can develop income and improve the quality of life of members by easy credit access. Moreover, people in group could develop confidence level. The SHGs will help in empowering the poor, develop social aspects, employment generation and ultimately facilitate the improvement over the quality of life of its members.

Now a day's formation of SHGs are the main strategy in India and most developing countries for credit linkage and self employment generation. There are large number of government institutions like District Rural Development Agencies (DRDA), Non Governmental Organisation (NGOs), banks are promting these SHGs in rural area .

The total number SHGs formed since inception in Bihar is 60,075. Out of which 8,957 have passed grade I (14.90%) and 2,693 groups have passed Grade II (4.48%) only 2,052 groups have taken up the economic activity (3.41%) the number of women groups is 10,779 (17.94%) out of which 3,149 (29.21%) women SHGs have taken up economic activity.

Bihar is located in the eastern part of India. As per 2001 Census the total population of the Bihar State was 8,28,78,796 (M 4,31,53,964, F 3,97,24,832). The literacy rate is 47.53% (M: 60.32%, F: 33.57%).

In the present study the Self Help Groups (SHGs) promoted by District Rural Development , NGO supported by UNICEF are studied. In Bihar Sarif (*Nalanda)* District 13 self-help groups studied were promoted by DRDA, while 8 SHGs were formed by *Jan Jagran Sansthan* (NGO).

The bank as supporting agencies could not be studied, as the SHGs promoted by them were eighter not available or were formed very recently (about 6 months old promoted by NABARD were available in Nalanda District).

Methodology

Study Area

In Bihar Sarif (Nalanda) District study was confined to the SHGs spread in 12 villages in four blocks viz. *Asthama, Biharsharif, Giriak and Rohi.*

Table 1
Study Area

Districts	*Blocks*	*No. of Villages*
Nalanda	AsthamaBihar SharifGiriakRohi	12

Sample

Table 2 shows the sample of SHGs studied according to Self Help Promoting Institutions (SHPIs). Altogether 21 SHGs were studied in Nalanda. Except one SHG all the remaining members of 12 SHGs promoted by DRDAs were male. However, all the members of 08 SHGs promoted by NGOs in the district were female.

Table 2
SHGs According to SHPIs

SHPIs	*Nalanda Distt.*
DRDA	13 (12 M; 01 F)
NGO (UNICEF)	08 (all Female)

As far concern the SCs/STs except one SHG where all the members were SCs rest all the SHG members were of mixed Caste Categories.

The major Income Generating activities of the SHGs promoted by DRDAs were cattle rearing (more than 95%), only few activities of SHGs were as leather Industry, Vegetable Cultivation, Borewell, Bangle Making, Organic Farming, Petty shop and Goat rearing.

Result and Discussion

Social Mobilisation by SHGs Promoted by DRDAs

NGOs involvement

The DRDA promoted SHGs were mobilized by a volunteer, who worked in literacy and DRDA Officials, also participated in this. The participation of officials in group mobilization left much to be desired as they were not adequately trained for their task.

Wherever NGOs were involved in formation and mobilization of SHGs in the group became more cohesive and concerned about social development aspects.

PRIs Involvement

PRIs role were limited to get their formal approval as members of B.P.L. family only . PRIs need to be oriented from the initial stage. So that they can be helpful in mobilization of group along with NGOs and officials.

Mobilization of SHGs Promoted by NGOs

NGO promoted SHGs were mobilized by specialized staff appointed and trained intensively in the aspects like Community Organization, Participatory Rural Appraisal, and Panchyat Raj Institutions etc.

The SHGs promoted by NGOs were better mobilized and developed cooperation, Communication, decision making skills, leadership and motivation to get involved in Community activities such as education, health, sanitation etc in comparison to the SHGs mobilized by the Officials.

Employment–Income Generating Activities

As stated earlier the major activities of the SHGs promoted by DRDA was cattle rearing. This suits to the *Swarojgaris* in view of the fact that they are not having any vocational skills in other trade. Moreover, there were huge infrastructure created in the district with coordination with Patna Dairy Development Project and Swajal Dairy Project. Wherever city is nearby or milk collection center is there in the village this activity (cattle rearing) is profitable.

By and large it is observed that average credit per *Swarojgari* under cattle rearing is about Rs.10,000- 12,000 for one cattle. The average profit per *Swarojgari* will be about Rs.1000–2000 p.m.

The cattle rearing are mainly individual activity. The money is divided equally among all members. Even the selling of milk is also taken up individually.

There is often delay from six months to one year in disbursement of credit also demotivating the group members.

The intensive training on the veterinary aspects for a week's time were given to the *Swarojaries* at district level by APO (Vet) with the help of Veterinary departments. Besides 2–3 days orientation were also given to each *Swarojgaris* in maintenance of accounts etc, at District/Block level.

The other few activities of the SHGs promoted by DRDA were *leather industry* and *Borewell.* These two activities were taken-up by group members jointly and were found profitable.

The major share of the credit has already been repaid by the *Swarojgaris*. The DRDA is helping leather industry by providing funds to SHGs for construction of a building, a three wheeler, and shops (*pucca)* on subsidised rent basis and inform about fairs and provide subsidies in transport for display of shoes in fairs. This is helping the *swarojgaries* in preparation of shoes. The *Swarojgaris* undertaking leather activities are already possessing required skills for preparation of shoes. Marketing is still the major problem for most of the *Swarojgaries.* These *swarojgaries* still need more credit in future for expansion of their activities.

Income Generating Activities (IGAs) and Credit Linkage for SHGs Promoted by NGO

The other activities undertaken by SHGs promoted by *Jan Jagran Sansthan* (with UNICEF assistance) were petty shop and goat rearing. The most of the members of these SHGs promoted by *Jan Jagran Sanstha* (NGO) were below poverty line but they were not enlisted in official BPL list. Hence, they did not get any subsidy from any agency. The credit linkage was problem with these SHGs. Even if linked with bank they get meager credit. The average credit was Rs.1000 per SHGs. So, the average income generation per swarojgari was about Rs. 100/- p.m. only.

It is pertinent to mention here that the *Jan Jagran Sansthan* has withdrawan for the last two years, as they did not get any assistance from UNICEF. Although NGO is helping them informally even now occasionally on the request of members of SHGs.

Empowerment through SHGs

There is certainly increase in level of awareness, participation, mobility of women, economic independence, collective decision making and increase in self-confidence, bargaining capacity and communication skills among the members of SHGs. But empowerments on these aspects were more in the SHGs promoted by NGOs in comparison of the SHGs promoted by DRDA/Block Officials.

Bankers Perception

The bankers were keen to assist women groups as there repayment are more secure. They were of the view that the main reason for failure of the enterprise is lack of entrepreneurship skills, training, infrastructure and marketing facilities. The illiteracy among the selected swarojgaries was also indicated as main reason of failure of the enterprises taken-up under the SHGs. Bankers stated that identification of a person who is taking credit is difficult at time for the bankers, is also the main cause of less recovery particularly in case of individual credits.

Present Status

The movement of SHGs promoted by DRDA is picking up now lately. For the past about six months NABARD with the involvement of NGOs has started forming SHGs with thrift activities in Bihar Sarif (Nalanda) District.

Case Studies

Unemployment (*Berojgar*) SHG

This SHG is working in *Jorarpur* village of Bihar Sarif (Nalanda) district in Bihar. The *Berojgar* SHG was formed in the year June 2002. There are 10 members in the group. All the members belong to below poverty line and are of backward caste (*Kushwaha*). Only two members were found illiterate.

The selection of President, Secretary and treasure were done with the consensus of all the members. The same elected executives of SHG are continuing since inception.

Each member of SHG is contributing Rs. 50/- per month. All the ten members has saved an total amount of, Rs. 1450/- and this amount are deposited in the bank . The group got revolving fund of Rs. 20,000 (Rs. 5000 from SHG and Rs. 15000 from Bank). The Bank has given total loan of Rs. 2.5 lack to this SHG. In this the subsidy was Rs. 1 lakh out of which 70,000 is returned by the group to the bank. The members are paying the loan in time. The secretary is maintaining the record properly and he is graduate. The bank pass books are also find in order and updated.

The each number of the group got two installments of an amount of Rs. 12,500/- each for purchase of Buffalo's.

The only problem stated by members in selling of milk. The city is about 6 km from village. Some milk they are selling in village and rest in the nearby city. Under SGSY infrastructure fund milk collection center is under construction through SHG. These centers will be linked with Patna Dairy Project – once this collection is in operation, the problem of selling the milk will be solved to large extend.

A member of SHG was associated with the panchayat samities and *school education samities* . The other member of

SHG seems to be quite active in the running of school and primary health center in the village.

Leather Uddyog Self Help Group

This SHG is situated in B.N.Pahari village . This village is situated about 7 km away from Nalanda, District Head Quarters *Bihar Sarif*.. The village possesses about 75 house holds all belongs to Scheduled Caste Community. Except 4-5 household, remaining all the house hold engaged in preparation of leather shoes and other leather items . They have no agriculture land. The most of the familie's living condition were found very poor (i.e. below poverty line).

The SHGs was established in February, 2000. This leather Uddyog Self-Help-Group has ten members all belongs to scheduled caste community. Out of these, 6 members were engaged whole time in preparation of leather shows and remaining members were in addition to *shoes* making, so far agriculture layout also in between when ever labour work is available in plenty.

Before joining this self help group the level of income of these members was very low they started it as Rs. 100/- to 200/- per month only. But the level of income from the *shoes* making has increased around 4 times i.e., Rs. 500/- to 1000/- per month after joining the group. They stated that now they are able to get cheap raw material and is available in time enhance their level of production thereby increased their production and profit substantially.

The group was formed by a local NGO "Sarva Hara Seva Samiti" this NGO has created by a local scheduled caste youth.

The group monthly saving of Rs. 20/- is made by each member. The total amount of groups' own saving was Rs. 3000/- only. The group got Rs. 10,000 as revolving fund from DRDA. An amount of Rs. 2,50,000 (Rupees two lakes fifty thousand only) as bank credit in five installments (25,000, 70,000, twice 40,000 and 1,75,000 respectively) out of the Rs. 85,000 returned to the bank. The members informed that to get released the fund, the group members with consensus took out Rs. 40,000 and purchased various raw material from

Calcutta. Members informed it that the material brought from Calcutta is about 60 per cent cheaper as compare to local market. The material is equally distributed among the members there is no conflict among the members. It benefited them immensely. Out of own saving group members take small loan. The decision to take loan is taken in a monthly meeting or in a special meeting conveyed for the purpose. The internal landing to the members is done on the guarantee of minimum two members on written papers. In case there is delay in return of money. The members of SHG press jointly and it works as most members return their loan.

The meeting of all members of SHG takes place twice in a month. Most of the members attend this meting.

All the records are found in order. The record is maintained by treasure that is studied up to primary level.

The shoes making is traditional occupation of all the members of SHG. Their families are engaged in leather works for the last 17-18 years. Hence SHG members have technical knowledge about shoes making. The members had technical training in *Mumbai* and or *Mukama* at their own. After joining the SHG the members had only two day training at *Bihar Sari* (District HQs Nalanda). The training was mainly related to the advantages of forming SHG and details about credit linkage with the bank.

Under infrastructure development DRDA has provided a grant of about Rs. 8 lakhs for construction of double story building through an other SHG in *Pichasa village*, which is about a Km from B.N.Pahari Village. The building is constructed by SHG working in Pichasa. The building was supposed to use as store house as well as a workshop for two SHG. But it is observed that building is neither used as storage nor as workshop place for both the SHGs. The location of building is not suiting to the members for shoes marking purpose hence members wanted to seat in their shop on the Bus stand. Moreover, the building is in possession of other SHG. At the time of visit building is remains as untitled and some portion is being used for taking bath by villagers. A local NGO *Sarvahara's* secretary told that he has plan to open school for village children on the house as it has not used presently. Besides a three-wheeler is also given to another SHG group in *Pichasa village*, which is also engaged in shoes making. But on enquiry it is found that till date this group has not used the three-wheeler for marketing purpose.

Marketing is the main problem revealed the *Swarojgaris* of the SHG. The main source of marketing is truck drivers. Besides, they go to some exhibition in *Gaya* and *Rajgir* and *Sonpur. Harldy,* some orders were also got from city to sell the *shoes*.

The members does not have their own shops. They wanted shop at *Bihar Sarif* (District Head Quarters,Nalanda) for selling their shoes. Moreover DRDA should assist and inform them about the different exhibitions organised in and around the city for better sale of their product.

The group wanted that the three wheeler given to other group in *Pichasa village* should be made available to them also free of cost for taking their product in exhibition and for sale outside.

The illiteracy was the main problem. The SHG is not mobilising any activity related to health, education etc. Although the group members informed that all children's are going to school in their village .

The members of SHG does not have membership in other village organization. The PRIs has not played any role in the development of group activities. PRIs were not involved in the group activities. There is caste conflict in the village. The *Mukhia* (*Sarpunch*) belongs to other caste communities (General).

The members have cordial relation among themselves and help each other during crises. They want to develop their business for that they wanted DRDA to provide latest automatic leather stitching machine and show room in city.

DRDA officials informed that they have tried to procure rates for automatic leather stitching machine but could not get authorized dealer in the country, hence are unable to procure the same. They informed that they are helping group by assistance in showing their product in different exhibitions in the state. The members reported that they are facing problem of sales tax by local officials.

Suggestions

1. The participation of officials in group formation and mobilization left much to be desired, as they were not adequately trained for this task. Hence, as far possible NGOs should be involved in formation and mobilization of SHGs. Moreover all concerned officials and bankers need to be trained on priority.
2. The PRIs were also not involved in the mobilization phase. Moreover, there were no training given to elected representatives. So they should be oriented in the initial stage for their participation.
3. SHGs formed by *Jan Jagaran Sansthan* (NGO) at Nalanda did not get any subsidy and banks were reluctant to provide credit. Wherever credit was provided it was meager amount. Hence members of such SHGs may be included in newly-formed SHGs by DRDAs.
4. Most of the groups has not yet reached to the stage of such maturity when they can be merged into federation. It will help group in developing leadership qualities and empowering them if they are linked with other groups and formed in federation on experimental basis .
5. The major activities undertaken by *Swarojgaries* under SHGs were cattle rearing. However, it was observed that Veterinary services were not provided adequately. The *Swarojgaries* has to spent lot of money for consultation and medicine. Hence, efforts should be made to provide better Veterinary services.
6. There is no provision to provide cattle shed in the villages. The *Swarojgaries* suggested that cattle shed might be provided on cluster basis as most of the members do not have enough space for the same.
7. Marketing is the major bottle neck in income generating activities. Particularly the leather industry members of SHGs wanted DRDA to provide automatic leather sewing

machine for quality improvement and show room in the big city.

8. Most of the members of the SHGs promoted by NGOs were though poor were not enlisted in official BPL list. Hence efforts should be made to include genuine poor in the list of B.P.L.

Note

Paper is based on an first hand information of the author conducted during a NIRD study on "Social Mobilisation, Employment and Empowerment through SHGs in Bihar".

31

RURAL CREDIT AND AGRICULTURAL DEVELOPMENT IN INDIA: AN ANALYSIS OF ITS STRUCTURE, NEED AND GROWTH

JAYASHEELA & SHOUKAT ALI M

Introduction

IN this paper an attempt has been made to study the structure, credit need and growth of rural credit delivery system for agricultural development in India. The existing literatures and data on the said subject was reviewed and analyzed to understand the credit need and growth of agricultural development in India. (Provision of adequate and timely credit to the peasant communities plays an important role in balanced and sustainable growth of agriculture and allied activities in the countryside. Most of the rural area people depended on primary sector; therefore, primary sector is considered to be the backbone of the economy.) Agriculture is the most important constituent of the primary sector. If we look at the history of the economic development of the most of the present developed nations, which have embarked on the development path, it is the development of agriculture that has laid foundation for development of other sectors. It plays a basically passive and accommodating role for the requirements of modern industrial sector (Lipton, 1977)[1] and has a considerable impact on non-agricultural growth (Killick, 1985[2]; Chadha, 1986[3]; Biradar, 2006[4]). Although a large share of the economically active population in developing and transitional countries is still active in agriculture, its importance as an income source shows a steady decrease worldwide, with significant differences between continents, countries and specific areas within countries.

Even civilization began with agriculture. When our nomadic ancestors began to settle and grow their own food, human society was forever changed. Not only did villages, towns and cities begin to flourish, but also so did knowledge, the arts and the technological sciences. And for most of history, society's connection to the land was intimate. Human communities, no matter how sophisticated, could not ignore the importance of agriculture. To be far from dependable sources of food was to risk malnutrition and starvation.

The agriculture remains central to the economic and social life of much of the developing world (Rahaman)[5]. It is par excellence, the fundamental industry (Baker, Barasodi and Wilson, 1953)[6], because it is the basis of the existence of human race and plays an important role in generating employment opportunities and supplementing includes of small, marginal farmers and landless labourers, especially in rainfed and drought-prone areas. Effective control of animal diseases, declaration of disease-free zones, and scientific management of genetic stock resources, breeding, quality feed and fodder, extension services, enhancement of production, productivity and profitability of livestock enterprise will be given greater attention in this sector.

The agriculture was given highest priorities even before the Adam Smith's 'Wealth of Nations'. Physiocrats[7] believed that 'the origin of all wealth lay in agriculture and this wealth consisted of real produce (Servaas Storm, 1992)[8]. *Produit net* was conceived as an excess of output over the inputs, which showed that industry and trade were sterile or unproductive. They were very important but they did not add to the net wealth of the economy' (Bhatia, 1992)[9].

All the three basic objectives of economic development of the country, namely, output growth, price stability and poverty alleviation are best served by growth of agriculture sector. The agricultural productivity increase has a major effect in reducing poverty, (which is the major concerns of third world countries) and the effect is relatively greater in its impact on the poorest and the distribution of income among the poor. Industrial growth has much less or even no effect in reducing poverty (Ravallion and Datt 1996[10] and Timmer 1997[11]) rather dynamic and vibrant agriculture alone will effectively address the problems of rural poverty (RBI, 2004)[12]. Therefore it is rightly regarded as an indicator of the quality of life at the grassroots level making it what may be called 'peoples sector' (Reddy, 2001)[13]. In the globalisation era agricultural trade and investment regime has provoked a new agricultural agenda (Barbara, 2002)[14].

In India, One of the reasons for the slow grow th of economic development is neglect of rural development prior to dependence, particularly agriculture sector. (Jayasheela, 1997).[15] Here agriculture is way of life rather than a business. More than one third of the people directly or indirectly engaged in this sector. It continues to be the mainstay of the Indian economy. Therefore 'agriculture is not a commodity machine but the backbone of the livelihood security system in India, where 70 per cent of the population living in the villages. So, agriculture is not just a question of economics and trade but of dignity and survival' (Swaminathan, 2004)[16]. It feeds human and non human in the country. The agriculture is the root of prosperity in other fields (Sing, 1994)[17].

The Phases of Rural Banking Policy Since 1969

The banking policy in India has undergone several changes. It has witnessed mainly three phases under which the KCC system has been evolved. The first was the period following the nationalization of India's 14 major commercial banks in 1969. This was also the early phase of the green revolution in India. During this period, nationalized banks attempted to mop up new rural liquidity. The declared objectives of the new policy, known as "social and development banking", were to provide banking services in previously unbanked or under-banked rural areas; provide substantial credit to specific activities including agriculture and cottage industries; and to provide credit to certain disadvantaged groups such as, for example, Dalit households (Wiggins and Rajendran, 1987)[18]. The Government of India and the Reserve Bank of India (RBI) issued, from time to time, specific directives regarding "social and development banking". These included setting targets for the expansion of rural branches, imposing ceilings on interest rates, and setting guidelines for the sectoral allocation of credit. Given the new farming practices associated with the green revolution, the first post-nationalization phase of expansion in rural banking saw growth in credit advances for agriculture. Specifically, a target of 40 per cent of advances for the priority sectors, namely agriculture and allied activities, and small scale and cottage industries, was set for commercial banks. In addition, a decision was taken in 1972 to introduce regional rural banks, institutions that would specialize in social and development banking for rural areas was examined in 1993 by Binswanger, Khandker and Rosenzweig (Narayana, 2000)[19]. Advances to the countryside increased substantially, although they were, as was the green revolution itself, biased in respect of regions, crops and classes.

In the second phase, which began in the late 1970s and early 1980s, the rhetoric of land reform was finally discarded by the ruling classes themselves, and the two major instruments of official anti-poverty policy were developed: loans-cum-subsidy schemes targeted at the rural poor and state-sponsored rural employment schemes. Thus began a period of directed credit, during which credit was directed towards the so-called weaker sectors. The most important new scheme of this phase was the Integrated Rural Development Programme (IRDP), a scheme for the creation of productive income bearing assets among the poor through the allocation of subsidized credit. Initiated as a pilot project in 1978-79, it was extended to all rural blocks of the country in 1980.

The second phase also involved an expansion and consolidation of the institutional infrastructure for rural banking. "Even ardent critics of India's growth strategy," wrote a noted scholar of India's banking system, "would admit that what the country achieved in the area of financial sector development before the present reform process began, particularly after bank nationalization, was unparalleled in the financial history of any other nation in the world" (Shetty, 1997:253)[20]. According to Shetty, there was, after bank nationalization, "an unprecedented growth of commercial banking in terms of both geographical spread and functional reach". Finally, the third phase was that of liberalization, particularly after 1991. The policy objectives of this phase were encapsulated in the Report of the Committee on the Financial System chaired by M. Narasimham. In its very first paragraph, the report called for "a vibrant and competitive financial system...to sustain the ongoing reform in the structural aspects of the real economy" (RBI 1991)[21]. The third phase inevitably saw a reduction in rural banking in general and in priority sector lending and preferential lending to the poor in particular. The new policies also contributed to other distortions in the financial system (Shetty, 1997)[22].

Structure, Need and Classification of Rural Credit for Agricultural Development

Credit, an old French proverb says, "Support the farmer as the hangman's rope supports the hanged" (AIRCS 1951)[23]. Similarly, Darling's statement (1925)[24], states that "the Indian peasant is born in debt, lives in debt and dies in debt," still remains true for the great majority of the peasant communities in rural areas. The rural credit structure can be classified into the Institutional and Non-institutional credit lending agencies. The structure of non-institutional credit delivery system includes moneylenders, agricultural-cum-moneylenders, traders and commission agents, agro-shop dealers, friends and relatives, who charge exorbitant rate of interest and tend to keep their eyes on grabbing the assets of borrowers. The institutional credit delivery system on the other hand, is presented in Figure 2.1. It is evident that there has been a "multi-agency approach" to meet the credit needs of the rural households in general and the farming communities in particular.

Agricultural production (output) and productivity in any country depends upon various factors like stable monsoons, proper rain, fertility of soil, availability of irrigation facility, proper use of fertilisers, insecticides scientific use of implements (i.e. tractors, cattle carts, ploughing machines, harvest machines etc.), modern technology, finance for payment of wages and purchases of required implements and others. Among all these inputs, finance or credit is an important linkage for higher productivity, complemented by other factors like technology, management, marketing and follow up. It plays an accelerator role in the agricultural development if it is adequate in quantity, cheap, and timely provided for the development oriented (Belshaw 1931[25]; Galbraith 1952[26]; Myrdal 1968[27]; Schultz 1964[28]).

Peasants need adequate and timely credit for improvement of inputs, improvement of productivity of land and other resources. Prices for agricultural products tend to decrease while the costs of inputs tend to increase[29] in the present wake of liberalisation, privatisation and globalisation (LPG) era and also Economic Reforms since 1991, demand for credit in agriculture has increased.

The demand for credit further increase due to emergence of new areas of investment in agriculture such as adoption of high yielding verities of seeds, early maturing, disease resistant verities of food as well as non-food crops, adoption of latest technology requiring improved irrigation systems and other machinery establishing commercial farms of dairy, poultry, piggy, fishery, etc., equipped with adequate linkages for processing, packaging, transport, marketing etc., tapping commercial avenues in the areas of horticultural plantations, floricultural, aquaculture, bee-keeping, sericulture, mushroom cultivation, developing capital intensive, hi-tech, non-conventional, export oriented projects in the field of bio-technology, tissue culture, embryo-transfer technology, plasticulture, green house plantation of aromatic and medical plants etc (Singh 1996).[30]

According to Dantawala (1966) and Dandekar (1993) credit *per se* (with respect to its inherent nature) does not influence agricultural development because it is merely a means to an end. But when it results in investment in real resources including human labour, it influences output growth in agriculture. The new technology led inputs like HYV, fertilizers, pesticides, diesel, electricity, form implements, certain machines etc., and complement to the agricultural production. Institutional credit that would encourages investment in these new inputs and helps in utilization of capital and also output in agriculture (Desai (1994).[31] The credit needs of modernising India's agriculture have to be tailored to take account these systemic changes, particularly in the marketing infrastructure and generally in the output mix. It goes without saying that deregulation of marketing structures, removing the heavy hand of government and the amendment of the Essential Commodities Act is also essential to modernising agriculture by opening out markets to farmers (Venkitaramanan 2004).[32]

Credit Flow for Agricultural Development

As mentioned earlier, there are mainly two source of credit to agriculture, one is institutional/formal source and another is non-institutional/informal source. Non-institutional includes moneylenders, landlords, traders, commission agents and others. Institutional includes Government, co-operative banks, commercial banks and regional rural banks. In chronologically the growth of agricultural delivery is studied pre independence and the post independence era.

Credit Flow during the Pre-Independence Period

During pre-independence era non-institutional or informal sectors were playing a vital role in disbursement of credit to agriculture sector. The share of non-institutional source of agricultural credit was as high as 97 per cent. But informal sector dealing system was not suit for the welfare of the farmers. They were charging higher rate of interest, they were maintaining the vernacular system of accounting, harassing the farmer in repayment of loans, some times they used to grab the land of poor farmers which they mortgaged the lands of the farmers and others.

To overcome these defects institutional source was invented. Historically institutional source of finance starts with *taccavi loans* of State Governments 1793. There was also aimed at relief to the drought measures. In 1870s The British colonial government extended institutional credit to the peasants to fight the natural calamites. In the beginning of 19th century there was thinking to words establishment of cooperatives. In 1904 Cooperative Societies Act was passed. Finally, in 1904 and cooperatives were seen as the premier institutions for disbursing agricultural credit. "For some decades, that is, since long before the organisation of the Reserve Bank, great faith has been placed in India in the potentialities of the cooperative organisation to serve the credit needs of the country, especially of the rural sector" (RBI 1970)[33].

In the beginning of 20th century special and continuous official attention was given to the rural credit in general and agricultural credit in particular, in this direction a new Act was passed in 1912 giving legal recognition to credit societies and the like (a precursor of micro-finance); the Maclagan Committee on Cooperation in India issued a report in 1915 advocating the establishment of provincial cooperative banks, which got established in almost all provinces by 1930 thus giving rise to the 3-tier cooperative credit structure; the Royal Commission on Agriculture further examined the programme of rural credit in 1926-27; In 1928, introduced the land mortgage banks in the cooperative system to provide long-term loans for redemption of debts to money lenders. Sir Malcolm Darling submitted another report on cooperative credit to the Government of India in 1935, just before the founding of the Reserve Bank of India. This continuing concern reflected the intrinsic problems of extension of rural credit, which, to some extent, find resonance even today. It was then reported that in many provinces credit overdues to these credit cooperative institutions constituted to 60-70 per cent of the outstanding principal due (Rakesh 2004)[34].

"It was in 1935 that the Reserve Bank was founded: the Reserve Bank of India Act, 1934 is unusual among central banks to have specific provision for attention to agricultural credit. Section 54 of the Act enjoined the Reserve Bank to set up an Agriculture Credit Department which was to have an expert staff to advise the central government, state governments, state cooperative banks, and other banks; and to coordinate RBI functions for agricultural credit. Section 17 of the Act empowered it to provide agricultural credit through state cooperative banks or any other banks engaged in the business of agricultural credit" (Rakesh 2004)[35]. During the period between 1935 and 1950, the RBI played a central role in the task of building the cooperative credit structure, which gradually evolved into two separate arms: short-term and long-term credit.

Credit Flow to Agricultural Sector during the Post-Independence Period

After Independence, the benign and paternalistic attitude towards changes in agricultural credit policies continued but with more significant ideological inputs, which in retrospect did more harm to the rural credit delivery system. Various reports of the Committees made 'forced growth' leading to quick changes and policy 'turnarounds,' (Karmakar 2002)[36] in this direction, agriculture was considered top priority in the First Five Year Plan. As per AIRCS (1951)[37] "Agricultural credit is a problem when it cannot be obtained; it is also a problem when it can be had but in such a form that on the whole it does more harm than good. It may be said that in India, it is this twofold problem of inadequacy and unsuitability that is perennially presented by agricultural credit".

The continuing intense concern with the provision of rural credit continued in the post war years: more than half a dozen committees were appointed between 1945 and 1950 and important one was Report of the All India Rural Credit Survey (1954). The Committee of Direction that conducted survey and observed that the provision of credit through cooperatives remained meagre with only 3.3 per cent of the cultivators having access to credit from cooperatives, and 0.9 per cent from commercial banks. Agricultural credit fell short of the right quantity, was not of the right type, did not serve the right purpose and often failed to go to the right people. The Committee also observed that the performance of co-operatives in the sphere of agricultural credit was deficient in more than one way, but at the same time, co-operatives had a vital role in channelling credit to the farmers and it suggested various measures to strengthening the co-operatives because the roots of cooperatives lies in rural areas and farmers too. Therefore summed up that, "Cooperation has failed, but Co-operation must succeed"(AIRCS 1954)[38].

In 1955, State Bank of India was formed as an 'Imperial Bank'. SBI was asked to concentrate the agricultural sector. In this view SBI had opened its Agricultural Development Branch to give to special attention and extension of commercial banking facilities to rural and semi-urban areas with the agricultural credit as a special focus. In 1960, Committee on Cooperative Credit was appointed and in 1963 the Agricultural Refinance Corporation (ARC) was set up by the Reserve Bank to provide funds by way of refinance to the agricultural growth. It was changed into ARDC in 1975 and then NABARD in 1982.

In July 1966, the All India Rural Credit Review Committee (Chairman: Shri B. Venkatappiah) was set up to, *inter alia*, review the supply of rural credit in the context of the Fourth Five Year Plan in general, and the requirements of the intensive programmes of agricultural production in different parts of the country, in particular, and to make recommendations for improving the flow of agricultural credit. After a comprehensive review, the Committee recommended that the commercial banks should play a complementary role, along with co-operatives, in extending rural credit. In 1968, National Credit Council Study Group was appointed to seek on organisational framework for implementation of social objectives. In 1969, Rural Credit Review Committee recommended to nationalise the private sector banks with view of social control. In this connection on 19th July 1969, 14 major banks were nationalised, and 6 more banks on 15th April 1980. The priority sector-a concept innovated in 1969, and priority sectors was sought to be achieved through the stipulation that a certain proportion of the total net bank credit be deployed in these sectors by specific target dates. This change was highlighted in Green Revolution and there was no doubt that the green revolution in Punjab agriculture brought about a significant reduction in rural poverty in terms of both the absolute number and percentage of poor and ultra-poor population in total rural population from the early 1970s (Singh 2004)[39].

In 1972, Banking Commission was set up and 1972-75 REC and SFDA were set up. The Lead Bank Scheme was also introduced to spearhead the credit allocation for, *inter alia*, agricultural lending in a lead district. In order to emphasise the developmental and promotional role assigned to the ARC in addition to refinancing, the Corporation was renamed as the Agricultural Refinance and Development Corporation (ARDC) by an amendment to the Act in 1975. In 1975, Narasimham Working Group recommended to set up Regional Rural Banks. Keeping in the views of the committee, RRBs were set up on October 2nd, 1975.

In 1977, all these three institutions (Cooperatives, Commercial Banks and RRBs) who are lending in the rural sector were termed as "multi-agency approach". In 1982, the National Bank for Agriculture and Rural Development (NABARD) was set up with the recommendations of the "Committee to Review Arrangements for Institutional Credit for Agriculture and Rural Development", for providing credit for promotion of, among others things, agriculture. It is the Apex institution, which has been entrusted with a pivotal role in the sphere of policy planning and providing, refinance facilities to rural financial institutions to augment their resource base. Since its inception, the NABARD has played a central role in providing financial assistance, facilitating institutional development and encouraging promotional efforts in the area of rural credit. NABARD also administers the Rural Infrastructure Development Fund (RIDF), which was set up in 1995-96; the corpus of RIDF is contributed by scheduled commercial banks to the extent of their shortfall in agricultural lending under the priority sector targets. NABARD has been playing a catalytic role in micro-credit through the conduit of Self-Help Groups (SHGs).

The Report of the Committee on the Financial System (Narasimham, 1991)[40] provided the blue print for carrying out overall financial sector reforms during the 1990s. Furthermore, weaknesses in the performance of rural financial institutions since 1991 resulted in setting up of various committees/ working groups/ task forces to look into their operations such as: "The High-level Committee on Agricultural Credit through Commercial Banks" (Gupta, 1998)[41], "Task Force to Study the Functions of Cooperative Credit System and to Suggest Measures for its Strengthening" (Capoor, 1999)[42], "Expert Committee on Rural Credit" (Vyas, 2001)[43], The Working Group suggested various amendments in matters of rural lending in general and agricultural lending in particular. The Standing Committee on Agriculture (2005)[44] also felt that though in order to provide greater financial autonomy to the cooperatives, the Multi-State Cooperatives Act has to be enacted, yet a lot more needs to be done to remove structural weaknesses and regional imbalances in the Cooperatives. The Committee urged that, the farmers should get the much required support and strength for their sustained development and prosperity.

The Various committees/ working groups/ task forces made far-reaching recommendations having a bearing on agricultural credit. While the Capoor Task Force suggested adoption of a Model Co-operative Act, setting up of a Co-operative Rehabilitation and Development Fund at NABARD and Mutual Assistance Fund at the state level, the Vyas Committee (2001) recommended restoration of health of Primary Agricultural Credit Societies (PACs) by scrapping the cadre system, selective delivering of cooperatives credit structure and integration of short and long-term structures. The Chalapathi Rao Working Group (Chalapathi Rao 2002)[45] had, in addition to suggesting diversification of the business of RRBs, recommended introduction of capital adequacy norms for RRBs in a phased manner, along with the RRB-specific amount of equity based on the risk-weighted assets ratio. The Standing Committee on Agriculture (2005)[46] are perturbed to note that 20 Public Sector Banks and 27 Private Sector Banks have not been able to reach the mandatory agricultural lending target of 18 per cent of the net bank credit. The Committee desired the Government to take stringent action against all such banks for neglecting this important sector.

The financial sector reforms formed an integral part of the overall structural reforms initiated in 1991 and included various measures in the area of agricultural credit such as deregulation of interest rates of co-operatives and RRBs; deregulation of lending rates of commercial banks for loans above Rs. 2 lakh; recapitalization of selected RRBs; introduction of prudential accounting norms and provisioning requirements for all rural credit agencies; increased refinance support from RBI and capital contribution to NABARD; constitution of the Rural Infrastructure Development Fund (RIDF) in NABARD for infrastructure projects; introduction of Kisan Credit Card (KCC) and stipulation of interest rate not exceeding 9 per cent for crop loans up to Rs. 50,000 extended by the public sector banks. In recent years agriculture credit policy has been progressively institutionalized for providing timely and adequate credit to the farmers for increasing agricultural production and productivity (GOI 2000)[47].

Table 1 presents that data on plan outlay for the development of agricultural and allied activities during different five years plans. It is evident that the percentage share of outlay for agricultural and allied sectors increased till fifth plan and begun to decline thereafter. This indicates that there has been a gradual decline in public expenditure for development of agricultural and allied activities.

It can be noted that banking sector reforms, during 2000-01, emphasized building the health of banks and financial institutions, improving their asset quality, strengthening prudential norms and supervision and monitoring developments with a view to securing the soundness and

Table 1
Plan Outlay in Agriculture and Allied Sectors (Rs Crore)

Plans	*Total Plan Outlay*	*Agriculture and Allied Sectors*	*Percentage of agriculture & Allied Sectors to Total*
I Plan (1951-56)*	2378	354	14.9
II Plan (1956-61)*	4500	501	11.3
III Plan (1961-66)	8577	1089	12.7
Annual Plans (1966-69)**	6625	1107	16.7
IV Plan (1969-74)**	15779	2320	14.7
V Plan (1974-79)	39426	4865	12.3
Annual Plan (1979-80)	12177	1997	16.4
VI Plan (1980-85)	97500	5695	5.8
VII Plan (1985-90)	180000	10525	5.9
Annual Plan (1990-91)	58369	3405	5.8
Annual Plan (1991-92)	64751	3851	6.0
VIII Plan (1992-97)	434100	22467	5.2
IX Plan (1997-2002)	859200	42462	4.9
X Plan (2002-07)	398890	20668	5.2

Note: * Includes Animal Husbandry, Special Area Programme, Rural Development and Forestry and Wildlife.

** Includes buffer stocks of Rs. 140 crore for 1968-69, Rs. 24 crore for 1969-70, Rs. 50 crore for 1971-72 and Rs. 25 crore for 1972-73 and Rs. 24 crore for 1973-73. Thus the figures for V Plan work out to be Rs. 124 crore against the original Plan provision of Rs. 225 crore

Source: Tenth Five-Year Plan 2002-2007.

stability of the Indian banking system comparable to international standards (RBI 2001-02)[48]. Table 1 provides the data, percentage of direct agricultural credit to agricultural GDP, total GDP and total credit. The data indicate that the direct agricultural credit as a percentage to total agriculture registered an increasing trend, but as a percentage to total income from all sectors of the economy registered a declining trend. Similarly, the agricultural credit as a parentage to total credit began to decline over the years. This decline itself reflects the lack of interest in agricultural sector among the policy makers and government representatives.

Table 3 provides the data on share of agricultural credit provided by different formal institutions in India. It is clear

Table 2
Percentage of Direct Agricultural Credit (Disbursements) to Agricultural Gross Domestic Product (GDP), Total GDP and Total Credit

Period	*Agricultural Credit as a percentage to Agricultural GDP*	*Agricultural Credit as a percentage to Total GDP*	*Agricultural Credit as a percentage to CS*
1950-51	0.5	0.3	NA
1960-61	3.3	1.3	NA.
1970s	5.4	2.1	10.8
1980s	8.3	2.6	8.5
1990s	7.4	2.0	6.4
2001-02	8.7	2.0	5.5

Note: NA: Not Available;

1. Agricultural Credit: Direct credit for agricultural and allied activities extended by Co-operatives, Commercial Banks and Regional Rural Banks;
2. Total GDP and Agricultural GDP are at factor cost and at current prices and
3. CS–Other banks' credit to commercial sector (outstanding) proxy for total credit.

Source: 1. Report on Currency and Finance: Various Issues and Handbook of Statistics on Indian Economy: 2002-03;

2. Rakesh Mohan (2004).

that the share of credit by co-operative banks started declining and that of commercial banks and RRBs continued to rise during 1999-2000 to 2004-05; the share of RRBs increased little faster than that of commercial banks during the same period. In 1999-00 the total agricultural credit by all instantiation was about Rs. 46,268 crores. Out of this advances 39.6 per cent by cooperative banks, 6.9 per cent RRBs, and more than half 53.5 per cent by commercial banks. As in 2006-07 the share of cooperative banks declined to 22.2 per cent, where as the share of RRBs gradually increased 10.2 per cent and Commercial Banks a tremendous achievement of 67.6 per cent. This itself indicate that the cooperative banks are performing very poorly, this is mainly might be failure of policies, lack of initiation of the governments, prudential norms of the

Table 3
Institutional Credit to Agriculture by Formal Banking Institutions in India (Rs in crore)

Institution	*1999-2000*	*2000-2001*	*2001-2002*	*2002-2003*	*2003-2004*	*2004-2005*	*2005-2006*	*2006-2007**
Co-operative Banks	18,363	20,801	23,604	23,716	26,959	31,424	39,404	33,174
	(39.7)	(39.4)	(38)	(34.1)	(31)	(25)	(21.9)	(22.2)
Regional Rural Banks	3,172	4,219	4,854	6,070	7,581	12,404	15,223	15,170
	(6.9)	(8)	(7.8)	(8.7)	(8.7)	(10)	(8.4)	(10.2)
Commercial Banks	24,733	27,807	33,587	39,774	52,441	81,481	1,25,859	1,00,999
	(53.5)	(52.6)	(54.1)	(57.2)	(60.3)	(65)	(69.7)	(67.6)
Total	46,268	52,827	62,045	69,560	86,981	125,309	180,486	1,49,343
	(100)	(100)	(100)	(100)	(100)	(100)	(100)	(100)

Note: *Up to December 31, 2006.
Source: NABARD, (the data in parentheses are percentage to total).

banking system. Hence why the formers are depending on informal agencies for their credit need, if they fail to repay due to failure of crops or other reasons they are committing suicides.

Kisan Credit Card System

Concept, History and Evolution of Credit Cards

The Oxford Dictionary meaning of "credit card" is an authorizing purchasing of goods on credit". The 'credit card is an identification document identifying the holder as possessing a credit account. It is simply a means to an end.... means through which a host of goods and services can be purchased on credit at the nominated business outlets in the market place; such credit system may allow short or business credit facilities within the ambit of rules and regulations of the card issuing institutions.

Lobo (1999)[49] in his thesis explains how the credit cards grown in India. In 1961, Mr. Kali Modi who was responsible for bringing the credit card system in India introduced the 'Dinner Club' and he can be called as 'father of credit cards in India' for consumer purposes. It took several years to reach a break-even point and make the operations profitable. After achieving a modest card membership of about 8000, Mr. Modi sold his credit card company to Mr. Shyam Sunder Agarwal in 1976. The growth process of credit card system in India is provided in Box 1.

Typology of Credit Cards

Several types of credit cards can be seen in modern world. There are three important types of credit cards, namely, in house card, debit cards and smart card. In house cards are those cards which are issued to regulate customers by or on behalf of hotels such as Taj, Holiday Inn etc. these cards act an auxiliary to their main business, which can only be used at the outlets of the hotel/establishments concerned. The charge cards or debit cards (ATM) are the banks cards, which provide credit only for the short period between purchase

Box 1
Evolution of Credit Card System in India

- In 1960s, credit card system introduced in India.
- In early 1970s due to increase in urban income and young executives the credit card business increased.
- In 1980s, central Bank of India launched 'Central Card' that is the first bank credit card in India. Further competition rose with affiliation of central card with both VISA and Master Card.
- In 1981, Andra Bank lunched 'Andra Visa Card' and Andra Gold in 1988. After this various banks issued their own credit cards. The ATM facility was extended to credit cards and ATM cards were issued.
- Credit cards have played a pivotal role in the development of plastic and electronic banking technology. Using credit cards banks have introduced various types of new serviced and found out effective solutions to their customers' problems. Various banks are issued the cards in their bank names like 'cancards' by Canara Banks.
- Initially it took time for its gain popularity; there is a spurt in number of cards issued from 1992 onwards as number of banks got into this business introducing their own cards or on bilateral agreement with other banks that had entered into this business earlier.

and billing during which time the cardholder is expected to settle the outstanding balance in full within 15 days from the date of the bill, failing with interest @ 2.5 per cent is charges as service charges along with the amount payable in the following month. Non-payment of dues beyond 60 days may result in hot listing of the card. Some times defaulters' amount is debited from their saving account. Lastly, the smart card is a plastic card with a tiny integrated-circuit chip embedded in it, will not only tell the cardholder bank balance, but also helps him to pay for the items he buy in store. This practically eliminates the need to carry cash. It is programmed against tampering and fraudulent. It is a typical electronic purse. This 'smart cash card' was launched in Dubai on February 15, 1996.

Credit Cards in Agriculture

The credit card concept is not so new in agricultural sector. In 1964, Syndicate Bank organised a separate "Agricultural Finance Department", through this it carried out various innovative methods to increase the agricultural production and productivity. "The more important of these schemes are those for financing the raising of hybrid seeds, production of export varieties of banana, purchase of pump sets, power tillers, tractors and other agricultural machinery. An innovation made by the bank, to issue of 'AGRICARDS' to farmers to enable them to get their requirements of seeds, fertilizers, pesticides and sphere parts for machinery, on credit from approved dealers"(AIRCRC 1999).[50] This was perhaps first "Agricultural Credit Card" in India.

After ACRICARD, the nationalized banks like Canara Bank, Vijaya Bank, Corporation Bank and Dena Bank launched their own 'Agricultural Credit Cards' follows the directive of the RBI. The cards for the welfare of the farmers are known as 'Farmer's Green Card'. This card enables the farmers to avail of short-term credit facility from the branches of the bank form where the card is issued for purchase of agricultural inputs. There is a right move by the Election Commission of India to provide with identity card for eligible voter in India. This credit card could have been used as an identity card instead of producing ration card, passport etc. to prove ones identity.

Kisan Credit Cards

The success of the benefit of the credit depends on many factors, including the availability of complementary inputs and services, sound credit policies, well-managed institutions and appropriate delivery channels. The agricultural credit is just one of the several key ingredients that can transform rural society. The institutional credit should emerge as in instrument of promoting growth with equity. The major schemes of the agricultural credit disbursement system in general have not produced the desired results in terms of direction, quantum and quality of the flow of credit. Banks have not been adequately effective in transforming credit structure of weaker sections because of the complex tiering of funds through RBI-NABARD–commercial banks-state co-operative banks-district Co-operative Banks-Primary Agricultural Credit Societies has tended a unduly increase the cost of service. Besides information imperfection have contributed to inefficiencies like high transaction costs and low regarding of credit the timely availability of credit rather than its cost with determine the success of all agricultural lending operation. (Joshi 1998)[51]

It was also observed that performance of rural financial institutions has been far behind the expectations both fulfilling objectives they were established for as well as in term of their own viability. Only one-third of the cultivators need was fulfilled (Tyagi and Sing 1998)[52]. It was also viewed that recent year the demand for investment in agricultural have not met, to give impetus to the flow of credit to agriculture, the RBI set up a one man High-Level Committee headed by Shri R.V. Gupta on agricultural credit through commercial banks in December 1997 to suggest measures for improving the credit delivery system as well simplification of procedures for agriculture credit.

The Gupta Committee (1998)[53] submitted its Report on April 21, 1998; opinion about the focus of credit appraisal should be on evaluation of the income stream of the borrower, and a comprehensive assessment of credit needs taking into account track record, credibility, capability, as well as technical viability of the proposal. Short-term credit needs of farmer should include all requirements directly and indirectly related to production, post harvest and household expenses. During cash rich periods, farmers have a propensity to invest in gold, land, implements, and livestock or incur expenditure of a consumption nature. As a result they are vulnerable during times of adverse price fluctuations and natural calamities. To address the issues of the farmers should be offered a liquid savings product with an appropriate return, which should be inbuilt in the loan product so as to provide them a cushion during lean periods, and also the banking scenario in the country has been fast changing.

Even the process of financial sector reforms highlighted the need for innovative credit interventions from financial institutions. Any such innovation should comprise timely credit in adequate quantity with operational flexibility to the borrowers and insurance protection. The banks while lending process have changed their methodology over the period of time. Various credit delivery innovations in the form of SHG-Bank Linkage Programme for making financial services available to the poor have been introduced. In this direction Kisan Credit Card was introduced then finance minister Sri Yashawant Sinha in his (1998-99) budget speech and NABARD was asked to formulate a model scheme for issue of Kisan Credit Cards to farmers on the basis of their holdings for uniform adoption by the banks so that the farmers may use them to readily purchase agricultural inputs such as seeds, fertilisers, pesticides etc. and draw cash for their production needs, "timely credit to farmers in a flexible and cost effective manner" was the main aim of the KCC Scheme (Singh 1998).[54] Based on the announcement, a model kisan card scheme was formulated by NABARD and was circulated among the banks in August 1998.

Kisan credit card scheme envisaged coverage of all the short-term credit needs of the farmers including crop loan and other items of production credit/working capital/short-term requirements for non-farm activities. The predominant idea behind this approach was to ensure farmers to get adequate credit to meet all of their short term needs through the single window of Kisan Card. Provision of timely and adequate credit has been one of the major worry formal banking institutions in India in dispensation of credit for agricultural and rural development. this idea is associated with the famous formula of Sir Horace Plunkett's "Better Farming, Better Business and Better Living" (AIRCS (1951).[55]

Acutely, the Kisan Credit Cards scheme, which was proposed by the United Front Government regime when Chaturanan Mishra was the Agriculture Minister, had run into rough weather. The Finance Ministry, then under P. Chidambaram, had expressed reservations over its feasibility. The sheer size of the beneficiaries, which envisaged the inclusion of any and every farmer, seemed untenable. This was partly due to the "conservative" thinking among bureaucrats when it comes to sop to the agriculture sector. Mishra then sought the intervention of the then Prime Minister I K Gujral, and the proposal was referred to a committee of secretaries, which concurred with the Agriculture Ministry's view. It was later forwarded to the RBI, which asked NABARD to formulate the scheme. In fact Mishra had meanwhile gone a step ahead and implemented a prototype in Kerala to prove his point (Nagaraj 1998)[56]. In the light of above problems in lending process, the Kisan Credit Cards Scheme was introduced. A Model Kisan Credit Card Scheme was prepared by RBI and circulated to commercial banks and by NABARD to Cooperative banks and RRBs in August 1998, with instructions to introduce the same in their respective area of operation.

Objectives of the KCC Scheme

A Credit Card is a mode of cash-less transaction that allows the user to pay for goods or services with the actual payment being made in installments, over a period of time (NABARD)[57]. Kisan Credit Card Scheme aims at provision of adequate and timely support from the banking system to the farmers for their cultivation needs including purchase of inputs in a flexible and cost effective manner. It has smoothened the flow of credit to the farmers overcoming delays in sanction and release of loans. "The borrowers' advantages were in the form of timeliness in availability of credit and reduction in interest burden due to flexible operation, while the implementing banks benefited by avoidance of repeat processing of loan documents every year and improvement in recovery, etc.". The salient features of Kisan credit system is presented in Box 2.

Beneficiaries covered under the Scheme are issued with a credit card and a pass book or a credit card cum pass book incorporating the name, address, particulars of land holding, borrowing limit, validity period, a passport size photograph of holder etc., which may serve both as an identity card and facilitate recording of transactions on an ongoing basis. Borrower is required to produce the card cum passbook whenever he/she operates the account.

Box 2

Salient Features of Kisan Credit System

- Farmers eligible for production credit of Rs. 500 or more are eligible for issue of KCC.
- Eligible farmers to be provided with a Kisan Credit Card and a pass book or card-cum-pass book.
- Provision revolving cash credit facility involving any number of drawals and repayments within the limit.
- Entire production credit needs for full year plus ancillary activities related to crop production considered while fixing limit. In due course, are activities and non-farm credit needs may also be carved.
- Limit to be fixed on the basis of operational land holding, cropping pattern and scale of finance.
- Sub-limits may be fixed at discretion of banks.
- Card valid for 3 years subject to annual review.
- Each drawal to be repaid within 12 months.
- As incentive for good performance, credit limits could be enhance to take care of increase in costs, changing in cropping pattern etc.
- Conversion/reschedulement of loans also permissible in case of damage to crops due to natural calamities.
- Security, margin, rate of interest, etc. as per RBI norms.
- Operations may be through issuing branch through other designated branches at the discretion of bank, through other designated branches.
- Withdrawals through slips/cheques accompanied by card and passbook.

Progress of Kisan Credit Card in India

Since introduction of the KCC Scheme in 1998 CBs, Cooperative Banks and RRBs have together issued 642.49 lakhs of Kisan Credit Cards up to 31st January 2006. {Cooperatives 319.6 lakhs

(49.75%), RRBs 79.18 lakhs (12.32%) and CBs 243.071 lakhs (37.93%)}. As against 1.56 lakh cards by the Cooperatives, 0.06 lakh by RRBs and 6.22 lakhs by the Commercial Banks for the year 1998-99. It is clear that the performance in the sanction of Kisan Credit Cards is improved over the year. In order to motivate the banks and to support their efforts to generate greater publicity for popularizing KCC scheme, NABARD has been providing financial assistance to Cooperative Banks and RRBs with an allocation of Rs. 6 crore and Rs. 1.1. crore respectively. To supplement to this NABARD has launched 10 lakh Meghdoot Post Cards with a message of KCC to be distributed through rural post offices all over India. This card costs a buyer only 25 paise as against normal post card @ 50 paise. Due to KCC Scheme farmers can get an adequate and timely credit with reduced interest rates.

Table 4
Agency wise Kisan Credit Cards Issued

(In Lakhs)

Year	*Co-operative Banks*	*RRBs*	*Commercial Banks*	*Total*
1998-99	1.56	0.06	6.22	7.84
1999-00	35.95	1.73	13.66	51.34
2000-01	56.14	6.48	23.9	86.52
2001-02	54.36	8.34	30.71	93.41
2002-03	45.79	9.64	27	82.43
2003-04	48.78	12.75	30.94	92.47
2004-05	35.56	17.29	43.95	96.8
2005-06	25.98	12.49	41.65	80.12
2006-07#	15.48	10.4	25.68*	51.56
Total	319.6	79.18	243.071	642.49
% Share	49.75	12.32	37.93	100.00

*Up to 30 June 2006, # Up to December 31, 2006.

Source: Economic Survey 2006-07.

There is a minimum paper work and simplification of documentation. The banks are also benefited in the form of reduction in workload for branch staff by avoidance of repeat appraisal and processing of loan papers. The transaction cost has reduced, fund can be utilized in a better way and also recoveries of loans become easy. There is improvement in

Banker-Client relationships. Keeping the above in view, the study would like to looking into how the Kisan Credit Card Scheme is being functioning and how it is helping the farming community in meeting the credit facilities.

Conclusions

In the history of banking growth various schemes/policies were invented over the time of period for overall growth of agriculture, in this direction Kisan Credit Card Scheme is among them. Innovative products can create additional value and expand the frontier of finance if they create access to the formal financial system by groups previously without access; reduce transaction and risk costs of the financial services provider or of the clients or both; increase the term of loans and of savings, and/or provide larger loans to clients by refining valuation processes. Rural lending requires greater effort to assess and design loans than in urban lending due to the greater complexity of rural households economies, which arises, from seasonality and diversified incomes.

Notes

1. Lipton (1977), *Why Poor People Stay Poor: A Study of Urban Bias in World Development*, London: Temple Smith.
2. Kellick, T. (1985), Economic Environment and Agricultural Development: The Importance of Macroeconomic Policy, *Food Policy*, 10, (1): 29-40.
3. Chadha, G. K. (1986), Agricultural Growth and Rural Non-farm Activities: An Analysis of Indian Experience. In Yang-Boo Choe and Fu-Chen Lo (eds.), *Rural Industrialisation and Non-farm Activities of Asian Farmers*. Korea: Rural Economics Institute, Asian and Pacific Development Centre.
4. Biradar, R.R. (2006), Rural Non-Farm Activities in India: Emerging Issues. In Sabanna Talwar (ed.) *Agriculture and Globalisation*. Serial Publications; New Delhi.
5. Rahman, Hussain Zillur (2002), New Arguments for and old problem: Re-thinking Land Reform in Bangladesh, Agri Reform 2002, *A Conference on Agrarian Reform and Rural Development*, Cairo, Egypt, March.

6. Baker, Barsodi and Wilson (1953), Agriculture in Modern Life, *App in Agricultural Economics* by Chauhan, D.S. Laxmi Narayan Agarwal, Edu, Pub, Agra.

7. Note; The Physiocrats defined agricultural surplus as the difference between the 'gross produce' of agriculture and 'productive consumption by farmers. The latter was thought to consist of material requisites of production of sustenance of labour employed in production for more see Bharadwaj, K. (1987); Analytics of agriculture-industry relation, *Economic and Political Weekly*, Vol. 17, No. (19-21).

9. Servaas Storm (1992), Macroeconomic Considerations in the Choice of An agricultural Policy: A study into sectoral interdependence with reference to India, Thesis Publishers Amsterdum. N.L.

10. H.L. Bhatia (1992), History of Economic Thought: Vikash Publication House Ltd. New Delhi, p. 55.

11. Ravallion, Martin and Gaurav Datt (1996). "*How Important to India's poor is the Sectoral Composition of Economic Growth*," *The World Bank Economic Review*. Vol. 10, No. 1.

12. Timmer, C. Peter (1997), "*How Well do the Poor Connect to the Growth Process*". CAER II Discussion Paper No. 17. Harvard Institute for International Development (HIID), Cambridge, MA

13. ———(2004), Report of the Advisory Committee on Flow of Credit to Agriculture and Related Activities from the Banking System, (Chairman; Vyas, Vijay Shankar), RBI, Mumbai, June.

14. Dr. Y.V. Reddy (2001), Indian Agriculture and Reform: Concerns, Issues and Agenda. A Speech Delivered at Conference of Indian Society of Agriculture Marketing at Vizag on February 3rd. *www.rbi.org.in*

15. Barbara Harriss-White (2002), Development, Policy and Agriculture in India in the 1990s, QEH Working Paper series Number 78.

16. Jayasheela, (1997), The role of Sericulture in Rural Development: A Study in two Districts of Karnataka, Unpublished theses of Bangalore University.

17. Dr M. S. Swaminathan (2004), Agriculture is backbone of livelihood security system: Business Line, Jan 28.

18. Rudra Pratp Sing (1994), NABARD Organisation, Management and Role: Deep and Deep Publications, New Delhi, p. 4.

19. Wiggins, S., and Rajendran, S. (1987), *Rural Banking in Southern Tamil Nadu: Performance and Management* (Department of Agricultural Economics and Management, University of Reading), Final Research Report.

20. Narayana, D. (2000), "Banking Sector Reforms and the Emerging Inequalities in Commercial Credit Deployment in India" (Thiruvanthapuram, Centre for Development Studies), Working Paper No 300, March.

21. Shetty, S. L. (1997), Financial Sector Reforms in India: An Evaluation, *Prajnan*, Vol. 25, No. 3-4, Pune.

22. RBI (1991), Report of the Committee on the Financial System, November.

23. *Ibid.*

24. ———(1951), All India Rural Credit Survey, Report of the Committee Direction, Vol. - II, The General Report RBI, Bombay, pp. 151.

25. Darling, M. L. (1925). The Punjab Peasant in Prosperity and Debt, Oxford University Press.

26. Belshaw H. (1931), The Provision of Credit with Special Reference to Agriculture, Cambridge: Auckland university Press, Texts No. 1.

27. Galbraith J.K. (1952), "The Role of Agricultural Credit in Agricultural Development" in Proceedings of the International Conference on Agricultural and Cooperative Credit, Berkeley: University of Clifornia.

28. Myrdal, Gunnar (1968), Asian Drama: An Enquiry into the Poverty of Nations, Volume II, The 2oth Century Fund Inc.

29. Schultz, T.W. (1964), Transforming Traditional Agriculture, New Haven, Yale University Press.

30. Prices of major agricultural commodities tend to decrease as technological innovations reduce the costs of producing them. Prices of inputs tend to increase as many are non-renewable resources or farmers become more sophisticated users of fertilizers and high yielding seeds. The recent evolution of some internationally relevant prices is presented at: http:// *www.worldbank.org/prospects/pinksheets/index.htm*

31. Singh O.N. (1996), Working Capital Finance in Agriculture, *Yojana*, Vol. 40, No. 11, p. 14-18.

32. Desai Bhupat M. (1994), "Contributions of Institutional Credit, Self-Finance and Technological Change to Agricultural Growth in India", *Indian Journal of Agricultural Economics*, Vol. 49, No. 3, July-Sept., pp. 457-475.

33. Venkitaramanan S. (2004), Agricultural Credit—Case for Mitigating Lending Risks, *The Hindu*, Monday, December 20.

34. ———(1970), Reserve Bank of India, p. 68.

35. Rakesh Monan (2004), Agricultural Credit in India: Status, Issues and Future Agenda, Lecture delivered by Dr. Rakesh Mohan, the then Deputy Governor, Reserve Bank of India on February 5, 2004 at the 17th National Conference of Agricultural Marketing, Indian Society of Agricultural Marketing, Hyderabad.

36. Rakesh Monan (2004), Agricultural Credit in India: Status, Issues and Future Agenda, Lecture delivered by Dr. Rakesh Mohan, the then Deputy Governor, Reserve Bank of India on February 5, 2004 at the 17th National Conference of Agricultural Marketing, Indian Society of Agricultural Marketing, Hyderabad.

37. Karmakar K.G. (2002), Ruraal Credit and Self-Help Groups: Micro-fiinance Needs and Concepts in India, Sage Publications India Pvt. Ltd., Delhi.

38. ———(1951), All India Rural Credit Survey, Report of the Committee Direction, Vol. II, The General Report RBI, Bombay, pp. 151

39. ———(1954), Report of the All India Rural Credit Survey. (Chairman: B.Venkatappiah).

40. Singh Sukhpal (2004), Crisis and Diversification in Punjab Agriculture; Role of State and Agribusiness, *Economic and Political Weekly*, December, pp. 5583- 5589.

41. ———(1991), *Report of the Committee on the Financial System (Chairman: Shri M. Narasimham).*

42. ———(1998), The High-level Committee on Agricultural Credit through Commercial Banks, (Chairman R. V. Gupta).

43. ———(1999), Report of the Task Force on Revival/ Restructuring for Co-operating Banks (Chairperson: Shri. Jagadish Capoor), Mumbai.

44. ———(2001), Expert Committee on Rural Credit, (Chairman V.S. Vyas).

45. ———(2005), The Standing Committee on Agriculture 2004-05, Ninth Report, Ministry of Agriculture, Department of Agriculture and Cooperation, Lok Sabha Secretariat, New Delhi, April, pp. 69-91.

46. ———(2002), *Report of the Working Group to Suggest Amendments in the Regional Rural Banks Act,1976 (Chairman: Shri M.V.S. Chalapathi Rao),* Ministry of Finance, New Delhi

47. ———(2005), The Standing Committee on Agriculture 2004-05, Ninth Report, Ministry of Agriculture, Department of Agriculture and Cooperation, Lok Sabha Secretariat, New Delhi, April, pp. 69-91

48. Government of India; Economic Survey 2000-2001

49. ———(2000-2001), Annual Report, Reserve Banks of India.

50. Lobo Wilfred John (1999), "Credit Card System in India–A Case Study in Bangalore City Unpublished Thesis Submitted to Mangalore University Mangalaganothri, January.

51. ———(1969), Report of the All India Rural Credit Review Committee, Reserve Bank of India, Bombay, (Chairmen, B. Venkatappiah), pp. 496-450.

52. Joshi Navin Chandra (1998), "Restructuring Credit System For Rural Development", *Kurukshetra* Vol. 46, No. 12, September, pp. 36-42.

53. Tyagi,Lalit Kumar and Sing, Rashmi (1998), "Rural Credit Delivery System: Neglected Dimensions and Needed Focus", *Kurukshetra.* Vol. 46, No. 9, June, pp. 5-7

54. ———(1998), Report of the High-level Committee on Agricultural Credit Through Commercial Banks. (Chairman Sri R.V. Gupta).

55. Singh, Jaswant (1997-98), Then Finance Minister Union Budget Speech at Parliament on 28th March.

56. ———(1951), All India Rural Credit Survey, Report of the Committee Direction, Vol. II, The General Report RBI, Bombay, pp. 139.

57. Nagaranj, B. S. (1998); Kisan credit card scheme finally takes seed, *Indian Express*, Tuesday, October 6.

32

INCOME GENERATION FOR THE POOR THROUGH MICRO ENTERPRISES

K. P. Kumaran

Introduction

Through various self-employment programs, the Government has been making several attempts to enhance the economic status of rural people living below poverty line. The major important Self employment programs implemented by the government include, Integrated Rural Development Program, Development of Women and Children in Rural Areas, Self employment for Educated Unemployed Youth, Sworna Jayanthi Gram Sworajgar Yojana etc. These programs have been under implementation for the past few decades, and definitely helped to create material asset and employment among the poor. Nevertheless, these programs could not enhance the economic status of poor beyond certain threshold due to the faulty implementation particularly associated with the selection of the beneficiaries or problem associated with delivery of credit.

Although there are several formal financial institutions operating in the country to meet the credit needs of weaker Sections, particularly the poor, our past experiences showed that the smooth delivery of credit to the poor was adversely affected due to the formalized procedure and apathy of concerned officers. Of late, amongst other measures to tackle poverty, self-employment through Micro finance program has evolved as a major approach to benefit low-income groups of society. The emergence of Self-Help Groups of the poor came handy for the effective delivery of micro finance to the poor. Studies have shown that SHGs are acting as an alternative mechanism for the smooth delivery of credit to the poor (Srinivasan: 1996; Kumaran: 1997).

Under the SHG mode, poor particularly the women are mobilised and organised in to informal groups. Of late, several agencies are coming forward to form SHGs among the poor through the process of mobilisation. The size of the group varies in the range of 10 to 20. Apart from other collective actions, the major focus is on thrift and credit. After six months of its formation, the group starts rotating their saving in the form of small loan for under taking micro enterprises and meeting important consumption needs.

Apart from serving as a viable organisation for the delivery of credit to the poor, studies have also shown that these organisations particularly managed by women, successfully demonstrated how to mobilise and manage thrift activities, appraise credit needs, enforce financial discipline, maintains credit linkage with banks and effectively undertake income generation activities. These, studies also shown that the poor as a group are quite credit worthy and repayment of loan is quite satisfactory. (Rao: 1992; Kumaran: 2002).

In a comparative study between the micro enterprises set up under DWCRA and through the SHGs promoted by NGO and Banks it is found that the enterprises set up by the later are more viable and sustainable as compared to those formed by the former. The reason being that the DWCRA is a loose knit organisation where it lacks saving and the micro enterprise set up were with out any proper logistic support. (Kumaran: 2002). The present study tries to examine the role of micro enterprises set up through SHG mode towards enhancing the income level of the rural poor particularly the poor women.

Methodology

The study was conducted in the state of Maharashtra and Assam. From these two states, one developed and one underdeveloped district were selected on the basis of certain development indicators. Thus from Maharashtra Pune (developed) and from Assam Morigaon(relatively under developed) were selected for the study. In this study, only those SHGs promoted by NGOs were examined. The NGOs selected for the study were BAIF and Chaitanya from Pune and Morigaon Mahila Mehfil and Morigaon Zilla Gramya Puthibharel from Morigoan. From the SHGs promoted by the first two NGOs, 15 groups on a random basis were selected which are five and above years old. Similarly, following the same procedure from the SHGs promoted by the other two NGOs 11 groups were selected. Among them, five groups were more than five years old and the rest around three years old. Further, from the selected SHGs, again following the same procedure 22 and_49 entrepreneurs were selected respectively from Pune and Morigoan for detailed study about the type of enterprise set up by them and the financial benefits accrued to them from these activities. Information about SHGs were collected by interviewing group leaders and micro enterprises by interviewing entrepreneurs with the help of an interview schedule. Information from available secondary sources was also collected, to support the primary data.

Profile of SHG

As mentioned earlier, from Pune 11 and from morigoan 15 SHGs were studied. As per the information furnished by the SHG leaders in Pune, 38 per cent of the SHG members belong to APL and 62 per cent BPL. It was informed in the course of survey that when the SHGs were initially formed most of them belonged to the category of BPL and in the course of time by accruing benefits some of them graduated in to the category of APL. While in the case of Morigaon, 84 per cent belong to the category of BPL and rest APL. As per the latest BPL survey undertaken by the department of Rural Development, in

Assam 70 per cent of the house holds in the district fall in the BPL group. Examination of managing committee showed that in each SHG there were two leaders and generally they are called President and Secretary who look after the affairs of SHG. In few cases, Treasurer was also appointed to take care of financial management. In Pune, in most of the cases, the Presidents post is filled up by forward castes and most of them are educated and agricultural labour by profession. While in the case of Morigaon, the Presidents post is mostly held by members belonging to OBCs. Most of them are educated to the level of primary and above and working as agricultural labour. Rotation of office bearers is rarely found in both districts, as a result, the same person continued in the same post for years.

Thrift and credit form the major activities of SHG. In the district of pune, initially the entire group started the saving at a rate of Rs. 10/- per month. Currently, the amount varies from Rs. 20/- to 100/-. While in the case of Morigaon, the monthly saving varies from Rs. 10/- to 50/-. Saving is regular in all the SHGs in both the districts and loans are disbursed to the members with certain interest as per the collective decision made by the SHG members. The saving capacity of SHG members in Pune is better than those in morigaon. In the district of pune, the major sources of loan were from group fund, bank and revolving fund. While in Morigaon the main source is from group fund and bank. In both the districts, repayment of group loan is cent per cent and that of bank loan above 95 per cent.

Profile of Entrepreneurs

In the following section socio-economic profile of the 71 entrepreneurs selected for the study is given. In the district of Pune, nearly half of them fall in the age group of 30 to 50 years .Those who are above 50 constitute 13 per cent and the rest below 30 years. While in Morigaon nearly half of them fall in the age group below 30 years and the rest above this. The age distribution in these two districts showed that the members are relatively younger in Morigaon as compared to Pune.

Information about marital status showed that in Pune all are married and one of them remained widow. While in the case of Morigaon 61 per cent of them married and 33 per cent unmarried. Widows constitute 6 per cent. Caste wise information showed that most of them belonged to other castes and OBCs. While in Morigoan, most of them belong to OBCs. Educational qualifications of the entrepreneurs showed that in Pune exactly half of them educated above primary level. Illiterates constitutes more than one fourth of them. While in morigoan, it is found that majority of them (69 per cent) educated between middle and higher secondary. Two of them had college education. Only two cases of illiterates were reported. This showed that the level of education among the entrepreneurs is on the higher side in morigoan as compared to Pune. Occupational status of the entrepreneurs in both the districts showed that they are predominantly agricultural labors followed by non-agricultural labors. Distribution of yearly House hold iincome from all sources showed that in Pune 41 per cent of them have income 24000/- and above. Those who earned income between Rs. 15,000-24,000 constituted 32 per cent of the sample and the rest had an income up to Rs. 15,000/- while in Morigoan, whose income below 15000/- constituted 49 per cent and between 15,000/- to 24,000/- constituted 26 per cent and the rest 25 per per cent had income above Rs. 24000/-.

Training of Entrepreneurs

Information about training undergone by the entrepreneurs after joining the SHG has been collected. In Pune, several agencies were involved in training The training on basic information about SHG, accounting and book keeping etc done by the promotion agency, while entreprenurship development programme (EDP) was conducted by agencies like Maharashtra Centre for Entrepreneurship (MCED), Maharashtra Industrial and consultancy Organisation (MITCON, Central Khadi and Village industries, and Banks. While in Morigoan, the training on the above subjects was imparted by the promotion agency in consultation with NABARD, SIRD and Banking Institutions.

In Pune, all the entrepreneurs and in Morigoan 68 per cent of them underwent training programme related to income generation.

Micro Credit and Micro Enterprises

In this study we have analysed 71 micro enterprises set up by 22 entrepreneurs from Pune and 49 from Morigoan. Information about various activities related to micro enterprises was collected for the year 2002-03. While undertaking the survey it was found that only one unit in pune was incurring loss and the rest of the units were showing profits with varying degree

Type of Micro Enterprises

In the district of Pune, the most common enterprises set up by the entrepreneurs is tailoring (26 per cent) followed by dairy and petty business set up by 27 per cent each of the entrepreneurs. The rest of the entrepreneurs pursued activities such as poultry and goat rearing. While in Morigaon the most important common activity was weaving pursued by nearly one fourth of the entrepreneurs. The next important activity was tailoring pursued by nearly 18 per cent of the entrepreneurs. Duckery was pursued by 4 per cent of them. The other activities include dairy, fishery, and land based agricultural activities pursued by the rest of the entrepreneurs. In Pune, most of the units were set up under the non-farm sector while in Morigaon basically traditionally pursued income generation activities at household level were undertaken.

Cost of Micro Enterprises

In Pune the cost of micro enterprises set up by the entrepreneurs varied from Rs. 600/- to 25000/-. Those who invested up to Rs. 5000/- constituted 41 per cent. The next highest investment was in the range of Rs. 5, 000 to 10,000/- was made 23 per cent of the entrepreneurs. Those who invested between Rs. 10, 000 to 20,000/- constituted 27 per cent. The remaining 9 per cent of them invested Rs. 20, 000 and above.

While in the case of Morigaon the maximum and minimum limit of amount invested was Rs. 600/- to 5,000/. What is notable in the case of Morigaon is that the investment made by lion's share of (85 per cent) the entrepreneur's do not exceed Rs. 5, 000/-. Those entrepreneurs invested between Rs. 5000/- to 10,000/- accounted for 6 per cent of them. Similarly, only 7 per cent of them invested in micro enterprises that cost above Rs. 10, 000/-. This shows that investment made in enterprises is relatively less in the case of Morigaon as compared with Pune. More than three fourth of the entrepreneurs invested below Rs.5, 000/-. While in the case of Pune, the same amount of investment was made by 41 per cent of the entrepreneurs.

In the district of Pune, all the 22 entrepreneurs cumulatively invested an amount of Rs. 2, 10,300/- indicating an average investment of Rs. 9, 560/- per entrepreneur. While in the case of Morigaon, the total amount invested by the 49 entrepreneurs amounted to Rs. 2, 81,400/- thus indicating that the per capita investment made by each entrepreneurs amounted to Rs. 5740/-. This showed that average investment in Pune is relatively on the higher side as compared to Morigaon.

Source of Finance

In the district of Pune 56 per cent of the total amount (Rs. 1, 77,700/-) invested in the enterprises was received from the SHG group loan. Another 33 per cent (Rs. 69, 400) was mobilised as bank loan. The total individual contribution made by each member for undertaking the economic activity amounted to 11 per cent (Rs. 23, 150/-) of the total invested amount. Where as in the case of Morigaon 56 per cent of the total finance (Rs. 1, 85,730/-) was mobilised collectively through SHG group loan and bank loan. The own contribution made by entrepreneurs constituted the remaining portion of 34 per cent of the investment (Rs. 95, 670/-).

Information collected from the entrepreneurs showed that in pune 5 per cent of them and in morigaon 2 per cent of them experienced problems in repaying the loan taken for setting up of micro enterprises. In such cases it was reported that the members either depended on moneylender or fall back on their friends or relatives to cope up with the situation.

As far as raw material required for undertaking income generating activities is concerned, most of the entrepreneurs admitted that they got the materials required for various activities with in the village and the rest got it from outside village. In response to another question related to market, only 2 per cent of them in each district faced the problem of marketing of their products.

Cost of Production and Return

In the district of Pune, the total turn over in a month during the year 2002-03 from all the 22 enterprises amounted to Rs. 81305/- indicating an average turn over of Rs. 3, 695/- per unit. The total cost of production for all the units stood at Rs. 37, 310/- showing an average cost of production of Rs. 1, 696/- per unit. Thus, the total net profit per month for all the 22 units stood at Rs. 43, 995/- indicating an average net profit of Rs. 2000/- per unit. The maximum and minimum net profit earned by the entrepreneurs varies from Rs. 150/- to 12,000/-. From the above analysis it is also found that 60 per cent of the units are earning a profit margin above Rs. 2000/-.

While in the case of Morigaon, the total monthly turn over from al the enterprises for the same year under reference amounted to Rs. 78, 000/- with an average per capita turn over of Rs. 1, 592/- per unit. The total cost of production was Rs. 36, 400/- indicating per capita cost of production at Rs. 743/-. Thus the net profit at aggregate level is Rs. 41, 600/- and the per unit is Rs. 849/- which is very low the net profit among the units varies from Rs. 100 to 2500/-. The profit earned by three fourth of the units is less than Rs. 1000/-. Only 10 per cent of the units could earn profit margin of Rs. 2000 and above.

Pattern of Expenditure

Information is also obtained on the pattern of utilisation of profit derived from the enterprises. In Pune, 25 per cent of the profit derived from the enterprises was used for repaying loan, 40 per cent towards meeting household expenditure and the rest 35 per cent meeting general and emergency expenses. While in the case of Morigoan, major share of the profit (73 per cent) was used for meeting household expenses. Around 19 per cent of the profit utilised for repaying the SHG and Bank loan and the rest used for meeting emergency needs. While in Pune, the major portion of the surplus has been reinvested for the purchase of assets like land, cattle, ornaments,etc

Summary and Conclusion

In this study an attempt is made to examine the role of micro enterprises set up through SHG mode towards enhancing the income level of the rural poor particularly the women. As part of the study we have analyzed 71 micro enterprises set up by entrepreneurs drawn from 26 SHGs. Out of this 22 units were setup in Pune and the rest 49 in Morigoan. Most of the finance required for undertaking the enterprises was channalised through SHGs wither for group loan or external loan from banks. We have seen that in the district of Pune the most important micro enterprises set up included tailoring, petty business, darying, and vegetable vending. While in the case of morigaon the most important activity was weaving followed by tailoring, petty business, poultry, dairy and duckery. Investment in terms of money made in setting up of micro enterprises was relatively less in morigaon where more than three fourth of the entrepreneurs invested less than Rs.5000/- per unit. While the investment made in Pune was relatively on the higher side. In both the districts the major source of finance was received from SHG group loan and bank loans. What is noticeable in the case of Morigaon is that nearly one third of the finance for setting up enterprises is contributed through own source, which is very low in Pune. The average net profit earned by each of the unit in Pune was Rs. 2000/-, while in Morigaon the same distribution is only 849/- which was very low. In Pune 60 per cent of the units earned a profit margin of Rs. 200/- in Morigoan more than three fourth of them earned less than Rs. 1000/- and only 10 per cent of the units could earn a profit above Rs.20000. The relatively low profit from the units set up in Morigaon is mainly due to the fact that many of the units were set up recently while those in Pune were matured by more than five years. The pattern of utilisation of profit accrued from the SHG showed that in Morigaon nearly three fourth of the profit was used for meeting household expenses and 19 per cent used for repaying SHG loan. The study showed that after becoming member of SHG and particularly after setting up micro enterprises the income of the entrepreneurs in Pune has increased considerably, while the increase in Morigaon was marginal. In Pune the entrepreneurs invested the surplus mostly to acquire fixed assets like land, cattle, ornaments. While in Morigaon, the same was used for procuring household items and facilities. But the important revelation of the study is that people of Morigaon could revive their traditionally performed house hold activities with the help of micro finance mobilised through SHGs which was otherwise discontinued due lack of house hold income. The study also showed that micro enterprises set up through micro finance also provided some sorts of economic support, whatever little it may be, but really helping them to fall back on during economic crisis.

References

Dinakar, Rao K. (1992), Women's Savings and Credit Schemes, Three Case Studies, NIBM, Pune.

Kumaran, K. P. (1997), Self Help Groups: An Alternative to Institutional Credit to the Poor, A Case Study in AP, *Journal of Rural Development,* Vol. 16 (3).

Kumaran, K. P. (2002) Role of Self Help Groups in Promoting Micro Enterprises through Micro Credit, *Journal of Rural Development,* Vol. (21), No. 2.

Srinivasan and Rao (1996), Financing of SHG by Banks-Some Issues BIRD, Lucknow.

INDEX

S